Oral Epics from Africa

African Epic Series

Thomas A. Hale and John Wm. Johnson, General Editors

Oral Epics from Africa
*Vibrant Voices from a Vast Continent*_____

edited by

John William Johnson
Thomas A. Hale
Stephen Belcher

Indiana University Press
Bloomington and Indianapolis

The paper used in this publication meets the minimum requirements of
American national Standard for Information Sciences—Permanence of
Paper for Printed Library Materials, ANSI Z39.48-1984.

Manufactured in the United States of America

Library of Congress Cataloging-in-Publication Data

Oral epics from Africa : vibrant voices from a vast continent / edited by
   John William Johnson, Thomas A. Hale, Stephen Belcher.
      p.   cm. — (African epic series)
      Includes bibliographical references, map, and index.
   ISBN 13: 978-0-253-21110-1

      1. Epic literature, African. I. Johnson, John William, date.
   II. Hale, Thomas A. III. Belcher, Stephen Paterson, date. IV. Series.
   PL8010.072   1997
   896—dc21   96-47367

1   2   3   4   5   02   01   00   99   98   97

To the memory of Goosh Andrzejewski
To the memory of Nouhou Malio
And to all our Teachers

And gladly would he learn, and gladly teach . . .

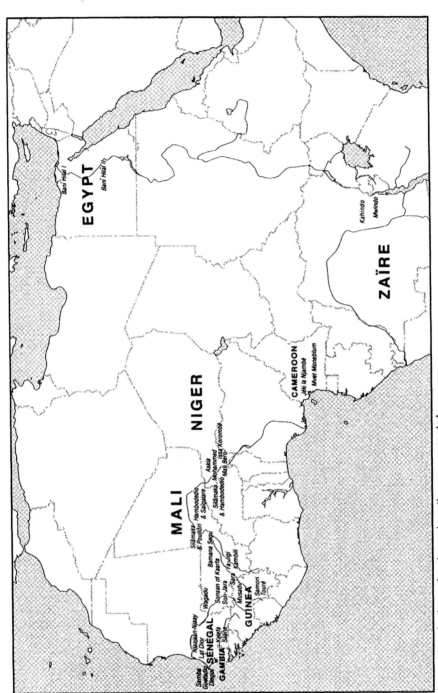

Short titles of epics and regions where they were recorded.

Contents

Contents

THIS ANTHOLOGY OF EXCERPTS from twenty-five African epics is the first of its kind to appear in the world and the third volume in the African Epic Series launched by Indiana University Press. It marks a significant step forward in the effort to shift the notion of epic from a Western to a global context. We hope that this volume will inspire readers to delve more deeply into epic traditions in Africa. The purpose of the present text is to offer a broad sample of the extensive epic traditions in Africa and to provide an overview of this important genre on this vast continent.

Books in this series provide affordable volumes of epic texts for a variety of uses. Teachers will find these books helpful for classroom use, and they will prove beneficial in a wide variety of courses where epic texts are needed at both the university and high school levels. Literary scholars who teach courses on the genre of epic will be pleased to have readable, authentic, linear translations of some of the world's great epics. Folklore and anthropology scholars who study the social use of text-based traditions and oral literature will also appreciate these volumes. Scholars of African written literature, who like to begin their courses with the flavor of oral performance, will find this book, and others in the series, inexpensive enough to include on their reading lists. Indeed, students in a wide range of related courses, such as mythology, history, communications, and linguistics will find an astonishing diversity of symbols, images, metaphors, and themes in these excerpts. We hope that all readers will encounter in these texts the same fascination that they hold for us.

Finally, for those who want to examine a particular African epic more thoroughly, scholarly editions of most of these texts exist. Two epics in this series, for example, *The Epic of Son-Jara* (collected, translated, and annotated by Johnson) and *The Epic of Askia Mohammed* (collected, translated, and annotated by Hale), provide complete texts and detailed descriptions. Two other studies that are now very close to completion, a detailed study of African bards (*griots* and *griottes*) by Hale, and another on African epic by Belcher, promise to provide even broader perspectives for the specialist and for the really curious reader with a more complete understanding not only of texts but also of their regional literary contexts and their narrators. When all these publications become available, a really thorough knowledge of epic in Africa will be available to Western reading audiences, long ignorant of the oral performance of this vibrant genre on that vast continent.

At the end of this volume, we have included a general bibliography on the African epic, and for each regional series of epics, the reader will also find short and more specialized listings of sources for further study. The general bibliography will give the reader a more extensive overview of the genre than we can supply here. The specialized listings include titles of more culture-specific works for the reader who wants to examine more closely what lies behind one of the epic traditions. The epic is a multi-functional genre not only for the societies that are reflected in the verbal mirror of its narrative, but also, we think, for readers outside of Africa. The generalist interested in literature will discover here an extraordinary universe of heroes, battles, and intrigues that matches anything produced elsewhere in the world.

For an anthology as varied and complex as this one, we have many people to acknowledge. We would like to thank the narrators of these texts as well as the collectors, translators, and editors who undertook the difficult task of conveying the oral performance to the print medium. Many of these texts are appearing in print for the first time. We are especially grateful to John Gallman, Director of Indiana University Press, for his sustained encouragement as well as for his patience, which must surely approach that of Job.

Just as the epic is a vast and interactive verbal form, so too we would like readers to consider this book as an opening statement in a continuing and expanding dialogue about the oral epic in Africa. Subsequent editions, with an even more diverse collection of excerpts, will depend on the responses of current and future scholars interested in this form. We would like to hear from you, and we may be reached via Indiana University Press, 601 North Morton Street, Bloomington, Indiana 47401-3797.

John William Johnson, Indiana University
Thomas A. Hale, The Pennsylvania State University
Stephen Belcher, The Pennsylvania State University

Acknowledgments

THE EDITORS GRATEFULLY ACKNOWLEDGE THE KINDNESS of the following individuals and publishers for granting permission to reprint previously published materials, as well as for permission to publish several original texts. It is through their generosity that this book has been made possible.

The Epic of Wagadu translated by Thomas Hale from mimeographed documents, by permission from Guy Sabouret and Youssouf Tata Cissé for the Fondation SCOA.

The Epic of Son-Jara reproduced from the published version of John William Johnson by permission from John William Johnson and Indiana University Press.

The Epic of Fa-Jigi from unpublished work by David Conrad, reproduced by permission from David Conrad.

The Epic of Bamana Segu reproduced from the published work of David Conrad by permission from David Conrad and the British Academy.

The Epic of Sonsan of Kaarta from unpublished work by David Conrad, reproduced by permission from David Conrad.

The Epic of Almami Samori Touré from unpublished work by David Conrad, reproduced by permission from David Conrad.

The Epic of Musadu from unpublished work by Timothy Geysbeek, reproduced by permission from Tim Geysbeek.

The Epic of Kelefa Saane from published work by Gordon Innes, reproduced by permission from Gordon Innes and the School of Oriental and African Studies, University of London.

The Epic of Kambili from published work by Charles Bird, reproduced by permission from Charles Bird and the African Studies Program at Indiana University.

The Epic of Sara from unpublished work by Charles Bird, reproduced by permission from Charles Bird.

The Epic of Askia Mohammed from published work by Thomas Hale, reproduced by permission from Thomas Hale and Indiana University Press.

The Epic of Mali Bero from unpublished work by Thomas Hale, reproduced by permission from Thomas Hale.

The Epic of Issa Korombé from unpublished work by Ousmane Mahamane Tandina, reproduced by permission from Ousmane Mahamane Tandina.

The Epic of Hambodedio and Saïgalare from published work by Christiane Seydou, translation and reproduction authorized by the Association des Classiques Africains.

The Epic of Silâmaka and Poullôri from published work by Lilyan Kesteloot; translation and reproduction authorized by L'Harmattan.

The Epic of Silâmaka and Hambodedio from published work by Christiane Seydou; translation and reproduction authorized by the Association des Classiques Africains.

The Epic of Samba Gueladio Diegui from unpublished work by Amadou Ly; translation and reproduction authorized by Amadou Ly.

The Epic of Njaajaan Nyaay from published work by Samba Diop; reproduced by permission from Samba Diop.

The Epic of Lat Dior from published work by Bassirou Dieng; translation and reproduction authorized by Bassirou Dieng and Editions Khoudia.

The Epic of Banī Hilāl: The Birth of Abū Zayd I from unpublished work by Dwight Reynolds; reproduced by permission from Dwight Reynolds.

The Epic of Banī Hilāl: The Birth of Abū Zayd II from unpublished work by Susan Slyomovics; reproduced by permission from by Susan Slyomovics.

The Epic of Mvet Moneblum from published work by Samuel Martin Eno-Belinga; translation and reproduction authorized by Samuel Martin Eno-Belinga.

The Epic of Jéki La Njambè Inono from published work by Tiki a Koulle a Penda; translation and reproduction authorized by the College Libermann.

The Mwindo Epic from published work by Daniel Biebuyck; reproduced by permission from Daniel Biebuyck and the University of California Press.

The Epic of Kahindo from published work by Daniel Biebuyck and Kahombo Mateene; translation and reproduction authorized by the Académie Royale des Sciences d'Outre-Mer.

The editors would also like to express their gratitude to Nicole Paulin for her assistance with preparation of the index and to David Barnes of Deasey GeoGraphics Laboratory at The Pennsylvania State University for his assistance in the preparation of the map facing the table of contents.

The Existence of Epic in Africa

AFRICAN EPIC TRADITIONS have not attracted much recognition from scholars in literature until recently because of the many barriers, intellectual and physical, that stood between the oral sources and their potential readership. For example, few people outside of Africa know any of the more than 1,000 languages on the continent. Even when a researcher knows one of these languages, it is difficult to transcribe an epic as it is being narrated. One must copy it on audiotape, a technology that came into wide-spread use only in the last few decades. Early collecting efforts, such as those of Leo Frobenius and others, may present the story but do not accurately reflect the performances. The consequence of these obstacles is that African traditions remain less well documented than those of Europe and Asia.

The epic is recognized as a primary genre of world literature. The earliest examples, such as the *Epic of Gilgamesh* or the Greek *Iliad* and *Odyssey*, attest to its age; the Greek literary tradition makes this genre almost equivalent to scripture. The influence of the classical literary tradition has associated the epic with written forms and until recently obscured its occurrence in the oral tradition. Unlike more universal forms of oral folklore, epics do not appear in the literatures of every culture, but they are far more widespread than is generally recognized. Readers will probably be acquainted with the written epics of Europe such as *Beowulf*, the French *chansons de geste*, and the German *Nibelungenlied*; they may also know the Sanskrit monuments of India, the *Ramayana* and the *Mahabharata*, or the Persian *Shahnama* of Firdausi. They are less likely to have firsthand acquaintance with the more recent textual versions of oral traditions, the result of an effort which began in the early nineteenth century with Elias Lönnrot's compilation of the Finnish *Kalevala* and Vuk Karadzic's compilation of Serbo-Croatian heroic narratives and continues to the present day with extensive research into the vast Turkic traditions, the discovery of epics among the Ainu of northern Japan, and the study of vernacular epic traditions in India. They are even less likely to know of African epic traditions, since a number of scholars, in spite of available evidence, have doubted their existence.

An early influential statement on the subject came from Ruth Finnegan in 1970. At the end of a chapter on "Poetry and Patronage" in her landmark study, *Oral Literature in Africa*, she offered a note on epic. She observed that "in the more obvious sense of a 'relatively long narrative poem,' epic hardly seems to occur in sub-Saharan Africa" (p. 108). Her objections were based on current assumptions, some of which were reasonable at the time but have since proven to be inaccurate. At the time of the publication of her book, there was very little evidence for the occurrence of epic in Africa for a number of reasons. First, compared to later decades, few epic texts had yet been collected and published; and second, almost all had been reconstructed into "novel-like" prose. Moreover, a number of collectors had published poems that purported to be epic but that were in fact panegyric, one of the dominant forms of African folklore, related but not identical to epic. Finnegan was also attempting to lay to rest the Western prejudice, born in theories of social evolution, that "epic is often assumed to be the typical poetic form of non-literate peoples . . . at a certain stage" (p. 108), and she concluded that "epic poetry does not seem to be a typical African form" (p. 110).

Finnegan's objection raised immediate protests. In successive order, Daniel Biebuyck ("The African Heroic Epic"), Isidore Okpewho (*The Epic in Africa*), and John Wm. Johnson ("Yes, Virginia, There Is an Epic in Africa") provided diverse critical responses. The best answer, of course, has been the publication of the evidence for African epics. In the past two decades scholars from Africa, Europe, and North America have recorded, transcribed, translated, and published many epic texts. Many of these texts, however, are inaccessible to a general public or only available in languages other than English. This volume represents the first attempt to assemble a representative selection of examples from the epic traditions of Africa. Our hope is to acquaint readers with the wealth of material available and to open the door for further recognition and study.

African Literature

Before focusing on the nature of African epic, we must place the study of the genre in the broader context of African literature. For many people, the notion of "African literature" still seems curious: they envision the Darkest Africa of Henry Stanley, an impenetrable jungle inhabited by isolated "tribes" speaking incomprehensible "dialects" and endowed with the most primitive level of material culture. It is an image reinforced by writers as diverse as Edgar Rice Burroughs, author of *Tarzan,* and Joseph Conrad, whose *Heart of Darkness* survived for generations on the reading lists of freshman English courses in the United States. If African peoples did not appear to have a literature, then it followed that they had no history either. Such a view was expressed by Hegel in the nineteenth century and was affirmed as late as 1963 by the historian Hugh Trevor-Roper.

Today, as both African literature and history emerge from behind a veil of ignorance maintained by the West, there are still questions about the definition of oral literature. Literature, after all, is based on the notion of "letters" and thus of writing. For some, the formulation "oral literature" is an offensive oxymoron. Modern African literature has found a more hospitable reception in the last three decades. Produced in the languages of the colonial powers (English, French, Spanish, Portuguese) and shaped in the genres of their European models (poetry, novels, plays), these literatures often appear as an extension or a variant of the respective European literature. In the last decade three writers from Africa have won the Nobel Prize for Literature (Soyinka in

1986, Mahfouz in 1988, Gordimer in 1991). The names Achebe, Ngugi, Sembène, Senghor, Kourouma, and Bâ now appear frequently on reading lists in universities around the world. But the relation of these emerging new literatures to their African roots and their accessibility to African audiences remains a subject of much discussion.

There are also literatures in Arabic produced in North and West Africa that draw on a variety of traditions. Written literatures in Swahili, Hausa, Amharic, and Fulfulde predate the arrival of Europeans. In many cases these literatures grew out of the introduction of Islam and the spread of literacy for local needs. But the elements of African verbal art most invisible to the outsider are those forms still transmitted through the oral tradition—in person, on the radio, and via cassettes. They do not necessarily conform to the accepted genres of European literature, for they exist within different social constructs and world views. To fully appreciate them, one must know their original languages and study the social organizations from which they emerge. All too often, anthropologists and folklorists are the only ones to invest the required time and effort to accomplish these goals.

To grasp the truly African element of African literature, we must turn to the oral forms of their verbal art and respect the diversity produced on a continent-wide scale. We cannot rely upon isolated, anecdotal images of single groups; nor should we be guided by our preconceptions or the familiarity of certain forms. And we must not be influenced by the poorly translated and highly selective publication of children's oral literature published by missionaries and others in the nineteenth and early twentieth centuries.

The African Epic Belt

Epics do not occur everywhere. They are the products of a combination of social and historical circumstances and various verbal genres. The opportunity to explore the roots of such a phenomenon is one of the great contributions Africa can make to the world-wide study of oral epic traditions. In various works, John Wm. Johnson has studied the documented appearances of epic across Africa (Johnson 1978, 1981). He has postulated the existence of an "African Epic Belt," running across the Sahel and down into Central Africa. The epics collected within this region possess features that link them with each other, although not necessarily in a continuous and historically related tradition. These traits set them apart from the widely documented panegyric tradition of Eastern and Southern Africa, as well as from the Arabic traditions of North Africa. Within this volume, however, we have been able to expand the boundaries of the epic belt as originally conceived, a process which we hope will continue as more and more information about the existence of this genre in Africa becomes available.

The term epic has often been applied to any tradition that is "national" or "heroic," regardless of form and length. The texts included here do not reflect this wider usage of the term. For instance, the Akan drum histories of their kings have not been included, although they may be viewed by some scholars as epics. We hope that our volume may inspire continuing lively discussions on the meaning of this term, as well as the publication of more texts recorded from the oral tradition.

Sources

Researchers encounter many difficulties in the translation of oral performances to book form. Some have proposed solutions ranging from variations in typography to extensive annotation. This volume offers no radically innovative solutions. Ideally, one should expect a "text" to represent the accurate transcription of an artist's production at a "natural" or "induced natural" performance (i.e., an occasion for which such a performance would be expected within the culture of origin). The printed text should reproduce faithfully the various elements of the performance: principal narrator, supporting personnel—backup singers, respondents, patrons, and intrusive audience members—as appropriate. But such texts are not always available; nor, often, are they accessible to a foreign audience unacquainted with the local idioms, norms, and expectations. One must strike a balance between the ideal representation of a communal event and the literary and textualized presentation of a verbal tradition. Such a balance requires the audience, in this case the readers, to attempt to recreate the performance context in their own minds.

Our concern has been to provide texts whose origin from the oral tradition can be reliably traced. We should know the name of the performer and the circumstances of the performance. We should have available the original language transcription (if not a tape). But our concern is also to recognize the material already available and the research of the scholars who have worked so hard to process these texts. In a few cases we have translated from a French version of the original transcription. Where possible, we have checked these translations with the collectors and editors who worked with the original recording in an African language. We feel that our inclusion of these selections justifies itself from the intrinsic merits and importance of the material, as well as from the stature as African men-of-letters of the individuals involved: Amadou Hampaté Bâ, in one case, and Samuel-Martin Eno-Belinga in another. We have also drawn on the recent collection efforts of scholars and their unpublished texts, for example the epic of Samori collected by David Conrad.

But the principal concern that has been respected is that the selections be traced, by whatever route, to an original performance. We do not present reconstructed conflations of variants or the transcriptions of anonymous informants. We wish to credit the original artists whose performances we are attempting to bring before a wider public.

Regional Similarities

Through this collection, we wish to lead the reader to an appreciation of the nature of local, regional, and universal traditions. For example, within the vast Mande world of West Africa, and in its neighboring and related areas (the Songhay, for example), one finds considerable cultural continuity as the result of two thousand years of contact through wars, trade, migrations, famines, and droughts. One is entitled to describe the features of this region, in Paul Stoller's term, as elements of a "Deep Sahelian Civilization." We must recognize that one feature common across this space is the narrator, the bard or *griot*, known by a variety of local names: *gewel, gawlo, jali, jeli, mabo, geseré, jeseré*, and others.

The Central African traditions are somewhat different. The link with human social and political institutions is less prominent. Instead, the epics present prodigious heroes with supernatural powers who move through an essentially mythical landscape. There are some exceptions—for example, the Mvet Moneblum reveals concerns that are also purely human. The style of performance is also distinctive. In this general region, the performances are far more dramatic and involve a wider cast. The lead performer will move about, miming the actions of his subjects, and he will be accompanied by musicians and singers as well as by the audience.

The contrast of the intercalated lyrics and the ongoing narrative has led some collectors in the region to present their material as prose rather than in set lines, as is the standard practice for West African texts. This difference raises a number of questions about textualizing epics, and needs to be studied in more detail. On a deeper and so for unexplored level, one can perceive similarities between the precocious heroes, Mwindo of the baNyanga or Lianja of the Mongo, and the troublesome children of the Sahel, such as Maren Jagu of *La dispersion des Kusa* or even Sun-Jata, bone-breaker and uprooter of baobabs. Within the local context, these Central African narratives also present an image of the past that is in many ways the functional equivalent of what we see in the Sahelian epics.

Inclusion of the North African epics opens the door to comparisons of the Arabic and sub-Saharan epic traditions. We offer no hypotheses here on influences or parallels, but we invite study of the question. The geographic proximity and elements of the narrative material—for example, Abū Zayd, like another Arabian hero, Antar, is black—suggests that such study might be richly rewarded.

Women and Epic

The world of the epic appears at first to be dominated by men. One soon discovers, however, that the heroes of many of these epics—Son-Jara and Askia Mohammed, for example—depend on women both in childhood and later at key points in their lives. One question emerges from the role of women in the epic: do women griots also recount epics? When asked if women narrate epics, male griots usually respond that the role of women is to sing songs, not epics. The man may sing or speak the narrative, while women contribute songs at the appropriate points during the same performance. In Central Africa, the very sketchy evidence available to us at this point suggests that women there may fit more easily into the role of performers of long narrative poems.

There is a growing debate, led by Lucy Durán, over this apparent gender division in the epic. The discussion is in some ways clouded, because local sources do not distinguish clearly between praises, sung by both men and women, and narrative, traditionally the province of men. Durán argues that women will sing an entire epic if no man is available for the task. Although no epic by a woman has appeared in print, Durán reports that some songs by women extend over long periods of time—as much as two hours—and contain in essence all of the elements of epic. The short narrative by the late Siramory Jabaatè, one of the most famous Malian griottes, or *jelimusow*, that we have included, gives some idea of the nature of epic songs by women. Future research on this question by Durán and other scholars will provide, we hope, evidence to explain more clearly the role of female bards in relation to the epic.

Definitions of Epic

Ruth Finnegan based her skepticism about the epic in Africa on formal criteria. She felt, essentially, that in many regards the examples she had examined of African epic at the time did not match the characteristics displayed by Eurasian examples of the genre. We do not wish to assert that African epic is identical to Eurasian traditions—such an assertion, in fact, would diminish the interest of these texts for a wider community. John Wm. Johnson has outlined features which he finds common to African epic and useful for analysis. Epics are poetic narratives of substantial length, on a heroic theme (so far we are on familiar territory); they are also multigeneric and multifunctional, incorporating more of a community's diversity than might have been expected; and they are transmitted by culturally "traditional" means. They are not the overnight creation of visionaries, whatever the role of individual creativity in the generation of a specific performance version.

The term epic, deeply rooted in the Western literary tradition, certainly fits the texts we present here; but readers need to keep in mind that the peoples who produced these African epics have their own words and generic boundaries for this genre. Just as we have employed the regional and global words griot and bard along with more ethno-specific terms such as *jali* to identify the narrators of some epics, we feel it is time for scholars to learn more about the particular ethno-poetic features represented in local terms for these texts. The Wolof term for epic is *cosaan* or *woy jallore*, praise song, tale of great exploits, and genealogical song (Kesteloot and Dieng, 1989, 13). For the Fulbe, it is *hoddu* (epic story as well as the lute played to accompany it; Seydou, 1972, 47). Among the Moors, who have a very rich and complex tradition of both oral and written poetry produced by different members of society, *thaydina* is a musical and poetic form of some length that contains both praises and accounts of deeds. It is sung mainly by *iggawen*, griots from the sub-Saharan oral tradition (Guignard, 36; Norris, 41). For the diverse peoples of the Mande world, there are many different terms. In the Mandinka region of The Gambia, *tariko* refers to spoken narratives. In Upper Guinea, David Conrad reports that *tariku* is commonly applied to long narratives. Both of these words come from the Arabic term for history, *tārīkh*. Elsewhere, for example among the Bamana and Maninka, the most common words for epic are *wasala* or *maana*. *Wasala* suggests completeness, inclusion, and thorough interpretation of all events and people in the narrative. *Maana*, a more typical term for epic, does not imply such great detail. In Songhay, the noun for a long narrative is *deeda*, or story about the past that often involves a blend of genealogy and narrative. Other terms in Central Africa include the *mvet* among the Fang and related peoples of Cameroon and Gabon, *munia* for the Jéki tradition of the Douala in coastal Cameroon, and *karisi* for the baNyanga performances. The variety of terms for long poetic narratives suggests that we need to redefine the notion of epic from a global rather than a Western perspective. Let us read the texts first and then derive the definitions.

Epic and History

Many of the heroes portrayed in epics have been described in documents ranging from medieval chronicles written in Arabic (*Askia Mohammed*) to French colonial reports from the late nineteenth century (*Lat Dior*). Those who read these texts for the first time, as well as Africanist historians who are quite familiar with the societies portrayed, often want to know what is of historical value in them. Attempts to reconstruct the past from these oral epics are severely limited, however, by a wide range of factors influencing the performance—the origin of the narrator, his or her knowledge of the different traditions, patterns of migration in the region, the location of the performance, the relationship of the bard to the audience, and the biases of the listeners. A version of the Sunjata epic in Kita, Mali, may differ considerably from one recounted in Brikama, The Gambia, for all the reasons cited above.

A more productive approach to the question of historicity is to view these epics as windows on the past that reflect contemporary values conveyed by one group in society, the narrators, who have a vested interest in promoting a particular version of events. That interest is closely tied to the patrons of these wordsmiths and to complex clan relationships. If we frame the question of historicity in a much broader temporal and geographical context, where the image of the past may change from generation to generation (example: African American history today versus that which appeared in textbooks half a century ago) or from people to people (example: British versus Russian views of who won World War II), then we can begin to understand why there may be such variability among performances of the same epic.

Our view of the historicity of epics may differ from that of many African listeners for whom the version of the past recounted by a griot constitutes the accepted representation of events. But we share both a common appreciation of the verbal art displayed by the narrators and a keen awareness that at bottom all historical accounts, written or oral, are interpretations of events subject inevitably to variation, revision, and reinterpretation, depending on who is telling the story and to whom it is recounted.

Terminology

The reader of these epics will quickly discover a confusing inconsistency in terminology and spelling for ethnic groups, places, and other terms. There are several reasons for this lack of a common nomenclature. First, the parts of Africa represented in this anthology reflect various external influences. The Wolof, Mande, and Songhay texts, for example, all come from French-speaking Africa, but Mandinka texts tend to come from English-speaking Africa. We have adopted French or English spellings depending on the country of origin of the text. But some of our contributors, notably Conrad, an American, have used English spellings in place of French when editing texts from French-speaking countries—for example Segu instead of Ségou. At other points, readers will note several different spellings for spirits known in English as genies—djinns, jinns, etc. Again, we have decided to maintain the original spelling in the text. A more complex problem arises with the names of peoples. The Bamana have long been known as Bambara to the outside world. The Fulbe are sometimes called Fulani, Fula, Poular, and Peulh, and they speak the Fulfulde language. The Maninka, a Mande people, are called Malinké by the Fulbe, a term that has been adopted by the French for that people. Within these groups, there is considerable variation depending to a large extent on who is talking and the distance between his or her maternal language and the local lingua franca. The Zarma, for example, speak a dialect of Songhay that is fully understandable by anyone who speaks that language. But the Zarma refer to their language as Zarma not Songhay. For comparison, note that Americans say they speak English, but when a French translator translates an American novel into French, the cover page reads "traduit de l'américain"—translated from American.

Another variation occurs in the names of clans. Diarra, a province of the ancient empire of Ghana as well as the name of a clan, is also spelled Jarra. The Keita clan is sometimes spelled Keyta by English speakers, and the village of Kéla in Mali is often spelled Keyla by anglophones. The profession of griots not only has different names, as indicated above under regional similarities, but also different spellings—for example *dieli*, *djeli*, and *jeli* for griot in the central Mande area, and *djali* or *jali* in the western Mande.

Another kind of vocabulary that may be confusing at first falls into the category of ideophones, which we have not attempted to translate. These are words that convey movement or action by their sound. An example in English would be "plop" for when something falls on the floor. The reader will find many different ideophones from a variety of languages in these excerpts—*bilika* (sound of weeping), *faat* (sound of an arrow striking), *bari* (sound of speed), *wuu* (sound of musket firing), and *farak* (sound of a horse drinking). In nearly every case, the context will help the reader to understand the ideophone. We might have modified all of these diverse terms to fit a uniform linguistic pattern. But such an approach would have done violence to the texts that we are including and would have robbed the reader of a full appreciation of the great diversity that marks the world of epic in Africa.

Finally, a few words of explanation about the use of the word tribe are necessary. "Tribe" is one of those anthropological terms that has taken on an extraordinarily wide range of meanings outside that field. Anthropologists cannot agree on just what it means, though the terms "common language" and "common ancestor" turn up often in attempts to define it. In the historical context, a people living as a tribe were usually viewed as fairly low on the scale of social development. Thus, until recently, it was quite common for scholars and journalists to use tribe in referring to Africans. Tribalism still appears in the media as the bane of African countries. In some parts of Africa a space for tribe is included on passports, and many Africans use tribe to describe their own peoples. The Bedouins, who are the source of the Banī Hilāl epics, refer to their own people as members of tribes. But today tribe is too vague a descriptor for most other contexts. The extent of the controversy over the use of tribe can be seen in the large number and generally negative tone of message postings in May and June 1995 on the H-Africa electronic network based at Michigan State University (H-Africa@MSU.EDU). The British Broadcasting Corporation and the Library of Congress have dropped the term as a descriptor for Africans. With few exceptions, then, we have adopted other words such as clan, people, ethnic group, or nation, to refer to the extraordinarily diverse collectivities that have produced these epics.

Presentation of the Texts

With such a diverse collection of texts, we have not imposed a particular format on our contributors. For many of the epics, a series of excerpts linked by transitional paragraphs written by the collectors or translators provides the flavor of the narrative in the few pages available. For shorter narratives, the entire text has been included. In a few cases—Charles Bird's excerpts from *Kambili* and the full text of *Sara*—the commentary is somewhat more extensive than for others because of the density or unusual nature of the narrative. Throughout, we have attempted to respect the original format. For some epics, the breaks between lines or sections simply indicate a pause. In other cases, however, these spaces reflect a shift from one episode to another or the omission of lines. The reader can judge from the sequence of line numbers whether the break indicates a pause or a shift to a new section of the epic.

We have adopted the same line numbers that appear in the original, but with a few exceptions—for example, the prose texts from Central Africa are not numbered. Two of the three Fulbe epics (*Silâmaka and Poullôri* and *Silâmaka and Hambodedio*) did not have line numbers in the original, so we have added them for the excerpts. The third Fulbe text, *Hambodedio and Saïgalare*, carries line numbers in the original, but for typographic reasons they do not distinguish between lines and line fragments. In the excerpts provided here, we have chosen to recount runover fragments as part of the line to which they belong rather than as separate lines. For this reason, our numbering system does not match the original. The problems of line numbering reflect in microcosm the highly complex task of transforming a recording of an epic to the print medium. Our goal is to facilitate the activities of reading, discussion, and analysis of these narratives.

We hope that this brief introduction to the issues rooted in the study of African oral epics, as well as the excerpts from the texts that follow, will inspire readers to explore in more depth both the general subject of this relatively unknown form and the particular traditions presented here. We believe that the excerpts and the references in the bibliography at the end of the volume will enable the reader to discover what we have learned during the past two decades: that the oral epic in Africa represents one of the most vibrant voices from this vast continent today.

PART ONE

WEST AFRICA

The Soninké Epic

THE SONINKE KINGDOM OF GHANA IS THE OLDEST KNOWN West African kingdom on the written record. It was described by Arab travelers in the ninth century a.d. as "the land of gold." With its capital in southeastern Mauritania, Ghana controlled trade in gold, ivory, salt, and slaves between North Africa and the forest region to the south. By the eleventh century, Ghana had declined and was eventually replaced by Mali in the thirteenth century under the rule of Sunjata (Son-Jara). The decline of Ghana had many causes, including wars and draught. Groups of Soninké began to disperse from the eleventh century onward over a large area of the Sahel and Savanna regions. These people, their descendants, fragments of their oral tradition, and in some cases just echoes of their language may be found today from Senegal to Niger. There is some evidence to suggest that Soninké oral traditions may well underlie many of the royal traditions of origin throughout the area.

The Soninké epic tradition, one of the oldest in the region, is not as well recorded as one might wish. At the start of the century, the German anthropologist Leo Frobenius collected a number of traditions on Wagadu and Dama Ngille of Jaara. He believed that he had uncovered a West African *Heldenbuch*, or book of heroes, but his sources, and indeed the language of his texts, are open to question.

The story of Wagadu is the central moment for Soninké history, a period of unity before its fall and dispersal. We have many short versions recorded over the past century. In a recent study, Germaine Dieterlen republished some older accounts, along with an annotated, 453-line text recorded from Diarra Sylla. Our principal lengthy example of Soninke oral performance is excerpted from a 1,220-line narrative by Diaowa Simagha entitled *Légende de la dispersion des Kusa*. It was published by Claude Meillassoux and Lansana Doucouré and gives the origin of a subordinate group of Soninke speakers who are not directly connected with Wagadu. Otherwise, we are left with more fragmentary and regional traditions: the story of Dama Ngille and the kingdom of Jaara, the history of the Kagoro, which in current form appears to reflect historical narration rather than epic performance, and a variety of tales, legends, and songs edited by Oudiary Makan Dantioko and published in often hard-to-obtain formats in 1978, 1982, and 1987.

These and many other examples of the Soninké oral tradition mentioned above convey parts of the legend of Wagadu, the story of how the empire was founded, the role of the Bida snake in providing wealth for its peoples, and the incident that led to the destruction of Ghana. This legend is known among many Soninké-speaking peoples from the Guidimaka region in Mauritania to the Borgu region in northern Benin. In many cases, however, it has been replaced by local oral traditions. We may still recognize historical elements in this legend—the production of gold, the decrease in rainfall, and the migration south toward the Senegal River and then eastward. In some versions, we also encounter historicized myth, incidents borrowed from the Judeo-Islamic tradition, and a unique twist on the pattern of the dragon-slayer story.

3

1. The Epic of Wagadu
Narrated by Diarra Sylla and Jiri Silla

Diarra Sylla text recorded in 1977 in Yéréré, Mali, transcribed and translated into French by Mamadou Soumaré. Jiri Silla text recorded in 1965 in Yéréré by Malamine Cissé, transcribed and translated into French by Abdoulaye Bathily. Each published in separate mimeograph form by the SCOA Foundation for the 1977 Colloquium at Niamey, Niger. This excerpt edited and translated into English by Thomas A. Hale.

THESE EXCERPTS ARE FROM TWO NARRATIVES about the rise and fall of the Ghana Empire, known locally as Wagadu because the first city was the home of the Wago, one of the three main peoples who claim descent from the empire and the group that is most closely associated with its founding.

Although no one has published an epic that gives the full story of the Ghana empire, the following two excerpts from two different versions of shorter narratives, the first by Diarra Sylla, 257 lines, and the second from Jiri Silla, 800 lines, taken together, give the reader the outline of what happened to the people of Wagadu. These texts constitute a partial reconstruction of what must have been a somewhat longer epic about events nine centuries ago.

Because the excerpts from the 1977 texts presented here are divided into separately numbered chapters and come from two different sources, the line numbers do not follow sequentially. But the shift from the first narrator to the second will be indicated below.

[Diarra Sylla first tells his listeners about Dinga Khoré, ancestor of the descendants of the Ghana empire. In this version, they came from India via Yemen and Israel to an unidentified place in Africa approximately 1,000 miles east of present-day Mauritania. Toward the end of his life, Dinga left a message for a vulture to convey to his descendants:]

75 . . . I have a message I would like to entrust to you.
    The vulture replied, "We are at your service."
    Dinga spoke again: "After my death, when all the sacrifices have
        been made, you will tell my descendants to go toward the
        West.
    "There is a place there called Kumbi, there is a well at that place,
        and there is something in the well, people talk with that
        creature, for it is not an ordinary creature, they only settle
        down there after they have reached an understanding with the
        creature in question."

[The vulture transmitted the message to one of Dinga's sons, Djabé Cissé.]

    Djabé Cissé asked, "How can one find this place? "

4

The vulture replied, "You will kill forty fillies for us, one a day.
125 "The lungs and the liver are for me, the vulture, and the remainder
of the meat you will give to the hyena "

[After the sacrifices were made, the vulture explained what the
descendants of Dinga would find at Kumbi.]

... after their arrival at Kumbi, they will find there a well and inside the well a monster.
15 They will be called upon to make a contract with this creature.

[Djabé Cissé and his people set off with the hyena and the vulture for
Kumbi.]

They walked for forty days before reaching Kumbi. At their arrival
the hyena stopped at the edge of a well and the vulture
perched at the top of a tree near the well.
20 The vulture said then to the children of Dinga, "Here is Kumbi,
here is the well."
Then a loud noise arose from the well.
The voice asked who was there, and the vulture replied that they
were the children of Dinga and that they had come to settle
there.
At these words, an enormous snake rose out of the well. He was
very black, he had a crest on his head like that of a rooster, and
the crest was very red.
He said, "No one will settle here."
25 Djabé replied, "We will settle here, for our father at the end of his
life ordered us to come to Kumbi. And this is certainly Kumbi:
here is the well! We shall settle here."
"Agreed!" said the snake called Bida. "But there are conditions for
that."
Djabé declared then, "We are ready to listen to these conditions."
"Fine!" replied Bida.
"Each year," he said, "in the seventh month, on the seventh day of
the seventh month, you will offer me 100 heifers, 100 fillies,
and 100 girls."
30 "Agreed," said Djabé, "but each year, the loss of 100 heifers, 100
fillies, and 100 girls will amount to the ruin of the country."
They bargained and finally agreed on one filly and one girl—but
the filly will be the best in the entire country and the girl the
most beautiful in the entire country.

[Djabé won the title of King of Wagadu as the result of a competition to
lift four heavy drums. The snake then gave him conditional power to
rule.]

47 When Djabé was installed as ruler, Bida declared to him that he
      would be supplied with people and goods as long as he honors
      the contract that linked them together.

[The Jiri Silla version follows from here on. When the time for the
sacrifice came next year, the people prepared themselves.]

15 At the end of the rainy season, in the seventh month and on the
      seventh day, all the people gathered and the sacrifice was
      carried out.
      The morning of the sacrifice, the morning of the solemn day, every-
      one turned up before the door of the ruler, drummers as well as
      citizens, all gathered in this spot.

18 As for the girl, she was already dressed, dressed in such an extra-
      ordinary way that you had to see it to appreciate it.
      The filly was so fat that it was beyond commentary.

25 When they arrived near the well, the cortege divided in two.
      The griots were always in front of the ruler, competing with each
      other in turn until they arrived at the edge of the well.

28 Before the griots could return to the ruler with their songs, Bida the
      snake suddenly surged out of the well and made a terrifying
      loud noise.

[After coming out and going back into the well twice, the snake
appeared again for a final time.]

30 He wrapped himself around the girl and the filly; he carried them
      into his lair.
      The ruler and his people returned to the town.

[The snake kept his promise. Gold rained down on the country and the
people prospered. But during the annual sacrifice to Bida another year,
after the third appearance of the snake from the well, a man attacked
it.]

690 Mahamadu the Taciturn cut off his head with his saber.
      At the very moment his head fell away, the serpent cried out:
          "Seven stars, seven luminous stars,
          "Seven famines, seven great famines,
          "Seven rainy seasons, seven entire rainy seasons,
          "No rain will fall in the country of Wagadu.
695   "And even less gold.
          "People will say that Mahamadu the Taciturn ruined Wagadu!"

[After the flight of the Wagadu people from the land, some of them returned home to see what was left.]

They found that everyone was dead.
775 Wagadu emigrated.
It divided into three groups.
One went along the banks of the river.
One group headed toward the Sahel.
And the third left by the middle way.
780 The one that left by the middle maintained the use of the Soninké language.

[Today, all that remains at Kumbi are some ruins. But the Soninké people live on in many parts of the Sahel from Senegal to Niger. An archaic form of their language has become the occult tongue of Songhay sorcerers and griots.]

Mande Epics

THE MANDE PEOPLES MAY BE DEFINED either linguistically, as a group of peoples speaking closely related languages, or historically, as a group of peoples defined by belief in a common origin, generally centered on the towering figure of Sunjata (Son-Jara in the version presented in this anthology), the thirteenth-century hunter-warrior-hero who founded the empire of Mali. The epic of Son-Jara is the best known example of this rich epic tradition and may be the most important piece in some respects, but it hardly represents the full range of possibilities found from The Gambia to Segu, from the Sahara to the forests of Côte d'Ivoire and Sierra Leone.

Some distinctions apply within the corpus. Most of the pieces are performed by *jeliw*, musicians who are members of hereditary status groups; the jeli functions within the community as a repository of shared, public, historical and genealogical knowledge (as opposed to private, familial traditions) and verbal arts. In the past, specific alliances linked noble and jeli clans and lineages, and the patron-retainer relationship was personal as well as commercial; the jeli served as confidential advisor as well as entertainer. Those days and patterns of patronage are gone, and the jeli now seeks a living where it may be found, though some jeli clans cling to old ways and claim a relationship to a noble clan, as do the Jabaatè clan of Kela, who remain loyal to the Keytas.

Another entirely separate epic tradition also exists among Mande peoples, that of the *dònsòn-jeliw* or hunters' bards, who are not jeliw by birth; they serve as bards for initiatory societies such as the hunters' groups or the Komo; such a one was Seydou Camara, the blacksmith, singer of *Kambili* and *Makantaga Jigi (Fa-Jigi)* in this anthology. In such a case, talent, practice or training, as well as knowledge of the occult and loyalty to a specific group or groups, define the role of the bard.

A similar distinction may apply to the corpus of performed pieces. Many are said to be historical in reference. These epics and songs are generally the product of the hereditary performers, the jeliw. Others are less time-bound and perhaps more popular both as to the story line and to a performance style which will readily incorporate songs and even some forms of dancing.

The selection of texts presented here offers a geographical and generic sampler of the Mande epic traditions. The tradition of Son-Jara is represented by a Maninka version from Kita in present-day Mali. Kelefa Saane comes out of The Gambia; this hero is typical of the bellicose aristocracy of the nineteenth century, remembered across West Africa as a time of tumult and war. Almami Samory Turé, coming on the scene somewhat later, was a war-leader from Upper Guinea and undoubtedly the fiercest opponent of French colonial penetration. He was indeed the most effective ruler the region had seen for some time. Musadu comes from a region lying southwest of Samory's territory, in modern Sierra Leone; the epic is comparable to that of Kelefa Saane in its local focus and style of presentation. The same is true of the epic of the Kaarta, which, together with the epic of Bamana Segu, takes us to the eastern fringe of the Mande world.

The epic of Bamana Segu is but a small portion of a wide and rich epic cycle dealing with the history of the kingdom that arose along the middle Niger in the early eighteenth century, under Biton Kulibali, and lasted some 150 years until it fell to the advance of the Islamic Fulbe and Tukolor. The cycle may be divided into many discrete episodes (particularly for the stories of the conquests of Segu), but is also presented as a grand and finite unit by its performers. Tayiru Banbera was a widely recognized and talented performer, and his version of the cycle is perhaps the most circumstantial and detailed available.

Seydou Camara, blacksmith, French army veteran, and hunters' bard extraordinaire, was a well-documented performer and a widely respected master of occult lore. The pieces presented here come from his adopted function of singer; *Kambili* is a classic hunters' tale which involves mastering the bush not through physical strength, but through the proper regulation of social relations and the discovery of secrets of power. *Makantaga Jigi (Fa-Jigi)* is, in some sense, the legend of origin for the occult power, which moves so much of Mande spiritual thought. The legend serves as a myth of origin for blacksmiths but is recognized beyond that group as an account of the introduction of magical knowledge into the Sahel.

The world of Mande oral tradition goes well beyond the canonized figure of Son-Jara, and we are fortunate that it has been relatively well documented so that we can provide such a diversity of texts. Each of the following texts, of course, is but the tip of a greater tradition. Beyond Kelefa Saane one finds a generation of Mandinka heroes in The Gambia. Accompanying Samori one finds his generals and his brother. In Segu we have a series of four kings and innumerable conquests. And finally, the corpus of the hunters' bard is potentially infinite. The traditions of performance and content change in response to new conditions brought about by recording technology and the transformation of the micro-economy, but they are not dying. They remain vital and enthralling.

While on one level, the Mande world is marked by broad cultural unity over great space and time, one should also note a number of tensions and divisions within the society, identified by analysts and recurring within the texts that follow. Within the frequently polygynous family, two tendencies may be observed: *badenya*, or 'mother-childness,' a spirit of unity and cooperation which marks the children of the same mother and binds them together; and *fadenya*, or 'father-childness,' which points to two sources of rivalry and tension—against the half-siblings, with whom one competes, and also, in the case of the sons, with the father whom one will strive to surpass. *Fadenya* is seen as a spirit of competition and ambition; it may lead to success, but it may also be socially disruptive.

Within the society at large, a number of other distinctions recur. The nobles, *hòròn*, will consider themselves above all others; their ancestry is free of the taint of servility or of professional status. The professional status groups, known collectively as *nyamakalaw*, have elicited copious analysis and discussion. The term "caste" has been used in reference to these groups, as a consequence of their endogamy; but we consider it inappropriate. The names of the different groups involved describe professions or economic activities, and these recur throughout the epic selections presented below. The *jeli*, or bard/griot, is the master of verbal arts, the praise-singer, the loremaster, genealogist, and mediator between troubled parties—and the source of our texts. The *numu* is the blacksmith, a figure of great occult power and authority. The *garangè*, or leatherworker, is less visible and claims a Soninké origin; the *kule*, woodworkers, are equally low profile. Finally, one should mention the *finè* (*funè*), who appear to be professionally related to the jeliw in that they are bards of a sort; but their specialization is not local genealogy but Islamic lore outside the recognized Muslim lines of authority.

2. The Epic of Son-Jara
Narrated by Fa-Digi Sisòkò

Recorded in Kita, Mali, on March 9, 1968, by Charles Bird. Transcribed and translated into English by John Wm. Johnson with the assistance of Charles Bird, Cheick Oumar Mara, Checkna Mohamed Singaré, Ibrahim Kalilou Téra, and Bourama Soumaoro. Edited by John Wm. Johnson, published by Indiana University Press in 1986 as The Epic of Son-Jara: A West African Tradition, *and reprinted with a new introduction in 1992 as the first volume in the African Epic Series. This excerpt edited by John Wm. Johnson.*

THE EPIC OF SON-JARA (SUNJATA, SOUNDIATA) KEYTA celebrates the exploits of the founder of the empire of the Manden, Old Mali, some 750 years ago. It is recited in several languages, among which are Mandinka, Bamana (Bambara), Jula, Khasonke, Wangara, and Maninka (Malinké). Professional bards (*jeli, jali*), well known to some readers by their French designation *griot*, recite this epic over a widespread area in West Africa: Mali, Senegal, The Gambia, Guinea, Guinea-Bissau, northern Côte d'Ivoire, northern Liberia, southern Mauritania, and anywhere else the well-traveled bard can find an audience of Mande language speakers in the commercial centers of West Africa and Europe.

Running some 3,084 lines of poetry, this version was recited in 1968 by the renowned bard Fa-Digi Sisòkò in the town of Kita in west central Mali. The plot opens with a remarkably similar structure to that of the book of Genesis in the Bible. It begins in heaven with the creation of Adam and Eve (*Adama* and *Hawa*) and proceeds through genealogies of Islamic and Mande families down to Son-Jara's father, thus establishing his royal heritage. The plot then shifts to another part of Old Mali to pick up the hero's mother's clan and his heritage of occult power from her, later to become the key to his successes as a ruler. The narrative goes on to describe Son-Jara's miraculous birth, his sibling rivalry, his exile and return to power through the defeat of his major adversary, Sumamuru Kantè. A final episode describes the conquest of The Gambia by Tura Magan Tarawere (Traoré), one of Son-Jara's generals.

In the following excerpts, we have selected passages which will take the reader through the career of Son-Jara, who is the most important culture hero of the Mande peoples. Indeed it is the recitation every seven years of a long variant of this epic, which lasts over several days, in the village of Kaaba (Kangaba) in the Mande heartland that acts as a "cultural cement" to many Mande peoples of West Africa by celebrating their common origin.

[The origin of Mali is recounted by the bard from the beginnings of humankind and recounted through the birth of the Prophet Muhammad. The Prophet's third convert and personal servant sired three sons, who go from Mecca to a strange new land and found the kingdom of the Mande. Note the italicized pronouncements to the right of the page.

These comments are spoken by the *naamu*-sayer, sometimes an apprentice bard, who represents the audience to the bard by responding after most lines, as is common in speech. Such pronouncements indicate atteniveness to the speaker.]

	Our grandparent Eve and our ancestor Adam,	*Indeed*
155	Conceived some forty times,	*Mmm*
	And begat eighty children!	
	Ben Adam,	*Indeed*
	His first grandchild was Noah,	*Indeed*
	And he had three sons,	
160	Ah, Bèmba!	*Indeed*
	Noah begat three sons:	*Indeed*
	Ham, Shem, and Japheth.	*Indeed*
	Japheth went forth and crossed the sea.	*Indeed*
	His descendants became the Masusu and the Masasa.	*Indeed*
165	Ham, black people descended from him, my father.	*Indeed*
	Shem, the twelve white clans	*Indeed*
	Descended from him.	*Indeed*
170	The Messenger of God, Muhammad, was born,	*Indeed*
	On the twelfth day of the month of Dònba.	*Indeed*
	On the thirteenth day,	
	Tuesday, Bilal was born in Samuda.	*Indeed*
	Ask the ones who know of this.	*Mmm*
175	That Bilal,	*Indeed*
	His child was Mamadu Kanu.	
	That Mamadu Kanu,	*Mmm*
	He had three sons:	*Indeed*
	Kanu Simbon,	*Indeed*
180	Kanu Nyògòn Simbon,	
	Lawali Simbon.	*Indeed*
	That Kanu Simbon and Kanu Nyògòn Simbon,	*Indeed*
	Settled in Wagadugu.	*Indeed*
235	They left Wagadugu,	*Indeed*
	And they went to Jara.	*Indeed*
	They left Jara	*Mmm*
	And went forth to found a farming hamlet,	*Mmm*
	Calling that village Farmtown.	*Indeed*
240	That Farmtown is Manden Kiri-kòròni,	*Indeed*
	The very first Manden village was Manden Kiri-kòròni.	*Indeed*
250	Kanu Nyògòn Simbon	*Indeed*
	Begat King Bèrèmu,	*Mmm*
	King Bèrèmu begat King Bèrèmu Dana.	*Indeed*
	King Bèrèmu Dana begat King Juluku, the Holy.	*Indeed*

	King Juluku, the Holy, begat King Belo Komaan.	*Indeed*
255	Belo Komaan begat Juruni Komaan.	
	Juruni Komaan begat Fata Magan, the Handsome.	
	That Fata Magan, the Handsome,	*Indeed*
	Went forth to found a farm hamlet called Kakama,	*Indeed*
	And they called that place, my father, Bintanya Kamalen.	*Mmm*

[The king's second wife, the ugly Sugulun Kutuma, descendant of a powerful sorceress, has come from the faraway land of Du, where she has been given as a prize for the defeat of the same sorceress by a pair of hunters. Fata Magan's personal fetish has told him that the offspring of this wife will bear the most powerful king the Manden will ever know, but he must first convince the hunters to give her to him. He trades her for his sister, Nakana Tiliba. A struggle for the throne ensues, as Fata Magan's two wives, Saman Berete and Sugulun Kutuma, both bear him sons nearly at the same time.]

	That Fata Magan, the Handsome,	
	He married the daughter of Tall Magan Berete-of-the-Ruins,	
	Called Saman Berete, the Pure.	*Mmm*
265	They called her Saman Berete.	*Indeed*
	She had not yet borne a child at first.	*Indeed*

[Speaking to the hunters, King Magan, the Handsome, says:]

	"You must give me your ugly little maid."	
	That token was added to Nakana Tiliba,	
	Exchanging her for Sugulun Kòndè.	*Indeed*
	It is said that Fata Magan, the Handsome,	
1045	Took the Kòndè maiden to bed.	*Mmm*
	His Berete wife became pregnant.	*Indeed*
	His Kòndè wife became pregnant.	*Indeed*
	One day as dawn was breaking,	*Indeed*
	The Berete woman gave birth to a son.	*Indeed*
1050	She cried out, "Ha! Old Women!	*Indeed*
	"That which causes co-wife conflict	
	"Is nothing but the co-wife's child.	*True*
	"Go forth and tell my husband	*Indeed*
	"His first wife has borne him a son."	*Indeed*
1055	The old women came up running.	*Indeed*
	"Alu kònkòn!"	*Mmm*
	They replied to them, "Kònkòn dògòsò!	
	"Come let us eat."	*Mmm*
	They fixed their eyes on one another:	
1060	"Ah! Man must swallow his saliva!"	*True*
	They sat down around the food.	*Indeed*
	The Kòndè woman then bore a son.	*Indeed*

	They sent the Kuyatè matriarch, Tumu Maniya:	*Indeed*
	"Tumu Maniya, go tell it,	*True*
1065	"Tell Fata Magan, the Handsome,	
	"Say, 'the Tarawere trip to Du was good.'	*True*
	"Say, 'the ugly maid they brought with them,'	
	"Say, 'that woman has just borne a son.'"	*True*
	The Kuyate matriarch came forward:	*True*
1070	"Alu kònkòn!"	*Mmm*
	They replied to her, "Kònkòn dògòsò!	*Indeed*
	"Come and let us eat."	

[The female bard Tumu Maniya goes to find the king and, like the old women who preceded her, is also invited to eat; but she rejects the food until her message is delivered. The announcing of the birth of Son-Jara first, though he was actually born second, causes the father to designate him as first-born. The old women then burst out their message of the Berete woman's child, but alas, they are too late. The reversal of announcements is viewed as theft of birthright; the Berete woman is furious at the old women, and co-wife rivalry is born for all time.]

	Saman Berete,	
1100	The daughter of Tall Magan Berete-of-the-Ruins,	
	Saman Berete,	*Indeed*
	Still bloodstained, she came out.	*Indeed*
	"What happened then?	
	"O Messengers, what happened?	*Indeed*
1105	"O Messengers, what became of the message?"	*Indeed*
	The Kuyate matriarch spoke out:	
	"Nothing happened at all.*Indeed*	
	"I was the first to pronounce myself.	*Indeed*
	"Your husband said the first name heard,	
1110	"Said, he would be the elder,	*Indeed*
	"And thus yours became the younger."	*Indeed*
	She cried out, "Old women,	*Indeed*
	"Now you have really reached the limit!	*True*
	"I was the first to marry my husband,	
1115	"And the first to bear him a son.	*Indeed*
	"Now you have made him the younger.	*Indeed*
	"You have really reached your limit!"	
	She spoke then to her younger co-wife,	*Indeed*
	"Oh Lucky Karunga,	*Indeed*
1120	"For you marriage has turned sweet.	*Indeed*
	"A first son birth is the work of old,	
	"And yours has become the elder."	*That's the truth*
	The infants were bathed.	*Indeed*
	Both were laid beneath a cloth.	*Indeed*
1125	The grandmother had gone to fetch firewood.	*Indeed*

	The old mother had gone to he . . . , to fetch firewood.	*Indeed*
	She then quit the firewood-fetching place	
	And came and left her load of wood.	*Indeed*
	She came into the hut.	*Indeed*
1130	She cast her eye on the Berete woman,	*Indeed*
	And cast her eye on the Kòndè woman,	*Indeed*
	And looked the Berete woman over,	
	And looked the Kòndè woman over.	*Indeed*
	She lifted the edge of the cloth	
1135	And examined the child of the Berete woman,	
	And lifted again the edge of the cloth,	
	And examined the child of the Kòndè woman.	*Indeed*
	From the very top of Son-Jara's head,	*Indeed*
	To the very tip of his toes, all hair!	*Indeed*
1140	The old mother went outside.	*Indeed*
	She laughed out: "Ha! Birth-givers! Hurrah!	
	"The little mother has borne a lion thief."	*That's true*
	Thus gave the old mother Son-Jara his name.	*Indeed*
	"Givers of birth, Hurrah!	
1145	"The little mother has borne a lion thief.	*That's true*
	"Hurrah! The mother has given birth to a lion thief."	

[At the death of King Magan Fata, the Berete wife's son is declared heir to the throne, disregarding the earlier declaration of Son-Jara as heir. The Berete woman summons a Muslim holy man and has a hex placed on Son-Jara, which causes him to be lame for nine years. In spite of her efforts, however, sign after sign portends that Son-Jara will one day rule the Manden. Finally, the day comes when Son-Jara must overcome the hex and stand on his own two legs.]

	For nine years, Son-Jara crawled upon the ground.	*Indeed*
	Magan Kònatè could not rise.	*Indeed*
1255	In the month of Dòmba,	*Indeed*
	The very, very, very first day,	*Indeed*
	Son-Jara's Muslim jinn came forward:	*Indeed*
	"That which God has said to me,	*Indeed*
	"To me Tanimunari,	*Indeed*
1260	"That which God has said to me,	*Indeed*
	"So it will be done.	*Indeed*
	"When the month of Dòmba is ten days old,	*Indeed*
	"Son-Jara will rise and walk."	*Indeed*
	In the month of Dòmba,	*Indeed*
1265	On its twelfth day,	*Indeed*
	The Messenger of God was born.	*Indeed*
	On the thirteenth day,	*Indeed*
	Jòn Bilal was born.	*Indeed*

	On its tenth day,	*Indeed*
1270	Was the day for Son-Jara to walk.	
1290	On the tenth day of Dòmba,	*Indeed*
	The Wizard's mother cooked some couscous,	*Indeed*
	Sacrificial couscous for Son-Jara.	
	Whatever woman's door she went to,	*Indeed*
	The Wizard's mother would cry:	*Indeed*
1295	"Give me some sauce of baobab leaf."	*Indeed*
	The woman would retort,	
	"I have some sauce of baobab leaf,	
	"But it is not to give to you.	
	"Go tell that cripple child of yours	
1300	"That he should harvest some for you.	*Mmm*
	"'Twas my son harvested these for me."	*True*
	And bitterly did she weep: *bilika bilika*.	
	She went to another woman's door;	*Mmm*
	That one too did say:	*Mmm*
1305	"I have some sauce of baobab leaf,	
	"But it is not to give to you.	
	"Go tell that cripple child of yours	
	"That he should harvest some for you.	
	"'Twas my son harvested these for me."	*True*
1310	With bitter tears, the Kòndè woman came back, *bilika bilika*.	

	"King of Nyani, King of Nyani,	
	"Will you never rise?	*Mmm*
	"King of Nyani, King of Nyani,	
	"Will you never rise?	*Mmm*
1315	"King of Nyani with helm of mail,	
	"He says he fears no man.	
	"Will you never rise?	
	"Rise up, O King of Nyani!"	*That's true*

	"King of Nyani, King of Nyani	
1320	"Will you never rise?	
	"King of Nyani with shirt of mail,	
	"He says he fears no man.	
	"Will you never rise?	
	"Rise up, O King of Nyani!"	*True*

1325	"O Wizard, I have failed!"	*True*
	"Ah, my mother,	
	"There is a thickener, I hear, called black *lele*.	*True*
	"Why not put some in my sauce?	
	"'Tis the thickener grown in gravel."	
1330	She put black *lele* in the couscous.	

	The Wizard ate of it.	
	Ma'an Kònatè ate his fill:	*True*
	"My mother,	*Indeed*
	"Go to the home of the blacksmith patriarchs,	*Indeed*
1335	"To Dun Fayiri and Nun Fayiri.	*Indeed*
	"Have them shape a staff, seven-fold forged,	
	"So that Magan Kònatè may rise up."	*Indeed*
	The blacksmith patriarchs shaped a staff, sevenfold forged.	*Indeed*
	The Wizard came forward.	*Indeed*
1340	He put his right hand o'er his left,	
	And upwards drew himself,	*Indeed*
	And upwards drew himself,	
	He had but reached the halfway point.	*Indeed*
	"Take this staff away from me!"	
1345	Magan Kònatè did not rise.	*True*
	In misery his mother wept: *bilika bilika*:	*Indeed*
	"Giving birth has made me suffer!"	*Mmm*
	"Ah, my mother,	*Mmm*
	"Return to the blacksmith patriarchs.	*Indeed*
1350	"Ask that they forge the staff anew,	*Indeed*
	"And shape it twice again in size.	*Mmm*
	"Today I arise, my holy man said."	*Mmm*
	The patriarchs of the smiths forged the staff,	
	Shaping it twice again in size.	*True*
1355	They forged that staff,	
	And gave it to Ma'an Kònatè.	*Indeed*
	He put his right hand o'er his left,	*Indeed*
	And upwards Son-Jara drew himself.	*Indeed*
	Upwards Nare Magan Kònatè drew himself.	*Indeed*
1360	Again he reached the halfway point:	*Mmm*
	"Take this staff away from me!"	
	Ma'an Kònatè did not rise.	
	He sat back down again.	*Indeed*
	His mother wrung her hands atop her head,	
1365	And wailed: "*dendelen!*	
	"Giving birth has made me suffer!"	*True*
	"Ah, my mother,	*Mmm*
	"Whate'er has come twixt you and God,	*Indeed*
	"Go and speak to God about it now!"	*Indeed*
1370	At that, his mother left	
	And went to the east of Bintanya,	*Indeed*
	To seek a custard apple tree.	*Indeed*
	Ah! Bèmba!	*Indeed*
	And found some custard apple trees	*Indeed*
1375	And cut one down.	*Indeed*

	She cut down that staff,	
	Going to give it to Nare Magan Kònatè,	
1405	To the Kòndè woman's child, the Answerer-of-Needs!	*True*
	The Wizard took the staff,	*Mmm*
	And put his right hand o'er his left,	*Indeed*
	And upwards drew himself,	*Indeed*
	And upwards drew himself.	
1410	Magan Kònatè rose up!	*Mmm*
	Running, his mother came forward,	
	And clasped his legs	
	And squeezed them,	*Indeed*
	And squeezed them:	*True*
1415	"This home of ours,	
	"The home of happiness.	*Indeed*
	"Happiness did not pass us by.	
	"Magan Kònatè has risen!	*Indeed*
	"Oh! Today!	*Indeed*
1420	"Today is sweet!	*Indeed*
	"God the King ne'er made today's equal!	*Indeed*
	"Ma'an Kònatè has risen!"	*Indeed*
	"There is no way of standing without worth.	
	"Behold his way of standing: danka!	
1425	"O Kapok Tree and Flame Tree!"	*Fa-Digi, that's true*

[Even more potent signs follow, foretelling that Son-Jara will one day rule the Manden. Finally, Saman Berete convinces her weakling son, the king, that Son-Jara must be exiled from the Manden. He is forced to flee with his mother and his younger sister and brother. After passing through several lands, they settle in Mèma, where eventually messengers come from the Manden to beg his return. In his absence, the sorcerer king of Susu, Sumamuru Kantè, has conquered the Manden and driven his weak brother from the throne. It is at this point that Son-Jara's mother dies, some say in order to enter the next world to better serve him through powerful occult. Son-Jara asks Prince Birama Tunkara of Mèma to give him a place to bury his mother. The king is at first reluctant, but gives in after a veiled threat. Actually, Son-Jara has buried his mother in a secret place so that her amulets will not be stolen by those who would steal her power.]

	Son-Jara looked on the Kòndè woman,	*Indeed*
2450	But the Kòndè woman had abandoned the world.	*Indeed*
	He washed his mother's body,	*Indeed*
	And then he dug her grave,	*Indeed*
	And wrapped her in a shroud,	*Indeed*
	And laid his mother in the earth,	*Indeed*
2455	And then chopped down a kapok tree,	*Indeed*
	And wrapped it in a shroud,	*Indeed*

18

	And laid it in the house,	*Indeed*
	And laid a blanket over it,	*Indeed*
	And sent a messenger to Prince Birama,	
2460	Asking of him a grant of land,	*Indeed*
	In order to bury his mother in Mèma,	
	So that he could return to the Manden.	*Indeed*
	This answer they did give to him	
	That no land could he have,	
2465	Unless he were to pay its price.	*Indeed*
	Prince Birama decreed,	*Indeed*
	Saying he could have no land,	*Indeed*
	Unless he were to pay its price.	*Indeed*
	He took feathers of Guinea fowl and partridge,	*Indeed*
2470	And took some leaves of arrow-shaft plant,	*Indeed*
	And took some leaves of wild grass reed,	*Indeed*
	And took some red fanda vines,	*Indeed*
	And took one measure of shot,	*Indeed*
	And took a haftless knife,	*Indeed*
2475	And added a cornerstone fetish to that,	*Indeed*
	And put it all in a leather pouch,	*Indeed*
	Saying to give it to Prince Birama,	*Indeed*
	Saying it was the price of the land.	*Indeed, ha, Fa-Digi*

[Prince Birama summons his three sages, All-Seeing-Sage, All-Saying-Sage, and All-Knowing-Sage, to read the signs.]

2495	They untied the mouth of the pouch,	
	And shook its contents out.	*Indeed*
	The All-Seeing-Sage exclaimed,	*Indeed*
	"Anyone can see that!	*Indeed*
	"I am going home!"	*Indeed*
2500	The All-Knowing-Sage exclaimed,	*Indeed*
	"Everybody knows that!	*Indeed*
	"I am going home!"	*Indeed*
	All-Saying-Sage exclaimed,	*Indeed*
	"Everybody knows that?	*Indeed*
2505	"That is a lie!	*Indeed*
	"Everybody sees that?	*Indeed*
	"That is a lie!	*Indeed*
	"There may be something one may see,	
	"But if ne'er explained to him,	
2510	"He will never know it.	*Indeed*
	"Prince Birama,	*Indeed*
	"Did you not see feathers of Guinea fowl and partridge?	
	"They are the things of ruins.	*Indeed*
	"Did you not see the leaf of arrow-shaft plant?	
2515	"That is a thing of ruins.	*Indeed*

19

	"Was not your eye on the wild grass reed?	*Indeed*
	"That is a thing of ruins.	*Indeed*
	"Did you not see those broken shards?	*Indeed*
	"They are the things of ruins.	*Indeed*
2520	"Did you not see the measure of shot?	*Indeed*
	"The annihilator of Mèma!	*Indeed*
	"Did you not see the haftless knife?	*Indeed*
	"The warrior-head-severing blade!	*Indeed*
	"Was not your eye on the red fanda vine?	*Indeed*
2525	"The warrior-head-severing blood!	*Indeed*
	"If you do not give the land to him,	*Indeed*
	"That cornerstone fetish your eye beheld,	
	"It is the warrior's thunder shot!	*Indeed*
	"If you do not give the land to him,	
2530	"To Nare Magan Kònatè,	
	"The Wizard will reduce the town to ruin.	*Indeed*
	"Son-Jara is to return to the Manden!"	*That's the truth*
	They gave the land to the Sorcerer.	*Indeed*
	He buried his mother in Mèma's earth.	

[Son-Jara returns to the Manden and does battle with Sumamuru but cannot overcome him, because his adversary's occult power is stronger than that of Son-Jara. Finally, Son-Jara's sister steals into Sumamuru's camp, seduces him, and learns the key to his power. She returns to Son-Jara and reveals the secret, which Son-Jara uses to overcome Sumamuru.]

	Son-Jara's flesh-and-blood-sister, Sugulun Kulunkan,	*Indeed*
	She said, "O Magan Son-Jara,	*Indeed*
2670	"One person cannot fight this war,	*Indeed*
	"Let me go seek Sumamuru,	*Indeed*
	"Were I then to reach him,	
	"To you I will deliver him,	*Indeed*
	"So that the Manden folk be yours,	*Indeed*
2675	"And all the Mandenland your shield."	*Indeed*
	Sugulun Kulunkan arose	*Indeed*
	And went up to the gates of Sumamuru's fortress.	*Indeed*
2690	"Come make me your bed companion!"	*Indeed*
	Sumamuru came to the gates:	*Indeed*
	"What manner of person are you?"	*Indeed*
	"It is I, Sugulun Kulunkan!"	*Indeed*
	"Well, now, Sugulun Kulunkan,	*Indeed*
2695	"If you have come to trap me,	*Indeed*
	"To turn me over to some person,	*Indeed*
	"Know that none can ever vanquish me,	*Indeed*
	"I have found the Manden secret,	*Indeed*

20

	"And made the Manden sacrifice.	*Indeed*
2700	"And placed it in five score millet stalks,	*Indeed*
	"And buried them here in the earth,	*Indeed*
	"'Tis I who found the Manden secret,	*Indeed*
	"And made the Manden sacrifice,	*Indeed*
	"And in a red piebald bull did place it,	*Indeed*
2705	"And buried it here in the earth.	*Indeed*
	"Know that none can vanquish me,	*Indeed*
	"'Tis I who found the Manden secret,	*Indeed*
	"And made the sacrifice to it,	*Indeed*
	"And placed it in a pure white cock.	*Indeed*
2710	"Were you to kill it,	*Indeed*
	"And uproot some barren groundnut plants,	*Indeed*
	"And strip them of their leaves,	
	"And spread them round about the fortress,	*Indeed*
	"And uproot some more barren peanut plants,	*Indeed*
2715	"And fling them into the fortress,	*Indeed*
	"Only then could I be vanquished."	*Indeed*
2730	He lay Sugulun Kulunkan down on the bed.	*Indeed*
	After one week had gone by,	
	Sugulun Kulunkan spoke up:	*Indeed*
	"Ah, my husband,	*Indeed*
	"Will you not let me go to the Manden,	*Indeed*
2735	"That I may get my bowls and spoons,	
	"For me to build my household here?"	*Indeed*
	From that day to this,	
	Should you marry a woman in Mandenland,	*Indeed*
	When the first week has passed,	
2740	She will take a backward glance,	*Indeed*
	And that is what this custom means.	*Yes, Fa-Digi, that's the truth*
	Sugulun returned to reveal those secrets	
	To her flesh-and-blood-brother, Son-Jara.	*Indeed*
	The sacrifices did Son-Jara thus discover.	*Indeed*
2745	The sacrifices did he thus discover.	*Indeed*

[With these secrets, and with the assistance of Sumamuru's nephew Fa-Koli, from whom Sumamuru has stolen a wife, Son-Jara defeats Sumamuru by neutralizing his occult power. After fleeing Son-Jara's army through several villages, Sumamuru, with his favorite wife, arrives at the banks of the Niger River, where so many significant events take place in Mande folklore. Even in defeat, this great sorcerer cannot die a natural death. And if you go to Kulu-Kòrò even today, you may find the spirit of Sumamuru dwelling in a sacred stone, to which you may pray for a favor.]

Sumamuru crossed the river at Kulu-Kòrò,	*Indeed*

	And had his favorite wife dismount,	*Indeed*
	And gave her a ladle of gold,	
2865	Saying that he would drink,	*Indeed*
	Saying else the thirst would kill him.	*That's the truth*
	The favored wife took the ladle of gold,	*Indeed*
	And filled it up with water,	*Indeed*
	And to Sumamuru stretched her hand,	
2870	And passed the water to him.	*Indeed*
	Fa-Koli with his darts charged up:	
	"O Colossus,	*Indeed*
	"We have taken you!	*That's the truth*
	"We have taken you, Colossus!	
2875	"We have taken you, Colossus!	
	"We have taken you!"	*Indeed*
	Tura Magan held him at bladepoint.	*Indeed*
	Sura, the Jawara patriarch, held him at bladepoint.	*Indeed*
	Fa-Koli came up and held him at bladepoint.	
2880	Son-Jara held him at bladepoint.	*Indeed*
	"We have taken you, Colossus!	*That's the truth*
	"We have taken you!"	*Indeed*
	Sumamuru dried up on the spot, *nyònyòwu!*	*Indeed*
	He has become the fetish at Kulu-Kòrò.	*Indeed*
2885	The Bamana worship him now, my father.	
	Susu Mountain Sumamuru,	
	He became the sacred fetish.	*That's the truth, indeed,*
		father, yes, yes, yes, yes!

[Son-Jara now returns to the Manden in glory and governs the land until his death, when his descendants continue to rule over the empire. At this point a number of episodes may follow, describing how Son-Jara's generals conquer vast lands around the Manden, incorporating them into the empire. Son-Jara's own death is a secret that bards of today are not likely to discuss in public but rather keep as a secret. His burial place, which is reported to be in more than one location, is also kept a secret for the same reason that he kept his mother's grave site a secret: so that greedy power-seeking people would not come there and steal his powerful amulets and fetishes.]

3. The Epic of Fa-Jigi
Narrated by Seydou Camara

Recorded in Bamako, Mali, on September 29, 1975, by David Conrad. Transcribed and translated into English by David Conrad with the assistance of Sekou Camara, son of the performer. This excerpt edited by David Conrad.

DURING THE CENTURIES WHEN ISLAM was gradually being integrated into societies of the western Sudan and becoming "Africanized," the bards or griots, specialists in the oral arts of peoples such as the Soninke and Malinké, were assimilating elements of Islamic tradition. At the same time that Islamic elements from across the Sahara Desert were finding their way into local oral accounts, the western Sudan was engendering its own Muslim heroes, among whom were some early Malian kings (*mansaw*) who undertook the arduous trans-Saharan pilgrimage to Mecca. One of the most prominent of these was Mansa Musa, who made his historic journey in 1324. The general outline of the Fa-Jigi legend is probably based on rural, non-Muslim people's perceptions of pilgrimages to Mecca by high government officials, and it could have been engendered as early as the fourteenth century, though the earliest accounts probably differed greatly from those we know. Pilgrimage stories were recorded in writing by the mid-seventeenth century, but no traditions mentioning the name Fa-Jigi were recorded before the colonial era in the late nineteenth century.

In its most general form as presented in many variants, this narrative begins with Fa-Jigi desiring to atone for a sin, often described as incest or murder, that sometimes involves his mother. He undertakes a pilgrimage to Mecca where he acquires the spiritually powerful medicines, amulets and sacrificial objects of important Mande secret societies, including the prestigious Komo power association which serves as a regulatory agency in traditional village life. As the hero returns through the lands of Mande he distributes various potions and amulets to the people who help him. Upon reaching the rivers of Mali, Fa-Jigi uses a magic canoe to transport his spiritually powerful baggage. When the canoe encounters rough waters, some of the cargo falls into the water and is transformed into various creatures such as fish and scorpions. Arriving at home, the location of which varies according to the informant, the canoe sinks to the bottom of the lake or river where it remains to this day, itself a spiritual object that receives sacrificial offerings. It is interesting to note that *jigi*, which means "hope" in Bamana, is used in a number of word plays in this text, beginning with Fa-Jigi ("the father of hope").

The narrator of this variant of the Fa-Jigi tradition is the late Seydou Camara (d. 1983), of Kabaya in the Wasulu region of southern Mali. He was from a family of blacksmiths that has worked with iron for many generations. From 1937 to 1945 he was in the French army, serving in Morocco during World War II. Following the war and many years of apprenticeship with a master singer, Seydou Camara became famous in Mali as one of the great singers of hunters' praise music. In the 1960s and 70s, he could often be heard on Radio Mali, which had recorded his music. In some of his performances he would occasionally interrupt his singing to offer an explanation, but all of the lines presented here were sung as he played the hunter's *ngoni*, a large six-stringed harp. In this performance, Seydou Camara was accompanied by his wife, Numuso, who played the *narinya*, a small, ridged, cylindrical, iron percussion instrument.

> The blacksmith,
> The blacksmith ancestor was called Old Fande.
> His first wife was called Fanbukudi.
> No, no blacksmith is older than Old Fande,
> 5   No blacksmith is older than Old Fande.
>
> Koroma Numuso,[1]
> 255   I speak of the smiths.
> Ah, people!
> Eternal life is not possible.
> Kuda Jan Kali[2] gave birth,
> He sired Numuso who plays the *narinya*.
> 260   Play the *narinya* for me, Numuso.
> Let us look for success and fame in this world, Numuso.
> Death is inevitable, Numuso.
> The other world allows no debts, Numuso.
> Nufaramba is dead, Numuso.
> 265   Camara Jan[3] has gone back, Numuso.
> Eh! Allah is powerful.
> Ah, people!
> Kali Jan has left the world.
> Koroma-Jigi,[4]
> 270   Jigi was a smith at Nora.[5]
>
> 305   Heeee!
> Koroma-Jigi got up,
> Fa-Jigi.[6]
> Fa-Jigi was handsome as a genie.
> Fa-Jigi was pretty as a European.
> 310   Fa-Jigi was prettier than a woman.
> Koroma-Jigi,
> The first woman who fell in love with Jigi was his mother.
> She wailed, "Jigi is so handsome,

1. The performer's wife. 2. The father of Numuso. 3. Late father of narrator.
4. "Hope of the Koroma." 5. Large town in upper Guinea. 6. "Father of hope."

Jigi's mother had a passion for him.
315   "They say he could not have come from my loins!"
Ah, people!
It was a miracle.
Ah, eh!
Nighttime is bad,
320   Nighttime is bad!
The night is a serious thing.
Fa-Jigi,
Leave the millet beer alone, Fa-Jigi!
Do not drink the millet beer, Fa-Jigi!
325   Do not get drunk, Fa-Jigi!
It is risky to drink, Fa-Jigi!
Koroma-Jigi filled himself with millet beer.
Jigi had no lover at Nora except for one girl.
This girl had gone to a hamlet for millet.
330   She had gone with her father,
Away for the night.
Before Fa-Jigi came home,
His mother took a supporter and fastened it to her breasts.
What else did she do before Fa-Jigi came home?
335   She took a bracelet and attached it to her wrist,
She took some waist-beads and put them around her waist.
On a dark and rainy night,
She went and stretched herself on Jigi's bed.
Ah, people!
340   Man is not equal to Allah.
Koroma-Jigi came home from the millet-beer hut,
And he lay with his mother.
He made her his wife, Fa-Jigi!
Ah, people!
345   Fa-Jigi had an accident.
Heee!
Jigi did a very bad thing.
Aaah!
Fa-Jigi was upset.
350   Koroma-Jigi had made his mother his wife,
So he decided to go and see the village almami.[7]
Fa-Jigi said "Listen, village almami.
"Almami, I have lain with my mother.
"Almami, how can I avoid the darkness of hell?"
355   "Koroma-Jigi,
"Clear a field beside the road.
"Farm for three years, Fa-Jigi.

---

7. Muslim cleric.

"Give your harvest to the beggars without touching a single
　　　grain, Fa-Jigi.
"Then your sin will be absolved.
360　"If you cannot farm,
"Go and dig a well in the bush, Fa-Jigi.
"Fill a jar with cool water and put it by the well, Fa-Jigi.
"The thirsty people will come to drink, Fa-Jigi,
"And this will absolve your sin.
365　"Ah, Fa-Jigi,
"You have done wrong.
"If you cannot do that, Fa-Jigi,
"I do not know how to help you."
Fa-Jigi said he was no well-digger.
370　He said he could not farm or make a jar.
The almami said, "Eh!
"Fa-Jigi, if you cannot do all this,
"You must go to Mecca.
"Go to Mecca and wipe out your sin."
375　If it is said that Fa-Jigi went to Mecca,
He did not do it by chance.
Ah, people!
Fa-Jigi did not play around.

Heee!
Allah is a *faama*.[8]
460　Allah refuses to do some things,
But he is never unable to do those things.
They made the necessary sacrifices for Jigi, who must go to
　　　Mecca.
[His uncle] said, "Heee!
"Koroma-Jigi, go to Mecca,
465　"For you will not meet any danger."
Koroma-Jigi began his trip to Mecca with a ram.
He accepted everything [his uncle] told him.
[His uncle] gave one hundred and fifty bags of gold for Fa-Jigi's
　　　journey.
"Go on your journey, Fa-Jigi,
470　"The trip to Mecca will be a source of happiness, Fa-Jigi."

Heee!
Koroma-Jigi walked and walked.
Soso Bala Sumanguru told Fa-Jigi to go to Mecca
　　　and sacrifice four *jigiw*.[9]
Fa-Jigi had only one, the *saka-jigi*,[10]
510　But his uncle said he would find the others along the way.

---

8. King.　9. "(Animals of) hope."　10. "Ram."

Koroma-Jigi walked until he saw a male baboon,
Sitting in the dust of the road.
When the baboon looked up and saw Koroma-Jigi,
It said, "Jigi of men,
515   "You face the east and go *makasi, makasi*.[11]
"Where are you going?
"Ngon-Jigi,
"Bring your head near me," said Fa-Jigi.
"Anybody who has lain with his mother,
520   "If they do not go to Mecca,
"They will be unhappy, Ngon-Jigi.
"They will begin with hell, Ngon-Jigi.
"They will end with hell, Ngon-Jigi.
"Let us go to Mecca and wipe out our sins, Ngon-Jigi."
525   The baboon said, "Have you not heard about Ngon-Jigi?
"All the children around me were born of the love between my
        mother and me.
"Koroma-Jigi, do not take another step without me,
"Let us go together."
So Ngon-Jigi followed Koroma-Jigi,
530   And the number of *jigiw*[12] were three.
The baboon *jigi* walked ahead of the ram *jigi*,
And the man *jigi* followed on the way to Mecca.
Fa-Jigi's journey to Mecca is not a lie, my dear.
It is not a lie,
535   It is not a fiction.
It is not just a song by a player of the hunter's harp.
Koroma-Jigi walked and walked until he found a male
        porcupine,
Crouched in the dust of the road.
Fa-Jigi said, "Eh,
540   "Man of thorns."
The porcupine looked at the *jigi* of men.
He said, "*Jigi* of men,
"Where are you going so fast, *marata, marata*,[13]
"In the direction of the East?"
545   "Heee, good fellow porcupine,
"I am not lying to you.
"Anybody who has lain with his mother,
"If he does not make a journey to Mecca,
"He will begin with hell, Bala-Jigi,
550   "He will end with hell, Bala-Jigi.
"We are going to Mecca to wipe out our sins, Bala-Jigi.
"We are cursed."
"Ah, people!

---

11. Sound of footsteps. 12. "Hopes." 13. Sound of footsteps.

The porcupine told his children to choose a *jigi* among them,
555 A new family leader.
He said, "Awa, Koroma-Jigi.
"Do not take another step without me.
"All my children were born of the love between my mother
    and me.
"I will go to Mecca to wipe out my sins."
560 The *jigiw* of Koroma-Jigi were then three,
And he himself was the fourth.
They walked and walked until they met Nkonkodon-Jigi in a
    grassy plain,
Browsing on the fresh grass.
The antelope raised its head to look at Fa-Jigi.
565 "*Jigi* of men you walk quickly.
"Where are you hurrying to, Fa-Jigi?"
"I am going to Mecca," said Fa-Jigi.
"I have lain with my mother and made her my wife;
"I am going to wipe out my sins at Mecca."
570 "Eh, Fa-Jigi," said the antelope.
"You will not go without me,
"Thank you very much.
"My mother has seven children and they are all by me.
"I will go with you to wash away my sins."

575 Ah, people!
Thank the Father of the world for that walk.
They walked until they arrived at Mecca,
On the day of the *boli*[14] market.
There were amulets[15] everywhere in that market,
580 The *boliw*[16] were everywhere that day.
The *boliw* wandered through the market,
And the *Komo*[17] played at tripping them.
Ah!
Fa-Jigi and his people were astonished.
585 There was no sorcery in Mande,
There were no powerful sorcerers in Mande,
There was no Nama Komo in Mande,
The bird dance did not exist in Mande,
There were no stilt-dancers in Mande,
590 There was no Komo in Mande,
There were no magic powders in Mande.
All these things were brought from Mecca by Koroma-Jigi.
Salute the Fula patriarch for clearing many dark ways.

---

14. Power object, fetish. 15. Charms made of knots in a string. 16. "Fetishes."
17. Esoteric initiation society.

The burning deadly things would not have filled
    a red duiker's[18] horn.

595 Eh, weii!
Since Jigi died,
The world has calmed down.
Koroma-Jigi exchanged the antelope for magic powder.
Ah, *naamu*-sayer![19]

600 The porcupine was traded for magic powder.
The ram was traded for magic powder.
Fa-Jigi returned from Mecca with nine horns of magic powder.
Nine birds' heads dangled from his bonnet when he came from
    Mecca.
Fa-Jigi had a bark-dyed sorcerer's bonnet,

605 He had the mud-cloth sorcerer's bonnet,
And he had the sorcerer's shirt.
Fa-Jigi got all those things in Mecca.
Eeeh!
He who imitates a thing is different from the one who really
    owns it.

610 Fa-Jigi did not play around.
Patron, do not play around with the blacksmith's art.
Do your work well for the blacksmiths.
Sorcery came from smithing.
Ah, people!

615 Blacksmithing is no joke.
Eh, wei!
Numu Kulumba,
Jigi who went to Mecca,
He bought so many *boliw* that he could not carry them alone.

620 He asked the people of Mecca to help him find a canoe.
He said "Ah, people!
"There are too many *boliw* for me to carry alone."
They felled a *kolokolo* tree
To make a canoe for Fa-Jigi.

625 He put the *boliw* in the canoe,
Including the *ntamani* drum. [20]
The griot's *ntamani* drum was given to Fa-Jigi,
As well as the stick for playing it.
The *boliw* talk a lot, Fa-Jigi.

630 They are too talkative, Fa-Jigi.
If they break your eardrum,
Play the *ntamani* drum, Fa-Jigi,
Then the *boliw* will shut up, Fa-Jigi.
Hear how Koroma-Jigi's *boliw* chattered:

---

18. Dwarf antelope. 19. Respondant who encourages the narrator. 20. Hour-glass-shaped drum.

635   "Eh, Koroma-Jigi,
          "You have done well.
          "When I arrive at your father's yard,
          "I will fight your enemies.
          "I will make them swell up, Fa-Jigi.
640   "They will not be able to get out the door, Fa-Jigi.
          "I will give someone a hernia,
          "I will cut the heads off the penises of others,
          "I will cut off the testicles of many.
          "What will I do, Fa-Jigi?
645   "Do you not know, Fa-Jigi?
          "I will put worms in the living bodies of your enemies."
          That is how the *boliw* spoke.
          The *marabout* [21] vocation began at Mecca.
          The Komo began at Mecca.
650   The first Komo owner at Mecca was called Yamusa.
          There is a mountain east of Mecca.
          Even today,
          If a bee from this mountain stings you,
          You will die before you can open your mouth to scream.
655   This is the mountain of magic powder near Mecca.

          Heee!
          Bila Fa-Koli!
          Everything has lost its mystery,
          But the blacksmith things cannot be revealed.
660   Heee, wei!
          They have turned everything upside down,
          But the secret of Komo cannot be betrayed.
          People of the country,
          Everything has been scattered.
665   Heee, wei!
          People have revealed many secrets,
          But the darkness of the grave cannot be revealed.
          Heee, nowadays people scatter everything,
          But *sayasila* [22] cannot be scattered.
670   People of the country have finished scattering everything,
          But the hunters' things cannot be scattered.

675   Koroma-Jigi put the *boliw* into the canoe.
          He took the paddle himself and embarked from Jeddah.[23]
          From Jeddah he paddled to the Bagwe River,
          From the Bagwe he went to Lake Debo,[24]
          From Lake Debo he entered the Joliba.[25]

---

21. Muslim holy man. 22. Sacrificial object for the Komo. 23. Seaport near Mecca.
24. Lake on the inland delta of the Niger River. 25. Bamana name for the Niger.

680 The *boliw* chattered constantly.
   If they break your eardrums, Jigi,
   Play the *ntamani* and they will shut up.
   Ah, *naamu*-sayer!
   When Jigi arrived at Keka,
685 The *ntamani* drumstick was dropped there.
   Nobody could lift it but Turamakan;
   He picked it up and placed it on a tamarind tree.
   If the war was won they spoke of Turamakan.[26]
   If the battle was lost they spoke of Turamakan.
690 If the river flooded they spoke of Turamakan,
   On the other side of the river.
   If the river was dry they spoke of Turamakan.
   The Battle of Dibuntu had heated up.
   This is no lie,
695 Jigi Koroma returned from Mecca.
   Koroma-Jigi slowly returned to Nora.
   The journey had gone well for Fa-Jigi.
   Sad to say,
   The enemies had laid a curse on Fa-Jigi with a louse.
700 The louse was stuck into the mud of the river.
   The day Koroma-Jigi arrived on the lake,
   There would be a great whirlwind.
   The wind would enter the water and cause a hurricane.
   The wind would make Fa-Jigi's canoe disappear in Nora Lake.
705 The whirlwind entered the water near the main entrance of
     Nora town.

   There was a great struggle,
   But the canoe turned over in the flooded lake.
   The Somono came quickly to rescue Jigi,
730 And Jigi was not drowned.
   They fished for the *boliw* for days,
   The *boliw* completely filled a house.
   Jigi brought special divination from Mecca,
   Jigi brought the magic pebbles from Mecca.
735 Jigi had a special amulet on his toe,
   And this amulet became a scorpion.
   Fa-Jigi had a magic powder called "wasp sting" in his armpit,
   And this powder became a wasp.
   If it stings you,
740 You will run in place.
   Jigi had a magic powder[27] called "To-make-unconscious,"
   And this was given to the white men.
   Eeeh!

---

26. One of Son-Jara's greatest generals. 27. Apparently an anesthetic.

31

Fa-Jigi brought a powder called "Beware,"
745   And this became a bee that made excellent honey.
Eeeh!
The rescued *boliw* were distributed all over the Mande.
Koroma-Jigi brought the Komo from Mecca.
Fa-Jigi brought the dust-divining from Mecca.
750   He brought the divination pebbles from Mecca.
He brought the divination cowries,
He brought sorcery,
Sorcery for eating people.
He brought sorcery with him,
755   Sorcery for saving people.
He brought the magic powders from Mecca.
Even now Jigi's bonnet is at Nora,
And they make sacrifices to it.
Every Wednesday of the month of November they make those
    sacrifices.
760   This cap fits all the legitimate descendants of Fa-Jigi.
Ah, people!
Fa-Jigi was an unbeliever.[28]
Koroma-Jigi brought the power of preventing cannibalism.
Fa-Jigi gave that to the old women.
765   Fa-Jigi,
Koroma-Jigi took the sorcery of cannibalism,
He gave it to the evil sorcerers so they could eat people.
Fa-Jigi took the magic powder,
He gave it to the Komo masters,
770   He gave medicine to the great healers.
He gave *marabouts* the power to enfeeble.
He gave the Komo masters power to transform themselves.
He said, "Protect yourselves with this.
"However long the course of life,
775   "The last day will arrive."

830   Heee!
Naamu-sayer,
Koroma-Jigi threw deadly powder on his mother,
And before morning lice had invaded that woman's entire
    body.
Her head,
835   Her armpits,
Her pubic hair,
Everything was full of lice.
His mother swelled up so bad she could not get through the
    door.

---

28. He followed a local religion instead of Islam.

Eeeh, wei!
840 *Naamu*-sayer,
Jigi's mother left the earth.
She died,
And Jigi shouted like this:
"If destiny has chosen that you must go to hell,
845 "Do everything you can to be the little sister of Diahanama
Malikiba."[29]

Eeeh, wei!
Naamu-sayer,
They dug a grave for Jigi's mother.
860 Eeeh!
The shade-tree has fallen,
Death has removed it from me.
My mother was a shade-tree,
Death has taken her from me.
865 Bard of the Komo,
Death has taken the shade-tree from me.
Numu Camara Jan was a shade-tree,
Death has taken him from me.
I am not telling lies,
870 The shade-tree has fallen,
Death has removed it from me.
Numu Faraban was a shade-tree,
Death has removed him from me.
Aaayi!
875 Death has taken the shade-tree from me.
Sele of Koulikoro was a shade-tree,
Death has removed him from me.
Numu Kulumba the shade-tree has fallen,
Death has taken him from me.
880 Numu Camara Jan was one of the shade-trees,
Death has removed him from me.
Death is bad,
The shade-tree has fallen,
Death has removed it from me.
885 Heee, wei!
Kuda Jan Kali was a shade-tree,
Death has removed him from me.

---

29. Angel who escorts sinners to hell.

4. The Epic of Bamana Segu
Narrated by Tayiru Banbera

Recorded in Segu, Mali, between February 28 and March 11, 1976, by David Conrad. Transcribed and translated into English by David Conrad with the assistance of Soumaila Diakité. Edited by David Conrad and published in A State of Intrigue: The Epic of Bamana Segu *by Oxford University Press, 1990. This excerpt edited by David Conrad.*

THE DECLINE OF THE MALI EMPIRE by the fifteenth century and the fall of Songhay in the late sixteenth left a power vacuum on the upper Niger River that eventually came to be filled by a number of smaller states. One of these which flourished from the late seventeenth to the mid-nineteenth century was the Bamana Empire, whose capital of Segu (as the state was also known) is some 150 kilometers downriver (northeast) from where Bamako, the present-day capital of Mali, is located.

This version of *The Epic of Bamana Segu* was narrated by the late Tayiru Banbera, a famous jeli of Segu. Jeli Tayiru's performance was recorded during six sessions at Segu between February 28 and March 11, 1976, by David Conrad who, with the assistance of Soumaila Diakité, later translated it into 7,942 lines of English.

In one of the longest epics recorded in Africa, Jeli Tayiru describes the deeds of many memorable characters, including the hero Bakari Jan, the villain Bilisi, the heroine Sijanma, the bard Tinyètigiba Danté, and several rebellious chiefs such as Desekoro of Kaarta and Basi Samanyana. He also frequently interjects discussions on topics of Bamana culture ranging from beer drinking and cooking to hair styles and seduction. At irregular intervals, Jeli Tayiru would pause, either to collect his thoughts or for dramatic emphasis, while he continued playing the *ngoni*, a small four-stringed lute on which he accompanied himself. These pauses are marked in the text as "musical interludes."

In the interest of continuity, the excerpts presented here focus on kings (*mansaw*) of Segu. There were at least nineteen mansaw of Segu before it was conquered by the Tukulor Army of Al-hajj Umar Tal in 1861. However, Jeli Tayiru mainly talks about only four of those, whose deeds are most memorable: Mamari (Biton) Kulubali (c. 1712-55), Ngolo Jara (c. 1766-87), Monzon Jara (c. 1787-08), and Faama Da Jara (1808-27).

Jeli Tayiru was a Muslim, so his narrative begins with a blessing as part of his traditional introduction, which is followed by some ancestral legends. He then describes Biton Kulubali's rise to power (in which the new king's mother figures prominently), the origin of taxes, and how Biton acquires a slave child named Ngolo, future founder of the next ruling dynasty.

> May Allah bless our master Muhammad,
> Grant peace to him and his family,

Peace to our master Muhammad.
This knowledge is older than any other knowledge.
5 A slave[1] must know the Being who made him,
He must know the messenger of the Being who sent him,
If he wants to be blessed.
If he does this,
He will accomplish what he came to do.

MUSICAL INTERLUDE

10 I, Jeli Tayiru, I come from Ngoin.
Eh the stories I will tell you here in Segu,
They are stories of long ago.
The *mansaw* who performed these deeds,
They are now in *lahara*.[2]
15 They have gone to lie in their own shady places.
The dust from each of their heads could fill a calabash scoop.

MUSICAL INTERLUDE

What *mansa* and what *mansa* do we talk about in Segu,
In Segu of the *si* tree,
Place of the Jara,
20 Segu of the *balansa* trees?
Four thousand *balansa*,
And four hundred *balansa*,
And four *balansa*,
And one humpbacked *balansa*.
25 Not every native understands their significance,
To say nothing of a stranger.

MUSICAL INTERLUDE

In those days Segu was not named "Segu,"
It was called "Sekoro."
There was only one entrance and one exit,
30 Segu was enclosed by a special wall.
Nzan the dog merchant was in the market,
The Bamana sold dogs.
If someone did not sell his dog by mid-afternoon,
The market did him wrong.
35 His dog would be served to the *faama*[3] for breakfast.
The Bamana ruled in Segu for 200 years, less twenty years and
four months.

MUSICAL INTERLUDE

1370 When Biton Kulubali, the man-killing hunter, was in power,
His people ruled for forty years.
His people in power for thirty years were six in number:
Biton himself and his son Bakari and Cekoro,

---

1. Slave here means servant of God. 2. Paradise. 3. "King."

Pelenkene Kanubanyuma and Gasi Kalfajugu and Ngoin Ton
       Mansa.[4]
1375   They ruled for forty years.
       At that time Ngolo was at Nyola,
       At that time Ngolo had not come into this land.
       He was really a native of Nyola.
       Balikoro Jara's grandson was not yet in this land.
1380   If the world were a human being,
       All its hair would now be gray.
       Many great things have happened since it was created.

[Through divination Biton Kulubali and his supporters learn that the
slave child Ngolo, who is not of the Kulubali lineage, is destined to
become *mansa* of Segu. Plots to kill the child repeatedly fail, so he is
sold to Moorish salt traders, who take him north to Walata in the Sahara
desert. Ngolo goes from there to the powerful Muslim Kunta Family of
Timbuktu, from whom he eventually acquires the blessings that assure
his accession to kingship.]

2130   Finally Ngolo came to Segu.
       When the time came for Ngolo to return, Biton's day was done.
       After Biton's day there was an old man in Sebugu whose name
              was Donbila Nsan.
                                        MUSICAL INTERLUDE
       When Ngolo returned to Segu his rival was Donbila Nzan at
              Sebugu.
       Donbila Nzan was older than Ngolo,
       But Ngolo came to live at Segu earlier than Donbila Nzan.
       People said, "If we decide according to age, Donbila Nzan will
              become master of the land.
2140   "But if we decide according to the order of arrival, Ngolo will
              become master of the land."
       Finally they decided to place Ngolo in power.
       On the matter of Ngolo coming to power, the councilors said,
              "All right,
       "Very well, how will this be done?"
       Banbugu Nce was Ngolo's first son.
2145   He said, "Is it possible for someone to sit in power without
              calling the slaves?"
       "No one can sit in power if he does not call the *sofaw*."[5]
       Then Banbugu Nce organized the power to follow his father.
       He assembled the Bamana here to cross the river.
       On that day the Bamana swore an oath.
2150   They said, "Until the death of Ngolo,

---

4. Slave chiefs who ruled Segu during a time of turmoil, c. 1757-66. 5. Mounted
warriors.

"Until the end of Ngolo's descendants,
"Nobody will step between them.
"They will have the power until their line has ended,
"No one can interfere with them."
2155 The Bamana went across the river to swear that oath.
They chewed red kola nut,
They cut their arms to make the blood flow,
They put the red kola in the blood.
Everyone swore on the kola and chewed it:
2160 "If anyone spoils this alliance, may the four great *boliw* [6] of Segu
not spare him.
"May Bakungoba not spare him,
"May Nangoloko not spare him,
"May Kontara not spare him,
"May Binyejugu not spare him."
2165 After everybody swore they came home to Segu.
MUSICAL INTERLUDE
Ngolo settled his first son Nce in Banbugu.
His next son was Monzon and he settled him at Npeba.
His sons Jokele Nyankoro, Seri, and Mamuru were settled at
Sebugu.
Ben settled at Kirango, and Denba settled at Masala.
2170 Nalukuma and Torokoro Mari, all these were his sons.
MUSICAL INTERLUDE
He gave each of them a place to settle.
When each of them was settled, Banbugu Nce had something
on his mind.
He went to his father and said, "Baba."
Ngolo said, "I hear you."
2175 Nce said, "Baba the thing that has been said is indeed true."
He said, "It is said that before dying and going to *lahara*,
"Every old man strikes an axe-blow in his homeland.
"This is indeed true."
Ngolo said, "Why, *Cemogo*?"[7]
2180 Nce said "Eh, you divided up your sons and gave them each a
place to settle.[8]
"Where did you settle me, your son Nce?"
Ngolo said "I settled you at Banbugu."
"Where did you settle Monzon?"
"I settled Monzon at Npeba."
2185 "What about Jokele, Nyankoro Seri, and Mamaru?"
Ngolo said, "They are settled at Sebugu,
"Ben is at Kirango, and Denba is at Masala."

---

6. Objects of power, fetishes. 7. Literally "man," but here a nickname. 8. Each of
the king's sons ruled over a garrisoned town.

37

Nce said, "Ah yes, let us look at the problem together.
"The mouth can fail to say something but the thoughts show it
anyway."

MUSICAL INTERLUDE

2190 Ngolo said, "Cemogo, why do you say that?"
Nce said, "What about the distance between Banbugu and the
riverbank?"
Ngolo said, "It is far from the riverbank."
Nce said, "What about the distance between Npeba and the
river?"
Ngolo said, "It is close to the river."
2195 "What about the distance between Sebugu and the river?"
"It is close to the river."
"Oh," said Nce, "This is why I said the mouth can fail to say
something but the behavior shows it.
"You have shown that you prefer your other sons over me."
Then Ngolo said to Banbugu Nce, "Segu is a group of four
villages,
2200 "Marakadugu is a group of nine villages,
"Dodugu is a group of twelve villages,
"Six of them on one side of the river and six on the other side.
"Segu is a group of four villages,
"Marakadugu is a group of nine villages,
2205 "Dodugu is a group of twelve villages.
"We believe that Marakadugu begins at Kuku not far from
here.
"From there you reach Marakaduguba,
"And from there you go to Busen, then Koke.
"Oh the Fula come from Macina.
2210 "They ride horses and can easily come to Segu.
"Marakaduguba is an old town where believers, learned, wise
and worthy people live.
"If the Fula of Macina come here two more times, they will ally
themselves with Duguba.
"If they ever become allied with Duguba, Segu will spend the
night peering at shadows.
"This is why I settled you at Banbugu.
2215 "I want you to be our bulwark for Segu against Duguba and
the Macina Fula."
(Eh, we *nyamakalaw*[9] say, "Nce" and the Fula say "Hamadi" to
describe the first son.)
Ngolo said, "There are three kinds of Nce in Bamana land.
"Nce the sauce-eater is one of them,
"Nce the dog-seller is one of them,
2220 "Worthy Nce is one of them.

---

9. Craft specialist and artists, including bards, blacksmiths, and leatherworkers.

"You are the worthy Nce."
Nce said, "This is all right, Baba, I hear it."
Ngolo calmed the heart of the eldest son.
Banbugu Nce went back to Banbugu.

[Urged on by a famous female bard of the time, Nce constructs a canal reaching seven kilometers from the Niger River to Banbugu. Ngolo dies and his son Monzon comes to power, but his younger brothers insist that the kingdom must be divided among them. Monzon refuses, saying, "a hundred heads can wear the same cap only if they do it one at a time." The brothers start a war, which Monzon wins before embarking on a series of conquests, including the famous battle of Koré, which expand the empire.]

2710   At the time that Monzon fought against Koré, things were not like they are now.
The young *marabout* who did the blessings for the battle of Koré was Mamadu Bisiri.
He was a *dafin*[10] master.
The people of Segu went to tell him that they wanted to attack Koré.
They asked Mamadu Bisiri to give them a blessing.
2715   He agreed to do the blessing,
He raised a lighted straw to the sky.
The people heard a noise coming from the sky.
The *marabout's* novice began to moan.
The *marabout* said to the novice, "Child do not bring misfortune on yourself and choose me as the cause of it."
2720   The *marabout* did the blessing and gave it to Monzon.
Then Monzon left here with two times forty companies of warriors.
They went to station themselves there.
What a spectacle it was.
They spent the day at the gates of Koré.
2725   They sent word to Dugakoro that war had come to his town.
Dugakoro put a basket of kola nuts on somebody's head and sent it with a message to Monzon:
"If you plant these and wait until they sprout and wait until they bear fruit,
"If you wait that long you will be able to conquer Koré."
He said, "If you cannot do so,
2730   "You had better go about your other business.

---

10. Form of Muslim divination.

"I am not sure you will ever be able to conquer Koré."
The town was so big that if some people fired gunpowder all
    day in one part of the town,
And if some others beat wedding drums all day in another
part,
Nobody knew what the others were doing.
2735   Oh this had nothing to do with the failure of the three-month
siege.
The siege began.
The expression "Koré siege, Koré siege" was first spoken that
    day.
They tried every tactic but were unable to enter Koré.
They were unable to enter Koré though they tried every tactic.
2740   Monzon himself was frustrated.
He said, "Hey, the day Koré is captured,
"The first man to bring me the news will be made a chief of
    something."
That day Nangoyi Koné was here.
That day Jeli Gorogi Koné was here.
2745   The leadership of the *nyamakalaw* belonged to them at that time.
                                      MUSICAL INTERLUDE
Little by little the sacrifices and the blessings were answered.
One day Koré was captured and destroyed like an old calabash,
Like an old clay pot.
The man called "Possessor of truth" ran *bara-bara-bara* to where
    Monzon was sitting.
2750   He said, "What was said has been realized.
"The prayers have been answered.
"We have destroyed Koré like an old calabash.
"We have smashed it like an old clay pot.
"Things inside the houses are now things outside the houses."
2755   Monzon said, "Then I give to you leadership of the *nyamakalaw*
    of Segu.
"It was my own mouth that said the first man to tell me Koré
    was conquered would be made a chief."
Tinyètigi, "Master of truth," ran to tell Monzon that Koré was
    captured.
That day Monzon made Tinyètigiba Danté chief of the bards.
Before that there had been some people above him.
2760   That was the end of the war with Koré.

2925   Oh, a day came with the sickness that would send Monzon to
    lahara.
He sent for Jeli Tinyètigiba Danté.
Monzon told him to go and call his favorite son.
Oho, when that was done, when the son came,
Jeli Tinyètigiba began to recite the genealogy.

2930 He started praising Da with Wanasi and his nine generations.
  He ended with how the Koné left Sankaran.
  "Eh," people said, "there is no limit to the word of this man!
  "Is his word not accurate?
  "Is his word not true?
2935 "Is the form of his word not just right?
  "We cannot choose one of these at the expense of the rest.
  "Your word has no limit.
  "The word from your mouth is good.
  "You are also the possessor of truth.
2940 "You are the possessor of truth,
  "The word from your mouth is good,
  "Your word has no limit."
  Dan t'i ka kuma na, "There is no limit to your word."
  That became a family name,
2945 The word of this man was good.
  There was no limit to his word.
  Tinyètigiba Danté, "Big possessor of limitless truth."
              MUSICAL INTERLUDE
  The sickness bit Monzon.
  He said, "Go and call my favorite son."
2950 Tinyètigiba Danté said, "Who is your favorite son?"
  Monzon said, "Faama Da."
  "Where is he?"
  "He is at Banankoro!"
  Tinyètigiba Danté went to call Faama Da,
2955 To say his father had called him.
  Faama Da came.
  He said, "Father?"
  Monzon said, "I hear you."
  Da said, "Father?"
2960 Monzon said, "I hear you."
  Da said, "Is it true you are calling me?"
  Monzon said, "Yes, I am calling you."
  Da said, "Why are you calling me?"
2965 Monzon said, "The reason for calling you is not serious.
  "I, Monzon, have been caught by the illness that will take me
    to *lahara.*
  "This illness will not go away without me.
  "It will take me to *lahara.*
  "I have destroyed every town I had to destroy.
  "I have conquered every town I had to conquer.
2970 "But when I was in my prime there were three towns I failed
    against.
  "I want to tell you about those three towns.
  "Here are the keys to Segu.

"They are one hundred twenty and ten in number.
"Among them is the key of the old dog,
2975 "Among them is the key of the female dog,
"Among them is the key of the four slaves.
"Hers is the key to the four big *boliw*.
"These are the substance of power in Segu.
"Never lose them after I am gone.
2980 "If you lose them you will be separated from Segu ahead of
        your time.
"If you keep them in your hands you and Segu will spend your
        life together.
"The people of Segu will not oppose your power.
"Ah, as for those three towns,
"I will die with my regret.
2985 "Except for those few towns,
"I defeated every one my eyes saw.
"But I do regret those three towns!"
                                            MUSICAL INTERLUDE
Faama Da said, "Very well Father.
"I hear your word.
2990 "What town and what town are these?
"Name for me the towns you could not conquer."
Monzon said, "Nwenyekoro is at Npebala.
"Desekoro is at Kaarta.
"Basi is at Samanyana.
2995 "These are the three towns.
"I could not conquer them.
"If you are able to conquer them after I am gone,
"Bakungoba will bless you,
"Kontara will bless you,
3000 "Binyejugu will bless you,
"The four big *boliw* of Segu,
"The remains of Cekolo will bless you.
"I myself will bless you from *lahara*,
"I failed to conquer them."
3005 Da said, "So be it."
Then Da went out.
He went to see Tinyètigiba Danté.
He said, "Danté."
"I hear you."
3010 "Danté."
"I hear you."
"Eh, my father's illness is getting more serious but he will not
        die.
"Father's illness is getting more serious but he will not die."
Da was impatient for his father to die because he wanted the
        power here in Segu.

3015   He had that in his heart.
        A week passed.
        Within that week the illness became more serious.
        In the second week the illness became 'Go and meet me.'
        In the third week Monzon set down his burden here in Segu.
3020   They began to beat the big ceremonial drum.
        Men gathered together,
        Women went into their houses.
        The *nyamakalaw* were shouting that the world had become
                troubled and confused:
                    The goat is sick,
3025   The goat owner is ailing.
                    The knife is dull,
                    The goat's throat is tough.
                    The day is drawing to a close,
                    The ground is hot.
3030   We have no basket to sit on in the sky while we tell our
                troubles to the angels of Allah.
        Where will we go to bathe?
        Where will we go to dry off?
        Our bathing place is gone,
        Our drying place is gone,
3035   All that was left of Segu was one forked post.
        Now that forked post is broken.
        The crossbeams, roof timbers, and wall posts have fallen.
        Cemogo Monzon has set down the baggage.
        We *nyamakalaw* had nothing before,
3040   But now our whole life is gone.
        The one who gave us our riding horse is gone.

[Despite Monzon's wishes, the Segu elders repeatedly refuse to recognize Da as the next *mansa*. Finally, in an organized plot, Da's hatchetmen swarm into a council meeting and begin to massacre the elders. The surviving councilors accept Da, who soon launches military campaigns against the rebellious chiefs whom his father, Monzon, had failed to conquer. One of these is the formidable Basi Diakité of Samanyana, who is defeated when the slave girl Sijanma seduces him to learn the secret of his power. Among Da's other conquests is his destruction of Kaarta, a neighboring Bamana state founded by Kulubali ancestors who are thought to have been related to Biton's forebears (see l. 5598).]

        They moved on with their war and crept ahead as slowly as a
                bad marriage.
        (Once a marriage turns bad, there is much discussion about it.)

5505   Oh world, father of astonishing things,
They took the war to the gate of Desekoro's Kaarta.
When the war arrived at the gate of Desekoro's Kaarta,
They fired a warning shot at the walls.

MUSICAL INTERLUDE

They were sending a message to Desekoro.
5510   At Kaarta in those days Desekoro had two men.
They did the divining for him on matters related to his wars or
    his power.
The name of the first diviner was "Nobody-knows-himself-but-
    you-will-see-someday."[11]
The name of the second diviner was "A-willful-person-with-his-
    mouth-open-is-bad."
After the warning shot was fired at the town wall, there was
    turmoil everywhere from sky to earth.
5515   No one had to tell another that the mounted warriors of Segu
    were coming.
Finally, master, 'the name of the child is Marabout.'[12]
At that time Desekoro had a new calabash.
His seers did their divining using the water in that calabash.
The calabash was filled with water and placed on the ground.
5520   Then the grooms brought out their war horses.
They pulled some hair from under the saddles.
The wind blew it into the calabash of water.
Then on the day that the amount of hair increased to more than
    any other day,
They would take that as a sign and say,"Hum!
5525   "Something is coming near us today."
They made the sacrifice that was required against the
    approaching thing.
Then they could deal with whatever war that was.

MUSICAL INTERLUDE

Oh, when this had been done "A-willful-person-with-his-
    mouth-open-is-bad" went to Desekoro of Kaarta.
"Ha!" he said, "Today."
5530   Desekoro said, "What happened?"
"Ha, very well," he said.
"Dese, the horsehair has darkened the top of the calabash."
Desekoro said, "Aha, very well, pour it out and put in fresh
    water."
He poured out the water and refilled the calabash.
5535   Before he could begin to say, "The name of the child is
    Marabout,"

---

11. This sort of descriptive name usually indicates slave status. 12. An oath
confirming the truth of one's words.

More horsehair made the calabash look like there was no water
    in it.
"Aha, very well Desekoro," said the diviner.
"The matter has become worse than before."
Desekoro said, "Very well pour out that water."
5540   They did that three times.
Desekoro said, "Go out and look at the road."
MUSICAL INTERLUDE
He climbed a high tree and craned his neck.
He looked at the road and saw mounted Segu warriors every-
    where.
There were hammermen among them,
5545   There were hatchetmen among them,
There were spearmen among them,
There were musketeers among them.
Turmoil was everywhere,
People could not even see each other.
5550   Then "A-willful-person-with-his-mouth-open-is-bad" rode his
    horse back to Desekoro, *bari, bari, bari.*
He said, "Aha, very well, is this not Desekoro of Kaarta?"
Desekoro said, "Yes it is."
He said, "Today we have arrived at the matter of war."
Desekoro said, "What has happened?"

5555   "Hmm," said the diviner. "Very well,
"You must know that the matter of today,
"Hmmm, bwa! bwa!
"It is not like anything before."
He said the mounted warriors of Segu had arrived.
5560   He thought that Kaarta was smashed.
The diviner said, "Very well, Kaarta is smashed."
Desekoro said, "Hey!
"'A-willful-person-with-his-mouth-open-is-bad.'"
He said, "I hear you."
5565   Dese said, "Eh, have you gone crazy?
"Indeed is the smashing of a town the size of Kaarta something
    to be spoken of?
"Aha, very well, seize him!"
Finally they seized "A Willful Person With His Mouth Open Is
    Bad,"
They cut his head from his neck.
5570   His two shoulders became milk brothers,[13]
The rest of his body ran away.
The blood poured out like a sacrificial cow of Mande.

---

13. Children of the same mother; very close.

War is not good for a coward.

MUSICAL INTERLUDE

Desekoro said, to his other diviner, "Aha, very well,

5575   "Nobody-knows-himself-but-you-will-see-someday," get up.

"Go look at the road and see about what has been said."

MUSICAL INTERLUDE

Oh, "Nobody-knows-himself-but-you-will-see-someday" went
out.

He climbed a high tree and craned his neck.

There could not have been more turmoil.

5580   It extended from sky to ground.

He cast his eye as far as possible but could not see the end of
the crowd of warriors.

He climbed down and went to Desekoro.

He said, "Very well, Dese,

"It is the little warriors of the warrior Monzon.

5585   "They are approaching fearfully, *yoli, yoli.* . . .

"We will capture them all but we must have courage."

MUSICAL INTERLUDE

The diviner said, "Hah, very well Desekoro, we must have
courage."

Desekoro said, "For that I give you two baskets of millet.

"I give you two bars of salt,

5590   "I give you two male slaves to attend to your horse."

The mounted warriors of Segu were everywhere outside the
walls of Kaarta.

Only the sand of the river separated them from Kaarta.

The Kaarta horsemen dashed boldly out.

Mansa and Moriba,[14]

5595   Nya Ngolo and Barama Ngolo,

Mansa and Moriba Kurubari.

Oh, that Desokoro, his family name was Kurubari.

He and Biton Kulubali of Segu came from the same father,

But they did not share the same mother.

MUSICAL INTERLUDE

5600   Finally they met on the sand of the river.

They were not in Kaarta,

They were not in Segu.

Hard things and difficult things,

They clashed nine times.

5605   Painful things and porcupine quills,

When mature men meet in battle there is no mercy.

Men were fighting so the winner would soon be known.

In those days a Bamana musket would fire only one shot at a
time.

---

14. Praise-names of inspirational ancestors.

But once the battle started the warriors on both sides stood fast
    in their positions,
5610   They were ready to go to *lahara.*
MUSICAL INTERLUDE

When the battle companies came together,
When the Kaarta muskets spoke *wuu!*
There were so many Segu muskets.
5635   The Kaarta bullets, powder, and wadding flew into the mouths
    of some Segu muskets
When the Segu muskets spoke *wuu!*
The bullets, wadding, powder, and smoke flew into the mouths
    of some Kaarta muskets.
Between them was river sand.
MUSICAL INTERLUDE

Hah, it became a very serious matter.
5640   The men took each other,
They took each other,
They took each other.
At one point Segu took Kaarta,
Then Kaarta took Segu.
5645   Segu would take Kaarta,
Then Kaarta would take Segu.
When the battle heated up,
Faama Da said, to Tinyètigiba Danté, "Danté!"
He said, "I hear you."
5650   "Tell them to let the battle rest."
Segu let the battle rest.
Da came to them and said, "Segu!
"Gather round while I give you a message about *lahara.*
"Hot bullets can take somebody to *lahara,*
5655   "Or a cold sword can take somebody to *lahara.*
"You will have to choose which one is better for you.
"If Segu takes Kaarta, I am not talking about that.
"But if Kaarta pushes Segu all the way back to me,
"I, Da, will take the men at the back and send them to *lahara*
    with a cold sword.
5660   "You know if I am able to do that or not.
"There are plenty of others to take your place.
"I do not want to take all day attacking one town.
"I will not spend a whole year laying siege to one town."
Then the warriors discussed this among themselves.
5665   That day the Bamana swore an oath to one another.
They said, "Well, from now on a hot bunch taking somebody to
    lahara,
"That is better than the throat cut with a cold sword.
"From now on any man who runs away,

47

"A dog has spent the night with his mother.
5670 "Any man of Segu who runs away after this,
"A dog has spent the night with his mother."
The Bamana carried their insult to this extent.
Oh, after that, death would find people there.
For any man they said this to, retreat became shameful.
5675 After that Segu pushed Kaarta and Kaarta pushed Segu.
Segu pushed Kaarta and Kaarta pushed Segu.
Segu pushed Kaarta and Kaarta pushed Segu.
Segu faltered but nobody retreated toward Da.
MUSICAL INTERLUDE

Oh some were impervious to bullets,
5680 Some were impervious to bullets.
Those who did not need muskets used axes.
Some who did not need muskets used battle hammers.
Oh, the hammermen finally said, "Hey musketeers!
"You are slowing our battle.
5685 "Get out of our way.
"We will look for them word for word.[15]
"This battle will soon be settled."
The musketeers stayed behind the hammermen.
MUSICAL INTERLUDE

Eh, when the hammermen seized someone by the shirt, they
     would ask him:
        "Elder brother are you one of us?"
5690 You would hear him, "Eh, little brother, are you going crazy?"
You would hear him, "Yes, all right, these are Segu words."
When they seized someone by his shirt and forced him to stop,
His eyes would pop out,
You would say like those of a frog carrying a clay pot on his
     head.
5695 You would hear them, "Elder brother are you one of us!"
You would hear him, "Yes, *i lanbè*, I am one of you."
"Among us you say *i lanbè*?
"That is not all right.
"*I lanbè* is not of Segu!"
5700 Pow! They would hammer him on the head.
He would go to *lahara*. . . .
The hammermen did this again and again.
5715 They were doing to people, you would say, like breaking
     chicken eggs.
They were doing to people, you would say, like breaking
     guinea fowl eggs.
They were doing to people, you would say, like breaking par-
     tridge eggs.

---

15. Recognizing them by their idiomatic speech.

They were doing to people, you would say, like breaking
    chicken eggs again and again.
A skillful horseman came riding *ban, bari, bari.*
5720   He went and said, "All right, is this Desekoro?"
"Yes it is."
"Are you just sitting here?"
"I am sitting here."
"Huh, all right, if you are sitting you must get up.
5725   "Get up!"
"What is the matter?"
"Ah, ayee, the Segu people have a weapon called a hammer.
"Aha, all right, many people have amulets against muskets,
"But they have nothing against the hammer.
5730   "Oh, they will break your head, you would say, like that of a
    dog.
"We are going.
"No one has amulets against the hammer.
"We are going."
Finally Segu took things inside the house of Kaarta,
5735   They made them things outside the house of Kaarta.
They came and sat down and snuffed tobacco.

[After more campaigns Da succeeds in conquering all of the towns
Monzon had named on his deathbed. Later Segu is troubled by the
slave-raider Bilisi and by invading Fula warriors from the kingdom of
Macina to the north. In additional episodes totalling more than 1,850
lines, Jeli Tayiru Banbera's narrative concludes with his story of how
the great hero Bakari Jan rides to the rescue on his wondrous horse,
Nyoté. There is no mention of the last seven rulers or of the conquest of
Segu by Al-hajj Umar Tal in 1861.]

5. The Epic of Sonsan of Kaarta
Narrated by Mamary Kuyatè

Recorded in Kolokani, Mali, August 19-21, 1975, by David Conrad. Transcribed and translated into English by David Conrad with the assistance of Sekou Camara and Jume Diakité. This excerpt edited by David Conrad.

ROUGHLY CONTEMPORARY TO BAMANA SEGU was a second Bamana state known as Kaarta, which for a time played a less significant role in filling the power vacuum left by the sixteenth-century decline of the Songhay Empire. Because Kaarta was much less successful than Segu, it left very little in the way of a historical record. It was apparently located in an area northwest of Segu in the general area of today's Beledugu region north of Bamako. The prosperity of the neighboring Bamana state of Segu can in great measure be attributed to its advantageous location, with many towns strung along the Niger River on the trade route between the land of Manden to the southwest and the inland Niger Delta to the northeast. Some north-south trade must have gone through Kaarta, but this state never had the level of prosperity that allowed Segu to maintain a powerful army and expand its borders in all directions. Indeed, despite the fact that the founders of Segu and Kaarta are said to have descended from the same distant ancestor (they were both of the Kulubali clan), the oral sources indicate that Segu attacked Kaarta on more than one occasion, and some informants believe that Kaarta was soundly defeated by its stronger neighbor during the reign of Desekoro Kulubali (1788-99).

The excerpt presented here is a rare example of epic discourse about Kaarta, and it focuses on a single character, the ancestor Sonsan, who is credited with founding the town of Sonsana. Sonsan's origins go back to the earliest ancestor of both Kaarta and Segu, recalled as the great hunter Kalajan, who is identifiable as one of three brothers known as Simbon, said to have come from "the east." Among Kalajan's descendants, two brothers, Nya and Barama, are usually recalled as important ancestors, and the performer of this text says Barama was the father of Sonsan. Sonsan's own son was Massa, whose descendants became the ruling lineage of Kaarta, including Desekoro who appears in the Bamana Segu epic.

The narrator of this discourse is Jeli Mamary Kuyatè of Kolokani, Mali, a sightless jeli who accompanies himself on the *ngoni* or four-stringed harp-lute like the one used by Tayiru Banbera, narrator of the Segu epic. His narrative is frequently punctuated by songs and musical variations. Jeli Mamary's text reflects the dangerous rivalry that can develop in Bamana society between brothers of the same father but different mothers. Also important here is the fact that unlike many cultures in this part of West Africa, the Bamana resisted conversion to Islam until long after the events of this story. However, for the past century Islam has been an important presence in Bamana society, which is why the bard (who is himself a Muslim) commences his tale by asso-

ciating early Kaarta and Segu ancestors with the Prophet Muhammad.
Nevertheless, he makes it clear that while they were willing to fight for
the Prophet (in a battle that the bard locates in Kayes, Mali, rather than
in Arabia), these fierce hunter-warriors were not interested in adopting
a religion that would require them to "bob up and down" in prayer.

       If you hear "Kulubali,"
The first village they settled here at Beledugu was Kulikòròba.[1]
In those days of the Kulubali, nobody had a family name.
There were twelve families in Mande.
5   They were headed by sons of the same parents.
These twelve men helped our king [the Prophet Muhammad]
      in the battle of Kaybara.
When people hear "Kaybara," they think it means another
      town.
They think Kaybara is another town far away.
Kaybara is not a remote town, it is Kayes.
10   Even today the sun has more force at Kayes than at any other
      place.
After the battle of Kaybara,
Only seven of the twelve men remained.
Among them, three were named Simbon.
When the country had been destroyed the leader asked them if
      they wanted a place in paradise.
15   This was not just any king,
This was the Prophet.
They had helped him in the battle of Kaybara.
He said, "Do you not want a place in paradise?"
They replied, "Bobbing up and down all night,
20   "Bobbing up and down all day to gain such a reward,
"We have no time for that."
So the Prophet said, "Very well,
"What would you like instead?"
"We want powder and bullets," they said.
25   "Very well, they are yours," said the Prophet,
"And good luck to you."
The three Simbon traveled to the Somono country on the bank
      of the river.
They were hoping to get across.
The Somono and Bozo fishermen said this would be no prob-
      lem.
30   "We will take you across," they said,
"On the condition that you unpack your loads and divide them
      among us.

---

1. Historic town on the Niger near Bamako.

"Then we will take you across the river."
But the Simbon did not want to do this so they refused.
In those days there was very dangerous sorcery.
35   This sorcery was very powerful.
Such a thing still exists, but it is not as strong.
On that day of sorcery the Joliba[2] was full to its banks,
But the three Simbon walked across it and the water was not up
    to their hips.
There were many people on the riverbank and they were
    astonished by this deed.
40   Ah! Those three men went ahead of the canoe,
They did not bother to use a canoe.
Ah! Those three men went ahead of the canoe.
Where the mountain sits by the river,
They built three houses near that mountain.
45   They cut down groves of trees to build three houses.
When you go out,
When you go out to those houses,
When you are asked, "Where are you going?"
You who go to those houses,
50   You say, *"mun ye kurun beli,"* 'those who precede the canoe,'
"I am going to their place."
Later that was shortened.
They just said *"Kurun beli"* or Kulubali.
That is how they got their name.
55   They got that name at Tufin Kumbe,
The shady place.
The Malinke call Kulikoro "the shady place."
It was there that they got their names.
The names of those three Simbon became famous.
60   There was Lawali Simbon,
Kanu Simbon,
And Furu Simbon,
All of the same parents.
In those days children were called by the father's or mother's
    names.

[Before they come by the name of Kulubali, Sonsan's ancestral lineage is identified as Wolo. Soro Wolo and his wife Nya give birth to the brothers Nya (named after his mother) and Barama Wolo. Seeking less populated lands, Nya and Barama go off in different directions to establish new communities. Sonsan is born and begins to mature at Gwegwa, where his charisma soon arouses the potentially deadly jealousy of his step-brothers, led by Kuntu, the eldest.]

---

2. "River of Blood." Bamana name for Niger River.

[Barama] passed near Banamba[3] and went on north of there.
310 They cleared the trees and founded a village called Gwere-
        gwena.
     This was hard for the Maraka of the area to say,
     So later it became known as Gwegwa.
     Barama Wolo had seven sons in that place.
     The first of them was Kuntu.
315 The second son was Banfo,
     Then there were Gweneke and Sonsan.
     Sonsan and his sister were the only two children of one of
        Barama's wives.
     But the seven boys and the girl all had the same father.
     There were seven boys in all,
320 But Sonsan was the favorite because of his ways.
     He was loved by everyone.
     From the time he knew his right hand from his left,
     Even if he was just walking through the village in the morning,
     Even if he was on his way to wash his face,
325 He would be accompanied by a group of friends,
     Sometimes as many as ten of them.
     Even now you will see children doing this.
     If you want to send a child on an errand to another compound,
     The father of the house can explain to the child where he wants
        him to go,
330 Just by telling him the name of the boy his age who lives there.
     Then he will make no mistake.
     If the child did not know the place from the name of its family
        head,
     He would say, "Oh yes, the father of my friend."
     He would always know it by the boy in his own age group.
335 It was like that until Sonsan had been circumcised,
     But even when that was done,
     The other boys and girls of the village would go around with
        him.
     At night the children of his age would meet at Barama Wolo's.
     They would enliven his compound.
340 When a Fula would come to Gwegwa,
     He would be sent to stay with Sonsan's family.
     When a Maraka came,
     He would also be lodged with Sonsan's family.
     When the blacksmiths came,
345 They would stay with Sonsan's family.
     When the griots came to Gwegwa,
     They would stay with Sonsan's family.
     When the *funew*[4] came,

---

3. Town north of Bamako. 4. Bards specializing in Islamic oratory.

	They would be sent to stay with Sonsan's family.
350	When the Suraka[5] came,
	They would be lodged with Sonsan's family.
	This had an effect on Sonsan's brothers.
	In those days the way that they built houses in Bamana country,
	They had small and large houses.
355	One day Sonsan's elder brother,
	The one named Kuntu,
	He called his five younger brothers into the small house.
	He said, "There is something for which we must find a remedy.
	"That is Sonsan.
360	"The back feet have passed up the front feet.
	"Eh!
	"The Fula,
	"The blacksmiths,
	"The griots,
365	"The *funew*,
	"The leatherworkers,
	"The Kakolo,[6]
	"All the strangers who come and go,
	"They stay at the house of Sonsan.
370	"The father is not yet dead,
	"But if it is like this while he still lives,
	"When he dies Sonsan will surely become head of the family.
	"Let us go after Sonsan and kill him.
	"Otherwise, when our father dies and things are like this,
375	"The way these strangers come and go,
	"I will not be head of the family."
	The rival brothers collected 6,000 cowries and gave them to Kuntu.
	This was so Kuntu could see the diviners and learn how to kill their brother Sonsan.
	They went to see the diviner.
380	The diviner sat down.
	He smoothed the dust in front of him to trace his magic signs.
	He would search in the dust for a message,
	An omen that would guide the step-brothers.
	The diviner cast some dust in different directions and chanted.
450	"The mouth begins by saying bad things,
	"It ends by saying good things.
	"Speak to Kuntu who respects his father's customs,
	"Speak to Kuntu who respects his mother's customs,

5. Bamana term for Moors or Berbers from the Sahara. 6. Mande-speaking people, east of Beledudu in Mali.

54

"Those who know Kuntu speak of him,
455 "Those who have seen Kuntu speak of him.
"He has taken his father's wealth and his mother's wealth,
"He has gone away from his father's family and his mother's
family.
"He has put his right foot in front of his left foot.
"He needs eight genies and eight humans to work as slaves
and nobles.
460 "He is doing harm to his younger brother, Sonsan, today,
"He will be doing harm to him tomorrow,
"Because he wants to kill him.
"If Kuntu is impatient,
"If he is impatient,
465 "He must be patient,
"He must be patient.
"He cannot do anything against Sonsan today,
"He cannot do anything against Sonsan tomorrow.
"He will just shake his head in regret,
470 "Slap his thigh in regret.
"He will regret it all night and be angry all day.
"When I move my hand up and down,
"Good sit and good rise.
"If the dust is good may the eight genies make it look good.
475 "If the dust is good may the eight humans make it look good.
"Show me if Kuntu's desire will be realized.
"Only a small omen in the dust can reveal the truth of the dust.
"May the truth of the dust grow so I can see it and speak of it.
"The bird flies, but not the tree where he perches.
480 "A little bad news is better than a lot of lies."
The diviner traced sixteen houses of *lateru*,7
The signs for the near future.
Then he said "Eh, Kuntu!
"You can do nothing against your younger brother.
485 "Allah has chosen Sonsan,
"So leave him in peace."
Kuntu was angry at this.
He said, "That big-headed diviner knows nothing.
"He sits in the dust and the dust is worthless."

[Frustrated at the unsatisfactory divination, Kuntu leads the step-brothers in a direct attack on Sonsan, lowering him into a well and then dropping large rocks which, unknown to them, fail to hit the boy who shelters under a ledge. They lower a white chicken on a rope, and when it comes back bloody (Sonsan cuts his finger and drips blood on it), they rejoice at his death and return home with the news.]

---

7. Divination signs.

610 The six enemy brothers held their heads in mock grief.
They said, "Oh, father!
"We are a long time finding our way back because we are so
  sad."
They returned to Barama Wolo like that,
Crying and rolling on the ground.
615 Barama Wolo said, "What is going on?"
The brothers replied, "Father,
"When we were at the well we let Sonsan down into it.
"The sides broke away and fell down on Sonsan."
The father said, "Didn't I tell you not to let your little brother
  down into the well?
620 "Your son has died, but not mine.
"Go back to that well and get Sonsan out.
"Why don't you get going?"
Kuntu said, "Father,
"Now the mud of the well is still falling inside.
625 "If somebody goes in again, there will be two dead instead of
  one."
They went to tell the mother of Sonsan.
She had Sonsan's sister with her.
The sister ran crying between the well and the house.
Messages were sent to tell everyone of Sonsan's death.
630 Sonsan's mother said, "Ah,
"Big well, you have had me.
"The bird has taken my only grain of millet and dropped it
  where it can be eaten.
"That was my son,
"He was the reason that I came to Gwegwa.
635 "But big well, you have had me."
People who came for the funeral said,
"May Allah not add to this tragedy any more of our village's
  strength."
For a long time there had been jealousy between the parents.
From the time the sun was high in the sky,
640 The mother and sister had no place to rest until night.
Until after the evening meal,
Sonsan's mother had no place to rest.
She also ran between the well and the house.
She let herself fall into the mud by the well,
645 She knelt there and wailed pitifully.
"Oh, the big well of Gwegwa,
"You have had me,
"Truly you have had me."
The mother continued to mourn like that into the night.
650 Even when a goat came into the mud with her,
She continued to wail:

"Big well of Gwegwa,
"If you have eaten Sonsan,
"If you have taken my only seed,
655   "You must also take us,
"You must also eat my daughter and me."
Sonsan heard what she said from down in the well.
He climbed onto a rock and said from the well,
"Is that Mama?"
660   The mother said, "It is me."
Sonsan said, "Ah, I am not dead."
As soon as his mother heard that,
She turned and ran to her house.
She had twelve meters of new cloth.
665   She called her daughter and said, "Come on,
"We are going to get your brother out."
They went with the twelve meters of cloth.
They stopped at the side of the well and unrolled the cloth.
They let it down to Sonsan in the well.
670   When it got to Sonsan he held on tight.
His mother and sister pulled him out of the well.
When they had lifted him out of the well and he was safely
       with them,
His mother said, "Is it really you, Sonsan?"
He said, "It is me."
675   His mother said, "Oh, Sonsan!
"Have you escaped the jealousy of the Kulubali?
"Sonsan, go wherever you want, my son.

"Wherever you put down and raise your feet,
"Where your brothers would find nothing,
"May you win good fortune there.
"Go, my son,
695   "Now that you have survived the jealousy of your brothers.
"My son,
"Go with my blessings and not my curses.
"If Allah brings you to manhood while I still live,
"I will come and join you."
700   Sonsan left Gwegwa and headed north.

[Sonsan travels to Dorko, a town of the Soninke people (whom the
Bamana know as Maraka), where he receives a warm welcome. At a
council of elders it is agreed that Sonsan may join their community.]

755   When the chief of the Maraka town had welcomed him,
Sonsan told him the story of his brothers' attempt to kill him.
Sonsan said, "Maraka,
"If that was not the end of life,

"Then death cannot happen.
760   "We the Bamana say, 'Death is hard,
      "'But it still leaves somebody to sit around the dinner bowl.'"

[Having no land of his own, Sonsan is unable to farm. Outside the town he encounters his spirit guide, the genie king (Jinna Magha). It is noteworthy here that the sacred grove to be destroyed in pursuit of Sonsan's destiny is the dwelling place of the same spirits who require him to do it. Also, note that although the Maraka people were among the earliest converts to Islam in this part of West Africa, they have protected the sacred grove out of respect for (and fear of) the indigenous spirits. This excerpt includes one of the bard's many songs.]

There was a grove of trees at Dorko.
It was known as the Jinna Mansa's grove.
That place was the grove of the genies.
Nobody could defecate there because it was a sacred place.
850   It was forbidden to gather chewing sticks[8] there,
      And nobody could enter that grove with an axe.
      As Sonsan passed near this grove on his way to the bush,
      The Jinna Mansa saw him.
      The Jinna Mansa said to his wife,
855   "When that Bamana man returns past here,
      "Change yourself into a Maraka woman
      "And meet him along the way.
      "After he greets you,
      "Tell him to ask the Maraka to give him this sacred land where
          our grove is standing.
860   "If they agree,
      "He will have to cut down the grove to clear his field for
          planting.
      "His destiny, his fame, and his life,
      "They are all contained in the earth of this grove."
      The genie wife did as she was told.
865   In those days we had good genies,
      But the corruption of man's innocence has spoiled all that.
      At the beginning of their friendship with genies men were
          good,
      But at the end they turned bad.
      The miser must die near his shop.
870   If the thief recognized the informer,
      He would not give him his daughter.
      A free woman asks Allah to let no evil come between her and
          her absent husband,

---

8. Sticks with soft, fibrous ends, used as toothbrushes.

Otherwise something worse than evil can happen between
    them.
875   Ha, if you kill your wicked dog,
            Another man's dog will bite you.
            If you kill your wicked dog,
            Another man's dog will bite you.
            If wicked neighbors urge Nyenenkoro to divorce his
                worthless wife,
            Someone else's wife will kick him.
880   If people urge you,
            If wicked neighbors urge you to chase your brother
                away,
            Someone else's brother will give you a kick.
            If people urge him,
            If wicked neighbors urge Nyenenkoro to disown his
                son,
885   The son of another will give him a kick.
            Kill a wicked dog,
            If you kill your wicked dog
            Somebody else's dog will bite you.
            Kill a wicked dog,
890   If you kill your wicked dog,
            Somebody else's dog will bite you.
            Ah, those blacksmiths were brave.
            We play for the brave blacksmiths.
            The fly sits on the dunghill of someone he does not
                respect,
895   But young blacksmiths put dung near the hearth all
                day,
            And the flies pass it by every time.
            Termites build their house on the dunghill of those they
                do not respect,
            Otherwise the dung may lie on the rubbish heap for
                ten years,
            Untouched until uncircumcised boys throw it on little
                girls' heads.
900   Salute the elephant,
            The bravest of the elephants is a great elephant.
            Salute the elephant,
            The bravest of the elephants is a great elephant.
            Salute the elephant,
905   The bravest of the hyenas is a great hyena.
            Salute the elephant,
            The bravest of the warriors is a great warrior.
            Two brave men do not know each other until they
                meet.
            Two heroes do not know each other until they meet.

910	The bravest of the elephants is a great elephant.
	Sonsan went out to cut the soft *nuan-nuan* bark for trimming his mats,
	He loaded it on his head and started home.
	When he got near the grove of the genies,
	The wife of Jinna Mansa changed herself into a beautiful Maraka woman on the path.
915	Sonsan approached wearing a big sun hat on his head.
	She greeted him, "*i ni ce*, Bamana man."
	Sonsan replied, "*i ni wula* , 'good afternoon,' Maraka woman."
	Then the Maraka woman said *nuwari*.
	That is a Maraka greeting.
920	Sonsan said, "Maraka woman,
	"I do not understand that language.
	"I am Bamana and I do not know Maraka."
	The Maraka woman said, "Bamana man,
	"If you hear the Maraka say *nuwari*,
925	"It means the same as *i ni ce*.
	They greeted each other in Maraka,
	But Sonsan repeated that he was a Bamana.
	He asked the woman to speak that language.
	She said, "Bamana man,
930	"You are afraid!"9
	Sonsan said, "No, I am not afraid.
	"I, Sonsan,
	"If I suspected that any part of my body was afraid,
	"I would take my knife and cut off that part,
935	"So do not say that again."
	Then the woman said, "Very well, Bamana man.
	"I am not really a Maraka woman,
	"I am a genie.
	"Do you see that grove of trees?
940	"That is the dwelling place of my husband,
	"He is chief of the genies.
	"He told me to come and tell you to ask the Maraka for that grove.
	"If they agree to give it to you,
	"You must return and cut it down to clear your field.
945	"That is how you will gain your destiny, your fame and your life.
	"All of this you will find in the earth of that place, oh Bamana man.
	"That is what my husband has sent me to tell you."
	Sonsan said, "That is all right.
	"When you go back, tell your husband that I understand,

---

9. A stranger met in the bush may be dangerous.

950   "That I will ask the Maraka to give me the land.
"If they agree to let me have it that is all right,
"But if they will not give it to me it is the end of the matter."

Sonsan returned from gathering his *nuan-nuan* bark.
He stored it in the rafters of his house.
1085   He passed that night and the following day without speaking of
        the genie grove.
Toward evening he went to see the Maraka village chief
And asked him to assemble the elders.
After the evening meal the elders came to the chief's house.
Sonsan said to them, "The reason you have been called today is
        not a serious matter.
1090   "It is I who asked for this meeting.
"I have seen something you have here.
"I would like you to give it to me,
"Nothing else will do.
"Because I am a Bamana,
1095   "Nothing pleases me so much as a good piece of land.
"I like your sacred grove very much, Maraka people.
"I pray that you will give me that grove of trees.
"I want to clear a field for planting."
"Safuru lai!" shouted the elders.
1100   "Do not say that again!
"Do not say that again!
"Leave it alone!
"Take care that your thoughts are not dried by the wind.
"You escaped your jealous brothers,
1105   "You came here asking for our protection,
"And yet you want us to give you that place?
"Since the time when our ancestors lived,
"Both fathers and brothers,
"That grove has stood there.
1110   "Nobody can defecate there,
"Nobody can cut chewing sticks there,
"Nobody can even enter it with an axe.
"Bamana man,
"That is the sacred grove of the spirits and it must remain
        untouched.
1115   "You look again in the bush,
"And if you find another place that you like,
"If it has nothing to do with that grove,
"Bamana man,
"Even if you decide to found a village there,
1120   "We will give you that place and everything around it.
"But we cannot give you that grove."

[Sonsan eventually convinces the elders of Dorko that they will be protected from the genies' wrath if he is allowed to cut down the sacred grove. He clears and farms the land, harvests his crops, and builds houses at the new location, which becomes the village of Sonsana. Next the genie chief directs him to choose Duba Sangarè for his wife, no matter how bad she looks to him. Sonsan rides to Dambala, home of his prospective father-in-law, a Fula chief named Alu Sangarè. Six daughters are exhibited for Sonsan's inspection, but none of them is Duba, who is regarded as too worthless for consideration.]

       At that time, Duba Sangarè had been suffering from an open
          sore for seven years.
       The only way she could move about was to scoot along on her
          buttocks.
       She could not even go out to urinate without scooting on her
          buttocks.

1690   When somebody brought her meals they would hold their
          nose,
       They would slide the food into the room and hurry away.
       Sonsan went to Duba's room, where she was sitting on a mat.
       He sat down and greeted her.
       He said, "Are you the daughter of Alu Sangarè?"

1695   Duba said, "I am."
       Sonsan said, "You see me here today,
       "But I do not bring any problems with me.
       "I have come seeking you to marry,
       "So tell me if you like me or not."

1700   Duba began to weep.
       She said, "Bamana,
       "Everyone who mocks a person does not say *kete kete*.[10]

       "You do not really want to marry me,
       "You only come to mock me."

1725   Sonsan said, "Duba,
       "I truly have not come to mock you,
       "I have come to marry you.
       "If you like me, say so.
       "If you do not like me, say so."

1730   Duba said, "Bamana,
       "If I say I like you, how will I go with you?"
       Sonsan said, "That is no problem.
       "Everybody knows I have a horse."
       "Very well," said Duba,

1735   "Go and tell my father that I like you."
       Sonsan went to Alu Sangarè.

---

10. Sound of laughter.

He said, "Your daughter says she is fond of me."
Alu Sangarè said, "Very well, Bamana.
"I thank you very much.
1740 "You will relieve me of a burden if you take that filth out of my house.
"It will please me very much."
Sonsan saddled his horse and removed its hobbles.
He asked for somebody to carry Duba out and put her up behind him.
Alu said to his slaves, "Get up and get that obscenity,
1745 "Put her on the horse behind Sonsan.
"Sonsan has relieved us of a big problem."
Duba was placed on the horse,
And Sonsan galloped away with her.
When they arrived at Sonsan's compound,
1750 He carried her into his house and placed her on a mat.
Sonsan took care of his horse,
Then he heated water and began to bathe Duba.
Before he had finished, the genie chief arrived with special medicines.
There was a red powder for cleaning Duba's sore,
1755 There was a white powder to heal it.
The genie's wife showed Sonsan how to use them.
Under this treatment the sore improved quickly.
After two weeks Duba could walk with a cane.

1810 When Duba had been with Sonsan for six weeks,
Her wound had healed and left only a white scar.
Duba could now fetch her own water and bathe herself.
She was ready for Sonsan,
But so far they had not shared a sleeping mat.
1815 When they had been at Dorko for three months,
Duba's sore had healed so completely that there was not even the trace of a scar.
Duba had changed.
Anybody who did not know she was a Fula,
They would have thought she was a Maraka woman.
1820 She gained weight and learned to speak the Maraka language.
One afternoon Sonsan and the genie chief were talking.
Sonsan said, "I have something on my mind.
"Tomorrow I want to take Duba and present her to her father,
"Then he can name the bride-price.
1825 "If he will not accept bride-price from me,
"I cannot appreciate Duba as I should.
"I am not a Muslim,
"I will not take a wife without paying the proper bride-price."
The genie chief agreed that this should be done because

1830   "A woman's power comes from the marriage."
That night when it was time for bed Sonsan said to Duba,
"Get ready to leave tomorrow morning.
"I am going to return you to your father so he can name a
    brideprice.
"If he does not do this I cannot hold you in proper esteem.
1835   "I would never accept a wife like a Muslim, without bride-
    price."
"There, Bamana," said Duba.
"I said you were only mocking me,
"That you never intended to marry me.
"My father has already told you he would not accept even a
    piece of kola for me,
1840   "And now you say you are taking me back to him.
"I will not go."
Sonsan said, "Wait until tomorrow."

[Returning to Dambala they astonish Duba's family with her recovery
and affirm her honor by paying the bride-price. Later she bears three
sons, the eldest of which is Massa, future ancestor of the Massasi ruling
lineage. In the final episode the Maraka capture a group of Bamana
men, which leads to conflict between Sonsan and his former benefactors.
Involving his wife Duba in the plot, Sonsan lays a trap for the Maraka.
Finally, the three sons depart in search of new lands and establish the
settlement known as Kaarta.]

2010   The genie chief came one day.
He told Sonsan to buy some muskets.
Sonsan bought fifty muskets and stored them in his compound.
In those days the villages were always preparing for war.
Sonsan had built a secure enclosed compound,
2015   And he had those fifty muskets.
One day fifty lost men were wandering near the Maraka
    village.
The Maraka took them captive.
They tied them together by the necks with rawhide
And locked them in Sonsan's compound.
2020   Captives were told that those who accepted slavery would be
    turned loose,
And those who refused slavery would be killed.
One afternoon Sonsan sat down where he could see the fifty
    men.
They were tied by the neck with ropes attached to the house
    beams.
When Sonsan looked at the fifty men,
2025   He lowered his head and wept.

When he raised his head and saw their eyes,
He lowered his head and wept.
Some of the captives saw this.
One of them said to Sonsan,
2030 "Why are you weeping?
"You are the owner of this house,
"So why do you weep?"
Sonsan said, "I must weep.
"I must weep because you are Bamana.
2035 "The only reason I am here myself,
"Is because of the greed of my brothers,
"The same sort of greed that touches you now.
"There are my three sons who are still young and can do
   nothing for themselves.
"If the Maraka decide to confiscate my property,
2040 "They will do the same thing to me that they have done to you,
"And my sons will have no chance in the world,
"For they will never benefit from my legacy.
"You are Bamana and I am Bamana,
"Yet they have captured you and imprisoned you in my com-
   pound.
2045 "This is the same kind of greed that brought me here.
"If you see me weeping it is because I am reminded of my own
   suffering.
"I have a plan.
"If you will agree to it I will be glad.
"I want us to plan together as Bamana."
2050 The captives wanted to know what they should do.
Sonsan made them swear an oath of loyalty before he told them
   his plan.
Sonsan put a spell on some water,
And all the men drank it and swore their oaths.
Any man who broke his oath would die.
2055 Sonsan said, "I have my own musket,
"But I also have fifty muskets for you men,
"And I have powder and ball.
"Tomorrow morning I will set you free,
"I will give you each a musket and a pouch with powder and
   ball.
2060 "After I have gone to greet the Maraka chief,
"You must send Duba to find me."

Then Sonsan went into the village of Dorko and greeted the
   Maraka chief.
The chief said, "Good morning.
2080 "Do you still have the fifty captives there?"
Sonsan said they were there,

65

But while they were talking Duba Sangarè came along and
said,
"I have told you the Maraka are doing you wrong.
"You live alone in your compound while they are in their
village,
2085 "But they have taken the fifty captives and tied them in your
compound.
"Now the fifty captives have cut their bindings.
"I and the children are left in the house with them.
"Why do you allow this?"
Sonsan said, "Leave me in peace,
2090 "Leave me in peace.
"How can men tied with fresh cowhide cut themselves free?
"Leave me in peace,
"Get away from me.
"You women think men must sit all day watching you.
2095 "Leave me in peace.
"What kind of nonsense is this?"
Duba went back home and the captives killed the horse.
They cut off the tail and gave it to her.
Duba went weeping back to the chief's house.
2100 She stopped at the door and threw the horsetail at Sonsan.
She said, "You say that during the day I want you to do
nothing but sit and watch me.
"Now they have killed your horse.
"Now you know you are mistaken!"
Ah, Sonsan began to wail.
2105 He said, "Chief, how can this be?
"I thought her words were nothing,
"And now I am truly unhappy because of it."
As the chief shouted for his men,
Sonsan ran to his compound and locked himself inside.
2110 Each of the fifty men took his musket,
They sat on top of the wall with their weapons ready.
The Maraka chief told the village men to go after the fifty
captives at Sonsan's,
He told them to leave nobody alive.
They were going to kill them like chickens.
2115 When the first men tried to open Sonsan's gate, the muskets
suddenly fired.
The villagers shouted, "It is a Bamana plot!
"Sonsan has betrayed us,
"Sonsan has betrayed us."
By the time the sun was high overhead the Maraka agreed to
Sonsan's demands.
2120 He told them they must change the name of the village.
They must call it Sontiana, which they did.

This is the same Sontiana that is north of Kolokani.
That is how it was named.
Sometime later Massa, Bakari, and Ceba Mana left Sontiana.
2125 They went west from Kolokani to settle.
They called their new settlement Kaarta.
All of those who are Kulubali at Kaarta,
They are descendants of Sonsan.
They came from Sonsan.
2130 Sonsan's father was Barama Wolo,
Barama Wolo's father was Tontigi.

There then, is the story of Sonsan.
Ah, my listeners,
2140 That brings us to the end of the Kulubali story.
I have told you all that I can remember.
That story ends here.

6. The Epic of Almami Samori Touré
Narrated by Sory Fina Kamara

Recorded in Kissidougou, Guinea, April 4, 1994, by David Conrad. Transcribed and translated into English by David Conrad with the assistance of Jobba Kamara and Lansiné Magasouba. This excerpt edited by David Conrad.

AMONG THE MANY AFRICAN LEADERS who resisted the nineteenth-century European conquest of Africa, Almami Samori Touré (c. 1830-1900) was one of the most determined and successful. Samori waged war against invading French forces from 1882 until they captured him in 1898. In 1861 Samori had acquired the Mande people's status of *kèlètigi* (war chief, war lord, commander). He was soon invading neighboring territories, conquering local rulers, and taking control of their lands and people. By 1876 Samori had established his first empire, mostly in what is now the Republic of Guinea, but extending into southern Mali to Bamako and Sikasso and into today's northern Sierra Leone and western Côte d'Ivoire. In 1892, as a consequence of his wars and failed treaties with French colonial forces, Samori moved eastward with many of his people. By 1886 he had succeeded in conquering a new empire extending over a large area of what is now northern Côte d'Ivoire. In 1899 the French exiled Samori to Gabon, where he died in 1900.

Sory Fina Kamara, a *fina* or traditional Mande bard specializing in Islamic subjects, is well known in Guinea for his fine vocal performances, especially his song and narrative of Almami Samori. In this performance Sory Fina is accompanied by two guitarists. The tune played by them is that of a praise-song, not for Samori, but for Samori's brother Kèmè Brèma, another important figure in this text. One of the guitarists, Sekou Kantè, also functions as the *naamu*-sayer, or respondent, interjecting remarks between some of the lines, as seen in other texts. *Naamu* may be translated as 'indeed' or 'yes.' Sory Fina's version of the Samori epic reflects the local African perspective rather than that of European observers. The narrator is mainly interested in describing Samori's imperial conquest against neighboring peoples rather than his battles with the French invaders.

> Good evening,
> Big men of the blackskin's land,
> Good evening.
> We are performing today at Kissi Faramaya.
> 5   This morning Sory Fina Kamara of Banko Wuladala is
>   speaking to you.   (Mm, hm)
> He is living at Kissi Faramaya.
> Sekou Kantè is playing the strings,
> Fadama Kantè is playing the accompanying strings,
> Because there is not such a performance every day,
> 10   There is not such speaking done every day.

[Before Samori is born, a diviner predicts that Kèmo Lanfia will sire a "doer of great deeds." Competing for the honor of bearing the future hero, Lanfia's three wives make sacrifices of their most valuable possessions. Ma Sona Kamara becomes the mother of Samori, winning out over her co-wives, Ma Kèmè and Manigbè. In these lines the bard employs some of Samori's praise-names, such as Manju and Sanakoro Faama (King of Sanakoro). The frequently repeated song lines about the "three big brides" of Samori's brother Kèmè Brèma refer to Brahima's wife, Mariama Sire, his horse, Joro, and his sword, Ju'ufa ("Enemy killer").]

       Allah blessed Ma Sona Kamara with that good fortune.
115   Ma Sona Kamara,
       Ma Kèmè,
       Manigbé.
       She gave birth to Almami.
       When he was born,
120   He was born with birthmarks.
       He had marks on both wrists,
       And over the eyebrow.
           Kèmè Brèma had three big brides,
           Joro and Mariama Siré and Ju'ufa,
125   When Almami was born he grew up a headstrong child,
       But some wise people observed him carefully.
       Almami was popular,
       With many children following him,
       Manju.
130   He and the other youth formed different societies.
       The children would collect around Manju to play.
       Some days they would catch chickens and make it their
          society's sauce.
       They kept catching domestic animals until they got up to cows.
       People went and complained to ancestor Kèmo Lanfia:
135   "Your son who is called Almami,
       "He has been doing bad things.
       "He often catches our cows and makes them into the society's
          sauce."   (Naam)
       Allah caused it, Manju!
       Sanankoro Faama said, "I'm going to become an itinerant *marabout*,
140   "In fact I'm going to become a trader,
       "I don't want to offend my father any more,   (Naamu)
       "I have to start trading."
       He loaded up his bundle of goods.
       His friends used to sell bolts of white cloth,

145	The cloth that used to be made in the *koré*.[1]
	He said to his friends, "Let's travel together,
	"I also want to sell white cloth."
	They went to one town and then came to Albadariah.
	Albadariah is what they refer to as Bakadayi.
150	They passed there and went on to Banko Wuladala. (Naam)
	They met the *ilimunu bajana*.[2]
	Sèdinu Kulubali.
	Ancestor Mori Soumaila,
	He was the master of the prayer beads at Banko Wuladala.
	(Naam)
155	He was the Almami's very first *marabout*.
	They came and lodged with ancestor Mori Soumaila.
	He had done his eight o'clock and bedtime prayers to Allah.
	(Naam)
	At three o'clock in the morning,
	He came and questioned the strangers.
160	He pointed at Almami, saying,
	"The boy among you whose left foot is sore,
	"Where does this youth come from?"
	Almami's friends woke him up.
	They told him, "Our host is waiting for you." (Mmm)
165	The host said, "My son, where do you some from?"
	He said, "I come from Sanankoro."
	"Very well, you stay with me because your left foot is injured,
	"So I can heal your foot, my son.
	"It is Allah who has caused me to love you, Manju." (Naamu)
170	Sanankoro *faama* said, "Very well."
	Tis Allah who causes his slaves to love one another.
	(That's right)
	Almami's wound finally healed.
	Ancestor Mori Soumaila told him,
	"This is what I have seen in you
180	"You must stop trading.
	"Trading is not for you. (Hm)
	"You have spent three months here and you haven't sold ten
	dalasi[3] worth of cloth.
	"Let me exchange this cloth of yours for one cow.
	"A cow is easier to sell than cloth."
185	Almami agreed and exchanged his white cloth for a bull.
	He took the bull by its lead rope and went to Saraya Wuladala.
	He tied his bull outside the town of Saraya,
	Then he entered to greet the people in traditional fashion.
	The cow got loose and ate some of the people's crops.

1. Esoteric initiation society. 2. A powerful Muslim cleric. 3. Five franc coin equivalent to a penny.

190   "Aah!"
They said to Almami,
"This cow is no longer yours.
"Your cow has eaten many people's crops."
He begged those people and begged them
195   But they refused to return his cow.

[Samori loses more cows in a similar fashion and suffers additional humiliation in other communities. These incidents provide the narrator's motives for Samori's later behavior when he returns with his army and brutally conquers each of the towns that gave him trouble. But Samori must also have the genies' approval, because for a hero to accomplish memorable deeds, he must be in accord with the spirit world. One sign of the genies' approval is Samori's possession of firearms, which are said to have been provided by twin female genies. Firearms were one key to Samori's success against both the French and the people he incorporated into his empires.]

Almami Samori said, "A slave who depends on Allah is never
    poor."   (That's right, mm)
He said, "The old man told me at Banko Wuladala that I should
    withdraw from business."   (That's right)
285   He went back to Mara at Kuriya.
He said, "I have lost my investment three times."
Mara took four bundles of kola nuts.   (Naamu)
He said, "Go and wander the land, my son."
In early times, people did not give grudgingly. (Never, walayi)
290   He took the four bundles of kola and headed for Sirin Setigiya.
He went to Namanji Kamara at Setigiya.   (Mmm)
Namanji Kamara was a big man at Sirin.   (Son of Kaman, mm)
Kèmè Brèma had three big brides,
Joro and Mariama Siré and Ju'ufa.   (Naamu)
295   Before people realized it, Manju . . .
Manhood had its *sabu*.[4]
Great deeds are not accomplished without a *sabu*.   (That's right)
Eeeyoooo,
Everybody has his special *sabu*.   (That's right, Sory)
300   Nobody must overlook his *sabu*.
He remained in Setigiya for three months.
Nobody picked up ten *dalasi*,
He did not sell ten *dalasi* worth of kola.   (Naam)
When people worry, they sleep too much.
305   Almami was worried.   (Ah, Allah! Naamu, mm)
He lay in the hammock,
Stretched out his legs,

---

4. Cause, foundation, source of good things.

	Took off his white cap and set it on his chest.	(Naamu)
	As Almami began to fall into deep sleep,	
310	Two young female genies came.	
	Their home was Takirini.	
	At that time Samawurusu . . .	
	Samawurusu was the ancestor of all the genies	(Naam)
	Samawurusu sent for all twelve genie families to come at the same time.	
315	"Let's have a meeting,	
	"Let's look for one trustworthy person,	
	"Let's give him the first musket in the blackskin's land."	
		(*Djassaow*, mm)
	It was that genie who authorized Almami to go to war.	
		(That's right)
	He did not attack people just for nothing.	
		(That's right, mm, mmm)
320	Samawurusu's first son is Jumanjujan.	(Naamu)
	"Send for your two twin sisters,	
	"Let them go all over Africa land,	
	"So we can entrust the musket to one trustworthy person."	
		(Naamu)

[Samori is not the genie's first choice as the person who deserves to receive the musket. The genie twins first approach other leading people of the time, but they fail the tests of worthiness. In the following passage Samori makes the correct ritual sacrifice and passes his test but receives the genies' blessing and the musket only on the condition that he swear never to attack three other rulers who are specially protected by genies. Meanwhile, Sere Brèma, powerful chief of the Sise clan, whose army already possessed firearms, has conquered Sanankoro and enslaved Samori's mother. Historically we know that Samori captured Sere Brèma and annexed his territory in 1881.]

620	A message arrived from Kankan:	
	"Those who are wise should build walls around their towns.	
	"If war comes and you don't have walls, you can become slaves in a single day.	
	"Everyone must build walls around their towns."	
	All the youths passed the word that nobody should go to market the next day:	
625	"We are going to build a wall tomorrow."	
	Almami heard this while he was still in Basando Moribaya,	
		(Naamu, naamu)
	Not knowing that it was for fear of Almami [himself] that the walls were being built.	
	At that time Almami had not yet acquired the musket.	
	At that time Sere Brèma was commanding,	
630	He was the first one to acquire the musket in this land of ours,	

La Guinée.
Karisi Manden Mori of Bakonko,   (Aaaaah)
Sere Brèma was the war lord.
When Almami set out to leave in the morning,
635 He met the youths on the road.   (Naamu)
The youths asked him, "Where are you going?
"Didn't you hear the announcement?"
He said, "Ah!
"I'm a stranger, that's why I was leaving."
640 They told him, "Go back to where the mud is being made,
"The law is not for only one person."
There was one hot-tempered man who hit Almami with a
            switch.   (Eeeh, beat him?)
Almami Samori smiled and went into the mud at Moribaya.
They were dancing in the mud until midday.
645 Almami asked them, "Is the work finished?" (Allah, mm, mm)
Almami had three bundles of ten kola nuts in his load.
He gave one to his host.
He took ten kola nuts and gave them to the workers.
He said, "Workers benefit everybody."
650 One old man called Kèmo Musa was there.
They told Kèmo Musa.
They said, "There was a stranger here who helped us dance in
            the mud,
"He had birthmarks on his wrists and above his eyebrows.
                                               (Mm)
"He helped us mix the mud.
655 "He has also given ten kola nuts to the workers.
"He said they don't work only in the interest of one person."
                                             (That's right)
"Haaa!" said Kèmo Musa,
"It was not a good thing for you to accept those ten kola nuts.
"We have been told about that man's signs.
660 "Anybody whom he helps to build a wall,
"He will break down that wall.
"Go after that Almami."   (Naam)
            Kèmè Brèma had three big wives,
            Joro and Mariama Sire and Ju'ufa,
665   The people searched for him.
            Descendant of the war lord.
            Good evening,
            It's Allah who makes a man the leader.   (That's right)
            The musket has its *sabu*.
670   Trading has its *sabu*.
            Expertise has its *sabu*,
            It is not just for nothing.   (That's right, Sory)
            Almamiii!

They went after Almami.
675 There was one old man called Suba Musa,
He was also a war lord.
He opened his closet and put Almami inside.
The Bananso people came searching for Almami,
They did not see Almami again.
680 After they went away,
Suba Musa let Almami out.
He said, "My son, go on."
"Aaaah!"
He met some people pounding grain with their mortars and
pestles.
685 He said, "I need to sacrifice a white cock."
He said to Suba Musa, "Loan me your musket,
"I want to go outside the town." (Naamu)
He went and shot one antelope,
Put it on his shoulder and carried it back to town. (Naamu)
690 He gave the animal to his host Suba Musa.
He took one of the legs and showed it to the women who were
pounding outside.
He asked, "Who can trade me a white cock for this?"
"Aah," he said, "this has more meat than a chicken."
[One woman said], "My workers will go to the farm tomorrow,
695 "Come and I will give you one white cock." (Naamu)
He took the cock and tied its two feet together. (Mm)
The genie twins said,
"Go to Kerouane,
You must go to Kerouane,
700 Arrive there between Thursday night and daybreak Friday,
When both sides of the night are equal,
When nobody is awake in Kerouane.
You must meet us by the Jigbé River at Kerouane.
Bring this white cock to offer as a sacrifice. (Allahu akbar)
705 Almami said, "Very well."
At midnight Almami took the cock by its two feet and
departed.
He said, "Fear is not the companion of manhood." (Never)
He arrived at the bank of the Jigbé at midnight.
The water changed to the color of fresh milk,
710 The water changed to the color of fresh blood, (Naamu)
The color changed as if the water had been dyed.
The genie twins rose out of the water. (Hetch . . . mm)
They called to Almami,
"We are the ones calling to you,
715 "Don't be frightened." (Eh, Allah)
Almami went into the water.
"Aah!" he said, "the water is not the place for me,

"I am afraid."
They made a rope bridge for Almami.
720 They told him not to be afraid. (Weii)
Almami walked and walked until he came to the genie twins.
They gave Almami the musket. (Naamu)
They said, "We are giving you the musket,
"But it is accompanied by three conditions:
725 "Thirty years, three months and three days,
"That's the time of your leadership in blackskins' land.
"Stranger in the morning,
"Host to strangers by evening."[5]
This is what they told Almami,
730 Almami said, "Very well."
Almami Samori climbed a *sida* tree.
There was a *sida* tree called Omisira. (Naamu)
The genie twins told Almami to climb that *sida* tree.
Almami Samori climbed the *sida* tree.
735 The genie twins transformed themselves.
One of them transformed herself into a python.
It started swallowing Almami from the hand to the armpit.
Almami Samori was not frightened.
The other one transformed herself and started licking his face.
(Naamu)
740 Almami Touré was not frightened of them. (Mmm)
"*Mba*,"[6] they said,
"We are giving you the musket for thirty years, three months
and three days.
"That's how long you will enjoy leadership in the blackskins'
land,
"But there are three conditions attached to the musket:
745 "When the war favors you, you must never attack Karamogo
Daye at Kankan.
"Karamogo Daye is our old friend. (Weiii)
"When the war favors you, you must not attack Sikasso Kèba.
"Our aunt does his genie work.
"When the war favors you, do not attack Gbon.
750 "Our sister does the genie work for the chief of Gbon.
"We have warned you about those three places,
"Do not attack Gbon.
"We have given you the rest of the Africa land."
Almami Samori said, "Very well."
755 He said, "Now that this is done,
"Let me go and see my old mother."
I want to go and see my old mother in Sanankoro,
Kabako! (Naam, naam, naam)

---

5. Standard praise for a conqueror. 6. Response to a greeting.

Sona Kamara,
760   Ma Kèmè Kamara,
Maningbè,
Kamara woman's son Sankun,
Mori the savior of everyone.
Before he could get there,
765   The warriors of Sere Brèma had already captured Sanankoro,
Including his mother Sona Kamara.   (Hmm)
Haaa!   (Hmm)
Almami went there and asked for his old mother.
"Aah!
770   "The warriors of Sere Brèma have taken your mother."
Blessings are good,
A blessed house is never empty.
Allah made the sky with abundant blessings,
Allah made the earth with abundant blessings,
775   And made the moon with abundant blessings,
He made the stars with abundant blessings.   (Sory, that's right)
He went to Sere Brèma,
Karisi Manden Mori,
He said, "I came for my old mother,
780   "Her name is Fani Sona.
"My father is living like a bachelor at Sanankoro.
"He was with Sere Brèma for three months,
"Then it became seven months.
"After those seven months it became seven years with Sere
        Brèma."
785   Ahah!
He had faith in Sere Brèma,
Sere Brèma had faith in Almami.
Whatever place Sere Brèma decided to attack,
Almami would go and capture it.
790   They would come and tell Sere Brèma. "Heeh!
"This stranger of ours is very powerful."
Sere Brèma became suspicious of Almami.   (Hmm)
Lack of confidence does not accomplish anything.
                             (There's truth in that)
He asked Almami Samori,
795   He said, "What do you want from me?"
Almami said, "I'm worried about my old mother.
"My father is living like a bachelor at Sanankoro."
"I will give you back your mother plus seven muskets.   (Weiii)
"If you wish, when you come back I will divide the army into
        two.
800   "You will have one division and I will have one division.
"I have come to like your ways very much Almami."   (Naamu)
Almami Samori said, "Very well."

76

A long time passed and Sere Brèma did not see Almami again.
He heard that Almami had organized some troops in Sanan-
    koro.   (Naam)
805   Almami said to the young men of Sanankoro,
"There is no special amulet for winning a battle."
He said, "Let's organize our own army."
Some of the young warriors were suspicious,
Some of them hesitated.
810   Those who were not afraid,   (Naamu)
Almami took them and attacked some people.
They captured three towns.
All the young warriors who were not married were each given
    a girl.
The word traveled from person to person:
815   "An army has been organized in Sanankoro,
"You can get a wife without paying any money."
Almami's army became popular.

[With his newly formed army, Samori launches a series of military campaigns, beginning with the towns that had humiliated him when he was a wandering merchant.]

When Almami's army was complete,
He said, "I still feel angry about the cow incident at Wasulu."
They mounted their horses and marched toward Wasulu.
915   At Wasulu they had put Almami's leg in shackles
Because he had gotten so furious about the cow,
But he was made exempt from the law.
Some had said, "Let's kill him."
There was one old man who said,   (Naamu)
920   "If one drop of this man's blood falls on the ground,
"Rain will not fall for seven years.
"Our eyes will not see rain fall in this land."
They had said, "Release him."
People are not alike.   (People are not alike)
925   Almami did not forget this,
Manju Touré.   (Naamu)
He said, "Since my army is ready,
"Let's go and ask them for the cow I loaned them.
"When I left there I told them I was only leaving it,
930   "Because I was unable to get it back from them,
"But that I was not satisfied."   (That's right)
He went and said to the people of Ton,
"Let me pass on the road through town,
"I am going to Wasulu."   (Naamu)
935   They said, "You can't use the road through the center of town,
"You must go around the outside of the town."

He said, "Nobody should disrespect a warlord,   (That's right)
"Ancestor of the warlord."   (Naamu)
He requested passage in the traditional way,
940   They did not allow passage to Almami.
In the morning he woke them up with muskets and gunpow-
            der,
What an amazing thing.
He took the road through the center of town,   (Paki)
He went on to Wasulu.
945   He told the Wasulu people, "I did not come to fight.
"The cow you took from me when I was a trader,
"That's the cow that I have come after."   (Hmm)
They asked him, "What did your cow look like?
"Was it a white cow?
950   "Or was it red?
"Was it a black cow?"
He said, "There is blood on my cow's face,
"And smoke is rising in front of it."   (Battle has come)
Everyone knows there is no cow like that.
955   He surrounded Wasulu with nineteen ranks with their gun bar-
            rels overlapping.
Whoever witnessed it saw a very big thing.
Anybody who failed to witness it missed something wonderful.
            Good evening warlord,
            Grandson of the warlord,
960   Manju Touré.
            Good evening,
            My presentation does not get interesting until late at
                night,
            Mm, hmm,
            There is a *sabu* for excellence.
965   There is a *sabu* for kingship.   (That's right, Sory)
            Everyone has his time.
After a time Almami asked the Wasulu people one question.[7]
He started destroying Wasulu,
He destroyed it like an old pot,
970   Like an old calabash.
That's why there are so many village ruins in the Wasulu
            country.   (There are many ruins)
If you can't help someone,
At least don't do him wrong.   (It's not good)

[Continuing his campaigns, Almami Samori violates his oath by attacking all three of the men who were protected by the genies. In one case
he ignores the genies' warning that if he attacks Sikasso (where Kara-

---

7. About the cow they took from him, ll. 185ff.

78

mogo Daye, one of the protected men has taken refuge), his army will
suffer great losses. Kéba, king of Sikasso, has a sister known as "One-
breasted Demba." (Physical deformity signifies special power.) She
falls in love with Samori's brother Kémé Brèma and sends him food
every day. Learning of this, Samori wrongly accuses his brother (who is
one of his greatest fighters) of treachery and strips him of his weapons.
In an earlier falling out, Kémé Brèma had sworn that he would never
again argue with his brother, so he removes his protective medicine
before the next battle and is killed. This motivates the one-breasted
woman to emerge as a heroine of Mande epic.]

> Kémé Brèma stripped off his protective amulets during the
>   battle of Sikasso.
> He purposely faced the gunfire without his medicine and was
>   hit by musket balls.
> They went and told the one-breasted woman.
>
> 1255   They said, "Kémé Brèma did not survive the battle at Sikasso."
> In his lifetime Kémé Brèma was never captured and abused by
>   the enemy.
> He gave himself up to the gunfire
> Because of what his brother did to him.
> People of early times lived up to their oaths,
>
> 1260   One-breasted Demba was told what happened.
> The one-breasted woman said, "At dawn I will ask my
>   brother."
> She did not sleep.
> She went and asked Sikasso Kéba.
> She said, "I want to know if it's true that Kémé Brèma has been
>   killed."
>
> 1265   She took off her *lapa*[8] and threw it at her brother.
> She said, "Give me your trousers."
> He took her *lapa* and wrapped it around himself,
> And gave the trousers to his sister.
> She put on his trousers.
>
> 1270   She said, "I invite you and Almami to the bank of the Kokoro,
> "So you and Almami can settle the account of Kémé Brèma."
> They let Karamogo Daye escape to Bamako.
> Sikasso Kéba said to Karamogo Daye,
> "You were here under my protection.
>
> 1275   "I don't want you to suffer from this turn of events."
> The Kokoro is in the region the Maninka call Woyowayanko.
> The battle at Woyowayanko was not sweet.
> Even up to tomorrow morning
> Musket barrels can be found in the Woyowayanko.
>
> 1280   It was that woman who organized the battle at Woyowayanko.

---

8. Wraparound cloth skirt.

7. The Epic of Musadu
Narrated by Moikè Sidibe

*Recorded in Kankan, Guinea, on December 1, 1993, by Timothy Geysbeek.
Transcribed and translated into English by Ansu Cisse and Faliku Sanoe
with the assistance of Timothy Geysbeek. This excerpt edited by Timothy
Geysbeek.*

MANY MANDE PEOPLE OF SOUTHEASTERN GUINEA and western Liberia
narrate a popular story of how a slave named Zo Musa founded the
town of Musadu near the provincial capital of Beyla in Guinea. They
also tell how a powerful Mande warrior named Foningama (Kamara)
later took control of the town. "Zo Musa" may have founded Musadu
between the thirteenth and fifteenth centuries during the time of the
Mande or the Mali empire. Most of the "Foningama" episodes seem to
date to a later period, perhaps during the sixteenth century or a little
earlier. The stories about Zo Musa and Foningama began as separate
accounts, but over time the Mande have compressed them into one narrative. The Musadu epic is as important to many of the Mande peoples
in this region for defining social, cultural, and historical relationships
between themselves and other peoples as the Sunjata epic is for the
Mande in Mali and neighboring lands.

Moikè Sidibe, the narrator, is Professor of History at the University of Kankan, Guinea. Sidibe's father is of the Fula ethnic group from
Futa Jallon, and his mother is a Kamara-Mande from Damaro in Kerouane province. The speaker can trace his ancestry through his mother's
father's line over ten generations to Foningama's son Fajala (Fènjala).
Moikè Sidibe thus provides a Kamara view of the Musadu epic.

Timothy Geysbeek recorded Moikè Sidibe in Lai Makula Mam-
madi Kamara's yard in Kankan on December 1, 1993. Toligbè Braima
Kamara and Fata Jiba Kamara encouraged Sidibe like *naamu*-sayers
throughout the narrative. Ansu Cisse and Faliku Sanoe helped Geysbeek translate the text. Sidibe divided his narrative into three major
parts: the Kamara migrations from the Mande to Côte d'Ivoire and
southeastern Guinea, Foningama's flight to Musadu after his father
died, and Zo Musa's founding of Musadu and exile after the Mande
forced him out of town. Sidibe usually said Masa instead of Musa and
Misadu instead of Musadu.

[The growth of Misadu.]

105	Damaro came from Misadu.	(Uhun)
	How did it come from Misadu?	(Uhun)
	Misadu was a town all by itself.	(Uhun)
	The Koniya people,	(Uhun)
	Loma,	(Uhun)
110	Kpelle,	(Uhun)
	Kono,	(Uhun)

They all lived in Misadu.	(That is right)
Misadu was a small town,	(Uun)
But Misadu later became a big town.	(Uun)

[The Kamara began to migrate south as the Mande became less secure. The Kamara ancestor's sons dispersed to different areas, and one, Foningama, traveled down to the town of Siyanò in Côte d'Ivoire. Foningama sired a son named "Small Foningama," who is the Kamara hero in this story.]

[The Kamara dispersal from the Mande.]

115	Later, Misadu	(Uun)
	The first Kamara who were there	(Uhun)
	Were not the same as the Kamara who came from up north,	
		(Uum)
	In Côte d'Ivoire.	(Uum)
	Foningama	(Uhun)
120	Came from Côte d'Ivoire.	(Uum)
	He came from a town,	(Uhun)
	From Siyanò.	(Uhun)
	They called it Silana.	(Uhun, Silana)
	How they came,	(Uhun)
125	Lets talk about that.	(Uhun)
	History	(Uum)
	Did not happen today.	(Uhun)
	Eh—Foningama,	(Uhum)
	Miakèdè Kamara,	(Uun)
130	Sonkoli Kamara,	(Uhun)
	Friki Kamara,	(Uhun)
	All came from one man.	(Uun)
	They came from Sibi,	(Uhum)
	From the north.	(Uum)
135	At that time,	
	There was trouble in Mande.	(Uum)
	The old people	(Uum)
	Say that many things were happening in Mande	(Uum)
	At that time.	
140	That did not happen in our presence.	(Uum)
	We only heard about it.	(Uhum)
	When they came from the north,	
	Some Kamara went and settled in a town in Côte d'Ivoire.	(Uun)
	It is called Siyanò.	(Siyanò)
145	The others went to Kouroussa.	(Uun)
	Sonabale	(Uun)
	Was founded on that side of Kouroussa.	(Uun)
	The other two went and settled, èh—near Fria.	(Uum)

81

The other went and settled in the Sigidi[1] region.   (Uhun)

[Kamara medicine, *saakèle.*]

150	The one who went left to the northern part of Côte d"Ivoire,	
		(Uhun)
	That was Foningama.	(Uhun)
	Foningama lived in Silana	(Uhun)
	And sired many children.	(Uhun)
	He died after his grandchildren were born.	(Uhun)
155	Those grandchildren were here.	(Uun)
	The name of an ancestor can be given	(Uhun)
	To a child.	(Uhun)
	After Small Foningama was born,	(Uhun)
	Confusion arose among his father's children.	(Uhun)
160	What was the nature of this confusion?	(Uhun)
	There was something in their family	(Uhun)
	That was called *saakèle.*[2]	(Uhun)
	The secret thing	(Uhun)
	Of the Jomani	
165	Was that *saakèle.*	
	After the father died,	(Uhun)
	It would be given to the first son.	(Uhun)
	That *saakèle*	
	Was medicine.	
170	It was a symbol of power.	(Uuun)
	The person who had it would rule.	(Uun)
	You would rule a region.	(Uun)

[The Kamara patriarch traditionally gave *saakèle,* or medicine-imbued sheep horn, to the oldest son in the family. Foningama's father, however, gave the *saakèle* to Foningama because of their close relationship. This caused resentment among Foningama's older brothers, particularly Kònsava. So, Foningama fled to his mother's family, the Kromah, who lived in Nèlèkòlò near Misadu. Foningama and the Kromah later moved to Misadu to secure more protection against Kònsava.]

[Foningama inherits the Kamara *saakèle.*]

	Concerning Small Foningama,	
	Eh, they said that Kònsava	(Uhun)
175	Was one of his father's children.	(Uhun, the Kònsava people)
	Tension rose between them	(Uhun)
	Because they were not near their father	(Uhun)
	And because they wanted to get their father's blessing.	(Uun)

---

1. Siguiri. 2. Sheep horn.

	The son who went near the father and was blessed	(Uun)
180	Was Foningama.	(Uun)
	That Kònsava	(Uhun)
	Left and went far away,	(Uhun)
	From his father.	(Uun)
	Life became difficult for his father.	(That is right)
185	His father got sick	
	And died later on.	(Uhun)
	Now after his death	
	Before he died,	
	He told his son [Foningama],	(Uhun)
190	"My son, you are the youngest of my children.	(Uhun)
	"I am not supposed to give the thing to you	(Uhun)
	"That I am going to give to you.	(Uum)
	"You are not the oldest,	(Uun)
	"But I am going to give it to you	(Uum)
195	"Because you have taken care of me,	
	"Because a good relationship developed between father and child.	(Uum)
	"I am giving this thing [to you],	(Uum)
	"And God will bless you in this world.	(Uun)
	"God will bless you at the time of judgment.	(Uun)
200	"If God agrees,	(Uhun)
	"And if there is nothing [bad] between the father and the child,	(Uun)
	"Nothing bad	(Uun)
	"Will come your way."	(Uhun)

[Foningama flees to his Kromah uncles in Koniya.]

	After they announced that he died,	(Uhun)
205	They sent a message for all the father's children to come.	
	They were thinking about . . .	(Uhun)
	They were thinking about	(Uhun)
	The *sani-saakèle*,	(Uhun)
	That medicine.	(Uhun)
210	But the man left the medicine with his son,	(Uhun)
	Small Foningama,	(Uhun)
	So the others went and tried to kill him.	(Uhun)
	He fled	(Uun)
	And went	
215	To his mother's home.	(Uum)
	He said, "If a child	(Uhun)
	"Can't be in his father's home,	(Uhun)
	"He should go to his mother's home."	(Uun)
	That did not happen recently.	(Uhun)
220	That happened a long time ago.	(That is right)

That is the parable that Konava gave.   (Uhun)
Layi Mako himself   (Uhun)
Said that if you see a man who is able to carry a load,
It means that he respects his mother's people.   (Uum)
225   If you respect your mother's people,   (Uum)
There are some things that you can do that others cannot do.
                                                  (Uhun)
You can become strong and powerful and have a good reputa-
      tion.   (That is right)

[Tumani Kromah and Foningama move from Nèlèkòlò to Misadu.]

Foningama fled and went to his uncles,   (Uum)
Who were the Kromah,   (Uhun)
230   The Kromah of Koniya.
His mother,
Her name was Dama Soloba.
His uncle was Tumani Kromah.
Tumani Kromah
235   Ruled Koniya at that time.
The Koniya
Was divided into twelve regions,   (Uhun)
And the Kromah ruled the whole area.   (Uhun)
In Koniya,
240   Foningama went to Nèlèkòlò,   (Uhun)
Which was Tumani Kromah's home.   (Uhun)
His uncle said, "I am happy that you came,   (Uhun)
"But I want us to flee   (Uhum)
"From the war   (Uhum)
245   "That is following you.   (Uhum)
"Let's go to Misadu   (Uhun)
"And settle in Misadu.   (Uhun)
"It is better than living in Nèlèkòlò."   (Uuhun)
250   That is why Foningama and his uncle went to Misadu. (Uhun)
Many people lived there.   (Uhun)
"[Let's move to Misadu] in case Kònsava decides to come and
      fight.   (Uhun)
"They say they want to take the *saakèle* from you (Uhun)
"And fight you."   (Uum)

[Plot to kill Foningama. This harks back to an earlier moment when
Foningama still lived with his family (l. 212).]

They had dug a hole   (Uhun)
255   In the house   (Uhun)
Even before he left,
And they put a spear and many other dangerous things

	In the bottom of the hole.	(Uhun)
	When Foningama came [into the house],	(Uhun)
260	They asked him to sit in the middle [of the room].	
	They hoped	
	That when he came and sat in the middle of the room	(Uhun)
	He would fall into the hole	(Uum)
	And that that would be the end of him.	(Uhun)
265	When he arrived,	(He came)
	He said, "Uun, this	(Uhun)
	"Is not my place."	(Uun)
	One old woman had warned him about the plot	
	Before he went to sit in the middle [of the room].	(Uhun)
270	Foningama listened and remembered what she said.	(Uum)
	When he went there,	
	They said, "Here is your seat."	
	He replied, "No, that place is reserved for important people."	
		(Uum)
	He went and sat at the back of the room,	(Uun)
275	And those who came in after him	(Uum)
	Went and fell into the hole.	(Uum)
	That is why Foningama fled to his uncle's place.	(Uun)
	That is what I have said today.	
	They left Nèlèkòlò	(Uhun)
280	And went to Misadu.	(Uun)

[As the Kamara were emigrating from Mande, a slave named Zo Masa ('chief') founded Musadu. Zo Masa acquired some powerful medicine and established a secret (*doo*) society to organize his followers against the Mande in a hilly area outside of Musadu called Doofatini. A *moli* or 'cleric' named Beyan Bèlète from Musadu finally defeated Zo Masa. Bèlète placed a more powerful medicine on a frog, and the frog swallowed Zo Masa's medicine. Zo Masa and the Loma, Kpelle, Kono, and Mano peoples associated with him later fled after Foningama defeated them in battle. Zo Masa moved to the town of Zota near N'Zerekore. The Kromah had granted Foningama the chieftancy of Musadu after he repulsed an attack from Kònsava. Foningama then extended his power and put his sons in control over twelve neighboring regions. Some of his sons, however, were executed for breaking a law. The survivors left and ruled other areas.]

[Zo Musa Kromah or Zo Masa Kòlò. Many say that Masa was a slave of the Kromah, and that his "last name" was Kòma.]

When they reached Misadu,	(Uun)
Zo Masa Kromah was there.	(Uun)
The people used to call him Zo-Zo Masa Kòlò.	(Uum)
He was the owner of Misadu at that time.	(Uhun)

285	He had medicine that could do anything.	(Uhun)
	The Kromah,	(Uhun)
	Bèlète,	(Uhun)
	Fofana,	(Uun)
	Zozo [Donzo],	(Uun)
290	Sumaro [Dole],	(Uum)
	They had all settled in Misadu by that time.	(Uhun)
	Misadu was mixed up by that time.	

[Kònsava attacks Foningama in Misadu.]

	Eh, when they attacked Misadu—	(Uhun)
	Kònsava and his people,	(Uhun)
295	Foningama fought very hard,	(Uhun)

[The Kromah make Foningama the *masa*[3] of Misadu.]

	And the Kromah appreciated what he did.	(Uhun)
	His older . . .	
	His uncle	(Uun)
	Helped him	(Un)
300	And said that they should make him that thing—the masa.	
		(Uhun)

[Moli Beyan Bèlète destroys Zo Masa's medicine.]

	But he asked how they would defeat Zo Masa and his people.	
		(Uhun)
	There was a *saakèle*,	(Uhun)
	Which Zo Masa had for medicine,	(Uhun)
	And it used to kill and do other big things there.	(Uhun)
305	They made medicine	(Uhun)
	From a frog.	(Uhun)
	The frog . . .	
	When it [Zo Masa's *saakèle*] swallowed the frog,	(Uhun)
	It was ruined.	(Uhun)
310	That is how Zo Masa lost his power.	(Uhun)
	That is how it is explained,	(Uhun)
	For the medicine was ruined.	(Uhun)
	Moli Beyan Bèlète	(Uhun)
	Was the one who fixed that medicine.	(Uhun)
315	He made the medicine.	(Uhun)
	He was a *moli*—	(Uhun)
	Somebody: [From] Misadu there.	
	Sidibe: [From] Misadu there.	
	The other person's power	(Uhun)

---

3. Chief.

320	Was destroyed	(Uhun)
	After he fixed that medicine.	(Uhun)

[Zo Masa's people go to Man, Bosu, and Lola.]

	Zo Masa Kòlò	(Uhun)
	Left	(Uhun)
	With his people.	(Uhun)
325	One group went	(Uhun)
	To Man in Côte d'Ivoire,	(Uhun)
	And they fought the people of Man	(Uun)
	When they reached Man.	(Uun)
	It was called Man.	(Uum)
330	That is what the people of Man did.	(Uum)
	Some went	(Uhun)
	To Zòò,	(Uum)
	All the way down to the region of Lola,	(Uhun)
	And settled in Bosu and Lola.	(Uhun)
335	Those are the Mano who live there.	(Uhun)

[Zo Masa takes water, roots, and rocks from Misadu.]

	The Kpelle,	(Uun)
	When Zo Masa Kòlò	(Um)
	Left Misadu,	(Uum)
	He took some water from Misadu,	(Uhun)
340	From the surrounding streams.	(Uhun)
	He also took some of its tree roots	(Um)
	And some of its rocks.	(Um)
	There were some rocks.	(Um)

[Foningama's sons are executed for breaking a law.]

	They passed a law	(Uhun)
345	And said that anybody who violated the law	(Uum)
	Would be killed.	(That is right)
	The persons who violated the law	(Uhun)
	Were Foningama's children.	(Uum)
	They killed them	(Uum)
350	At the rock near Misadu's mosque.	(Uum)
	That is their grave.	(They are there)
	They are the ones who were killed because they violated the	
	law.	(Uum)
	[They said,] "We have passed a law.	(Uum)
	"How can your children violate the law?	(Uhun)
355	"What should be done to them?"	
	Braima: Kill them.	

	Sidibe: They were killed.	(Uhun)
	Was there sympathy for anybody else?	(Uun)

[Zo Masa travels to Boola and Wenzu.]

	They left.	(Uhun)
360	When they reached the road,	(Uhun)
	They said, "*Kanikwekoe*."	(Uhun)
	[When they reached] the river near Damaro,	(Uhun)
	Zo Masa stood up and said,	(Uhun)
	"*Kanikookwe*."	(Uhun)
365	That means,	(Uhun)
	"God has saved me	(Uhun)
	"From Foningama and his people	(Uhun)
	"And separated me from them."	(Uhun)
	He passed	(Um)
370	And went to the region of Boola.	(Uhun)
	There are many mushrooms in the area	(Uhun)
	That are named *kpoola*.	(Um)
	They named Boola	(Um)
	After *kpoola*.	(Uhun)
375	The Kpelle settled there.	(Uum)
	They went to Wenzu.	(Um)

[Zo Masa settles in Zota.]

	After they left Wenzu,	(Uum)
	They went to Zèlèkole.	(Uum)
	They went and established a town	(Uhun)
380	There called Zota.	(Uhun)
	That Zota,	(Uhun)
	Ta,	(Uun)
	In Kpelle means 'town,'	(Uum)
	And Zo was Zo Masa Kòlò's name.	
385	That is why they call it Zo Masa Kòlò's town.	(Uum)
	Zèlèkole	(Uhun)
	Is not the real name of Zèlèkole.	
	The real name is Zaakolè.	(Uhun)
	Zaakolè	(Um)
390	Was a name given	(Um)
	To a small stream.	(Um, that is right)
	That is [Zota] where he [Zo Masa] went and settled.	
	He poured some water.	(Uhun)
	That water was like the water in Misadu.	(Uhun)
395	He put down the rock that he had,	(Uhun)
	And it became like the rock in Misadu.	(Uhun)
	The hill rose like the hill in Misadu.	(Uhun)

	The big tree also grew like the big tree in Misadu.	(Um)
	Even if that had not happened,	(Um)
400	The people knew that Zo Masa Kòlò left Misadu with his medicine	(Uum)
	And came here.	(Uun)

[Zo Masa, scarification, and *doo* in Misadu.]

	Scarification formed the basis of the *doo*.[4]	(Uum)
	Doo started in Misadu,	(Uum)
	In the Gbèi area.	(Uum)
405	The hill [Doofatini]	(Uum)
	Is by the road that leads to Sinkò.	(Uun)
	That is where *doo* was started.	(Uum)
	That is where they started to cut people's skin.	(Uum)
	His name was Zo Masa Kòlò.	(Uum)
410	Do you understand?	(Uum)

[The Mande people meet the Loma, Kpelle, Kono, and Mano in Koniya.]

	Foningama lived in Misadu.	(Uhun)
	Didn't I tell you that this area was divided into twelve regions?	(Koso-Kosobè)
	He put the Kamara[5] to rule over these regions.	(Uum)
	Braima: Now we come to Koniya.	
	Sidibe: Now we come to Koniya.	
415	What does Koniya mean?	(Uhun)
	Say, "Kòniya."	(Uhun)
	Kòni,	(Uum)
	Water, èh—'rock.'	(Uhun)
	Ya means this thing—	
420	*Braima*: 'Water.'	
	Sidibe: 'Water.'	
	That is where the name Koniya comes from.	(Uum)
	Otherwise, the children of the land of Koniya,	(Uhun)
	They are the Loma, the Kpelle, the Kono.	(Uum)
425	The people of Mani[6] came and met them there.	(Uum)
	All of the [Mande] people who can say,	(Uum)
	"*Ngo* (I say)," came and met them there.	(Uum)
	Do you understand? . . .	(Uum)

[Zo Masa Kòlò founds Misadu.]

How was Misadu founded?

---

4. Secret. 5. His sons. 6. The Mande.

89

	A man was there	(Uhun)
950	Whose name was Masa.	
	Some people called him Musa,	(Uhun)
	And some people called him Masa.	(Uuhun)
	Do you understand?	(Uhun)
	Masata Zo	(Uhun)
955	Was Loma.	

It is *masa so*,[7]
Masa kèla so.[8]
Musata Zo, Musa's town, Misadu.
The town of Musa.

960 How was it established?
You know that a stream was there.   (Uhun)
Now, Musa was a slave.
He used to go fishing there.
After he caught fish,
965 He would go and make a mat and put the fish on it.
People went and bought them.
People went and bought them a little at a time.
He built a house there.
After he built his house,
970 People started to go and settle there as his business became
      more prosperous.
The Dukule settled there.
The Kromah settled there.
The Sware settled there.
The Fofana settled there.
975 All of them went there and made the place become big.
But the Loma, Kpelle, èh-èh—Kono, Konè,
Braima: Mano [in the background].
Sidibe: They all lived—all lived in Misadu town.

[The Loma, Kpelle, Kono, and Mano flee when Foningama defeats Zo Masa.]

That is why they say
980 That all of the towns in the forest came from Misadu.
All of them came from Misadu.   (Uhun, Uhun)
Many people left Misadu when Foningama
Went to Misadu   (Uhun)
And fought, èh-èh—Zo Masa Kòlò.
985 They fought Zo Masa Kòlò.
That is what happened.
Now, the people left.
Some people went to the east.

---

7. Chief's town. 8. The chief man's town.

Some people went to the south.
990   Some went toward Macenta and Zèlèkole and Lola and Liberia
       and Côte d'Ivoire.
Do you understand?   (Uhun)
That is how Misadu was established.
That is how Misadu came to be.

8. The Epic of Kelefa Saane
Narrated by Shirif Jebate

Recorded for Radio Gambia sometime in the 1960s. Transcribed by Bakari Sidibe. Translated into English by Gordon Innes with the assistance of Bakari Sidibe. Edited by Gordon Innes and published in 1978 by the School of Oriental and African Studies, University of London. This excerpt edited by John Wm. Johnson.

KELEFA SAANE WAS A MID-NINETEENTH CENTURY WARRIOR of the aristocracy of Kaabu, a confederation of Mandinka states whose influence extended from the Gambia River southward as far as the Rio Corubal, but whose heartland was the state of Kaabu, which was located in the northeast of what is now Guinea-Bissau. It is puzzling that an epic is today recited by Mandinka bards about this figure, for he had no influence on events in which he was involved and in no way affected the course of history. Indeed, he loses the battle which is recounted in the epic and is killed. Moreover, he is described by the Mandinka bards as being a Jola, who are linguistically and culturally quite distinct from the Mandinka. The bards' practice of referring to Kelefa as a Jola is made even more puzzling by the fact that Kelefa's family name is Saane, the name of one of the lines of warrior aristocrats of the Mandinka state of Kaabu. Yet, in The Gambia, the story of Kelefa's career is one of the best-known and best-loved items in the bards' repertoires, and his principle praise-poem is traditionally the first piece a young bard learns to play on the kora, the twenty-one-stringed lute-harp so popular among the Mande peoples.

The text presented here is a transcription of a performance by a highly respected elderly Gambian, Jali Shirif Jebate who, like other Gambian bards, possesses a repertoire of historical narratives falling into two main parts. The first of these is the Sunjata epic, which recounts the career of Sunjata Keita, culminating in the defeat of his great adversary, Sumanguru, about the year 1235 and his establishment as ruler of Manding (or Mali), which expanded under his successors to become the most influential of all the medieval Sudanic empires. The second part of the bards' repertoire comprises accounts of the careers of various outstanding local figures of the second half of the nineteenth century who were active in The Gambia valley and in the area stretching south from there into Guinea-Bissau. The epic of Kelefa Saane falls in this second category.

Kelefa's military career can be briefly told. When war between Niumi and Jokadu appeared inevitable on the north bank of the River Gambia, King Demba Sonko of Niumi, a member of one of the three lineages which held the kingship of Niumi in rotation—the others were the Saanes and the Maanes—sent a request for help to Badora, one of the states in the Kaabu confederation. Kelefa Saane responded to the call and set off to Niumi. His arrival in Niumi seems to have been an embarrassment to the king, who had been forewarned by his Muslim diviners that he would be ill advised to have Kelefa by his side when he joined battle with Jokadu. King Demba Sonko therefore sent Kelefa off across the river on a pretext while the Niumi forces launched their attack. When Kelefa returned and caught up with his allies, who had gone off without him, he was not of great assistance. He certainly did not help the Niumi forces to victory, for the war was a disaster for both sides. In the fighting, Kelefa was rather ingloriously shot by a deformed leper (or albino) who lay in wait for him up a tree in the shade of which Kelefa rested from time to time.

Whatever the reality may have been, the princely ideal still has a powerful emotional appeal for the Mandinka. Kelefa seems to be the embodiment of the highest princely ideals, and in this lies much of his popularity with Mandinka audiences. Kelefa displays unselfishness of the highest order; he responded to the king of Niumi's call for help, because the king was in trouble, and it therefore behooved a prince to respond, regardless of his own circumstances. Kelefa clearly did not go to Niumi for personal gain; on the contrary, he repeatedly rejected the offer of generous gifts by the various rulers through whose territory he passed if he would abandon his intention of going to fight in Jokadu. These same rulers reminded him that war brings sudden death to many, but Kelefa remained resolute in his resolve to go and do battle on behalf of the king of Niumi, rejecting all offers of wealth. It would have been a betrayal of the princely ideal if he had chosen wealth rather than battle. The story of how Kelefa resisted all the offers of wealth and instead pressed forward to the hazards of battle to assist a friend in need must make a powerful impact on a Mandinka listener. Here are displayed loyalty to a friend, courage and unselfishness of the highest order. The popularity of the Kelefa story with Mandinka audiences must surely be due in large measure to the fact that Kelefa embodies in their highest form not only the ideals of the princes, but also ideals of everyday life such as unselfishness, loyalty to a friend, and courage.

> Kelefa summoned his men
> And said to them, "Let's go!"
> Kelefa took some wine and drank it.

> *Mm yee ee*, sit down and wait for me.
> 300   Ah, you seized him and you slew him.
> Yammadu the warrior, you are successful in war.

> When Kelefa Saane
> Arrived, he found all the Niumi forces assembled at the Mem-
>   meh bridge.
> They were arguing with each other;
> 305   Some were saying,

"Let's go to Dasilami," but Kelefa said to them, "The people
    there are Muslims, so don't let's go there."
Some said,
"Let's go to Tambana," but Kelefa said, "The people there are
    caste members."
Some said,
310   "Let's go to Bali."
But Kelefa said to them, "That area is upriver; if our attack fails,
    it will not be possible to get back to Niumi."
Some said,
"Then what are we to do?"
Kelefa told them,
315   "The best place for us to wage war is a place called Baria Koto.
"Let's go there."
As you approach Kuntair,
The small valley which you see
Marks the line of march of Kelefa Saane and the forces of
    Niumi; it is their passage which produced that valley.
320   They went to Madina Jiikoi,
Then they crossed the upper reaches of the creek at Fatakoo.
At the spot where the horses crossed, their hooves, which made
    the rock dry,
Have left prints which are visible to this day at low tide.
They crossed over and came to Baria Koto.
325   Saane Balaamang lies at Baria, Bobo Tuma, and Bobo
        Sankung.
    Great man of Tambana, a bee in sorghum wine, warrior in
        a foreign land.
    Not every child inherits his father's estate; I-haven't-got-it's
        griot is unfortunate, a mean man's griot is unfortunate.
    For what great men have I sung this? For great men, both
        friendly and hostile.
    But a Mandinka with his fickleness, if you do him a good
        turn, that will be noised abroad; if you do him a bad
        turn, that too will be noised abroad.

330   Kelefa said that they should not go to Tambana
Because the people there were caste members; but there were
    many men of high distinction there,
For at that time Mang Bandi was in Tambana,
Keni was in Tambana,
Keni Kumba was in Tambana,
335   Ngaali was in Tambana,
Kali Meta Suuko was in Tambana,
Jeenung Meta Suuko was in Tambana,
Hama Demba was in Tambana, Seeku Nufung was in Tam-
    bana, there were griots too in Tambana.

Mootang Maane,
340   Jata Banna Karte Was,
All of these were men of high distinction.
That was why
Kelefa Saane said that they should not go to Tambana.

They advanced,
345   The Niumi forces advanced,
They reached Baria Koto.
But before the Niumi forces reached Baria Koto,
King Demba took the mahogany writing board
Upon which the *marabout* had written
350   And he gave it to a messenger, who went and stood on the
        bank
Of the creek at Memmeh;
He took the mahogany writing board and threw it into the
        creek.
When he threw it in, a great sound filled the air,
A great noise was heard.
355   The Jokadu men shouted, "The men of Niumi are coming by
        river!"
Those who were first off the mark flung themselves into canoes
        and set off in the direction of the noise, but the canoes cap-
        sized with their occupants and they were drowned; they
        never arrived,
And they were not present on the field of battle.
The Jokadu men went
And manned the fence; Hamadada Seeka Ndemba and all the
        Jokadu forces
360   Along with the men from Bali manned the fence.
Kelefa Saane
And King Demba
Stood in front, side by side,
With all the Niumi forces behind them.
365   They launched their attack
On a Monday.
When Kelefa Saane
Fired his gun,
Three men, four men, ten men
370   Were laid low
With a single shot.
When Hamadada Seeka Ndemba
Fired his gun,
Five men, six men
375   Were laid low.
But when Kelefa Saane was fired upon,
The bullets failed to penetrate his body;

He picked them up, examined them and dropped them into his
    bag.
They fought
380   On Monday,
And on Tuesday,
And on the third day
The female jinn came to Hamadada Seeka Ndemba and said to
    him, "Hamadada!" and he answered, "Yes."
She said, "This Jola who confronts you," and he said, "Yes." "A
    bullet," she said, "Won't kill him."

385   When the two armies had met,
On the third day
The fighting was still going on;
On the fourth day
The fighting was still going on,
390   And the female jinn came and said, "This Jola who confronts
    you will not be killed by a bullet. But this Jola fellow—
"Before six days are up,

"This Jola." Hamadada said, "Mm. You must kill a one year
    old cock on Monday
"And remove its spur
"And soak it in poison.
395   "When you have soaked it in poison,
"You must put it in a gun.
"You must send a deformed leper without fingers
"Up a tree onto a platform.
"When you have sent him up onto a platform,
400   "Before he shoots Kelefa Saane on Monday morning,
"He must bend down with his back to him.
"But before you do all that,
"You must take a bead of a pure Fula
"And put it in a gun and shoot him with it."
405   They went to Hamadi Fall
And got a bead of a pure Fula
And put it in a gun.
They shot Kelefa with it,
But it made no impression on Kelefa.
410   They moved from there,
And the female jinn said to them,
"Ah, look, this bead of a pure Fula has made no impression on
    Kelefa.
"Now take the one-year-old cock."
On Sunday evening
415   They took the spur of the one-year-old cock
And soaked it in poison.

They sent a deformed man up a tree onto a platform
And told him,
"When dawn breaks,
420 "Before you shoot Kelefa,
"You must bend down with your back to him three times,
"And the fourth time,
"You fire."

Kelefa Saane—
425 On the Monday morning,
When the female jinn
Had given them those instructions,
They put the spur of the one-year-old cock in a gun.
The deformed man climbed up into a tree,
430 He bent down with his back to Kelefa Saane.

When the deformed man had bent down three times with his
     back to Kelefa Saane, the fourth time he took the spur of the
     one-year-old cock
And shot Kelefa Saane with it.
When Kelefa was shot,
The bullet hit him;
435 And he swayed forward,
And he declared, "This bullet which has hit me will be the
     death of me."
He said, "King Demba!" and the king said, "Yes."
Kelefa asked him, "Who are the men who are giving you most
     trouble in this battle? Tell me who they are, so that they
     can be my hosts in the next world when I have killed
     them."
Kelefa clutched the bridle.
440 When he was leaving Badora, his mother had given him a little
     horn,
And that horn now fell to the ground.
It went back to Badora.
If you remember, I have already told you about that. When
     Kelefa was leaving Badora, I told you about the horn; I said
     that his mother gave him a little horn. She said that he was
     to take that little horn with him to war;
If he died, it would return and report his death, but if he did
     not die, he would return home with the horn.
445 Kelefa Saane
Moved forward
And almost fell from his horse; but he did not altogether fall,
     for several men rushed to his aid.
When he had been helped to sit firmly in the saddle,

97

Those men who had been giving King Demba most trouble in
    the battle
450   Were shot by Kelefa
And carried off by him to the next world,
Where they became his hosts.
He suddenly fell from his horse
And his followers lifted him up;
455   And the spot where they were going to lay him down
Was under a mango tree.
Kelefa asked them, "What tree is this?"
And they told him, "This is a mango tree."
He said, "This tree is very cold.
460   "Don't bury me here,
"Because this is a mango tree
"And this is what children practice their climbing on."
He left there;
They bore him away
465   And laid him under a *santang* tree.
He asked them, "What tree is this?"
And they told him, "This is a *santang* tree."
He said, "If the ash of a *santang* tree is not bitter, it is still not
    palatable."
He left there,
470   And they carried him under a *sinjang* tree.
He asked them, "What tree is this?"
And they told him, "This is a *sinjang* tree."
He said, "Dig up its root and examine it.
"What is it like?"
475   They said, "It is bitter."
"What about its seeds?"
They said, "They are bitter."
He told them, "You must bury me here.
"But when you bury me here,
480   "At the head of my grave and at the foot,
"A termite mound will rise up,
"But upon my grave
"No grass will grow
"Till the end of time."
485   And to this very day,
Upon Kelefa Saane's grave
No grass grows.
The war was a disaster.

Then Kelefa Saane's spear was removed.
490   His spear is at Niumi Jufureh at the present time.
Whoever can do so should go and see his spear.
But in any case Kelefa's spear is at Jufureh at the present time.

The maternal grandfather of Alkali Nufung who died
    recently—
When Kelefa Saane and his followers arrived,
495   There was great poverty—
Was trading in European goods.
Some men took the spear
And pledged it with him.
That spear was pledged
500   And to this day it has never been redeemed.
It belonged to
Alkali Nufung Taali's maternal grandfather.
He died,
And the Alkali's father took it over.
505   He in turn died,
And Alkali Nufung took it over.
He in turn died,
And it is his son who is there now—
Mamadi Taali.
510   He has the spear.
The war was a disaster.
There was no one who could take
Kelefa Saane's place.
One Fula
515   Thought that he could take Kelefa's place.
That Fula—
Hamadada Seeka Ndemba
Took a spear against him,
And they wounded each other with their spears.
520   Hamadada wounded him with his spear
And drove him across the river,
And he entered Senegal.
He fled.
The war was a disaster.
525   Wounded men
Crawled back
To Niumi.
Wounded men
Crawled back
530   To Jokadu.
Ah, the nobles are finished,
War has finished the nobles
Civil war has finished the nobles.

9. The Epic of Kambili
Narrated by Seydou Camara

Recorded in Bamako in 1968 by Charles Bird. Transcribed and translated by Charles Bird with Mamadou Koita and Bourama Soumaoro. Published by the African Studies Program, Indiana University. This excerpt edited by Charles Bird.

I've seen a hunter; I've seen my friend.
I've seen a hunter; I've seen my brother.
I've seen a hunter, I've seen my sharer of pleasures.
Heroes, let's be off!
Eating the traditional dish is not an evil deed.
A man's learning and his ability are not the same.
Harp-playing Seydou from Kabaya has come.
Falsity is not good, Master.
Look to the Camara tree for the sacred tree of Mecca.
The wing descends, the wing and its captives.
The wing ascends, the wing and its captives.
Bow, Ancestor, your enemy-striking arrow!
You hit a *balenbon* tree.
From that day to this,
One side of the *balenbon* has yet to recover.
Should the wing move to the east,
You will hear its sound.
Should the wing move to the west,
You will hear its sound.
Ah! It's the voice of harp-playing Seydou!
The thing is not easy for all.
It's the sound of harp-playing Seydou from Kabaya.
Dugo's Kambili! The lion is evil!

The opening lines of Seydou Camara's Kambili

THE PRECEDING SELECTION IS FROM THE BEGINNING OF *KAMBILI*, an extended heroic epic of the Wasulu hunters in Mali. The published version available through Indiana University's African Studies Center consists of 2725 lines. The full narrative opens with events leading up to the birth of the hero, Kambili, during the reign of the Imam Samori Touré, whose rule in the nineteenth century extended over much of today's southern Mali and Guinea. The middle portion deals with aspects of Kambili's adolescence and the end deals with his marriage to the beautiful Kumba and his battle against the lionman, Cekura.

When the recording of Kambili was made in the spring of 1968, Seydou was about fifty years old. He had begun playing indigenous instruments of the Wasulu region as a young boy and had shown considerable promise, particularly on the *dan*, a six-stringed lute. He began his interest in the *donsonkòni*, the hunter's lute-harp, through his initiation and extensive interest in the Komo societies of the Wasulu region. In his early twenties, he was conscripted into the French army and went to serve in Morocco with the Free French Forces during World War II. After the war, he transferred to the Civil Guard in Mali and was stationed in Timbuktu, where he married his first wife, Kariya Wulen. While in Timbuktu, according to Seydou, he was poisoned by his enemies in the local community, the result of which was what we would probably call a nervous breakdown; Seydou said he was possessed by jinns. As a consequence, he was dismissed from the service and returned to his native village. Under the care of the famous Kankan Sekouba, Seydou gradually regained his health and devoted himself exclusively to playing the hunter's lute-harp, serving as a singer for the Wasulu hunters and as a bard for the Komo society. By 1953 he had developed his art to such an extent that he drew the attention of the influential deputy, Jime Jakite. Jakite brought him to a major political rally in Sikasso, where Seydou won the hunters' bard competition, which elevated him to national celebrity.

> *Speaking is not easy;*
> *Not being able to speak is not easy.*
> *I'm doing something I've learned,*
> *I'm not doing something I was born for.*

He recorded a number of songs for the national radio and his voice was frequently heard on Radio Mali's broadcasts when I was first in Mali in the mid-1960s. When I first met him, Seydou earned his living performing for hunters and their associations at their festivals, funerals, weddings, and baptisms, traveling to many of the major towns in southern Mali: Segu, Kutiala, Sikaso, Buguni. He got little for his services, usually receiving a *worosongo*, the price of kola nuts (about 500 to 1,000 francs, between one and two dollars), a traditional gift usually given as a greeting gesture. He performed wherever and whenever he could, often up to twenty times per month.

The most important part of Seydou's poetics was rhythm. He created his lines, unfolded his narratives against the rhythm of his *donsonkòni*, which itself was dependent on the forceful drive of the iron rasp scraper, among whom the best were his wives, Kariya Wulen and Nunmuso. Seydou's apprentices played the bass lines on their *donsonkònis* and Seydou played across the top. Seydou laid his language over the top of this as if his voice were the lead instrument in the ensemble, sometimes locking into the rhythm, sometimes in counterpoint, sometimes somewhere in between. In an effort to have the text reflect something of this rhythmic richness, I present the text in three different ways. Songs mark his performances like in a Broadway musical and are represented by indented lines with the choral responses further indented following them. Seydou delivered much of the narrative in a mode in which he organized the accented syllables of his language to coincide with the accented beats of the music, a variation of 4:4. This narrative mode is represented by an indentation. In a mode of delivery that

Seydou used to start his performances or to break between parts of performances, Seydou sang in a sprung rhythm, usually at breakneck
speed. The content of this mode of delivery consists mainly of proverbs,
aphorisms, wisdom of the hunters, and praise-lines. I represent this
praise-proverb mode in italics.

> Mother Dugo the Owl!
> I play my harpstrings for you.
>> *Master, you filled us with knowledge.*
>> *Ah! You've filled us with sorcery.*
> Man, I can't hear the sound of your harp.
> Is your harp not playing?
>> *Master, you filled us with knowledge.*
>> *Ah! You've filled us with sorcery.*
> Ah! Should you see a man with bad habits.
> You see a man who will die young.
>> *Master, you filled us with knowledge.*
>> *Ah, you filled us with sorcery.*
> Man, tighten that string!
> Tighten that string a bit!
>> *Master, you filled us with knowledge.*
>> *Ah, you filled us with sorcery.*
> All hunters go off to the bush,
> All are not masters of the powder.
>> *Master, you filled us with knowledge.*
>> *Ah, you filled us with sorcery.*
> Ah! Harpist, you're slowing down
> My words.
>> *Master, you filled us with knowledge.*
>> *Ah, you filled us with sorcery.*
> Some women give birth to sons,
> But all don't give birth to kings.
>> *Master, you filled us with knowledge.*
>> *Ah! You filled us with sorcery.*
> Hurry your hand on the strings!
> You make it hard for me to speak!
>> *Master, you filled us with knowledge.*
>> *Ah! You filled us with sorcery.*
> Ah! Dugo's Kambili, can't you stop
> The man-eating lion?
>> *Master, you filled us with knowledge.*
>> *Ah! You filled us with sorcery.*
> Ah! Rhythm man! Rhythm man!
> Slow down a little!
>> *Master, you filled us with knowledge.*
>> *Ah, you filled us with sorcery.*
>>> An excerpt from Kambili's wedding song

Seydou was always enigmatic to me. He was a consummate musician. I have yet to hear another lute-harp player with the mechanical mastery, rhythmic drive, and lyrical lilt that Seydou gave to his music. To some, Seydou was like a court jester, a buffoon. He loved to clown, to tell off-color jokes and stories that made his audience roar with laughter. Seydou loved women. He had two wives and would have had many more if he could have afforded it. He liked booze of all kinds and he could frequently be found at the local millet beer hall when he had a few francs in his pocket. He would say, from time to time, that he was a Muslim, but he loved to ridicule the Muslim clergy, whose hypocrisy he saw as ludicrous. I never did see him pray.

> Ah! All the holy men are by the mosque,
> But all of them are not holy men!
> > Master, you filled us with knowledge.
> > Ah! You filled us with sorcery!
> Ah! Some are studying at the mosque,
> But they all don't give birth to saints.
> > Master, you filled us with knowledge!
> > Master, you filled us with sorcery!
> All the holy men are by the mosque,
> But they all don't know how to read.
> > Master, you filled us with knowledge!
> > Master, you filled us with sorcery!
> Of all those who make the pilgrimage,
> They all don't know what it means.

He had a twinkle in his eyes that let you know, more than anything, that Seydou was having a good time doing what he was doing. To others, Seydou was like a priest. His services for the hunters were often of ritual nature, singing songs that empowered his hunter clients to overcome the obstacles of the bush and the wild game they sought to kill. On a number of occasions while I was sitting in his hut talking or listening to him play, a hunter would come in with dried or smoked parts of an antelope as Seydou's part of the kill. He sang the songs that calmed the unleashed spirits of those slaughtered beasts.

> *Born for a reason and learning are not the same.*
> *A man doesn't become a hunter if he cannot control his fear.*
> *A coward does not become a hunter,*
> *Or become a man of renown.*
> *Death may end the man; death doesn't end his name.*

To some, he was a traditional medicine man. His tiny hut was crammed full of powdered roots, leaves, dried unidentifiable animal parts and bones. He had a steady stream of clients to whom he delivered medicines for such ills as menstrual cramps or examination anxiety. He cast divination stones to guide people on new voyages, marriages, business ventures, and hunts. I was in awe of Seydou's effortless expertise and the efficacy of his arts. I came to see Seydou as my protector. In a place full of things I didn't and perhaps couldn't understand, Seydou was always there with talismans, poultices, incantations, and divinations, assuring me that I would be all right.

The extended text which follows is from the end of the epic.

> A hunter's death is not easy for the harp-player, Allah!
> A hunter dies for the harp-player.
> A farmer dies for the glutton.
> A holy man dies for the troubled.
> A king dies for his people.
> To each dead man, his funeral song, Kambili.
> And should an old bard die,
> Call out the hourglass drummer,
> Call out the iron rasp scraper,
> Call out the jembe drummer.
> Have them sing my funeral song.
> To each dead man, his funeral song, call Kambili!

Seydou Camara died in his village, Kabaya, in 1981.

	The Jimini nobles made a plan.
1900	Cekura had a wife.
	His wife's name was Kumba.
	They changed her mind, taking her from Cekura.
	Ah! They took Cekura's wife from him.
	And Cekura was a man who could change into a lion!
1905	Ah! *Naamu*-sayers!
	He sent word to all the lion people.
	He said, "Lionmen!" "Yes?" the reply.
	"Let us eat all the people of the village.
	"Let us eat all the cows of the village.
1910	"Let us eat all the sheep of the village.
	"Let us eat all the dogs of the village.
	"Let us make this a fight for my wife."
	The slave's wife had been taken from him.
	The fight for his wife wasn't sweet in Jimini.
1915	Don't you know Cekura was deeply hurt?
	So he sent word to the lionmen.
	Whoever went to defecate,
	He was made a toothpick.
	Whoever was going out to the fields,
1920	They turned him into a toothpick.
	Whoever went to water the garden,

	They turned into a toothpick.
	And made it hot for the village people,
	And made it hot for the cowherd,
1925	And made it hot for the sheep flock.
	Yes, they made it hot for the people.
	Ah! There seemed no end to the bits of people around Jimini.
	When night had fallen, Master,
	As soon as you had closed the door of your hut,
1930	He would pull out his sticklike tail
	And bang on the door with it,
	And do the best of greetings, Kambili.
	No sooner would you say, "Welcome,"
	And open the door a crack,
1935	He would jump in and grab one of you.
	He would turn him into a toothpick, Kambili Sananfila.
	Ah! The Jimini man-eating lion was really playing in Jimini.
	The lion was going to eat the whole army.
	He had already finished the water carriers.
1940	He had finished the best of the farmers.
	The lion had finished the horsemen.
	The lion had finished the learned holy men.
	The lion had finished the king's children.
	Ah! It was an awful situation in Jimini.
1945	The voice of death was in Jimini.
	Lots of noise was in Jimini.
	It's a story about Dugo the owl, the soul-seizing angel.
	There was no joy in the Jimini lion business,
	And the lion's name was Cekura.
1950	His apprentice's name was Faberekoro.
	Cekura was seizing people in Jimini.
	Faberekoro was finishing up their remains.
	This created a serious problem for Samori,
	And so he advised the hunters' group,
1955	"If you don't apply yourselves, if you don't apply yourselves,
	"I will come to doubt the hunters."
	This warning given once,
	This warning given twice.
	It was given before the harp-player, Yala the smith.
1960	Yala the smith took his harp
	And went straight to Kambili,
	The son of Dugo, the Owl Bird,
	The son of Dugo, the Night Bird.
	Ah! *Naamu*-sayers!
1995	At this time, kolas had been sent out for Kambili's wife.
	And what was Kambili's first wife's name?
	Her name was said, Kumba.

They tied up ten kolas,
And went off to marry the beloved Kumba.
2000   And brought her and gave her to Dugo's Kambili.
It was the way of doing a marriage.
Man, pay attention to the rhythm!
Don't miss the rhythm whatever you do!
To each slave his reason for coming.
2005   *To each his destiny.*
Putting tradition aside for one day's pain is not good.
Hot Pepper of the Game, Kambili Sananfila!
Speaking is not easy;
Not being able to speak is not easy.
2010   *I'm doing something I've learned.*
I'm not doing something I was born for.

[Seydou sings the wedding songs.]

They finished the wedding procession.
2110   The wedding speeches had been given, Allah!
When the message had been given to Kambili,
He spoke out saying,
"This man-eating lion, Allah!
    "If this man-eating lion is going to die,
2115   "Pay attention to the rhythm!
"Ah! If this man-eating lion is going to die in Jimini,
"That lion will die with one shot in Jimini."
Look to the cat for the wild hunting cat.
The dancers of the war dance have decreased.
2120   *The dancer of the warriors' dance has gone to rest.*
Soloba Jantumanin has gone to Last Judgment.
No reason was given for the powderman's going to rest.
Soloba Jantumanin has gone to Allah.
The bullet master has gone back for sure.
2125   *The darkness of Last Judgment is never empty of strangers.*
It's the call for Dugo the Owl, Kambili Sananfila.
Greet the tracking dog as the hunting dog.
Look to the chair for seizing all the smells.
A sandal that's stepped in dung leaves its bits behind.
2130   They finished with the wedding ceremony.
Toure ni Manjun came out.
    He came out with ten red kolas
    And went to give them to Kanji.
He said, "Kanji!" "Yes?" the reply.
2135   "Go tell the hunters in Jimini,
"If the man-eating lion doesn't die in Jimini,
"The vulture will settle on the hunters' children."
"Ah! The totem of the man-killer king is not broken

"If the Jimini man-eating lion doesn't die!"
2140   The vulture will finish eating the children;
          The beast will finish all the good children;
          The beast will finish the grass cutters,
          The beast has finished the horsemen;
          The beast has finished the wood gatherers,
2145   The beast has finished all the good farmers.
          The beast will finish all the good children;
      Don't you see there's no way to get to the market?
          The beast finished eating all the market people.
      Don't you see that this powder business has heated up.
2150 ⸸ The Jimini battle was no pleasure, Kambili.
      Greet the tracking dog as the hunting dog.
      Greet the chair for seizing all the smells.
      Look to the drying sun for the sun of midday meal.
      Greet the loincloth as breeze-catching cloth.
2155 *The man's totem cannot be the loincloth.*
      Neither can it be the women's totem.
      The loincloth is but breeze-catching cloth.
      Look to the undryable for the unburnable.
      Mother Dugo, it's the call for early death in the Terende bushes.
2160 *The brave, seated, a dangerous thing.*
      The brave standing, a dangerous thing.
      A small deadly thing burned up wouldn't fill a horn.
      Although the great snake makes like to coil,
      He can't be used as a head coil.
2165 *Who has ever seen a snake as a head coil?*
      It's the call for the Hot Pepper of the Game.
      It's the call for the Hot Pepper of the Beast.
      Buffalo fighting is not easy for the coward.
      Buffalo fighting is not easy for the trembler.
2170 *The voice of the wild dog of the plain, "Arise and fight!"*
      The wild dog's voice in the plain, "To the attack!"
      Great stallion of the plain without saddle,
      His belly great; it's not from begging.
      His mouth, white, but not from the worthless one's mother's flour.
2175 *His tail, close to the ground, not to be seized by the worthless one's*
          hand.
      His ear, great, it will never be the worthless one's mother's scoop.
      My hand is now in my traditional thing.
      Kabaya Seydou's hand is now in his traditional thing, no lie.
      A man dies for his sharer of secrets, Father.
2180 *A man dies for his sharer of hopes, Allah.*
      A man dies for his sharer of wealth, Man.
      A man dies for his sharer of secrets, no lie.
      Kanji took his harpstrings there.
      Kanji took his harpstrings to Jimini,

2185   And presented himself to Dugo's son.
He said, "Dugo's Kambili!
"The king brought out the man-killing kolas,
"Saying to give them to my men,
"To give them to my hunters' group,
2190   "Saying, if the Jimini man-eating lion doesn't die,
"Come next Thursday,
"The vulture will descend on the hunters, Kambili."
Ah! The speech was bad!
Ah! I'm afraid of the widow's headband, Kambili.
2195   I'm afraid of one blast of the whistle, Kambili.
I'm afraid of one blast of the whistle, Kambili.
I'm afraid of cold tears, Kambili.
"Ah! That's no lie!" said Kumba.
"I don't ever want to become a widow. Allah!
2200   "There is no one to inherit me, father.
"I don't want to get mixed up in it.
"Ah! Do your best, Kambili. Do your best!"
Born for a reason and learning are not the same.
Putting tradition aside for one day's pain is not good.
2205   *Hot Pepper of the Game!*
The brave sat down and thought.
He said, "Kumba! Beloved Kumba!" "Yes," she replied.
She said, "Kambili, the Hunter, Kambili Sananfila!
"The man-eating lion will die in Jimini.
2210   "I will go to the hair-dressing place at my namesake's house.
"With Cekura's mother, Marama.
"I was once the loving wife of Cekura in Jimini.
"I grew up by the side of his robe in Jimini.
"The wife of Cekura's host was my tutor.
2215   "I know Cekura himself.
"No other is seizing the people,
"If it is not Cekura."
So they called Bari the Omen Reader.
Bari began to read the signs.
2220   "Namusa
"Naburuma
"Woro dogolen
"Woro faransan
"Jitumu Mansa
2225   "Jitimu Forokoro
"Filanin Fabu
"Kenken Mamuru
"Jonyayiriba
"Twenty-four parts of the bow.
2230   "This is sigi.
"This is maromaro.

"This is karalan.
"This has become teremise.
"This has become regret,
2235 "Another regret.
"This is Nsorosigi.
"This, Yeremine.
"Here again is Karalan.
"Ah! This sign has become Maromaro, Man!
2240 "The omen has become a longbow sign.
"The earth-shaking reason has come out.
  "Bring me a head hair.
  "Yes, bring a hair of the lion's head.
  "And bring some hair from under his arm,
2245 "And bring some hair from his crotch,
  "And bring the sandal off his foot,
  "And bring a pair of his old pants,
  "And lay them on the omen board.
  "And when we find a means to the man-killer lion,
2250 "Should we do that, the man-eating lion will die."
Sleep has made your eyes heavy. Pay attention to the rhythm!
The debt of Last Judgment is never forgotten for the living.
A slave spends a late evening.
A slave doesn't stay long among you.
2255 *The omen for staying here is not easy on things with souls.*
A name is a thing to be bought: a name is not to be forced.
My hand is dipped in my habitual thing.
The thing is not easy for all.
Ah! It was none but Kumba's voice.
2260 "Kambili the Hunter," she said, "Kambili Sananfila!
"I will go have my hair done at Marama's place.
"I will never betray you."
  She took ten kolas,
  And came with the ten white kolas,
2265 And put them in a little calabash,
  And brought out greeting gifts,
  And put them in a little white calabash.
  "I'm doing this for my man, Kambili.
  "Please forgive me, Kambili.
2270 "I'm going for the hair on his head, Kambili.
  "I'm going for the underarm hair, Kambili.
  "I'm going for the sandal, Kambili.
  "I'm going for the old pants, Kambili.
  "That done, the man-eating lion will die, Kambili."
2275 *If you are not afraid of females, Master,*
If you are not afraid of females,
You're not afraid of anything.
The woman's hand knows how to strike a man's desires in any case.

Beloved Kumba went to meet Cekura,
2280 Entering his place at about two o'clock.
She called, "Cekura!" "Yes?" the reply.
"I have come to the hair-dressing place."
Don't you know this made Cekura happy?
It was none but the lionman's voice.
2285 He said, "The hunters will surely kill you this time,
"And I, Cekura, will cry.
"Ah! Little hypocrite, didn't I tell you
"Marrying a hunter will never succeed?
"A hunter is nothing!
2290   "When a hunter enters the bush,
"He may spend a whole week.
"He has no need for his wife.
"When a hunter sees some antelope,
"He has seen the game he will kill.
2295   "It's a case of coveting the game.
"He has no concern for having children, Allah."
This put Kumba in a difficult situation, beloved Kumba.
Kumba responded, saying, "So it is.
"You have just said my reason for coming.
2300   "Cekura, that's my reason for coming.
"I'm no longer in this hunter's marriage.
"I'm fed up with this hunter's business.
"Him and his shoulder talismans!
"The hunter and his side talismans are never far apart.
2305   "Saying you shouldn't touch the hunter's bag;
"A woman's taboo is inside it.
"Don't put your hand on his shirt;
"A woman's taboo is on it.
"When he has gone off to the bush,
2310   "He can come back and spend three nights,
"Without touching his wife;
"He has no desire for his woman."
She went on, "Cekura!" "Yes?"
"There's just one thing about what I've said,
2315 "I beg of you
"That you hurry up this matter between us
"So that I can go back soon.
"Kambili's funeral, I don't want to miss that."
So he called out, "Marama, Kumba's here to have her hair
        done."
2320   He went and bought some grains of rice,
And went and bought some white chickens,
And went and bought ten white kolas,
And came and gave them to beloved Kumba.
He had some rice prepared,

2325   And had those chicken's meat cooked up,
    And went and poured out some milk,
    And soaked the fresh milk with honey,
    And gave it to beloved Kumba.
    "Kumba, don't you see this drinking water?
2330   "As for me, I'm doing well these days.
    "What need have I for any of this?
    "As for me, I'm after these people, for vengeance."
    When night had fallen,
    As soon as they had finished eating,
2335   They lay down together.
    He put his leg over Kumba,
    But she said, "Get your leg off me!"
    He laid his hand on her,
    But she said, "Get your claws off me!"
2340   Ah! Cekura was in a hurry.
    "I have found the way,
    "I have found the way to destroy Kambili.
    "Those nights between Kambili and me,
    "I can count them.
2345   "They do not go beyond ten.
    "None of them ever accomplished anything beyond hunting
        game,
    "Charging off to game hunts.
    "I have no desire to be married to a hunter.
        "If you give me an old pair of pants,
2350   "They'll be used as a means against Kambili.
        "Bring me some hair off your head,
        "We'll find a means to Kambili today.
        "Bring me some hair from under your arm,
        "And get me some from your crotch,
2355   "And take off your old sandals,
        "Take those sandals off your feet.
        "We'll use them as a means to get the tough one, Master.
        "When all that is done, he'll be a corpse,
        "And I will begin marriage to Cekura once more.
2360   "Ah! Take up the weapon!
    "Don't you fail! Do not hesitate!"
    Words are like the writing of a holy man;
    They don't suit the heart of every young man.
    Speech is something to be learned in every day of this world.
2365   *Intelligence has become a thing hard to find, Master.*
    Look to Mother Dugo's ogre for that which scares the children.
    Cekura gave some of the hair off his head,
    And gave the hair from under his arm,
    And gave the hair from off his crotch,
2370   And gave the old pair of pants,

And gave the sandals off his feet,
    And went and took an old, used hat,
    And put it all in one calabash,
    An old cloth, wrapped around it for good.
2375   "After that, there is only me."
She said, "Cekura, oh, Cekura!
    "My hair has been dressed,
    "I am going right off with these means,
    "So that no one does it before me.
2380   "As soon as the hunter is killed,
    "I will come and marry Cekura.
    "There is no other person I want in this world,
    "If it is not Cekura."
These words were sweet in the old hyena's ears.
2385   He hunched back his shoulders.
    He tried to hold back his joy.
    He gave a little chuckle.
He said, "Don't betray me." He said,
"Don't betray me between this world and Last Judgment."
2390 And she replied, "I would never betray you in this world."
    Kumba brought back the things for her means
    And came to give them to Bari of the Omens.
    He laid them in the omen dust,
    And made an offering to the omen,
2395   An Earth-shaking Reason sacrifice,
    And went to bury it in the old market in Jimini,
By the old *nere* tree there.
Ah! Mother Dugo the Owl,
    Kambili took the magic black Nyaji powder.
2400   Kambili had become an expert, old hunter.
    Kambili took out a kola of red hue,
    And took out a white pullet,
    And went to sit at the crossroads.
    "If we are to go toward the east, Nyagi,
2405   "For me to kill the man-eating lion, Nyagi,
    "Turn the kola halves face to the ground."
    The two halves turned face to the ground.
    "If we are to go to the south, Nyaji,
    "For me to kill the man-eating lion, Nyaji,
2410   "Turn the two kola halves face to the sky."
    The two kola halves turned face to the ground.
    "If we are to go to the west, Nyaji,
    "For me to kill the man-eating lion, Nyaji,
    "Turn the two kola halves face to the sky."
2415   "The two kola halves turned face to the ground."
    "Should we go to the north, Nyaji,
    "For me to kill the man-eating lion, Nyaji?

"Turn the two kola faces to the sky."
"The two kola halves turned face to the ground."
2420   "Should I sit in the old market, Nyajij,
"To kill the Jimini man-eating lion, Nyaji,
"Have the kolas turn face to the ground."
And the two kola halves turned face to the ground.
Look to the talisman's Angel of Death for that's not easy for all.
2425   *The praise for Tears of the Game, Nyaji.*
No man becomes a hunter if he has no good talismans.
You don't become a hunter if you have no knowledge of magic.
Nothing is pleasing to a man without a reason.
Nothing is displeasing to a man without a reason.

[Kambili sets a trap for the lionman, tying a small boy to the base of the *nere* tree in the market. Kumba leads the lionman into the market. The lionman comes up, circles the young boy, and is about the devour him, but Kambili has fallen into a deep sleep under the influence of Cekura's sleep talisman. The young boy, however, sings a song invoking Kambili to awake. In the nick of time, he raises his musket, pulls back the hammer, and fires straight and true, killing the lionman with a single shot. The epic ends with Kambili's victory songs, the principle one of which sings the praises of Kumba.]

Ah! Kumba has charm, Jimini Kumba.
Kumba has charm.
2695   The gracious, the beautiful Kumba.
You've killed the man-eating lion!
The gracious, the beautiful Kumba.
A woman to surpass all women.
Kumba has no match among women.
2700   The gracious, the beautiful Kumba.
She lies beside a hunter brave.
The gracious, the beautiful Kumba.
Kumba did not betray the hunter brave.
The lion was left in the dust.
2705   The gracious, the beautiful Kumba.

Kumba was given to the hunter brave.
The lion cried in despair.
The gracious, the beautiful Kumba.
2725   Ah! The Jimini man-eating lion has been killed.
The reason was Kumba!
The gracious, the beautiful Kumba.

10. The Epic of Sara
Narrated by Sira Mori Jabaté

Recorded in Kéla, Mali, in 1968 by Charles Bird. Transcribed and translated into English by Charles Bird and Kassim Kònè. This excerpt edited by Charles Bird.

SIRA MORI JABATÈ WAS ONE of Mali's GREAT FEMALE BARDS. She was especially renowned for *Sara*. For this version, she was accompanied by her brother, Yamuru Jabatè, and a chorus of adolescent females. Sira Mori passed away in 1989, and fifteen head of cattle were sacrificed at her funeral ceremony.

We include this as an example of epic for a number of reasons. Sira Mori uses the formal style of the traditional bards to deliver this story of the heroic behavior of Sara, whose promise would not be denied. The form she uses is more melodic than the typical Mande male bard's narrative mode. As such it sounds more like praise song (*faasa*), of which Sira Mori was one of the great Mande masters. This is not, however, at all typical of praise song from the point of view of content. Praise songs do not tell stories. This is clearly poetic narrative, and heroic, and therefore, by any definition, it qualifies as epic. From the point of view of Maninka speakers, *Sara*, like the Sunjata epic, is called *maana*, the term they use when talking about poetic narratives.

The theme of *Sara* recurs in virtually all societies where marriages are arranged. In the Mande world marriages are officially arranged and sanctioned by the male authorities, often in conflict with the wishes of the bride and sometimes of the groom. In this story Sara has given the promise of her undying love to another, her "promise-sharer." The story is about the importance of that promise and what Sara does to protect it. The poetic density of this text requires detailed explanation and commentary.

"Ah! Sara! Sara is sung for those of one voice./Ah! Long-necked Sara!" 'Those of one Voice' translates *kankelentigi*, 'voice-one-master.' It means roughly 'someone who is true to his/her word.'

Mande poetry exploits polyphony. The word Sara itself is polyphonic. Sara is an Islamic woman's name probably borrowed very early with the introduction of Islam in West Africa in the eighth and ninth centuries. It is an Old Testament name, the wife of the patriarch Abraham. It is also a traditional Mande name given to the first-born girl. *Sara* is also the word for 'charm, grace,' and in this story, Sara's charm and grace constitute much of its understood content. *Sara* is also the word used to refer to 'payment, salary, reward.' This too is a subtheme of this story. Sara is rewarded for keeping her word.

> Chorus: Ah! Sara is sung for those of one voice.
>   Don't you see it?
> Sira Mori: Sara! Sara is sung for those with promises.
>   Long-necked Sara!

5   Chorus: Ah! Sara is sung for those of one voice.
      Don't you see it?
    Sira Mori: Sara! Sara is sung for those with promises.
      Long-necked Sara!
      Don't you see it?
10   Chorus: Sara is sung for those of one voice.
      Don't you see it?
    Sira Mori: Sara is not sung for "Money's in my pocket."
    Sara is not sung for "My name is gold."
    Sara is not sung for beauty.
15   Sara is sung for a person's behavior, Allah!
        (Yes! It's the truth! It's a matter of behavior. Sara
        was sung for the promise, for those who have seen
        tough days, for those who looked into fiery things.)

[The above paragraph presents Yamuru Jabatè's commentary on the story. It is not uncommon to have commentators who may from time to time contribute pieces to the performance. The phrase, *minw ye lon ye* translates literally as 'those who have seen the day,' which is used in Maninka to convey the sense of 'having met a challenge, having faced difficult times and come through them.' We used 'fiery things' to translate *ko wulen,* literally 'red thing.' *Wulen* has polyphonies extending from 'red' to 'hot, fiery, fierce.' As we read it, it refers to those who have suffered for a cause. An important theme introduced here is that the bards sing of a person's deeds. Their praise cannot be bought.]

    Sara is not sung for beauty.
    Sara is sung for a person's behavior.
    Sara is not sung for the charming.
    Sara is sung for a person's behavior
20   Behaving is hard!
        (Amazing! Amazing, Sira Mori!)
    Why union happens is that love is of paradise.
    Why union happens is that union is of paradise.
    No one should shame their sharer of secrets.
    Why union happens is that union is of paradise.
25   Why union happens is that union is of paradise.

[We have translated *yomali kiyama* as 'paradise.' It could be translated as 'heaven, the hereafter.' It is not difficult to see that Sira Mori's story constructs a strong argument for love and for marriage based on love. Love, she argues, is Allah's will. It is something of the hereafter, the eternal, something of paradise. The union of two people is first and foremost the will of Allah.]

    No one should shame their sharer of secrets
    Do not say your inner words to a gossip.

No slave knows Allah.

['Slave' (*jon*) is here understood as 'slave of God,' a human being. No one can claim to know the ways of God.]

    Giving your word is misery.
30   Ah! Giving your word is hard.
    Giving your word is hard.
    Nobles must hold to their word.
    Ah! Giving your word is hard.
    Nobles must hold to their word.
35   If you are not a bastard,
    Then giving your word is your misery, Allah!

[Sira Mori here is using *horon* to refer to a kind of noble behavior which is not limited to social structural categories. Anyone may be called *horon* if they behave in a certain way. As Yamuru said, a person becomes a slave by his or her behavior. *Horon* are those who can trace their patrilineal descent and be proud of it. This is opposed to *nyamogoden*, literally 'before-person child,' 'the child of someone who came before' (the wedding, we assume), hence, a bastard. Bastards cannot trace their ancestors through their fathers and are thus cursed by a biological lack of dignity and are therefore untrustworthy.]

    The wedding people came,
    Sara's wedding people came.
    Sara's husband-to-be did not please her,
    But she said, "I will not shame my fathers.
40   "I will not shame my grandfathers.
    "I will not shame my uncles.
    "If Allah is not in the matter
    "It does not happen,
    "Because my word has been spoken to another."
45   Sara's bride-price had been taken.
    The wedding cows had been taken.
    Sara's wedding date had been set.
    Oh Sara, Allah!

(This part calls to Sira Mori Nana.
They did not break their promise.)

    The wedding escort rose up.
50   Sara's promise-sharer spoke.
    He said: "Ayi! Giving your word is hard. Oh, la, la!
    "Oh, oh! Giving your word is hard.
    "Your bride-price has been taken.
    "Your wedding cows have been taken today.
55   "Your wedding escort has risen up.
    "Long-necked Sara, giving your word is hard.

"Do not think about those cows, my twin-alike.
"Do not think about this marriage, my pair-alike."

[We have translated *filanin-nyogon* as 'twin-alike,' which is a literal
translation of the Maninka. It is a term of endearment used for someone
who is like a twin to you, someone with whom you giggle, laugh, and
cry. The meaning of *ma-nyogon* is 'person-alike,' roughly 'each other's
person.' We wanted to preserve Sira Mori's Maninka parallelism in our
translation which explains the idiosyncratic English.]

      I will not shame my grandfathers.
60   Giving your word is hard.
      Do you not take me at my word?
      Do not hurry so.
      Giving your word is hard.
                (Amazing! If you spit out your saliva, it can
                not be gathered up again. That's the truth!)

[The following section describes the wedding party leaving Sara's village for the village of her husband-to-be, where she will reside. The
wedding party will be met outside the new village by a party consis-
ting mostly of her new female in-laws.]

      The wedding arrangers rose up, Sara.
65   They all went off passing the boundary.
      The birds in the trees were crying.
      The *ko-n-kan-ko* birds all were crying, Sara.

[*Ko-n-kan-ko* is held to be the cry of the messenger bird. It is a way of
gaining the floor when you have something to say: "Say, my voice
says. . . ."]

      The wedding arrangers said: "This is amazing!"
      This is what the *ko-n-kan-ko* birds sang:
70   "No slave knows Allah.
      "Giving your word is hard."
                (Your father makes you noble. You mother
                makes you that. You make yourself a slave.
                    This calls to Sira Mori Nana's child. Bati
                    Hayidara, this must call to him. He is noble.)
      Sara arrived outside the village.
      Those meeting the wedding party came.
      The *jembe*-drummers began.
75   The balafon-players began.
      The gong-playing bard women began.
      The bride who was being met . . .
      When those meeting the wedding party saw Sara,

80
>She said her belly was in pain,
>Ah! Those meeting the wedding came up.
>She said: "Laila! Laila! Mahamadarasurudilahi!"

[The above expressions are Arabic and mean, "There is no God but Allah, and Mohammad is His Prophet." In Maninka, it is used in situations similar to those in which an English speaker might say in swearing, "Jesus Christ Almighty God." We have not broken the expression up into its Arabic words, because we do not believe that the majority of Maninka who use it do so.]

>She said: "Ah! Allah! My belly pains me."
>The wedding arrangers said: "It's amazing!"
>Those meeting the wedding party having come,
85
>They said: "Sara says her belly pains her."
>"Get away from me!
>"My belly pains me, lalala layi!
>"My belly won't cool down.
>"Ah! My belly pains me!"
90
>One old brave spoke up:
>"Calm down!
>"Let the *jembe*-drummers return,
>"Let the bard women return."
>He took the end of Sara's staff to lead her.

[The image here is of Sara debilitated by her illness, leaning on a staff like a blind person who is often led around by a young boy or girl holding the end of the staff. There is a very material sense of language in this story. Sara's promise is embodied; it is in her belly. Words are things that enter into people and cause them to behave in particular ways. Some phrases, like the Arabic expressions above, are known only by their use, by their potential effects on one's life. They have no analyzable meanings independent of that.]

95
>They went to her groom's compound, Allah!
>They went there with Sara,
>Ah! World!
>The belly-pain men came up to her.
>The medicine-powder men came up to her.
100
>The string-knotters came up to her.
>The belly-spitters came up to her.

[There are hundreds, if not thousands, of practitioners of traditional medicine in the Mande world. They are brought into the story named for the devices they use. Some medicines, like ours, involve the use of powders: ground roots, bark, or leaves. Some medical interventions involve the knotting of string which may then be wrapped around the problem. The knots draw the badness out. They say that some of these knotted strings wrapped around a fetish can kill your enemies.]

She said: "My belly pains me.
"If you don't get away from me,
"My belly will not cool down, lalala layi!
105   "My belly pains me."
                     (Amazing! Her stomach does not pain her.
                     It is the sound of her promise that pains her.)
Sara's man said: "Laila, eee! Laila!
"Mahamadarasurudilahi!"
He said: "Ah! World! My bride who has come thus,
"Three days, her belly does not cool.
110   "Four days, her belly does not cool.
"Five days, a headache is added to it.
"Ah, Sara! What will cool your belly?
"Long-necked Sara!
"The medicine powder men have failed on you.
115   "The string-knotters have failed on you.
"The belly-spitters have failed on you.
"Ah! Long-necked Sara!
"What will cool your belly then?"
She said: "My belly pains me.
120   "If you don't leave me alone,
"My belly will not cool. Laila!
"Ayi! My belly hurts me. Allah!
"My belly will not cool."
Sara's man-to-be said: "Laila,
125   "No slave knows Allah.
"The wedding arrangers are troubled.
"Sara's bride-price should go back.
"I am shamed before my ill-wishing *faden*.
"I am shamed before my ill-wishing *baden*."

[*Faden* is literally 'father-child.' *Baden* is literally 'mother-child.' These terms, as you might expect, are polyphonous. Perhaps early meanings referred, in the case of *faden*, to the children of the same father but not the same mother in polygamous households. *Baden* refers from this point of view to children of the same mother. Perhaps by extension, *faden* came to refer to those people with whom you compete, against whom you measure yourself. *Baden* refers to those people with whom you cooperate, with whom you subordinate your self-interest and suppress matters of ego. Your *faden* pushes you away. Your *baden* pulls you close. We have translated the Maninka word *jugu* as 'ill-wishing.' As a noun, it can mean 'enemy.' Modifying a noun, it can translate 'mean, cruel, dangerous, bad,' and 'ill-wishing.']

130 "My bride having come
  "Three days, her belly does not cool.
  "Four days her belly does not cool.
  "Five days, a headache is added to it.
  "Let the wedding arrangers go back."
135 Two young boys had run up *biribiribiri*.
  And climbed out on a branch of a *dubalen* tree
  To look out on the world.
  "Well, the world is thus!"
  The two boys ran *biribiribiri*.
140 They came to stop before the promise-sharer's door.
  One said: "Cool off my mouth!
  "Sara's wedding is dead!
  "Those ten kola nuts in the container there,
  "That is the mouth-cooler, my father.
145 "Thus a promise is not paid just once."

[The expression *n da lafige*, literally, 'fan/blow on my mouth,' is used by the bringer of news, which, it is said, makes his or her mouth hot. The heat dispels with a gift. Thus, *n da lafige* means, in Wittgenstein the Elder's sense of the word, 'give me a tip.']

  Sara stood before her father.
  She said: "It's Allah's work."
  "Mama, this child of yours,
  "Long-necked Sara! . . . and her belly will not cool."
150 Sara's mother said: "Laila, no slave knows Allah.
  "Will your belly not cool?"
  She said: " Mothers do not cry!
  "Ayi! Mother, do not cry, ay!
  "King White Guts did this to me."

['King White Guts' translates word for word the expression *Mansa nagal-agwe*. This is a metaphor for God, whose white, gutlike clouds pass across his great belly, the sky.]

155 Sara said to her father:
  "Baba won't you gather the men for me today?
  "Gather the riverbank village men for me today.
  "Gather the men in the village for me.
  "Whoever will cool my belly today,
160 "Father, that will be my husband
  "And get you out of this talk.
  "Won't you gather the men?"
    (Amazing! Her belly does not hurt her. It's the spoken
    words that hurt her. Her spoken words are hurting her.)
  Iyo! He gathered the men,

Gathered the men in the village.
165   The medicine-powder men came.
The men of importance came.

[We have translated *cebakoro* as 'men of importance.' In some contexts, one might think of a *cebakoro* as a seasoned brave, a mature warrior.]

The big money men came.
The Koran men came.
The *nasi*-writing men all came.

[Islamic holy men are heavily involved in traditional medical practices. Some specialize in writing verses of the Koran on a chalkboard, which is then washed and the water collected. This *nasi* water can be used for washing or drinking, and its uses extend to all manners of illness and social problems.]

170   Three days, Sara's belly was hurting.
They all had failed. Sara remained in it.
Sara's mother said: "How is it going to go today, Sara?"
"Mother, hush up, my mother.
"King White Guts did this to me.
175   "Do not hurry Allah, my mother."
With the night half gone,
With the night half gone,
She stopped before her promise-sharer's door.
"Is there no one in the house, my twin-together?"
180   "There is someone in the house, my mother.
"Whose voice is that in the deep, dark night?
"Whose voice is that in the dawn?"
"It's the voice of your embrace-together.
"It's the voice of your sharer of inner words."
185   "Well, won't you sit, Long-necked Sara?"
"I am sitting down, my father.
"The powder medicine men have failed on me.
"The string-knotters have failed on me.
"The belly-spitters have failed on me.
190   "What will cool this belly,
"If there is no meaning to it?
"You should find ironstone tomorrow,
"And put it in the fire and embers.
"I say, when the ironstone gets hot,
195   "You should put it in drinking water, my promise-sharer.
"Wiii! My belly will cool tomorrow,
"Because of my spoken words, Allah!"

(Yes! That is just the answer she was looking for. Her
belly was not hurting her. The promise that she gave
him, that was what was hurting her. That is the reason
for this part, to detail it and show to the people. The
children of Adam must stick to their word.)

[There is certainly an interpretation of this story in which Sara is con-
strued to be duplicitous, faking her illness to avoid her marriage; but
both Sira Mori and Yamuru go to considerable pains to show that her
pain was real, coming from the promise she had given to another man.
The ruse that she constructs to allow her "promise-sharer" to cure her
and win her hand may, in the view of some readers, detract from her
moral standing somewhat, but her *horonoya*, her nobility, comes from
her keeping her promise; and it must be pointed out that the ruse is in
fact a way for her father to save face. Sara does not defy authority in this
story. Rather, like Brer Rabbit, she finds ways to use it to her
advantage.]

	From the time the cock cried,
	When the first cock cried,
200	He went to find the ironstone.
	Allah came to lay the stone before him. Iyo!
	Mid-morning prayer time arrived,
	He took the ironstone *co*!
	And put it in the fire and embers.
205	When the ironstone boiled,
	He put some in drinking water.
	He was off with the water an hour later.
	The men of importance said:
	"No one should even speak with you.
210	"The thing that caused the medicine powder to fail,
	"The thing that caused the *nasi*-waters to fail,
	"And you think it's just dead water that will cool it for you!"
	"I beg your pardon, big money men.
	"I beg your pardon, medicine men.
215	"Let her try the water for me.
	"Sara should try my fresh water for me."
	Ah! Sara! Sara drank the water, unnnh!
	She drank the water at midmorning.
	As the early afternoon prayer was called,
220	She went before her birth father.

[In the Mande social world, there are many people that you call *n fa*,
'my father.' To refer to the biological father, the Maninka use the expression, *wolo-fa*,' birth father.']

"Ah! Baba!" She said: "My belly has cooled,
"Baba, ah, my belly has cooled, lalala! Woyi!
"My belly has cooled today.
"I passed the night my belly did not rise up.
225   "Baba, my belly has cooled.
"Make this my true wedded husband."
Sara's mother said: "Won't you calm down?
"The late afternoon prayer has not been called.
"And you say your belly has cooled?"
230   "Mama, won't you prepare the baggage today?
"Prepare my wedding baggage today.
"Let my wedding arrangers come forward.
"This one will be my true wedded husband."

Sira Mori: Ah! Sara! Sara is sung for those of one voice.
235   Ah! Long-necked Sara!
    Chorus: Ah! Sara is sung for those of one voice.
       Don't you see it?
Sira Mori: Ah! Sara! Sara is sung for those of one voice.
    No slave knows God.
240   Chorus: Ah! Sara is sung for those of one voice.
       Don't you see it?

Songhay and Zarma Epics

THE SONGHAY AND THEIR COUSINS THE ZARMA constitute two related groups that are part of a much larger and more complex assemblage of diverse peoples who speak different dialects of a single language. These peoples—the Songhay, the Zarma, the Kourthèye, the Wogo, the Dendi, and others—live in an unusually elongated space that follows the Niger River for about 1,200 kilometers from Goundam, in the Timbuktu region of north central Mali, down to the Kandé-Parakou region in northern Benin. This area once stretched farther west to the ancient city of Djenné in Mali and east to include communities in the Agadez-In Gall region of northern Niger. Today, one can find Songhay and Zarma speakers in parts of northeastern Burkina Faso and northwestern Nigeria. Zarma is linguistically a dialect of Songhay, but the Zarma refer to their language simply as Zarma.

Some of these peoples trace their roots to the Songhay empire. It developed in the fifteenth century under the rule of Sonni Ali Ber (1463-1492), reached its apogee in 1493-1528 during the reign of Askia Mohammed Touré, and then declined during the sixteenth century before falling on April 12, 1591, to an invading force of 3,000 soldiers sent by the Sultan of Morocco. After the defeat of the Songhay, the leadership retreated southward from the capital in Gao, 443 kilometers upriver from Niamey, Niger, into western Niger and regrouped in small principalities. They mounted a sustained resistance against the colonial regime installed in Timbuktu by the Moroccans. In this effort, they were aided by their Zarma neighbors, who had migrated from Mali at some point in the distant past to the left-bank region of the Niger River in western Niger.

The Songhay and the Zarma share, then, a language and some common experiences in the past. One of those experiences is recurring conflict with some of their other neighbors in the region, the Tuareg and the Fulbe. The result is an oral tradition that often turns out to be a blend of heroes and events known by both peoples. In the *Epic of Askia Mohammed*, we find descriptions of the aid provided by the Zarma. In *The Epic of Mali Bero*, there are also descriptions of that mutual assistance. Both *The Epic of Mali Bero* and *The Epic of Issa Korombé*, narratives that describe events separated by several centuries, feature conflict with the Fulbe and the Tuareg. For those who seek to understand the rebellion of some Tuareg groups against the governments of Mali and Niger in the 1990s, the epics reveal early episodes of those conflicts.

Scholars in Niger, Mali, the United States, and Europe have recorded narratives about some of these heroes, but much of the published material is available only in mimeograph form from local research centers. In the 1960s and 1970s, the late Boubou Hama and Diouldé Laya published a series of short studies on the oral traditions of the Songhay and Zarma that included prose versions of *The Epic of Askia Mohammed* and *Mali Bero*. More recent poetic versions appear in Ousmane Mahamane Tandina's doctoral thesis on Issa Korombé, cited later, as well as in *Le mythe et l'histoire dans la Geste de Zabarkane* (Niamey:

124

Centre d'Études Linguistiques et Historiques par Tradition Orale, 1988) by Fatimata Mounkaila, a study that includes several fragments of the Mali Bero story, and in Thomas A. Hale's *Scribe, Griot, and Novelist: Narrative Interpreters of the Songhay Empire*, which contains Songhay and English versions of *The Epic of Askia Mohammed* (Gainesville: University of Florida Press, 1990). Indiana University Press published a slightly revised version of the English translation of that epic in 1996.

11. The Epic of Askia Mohammed
Narrated by Nouhou Malio

Recorded in Saga, Niger, on December 30, 1980, and January 26, 1981, by Thomas A. Hale. Transcribed by Mounkaila Seydou Boulhassane Maïga, Ousmane Mahamane Tandina, Moussa Djibo, and Thomas A. Hale. Translated into English by Thomas Hale with the assistance of Mounkaila Seydou Boulhassane Maïga, Ousmane Mahamane Tandina, Moussa Djibo, Fatimata Mounkaila, Abdoulaye Dan Louma, and Abdoulaye Harouna. Edited by Thomas A. Hale, published as part of Scribe, Griot, and Novelist: Narrative Interpreters of the Songhay Empire by the University of Florida Press in 1990, and reprinted in 1996, with a new introduction, as the second volume in the African Epic Series by Indiana University Press. This excerpt edited by Thomas A. Hale.

THANKS TO THE AGGRESSIVE LEADERSHIP of Sonni Ali Ber, the Songhay empire, based at Gao on the Niger River in southeastern Mali, expanded to absorb a part of Mali as that kingdom, founded by Son-Jara, declined in the fifteenth century. From 1463 to 1492, Sonni Ali Ber laid the foundation for Askia Mohammed Touré, a ruler of Soninké origin who, in turn, built a vast and complex empire from 1493 to 1528. At its apogee in the early sixteenth century, Songhay appears to have controlled in one way or another peoples and territory covering over 400,000 square kilometers, from eastern Senegal 3,000 kilometers eastward to central Niger, and from Upper Guinea 1,500 kilometers northward to the Mali-Mauritania-Algeria frontier region.

Our knowledge of Songhay history comes both from the Timbuktu chronicles, written in Arabic by Muslim scribes close to the ruling elite, and from griots, known in Songhay as *jesere*, a term derived from the Soninké word *geseré*. Songhay oral narratives were originally chanted in Soninké, probably because griots from the dispersed peoples of the much earlier Ghana empire gravitated toward a powerful ruler whose clan name, Touré, indicated a Soninké link. Today, some Soninké phrases survive in archaic and often untranslatable form in narratives and incantations from Songhay *jesere* and *sohanci* (sorcerers).

Askia Mohammed spread Islam to new areas of West Africa by force and by other means. He also offered support to Islamic scholars in Timbuktu, made a pilgrimage to Mecca in 1497-98, and corresponded with the North African theologian al-Maghili. It is not surprising, then, that Islam has a much higher profile here than in epics about earlier periods. But traditional Songhay beliefs and magic play equally significant roles in the story of Askia Mohammed. Like Son-Jara and other epic heroes, Askia Mohammed was born under extraordinary circumstances and had to overcome great obstacles. Called Mamar Kassaye (the dimunitive of Mohammed, son of Kassaye), he appears in the epic as the killer of Sonni Ali Ber, referred to here as his uncle Si. These excerpts come from a 1602-line version recounted in Songhay by Nouhou Malio and accompanied by Soumana Abdou, who played the three-stringed *molo*, a type of lute.

126

Kassaye is the woman.

It is Si who is the man, it is he who is on the throne, it is he who is the chief.

Kassaye is his sister, she is in his compound.

Any husband who marries Kassaye, and if she gives birth,

10   The seers have said "Listen"—they told Si it is Kassaye who will give birth to a child who will kill him and take over the throne of Gao.

It is Kassaye who will give birth to a child.

That child will kill Si and will take the position of ruler.

Si also heard about this.

Each of the children that Kassaye gave birth to,

15   As soon as Kassaye delivered it, Si killed it,

Every child that Kassaye delivered, as soon as it was born, Si killed it.

Until she had given birth to seven children,

Which her brother Si killed.

Kassaye had enough, she said she would no longer take a husband.

20   She stayed like that.

Si is on his throne,

While Kassaye remained like that.

Until, until, until, until one day, much later, in the middle of the night,

A man came who was wearing beautiful clothes.

25   He was a real man, he was tall, someone who looked good in white clothes, his clothes were really beautiful.

One could smell perfume everywhere.

He came in to sit down next to Kassaye.

They chatted with each other, they chatted, they chatted.

He said to her, "It is really true.

30   "Kassaye, I would like to make love with you.

"Once we make love together,

"You will give birth to a boy,

"Whom Si will not be able to kill.

"It is he who will kill Si and will become the ruler."

35   Kassaye said to him, "What?"

He said, "By Allah."

She said, "Good, in the name of Allah."

Each night the man came.

It is during the late hours that he came,

40   Each time during the coolness of the late evening,

Until Kassaye became pregnant by him.

Kassaye carried her pregnancy.

Kassaye had a Bargantché captive.

It is the Bargantché woman who is her captive, she lives in her house, and she too is pregnant.

45 They remained like that,
  Kassaye kneeled down to give birth.
  The captive kneeled down to give birth.
  So Kassaye, Kassaye gave birth to a boy.
  The captive gave birth to a girl.
50 Then Kassaye took the daughter of the captive, she took her
   home with her.
  She took her son and gave it to the captive.
  So the people left for the palace.
  They said to Si:
  "The Bargantché captive has given birth."
55 He said, "What did she get?"
  They said, "A boy."
  He said, "May Allah be praised, may our Lord give him a long
   life and may he be useful."
  Then they were thoughtful for a moment.
  They got up and informed him that Kassaye had given birth.
60 They asked, "What did she get?"
  They answered, "A girl."
  He said, "Have them bring it to me."
  They brought it to him, he killed it.
  It is the boy who remained with the captive and Kassaye.

[By this subterfuge, Kassaye saves her son, who becomes a servant working for his uncle. Of noble origin, he must nevertheless pass as a slave.]

  He became a young man, tall and very strong, a tall young
   man.
  The children in the compound,
  They are the ones who insult him by saying that they don't
   know his father.
  Also, they call him the little slave of Si.
110 "The little slave of Si, the little slave of Si."
  They called him "little slave of Si," and said, "We don't know
   your father, you don't have a father.
  "Who is your father?"
  Then he came home to his mother's house and told her that the
   children in the compound were really bothering him.
  They say to him, "Who is your father?"
115 She told him, "Go sit down, you'll see your father."
  He stayed there until the celebration at the end of Ramadan.
  It is going to take place the next day.
  Tomorrow is the celebration.
  Soon they will look at the moon.
120 The moon will appear in a short while, and they will celebrate
   the next day.

It is in the night that the jinn came to her,
For the man is a jinn.
He is also a chief of the town under the river, his land that he
    rules.
It is under the river that lies the country he rules.
125   That night he called her.
He came, the man came to Kassaye's house.
He took a ring off his middle finger.
He said to her that when daylight comes,
"Give it to your son."
130   He should hold it in his hand.
If he gets to the edge of the river, then he should put the ring
    on his finger.
He will see his father.
She said, "So it will be."
Daylight came.
135   The sun was hot, I think, the sun was hot.
Then Kassaye called Mamar.
She said, "Mamar."
He said, "Yes."
She said, "Come."
140   He came.
She said to him, "Look, take this ring in your hand.
"But don't put it on your finger
"Until you get to the river.
"Then you put it on your finger.
145   "At that moment, you will see your father."
Mamar took the ring to the river.
Then he put the ring on his middle finger.
The water opened up.
Under the water there are so many cities, so many cities, so
    many cities, so many villages, and so many people.
150   It is his father too who is the chief.
They too get themselves ready, they go out to go to the prayer
    ground.
He said, "That's the way it is."
His father greets him with an embrace.
There is his son, there is his son.
155   Yes, the prince whom he fathered while away,
The chief's son whom he fathered while away has come.
He said to him, "Now go return to your home, you do not stay
    here.
"Go return home."
His father gave him a white stallion, really white, really, really,
    really, really, really, really, really white, like, like percale.
160   He gave him all the things necessary.
He gave him two lances.

He gave him a saber, which he wore.
He gave him a shield.
He bid him good-bye.

[Armed by his real father from the underwater spirit world, Mamar Kassaye sets out to take power from his evil uncle. He chooses to do so on a Muslim holy day. Pretending to demonstrate his loyalty to Si, he races his horse up to the ruler three times in succession, stopping each time just before reaching his uncle.]

165   Si too and his people,
Si too has a daughter, two boys and one daughter that he has fathered.
He and his people go out, they went to the prayer ground.
They are at the prayer ground.
Then Mamar went around them and headed directly for them.
170   They were about to start the prayer.
They said, "Stop, just stop, a prince from another place is coming to pray with us.
"A prince from another place is coming to pray with us."
The horse gallops swiftly, swiftly, swiftly, swiftly, swiftly, swiftly he is approaching.
He comes into view suddenly, leaning forward on his mount.
175   Until, until, until, until, until, until, until he touches the prayer skin of his uncle, then he reins his horse there.
Those who know him say that he is the little captive of Si.
Actually, he does resemble the little captive of Si, he has the same look as the little captive of Si.
Did you see him! When I saw him I thought that it was the little captive of Si.
He retraced his path only to return again.
180   Until he brought the horse to the same place, where he reined it again.
Now he made it gallop again.
As he approaches the prayer skin of his uncle,
He reins his horse.
He unslung his lance, and pierced his uncle with it until the lance touched the prayer skin.
185   Until the spear went all the way to the prayer skin.

[Mamar Kassaye decides to atone for the killing of his uncle by making a pilgrimage to Mecca. On his way, he forces many peoples to accept Islam.]

In each village where he stopped during the day, for example, this place,

If he arrives in mid-afternoon, he stops there and spends the
    night.
Early in the morning, they pillage and they go on to the next
    village, for example, Liboré.
The cavalier who goes there,
280   He traces on the ground for the people the plan for the mosque.
Once the plan for the foundation is traced,
The people build the mosque.
It is at that time,
Mamar Kassaye comes to dismount from his horse.
285   He makes the people—
They teach them verses from the Koran relating to prayer.
They teach them prayers from the Koran.
Any villages that refuse, he destroys the village, burns it, and
    moves on.

[After his return from Mecca, Mamar Kassaye continues to impose Islam
on the territories he conquers. But he does not always succeed. He cannot escape the fact that when he was an infant he was nursed during
the day by a woman from another people, the Bargantché, who live in
northern Benin. This milk tie is as strong as the tie of blood that links
people together in families and clans. For this reason, when Mamar
Kassaye sets out to conquer the Bargantché, he encounters difficulty
and must call upon his mother for help. He sends a *sohanci*, who flies
through the air, to see his mother and ask advice.]

His mother, Kassaye, had told him, "Long ago,
"I told him not to fight against the Bargantché.
"He cannot beat them, for he has in his stomach the milk of a
    Bargantché."
435   However, she told him,
Now, she took some cotton seeds in her hand and said, "Take."
She took an egg, a chicken egg, and she said to him, "Take."
She took a stone, a river stone, she told him, "Take."
"If you go," if he goes to the Bargantché,
440   If the Bargantché chase him,
He should put all his horses before him and he should be the
    only one behind.
He should scatter the cotton seeds behind him.
They will become a dense bushy barrier between him and
    them.
If they chop it down,
445   This dense bush will not prevent anything.
They will clear the bush in order to find him.
If the bush does not help at all,
This time, if they are still hunting him,
He should put all his cavalry in front of him.

450   He should throw the stone behind him.
           It will become a big mountain that will be a barrier between
               them.
           If the big mountain does not help them,
           And if they chase him again,
           He should put all his cavalry in front of him again,
455   Leaving himself in the rear.
           He should throw the egg behind him.
           The egg will become a river to separate them.
           The river cannot—they will stop at the river.
           That egg will become a river that will be a barrier between
               them.
460   Before the cocks crow at dawn,
           When dawn has really come,
           The *sohanci* returns, he lands on the earth.
           He said, "By Allah, when I passed by Sikiyay I heard them say
               that Sana had given birth.
           "Then I said that if Sana gives birth—since Sana had given
               birth,
465   "They should name the child Daouda."
           He is the one who is Daouda Sana.
           They continued until they . . .
           He escaped from the Bargantché, the Bargantché who live along
               the river.
           He never again fought against them.
470   Now, he just passed through their country, to go and start again
               his reign.

[Nouhou Malio does not tell us what happened to Mamar Kassaye. But we know from the Timbuktu chronicles that he was overthrown by one of his sons, Askia Moussa, in 1528, and exiled to an island in the Niger River. He died ten years later. For the remainder of the century, the empire experienced a series of rulers descended from Askia Mohammed. A few, for example Askia Daouda, mentioned at the end of this excerpt, were extremely effective leaders, but most were not so talented. On April 12, 1591, an army sent across the Sahara by the sultan of Morocco defeated the Songhay, an event that destroyed not only their empire but marked the final chapter in the rise of a great Sahelian civilization whose stories still echo across the region in the narratives of modern griots.]

12. The Epic of Mali Bero
Narrated by Djibo Badié, known as Djeliba

Recorded by Thomas A. Hale on December 17, 1980, and April 1, 1980, at the home of Djibo Badié in Niamey, Niger. Transcribed and translated in first draft into French by Mounkaila Seydou Boulhassane Maïga. Translated into English by Thomas A. Hale. These excerpts edited by Thomas A. Hale.

MALI BERO, OR MALI THE FIRST OR ELDEST, is a legendary leader of the Zarma people of Western Niger who guided them in their migration from an unspecified region in Mali eastward to Western Niger several centuries ago. The story of Mali Bero has appeared in a variety of forms —poems, songs, and oral narratives. No one, however, has published a linear version of Mali Bero that is more than a few hundred lines long. Many of the shorter texts about him were assembled or collected and published by Fatima Mounkaila in the study cited in the introduction to this section. There, Mali Bero is framed in the broader context of a mythic Arab ancestor of all Zarma people who went to Mecca to convert to Islam and became a warrior fighting on behalf of the Prophet Mohammed before migrating to West Africa. Depending on the version, either Zabarkane or his son returned to Mali. One of his children or grandchildren was Mali Bero, known also as Zarmakoy [Zarma king] Sombo.

The following excerpts come from a 1,236-line epic narrated by Djibo Badié in two parts on two rather separate occasions. The long break between the two recordings was due in large part to his busy schedule. At the time of the recordings, he was the *jesere* most in demand in Niamey because of his great talent, the frequent broadcast of his songs on the radio, and his ancestry. He comes from one of the most respected *jesere* families in western Niger. It was very difficult for the researcher to arrange a recording session with him because he was either on the road every evening or performing at a special event in the capital.

The epic contains two episodes. The first is the story of the migration, an event that occurs in the distant past, though modern scholars now see it as taking place in the sixteenth century as the result of both a migration of Mande-speaking peoples from the West and the shift of a Songhay group to Zarmaganda, northwest of Niamey. The result of these two movements was the creation of the Zarma people. The second episode, occurring some time later, probably in the seventeenth century, tells of how the Zarma came to the aid of Songhay resistants who were fighting the Moroccan-led army that had defeated them in 1591 north of their capital, Gao, on the Niger River north of the Niger-Mali border. This episode also appears in *The Epic of Askia Mohammed*. In *The Epic of Mali Bero*, the migration and the support of the Songhay are separated by hundreds of lines of genealogy, a key part of the epic that links the heroes of the past to noble families today.

For the Zarma, the most important passage in this epic is the story of their migration eastward via a flying millet silo bottom. This is a flat and round surface perhaps two or three meters in diameter made of woven straw that serves as a foundation for a temporary silo. More permanent egg-shaped silos are crafted over a longer period of time out of mud. The incident that prompts the migration, the fight between Zarma, Tuareg, and Fulbe children, reflects the history of an off-and-on conflict that marks relations between these three groups until the present.

1   Mali the Great,
        Zarmakoy Sombo, he is the ancestor of all the Zarma people.

        One Friday,
        When Mali
10   Found some Tuareg children
        And some Fulbe children
        Who were taking a bath,
        Mali Bero
        Told each Zarma boy to steal his father's spear.
15   They arrived at the edge of the pond.
        Mali Bero
        Dug into the sand.
        He buried his spears in the sand.
        He told all the other Zarma children to do the same.
20   Mali,
        He and all the Zarma children went into the pond.
        They wash themselves.

        The Tuareg children
25   And the Fulbe children
        Run up to the edge of the pond.
        The Tuareg prince
        Grabs the cloth wrapper of Mali Bero
        And wipes his own body with it.
30   Mali Bero comes out of the pond.
        He tells him that he may lose his life.
        The Tuareg prince thinks that Mali Bero will grab the cloth
           from him.
        Mali slips his hand into the sand.
        He reaches the Tuareg prince
35   Who has taken his wrapper.

        Mali pierces him with his spear
        And kills him.
40   Mali Bero

Goes to look for his second spear.
He says to the Zarma children,
"Whoever among you allows the one who has taken your cloth
"To reach the dune,
45   "Know that I will strike you with my spear."
On that day, the Zarma children
Caused many lives to be lost at that pond.
"You, too, take your spear
50   "And strike the one who takes your wrapper."
Until they killed all the Tuareg children,
And all the Fulbe children around that pond.
Mali,
Whom they call Sombo,

57   On that day he came to the village.
He ordered that the drum named Sambonkon be beaten.
At that time, the Zarma had seven drums.

66   Sombonkon is the biggest of them all.

On that day the Zarma,
70   When the Sonbonkon is beaten,
Nobody asks why it is beaten
They simply come armed and ready for war.

75   On that day they had thirty horsemen.
He told the Zarma,
"I killed the Tuareg children,
"And the Fulbe children.
"And all the children of nobles who will follow a chief to war."
80   On that day, even those who arrived with courage
Found that their ardor cooled.
Those who arrived with *gris-gris*[1]
Found that their *gris-gris* no longer worked.
Going out in front will not work.
85   Hiding in the sand will not help.
Sombo, who is Mali Bero,
Had a man
Named Alamin.
Alamin is a sorcerer.
90   He is Mali Bero's slave.
On that day Alamin said to the Zarma people,
"Everybody should dismount."
Everybody dismounted.
He told everybody to go look for straw.

---

1. Charms.

135

95   They went and got straw and returned.
        He said that they should construct the bottom of a millet silo.
        He told everybody to climb on to it.
100   Only the cow should not get onto it.
        In those days it was only Alamin
        Who had a cow in Mali.

        Now, everybody climbed on board the millet silo bottom.
        The goats got in.
        The sheep got in.
110   The horses got in.
        The people got in.

        Alamin has a stick with a ring on it.
        Alamin strikes the millet silo bottom on the side facing the East.
        He says some words, he spits.
145   He strikes the millet silo bottom on the side facing the West.
        He strikes the millet silo bottom on the side facing the North.
        He says some words, he strikes it on the side facing the South.
        And the millet silo bottom begins to tremble with the people in
            it.
        He sits down in the center of the millet silo bottom.
150   Alamin makes the millet silo bottom rise.

[The flying millet silo bottom makes many stops on its trip eastward.
During a stop at Andéramboukane, a small town 225 kilometers northeast of Niamey, on the Niger side of the Niger-Mali border, Mali Bero's
jealous younger brother Bolonbooti informs the local Tuaregs that his
older brother has killed Tuareg children in Mali. Thanks to his own
gris-gris, Mali Bero becomes aware of his younger brother's betrayal.
He awakens the other Zarma, and they attack the Tuareg, who flee
along with his brother. The Zarma then take off on the millet silo
bottom without Bolonbooti. After more stops, it comes to a final rest at
Sargan, where the tomb of Mali Bero is located today. Sargan is a village seven kilometers south of Ouallam, a provincial capital seventy-
five kilometers north of Niamey. The narrator lists the many descendants of Mali Bero, tracing the lineage of some down to the present,
including Abdou Aouta, then the Zarmakoy, or chief Zarma, of Dosso,
the best known of the traditional Zarma chiefs in Niger. Djibo Badié
then shifts back to the narrative and to the period of Songhay resistance
against the Moroccan invaders who had toppled the empire in 1591.
The Zarma contribute to that resistance, and in so doing join their own
history to that of their neighbors. One of Mali Bero's descendants,
Hawayzé Mali, goes to the aid of the Songhay.]

        On that day, the Arabs of Morocco
        They swept through all of the Songhay region.

	They destroyed Gao.
	They captured Gao.
755	Until they entered the Zarma land.
	Until they arrived here.

	On that day he rose up at Dosso,[2]
	He came out to meet the Arabs.
	He took his army from Dosso.
	He gathered together the charlatans.
770	He gathered together the *marabouts*.
	He said to them, "Everyone will die in this battle except
	Yefarma Issaka."
	Yefarma Issaka is the son of his sister.
	On that day Yefarma Issaka
	Was sent to the Kebbi region in order to purchase a horse.

[Yefarma Issaka often appears in the oral tradition either as the nephew of Mali Bero or as the leader of the Golé people, a Zarma subgroup of Tuareg origin. Here, the narrator tells us he is a descendant of Mali Bero via his uncle, Hawayzé Mali. While Yefarma Issaka travels eastward, his uncle Hawayzé heads West with the army of Dosso to challenge the Moroccan-led force. He defeats them, forcing the invaders back to the Niger River, 100 kilometers westward. But the battle continues to rage along the river just south of present-day Niamey. Finally, Yefarma learns from a captive woman at a well that he has been sent away from the combat because he will die if he participates in it. Yefarma turns around and catches up with the Zarma army in the Niamey area.]

	He asks his uncle, "What are the fires on the edge of the river?"
	He replies, "They are the Arabs whom we are fighting."
905	Yefarma Issaka,
	He says, "Then you did not come here for war.
	"You came to get warm.
	"How is it that their fires are lit?
	"Your fires are also lit.
910	"But one fire must be extinguished."

	The uncle said, "Stop your mockery.
	"Stop your bravado.
915	"The people whom you will find here tomorrow,
	"You will find Zaw Zaw, he is a great Arab warrior.
	"You will find Bayero, he is a great Arab warrior.
	"You will find Sigsi, he is a great Arab warrior.
	"You will find here Mossoro, he is a great Arab warrior.

---

2. Provincial capital 107 kilometers east of Niamey.

920   "Among them all, one alone and his clan could fight both the
         Songhay and the Zarma for an entire day."
      Yefarma Issaka,
      He said, "Fine, tomorrow one fire will go out."

      The next morning the war began.
      Yefarma Issaka mounted his horse.
930   The Arab warrior named Zaw Zaw
      Mounted with his battalion.
      He chased all the enemies toward the dune.
      He found Yefarma Issaka who had stopped.
      They pierced Yefarma Issaka with two spears.
935   Yefarma Issaka cut off his head with a sword.
      He died.

[Bayero does the same thing, but is also beheaded by Yefarma. After the Zarma has killed six of the enemy, the Arabs take to dugout canoes. Yefarma goes after them on his horse and tries to capture one of them. He and the Arab end up in the water. He captures the young warrior, gives him to his uncle, and then goes back to the battle. By the end of the day, his body is full of spears.]

      Early in the morning they left,
990   They said that they wanted to remove the spears from the body
         of Yefarma Issaka.
      Yefarma said that they should not try to remove the spears
      Because if they are all removed, he will die.
      He spent the day fighting with the Arabs.
      They stopped to spend the night under the great baobab tree at
         Boubon.[3]
995   It is there that they removed the spears from the body of
         Yefarma Issaka.

1006   Under the great baobab tree of Boubon,
      Yefarma Issaka,
      His tomb is under the great baobab tree of Boubon.

[The battle continues as Hawayzé Mali and his army advance north up the left bank of the Niger River and defeat the invaders. From the Zarma perspective, it is they who saved the Songhay.]

1018   On that day the griots said of Hawayzé Mali,
      You are the one who freed the Songhay from their burden.

---

3. Town on the left bank of the Niger twenty-five kilometers north of Niamey.

[At this point, the narrator turns briefly to another hero of the Songhay-Zarma world, Issa Korombé, subject of the following epic, and links him to Mali Bero.]

1032   Issa Korombé,
       He is the descendant of Mali Bero.

1051   The mother of Issa Korombé is of blacksmith origin.

       Daouda Bougar
       He too is a warrior.
1055   He was the teacher of Issa Korombé.
       When Issa Korombé was a child,
       He learned to fight from him.

[The narrator continues the story of Mali Bero's descendants by evoking, a few lines at a time, the names of other heroes, towns, and villages where battles took place, and of peoples against whom the Zarma fought. He ends the narrative with the the oft-repeated question:]

1236   Who asks again about the deeds of Mali?

13. The Epic of Issa Korombé
Narrated by Samba Gâfisso

Recorded, transcribed, and translated into French by Ousmane Mahamane Tandina. Reproduced in "Une épopée Zarma: Wangougna Issa Korombeïzé Modi ou Issa Koygolo, 'Mère de la science de la guerre'" (Ph.D. diss., University of Dakar, 1984). These excerpts edited and translated by Thomas A. Hale.

A NINTEENTH CENTURY HERO OF THE GOLÉ, one of the Zarma-speaking peoples of Niger, Issa Korombé was born around 1810 in Koygolo, a town in the Boboye region of western Niger about 100 kilometers east of the modern capital of Niger and 50 kilometers north of the provincial city of Dosso. The Boboye is a dry riverbed that flows into the much larger Dallol Bosso, another dry riverbed that runs for 1,000 kilometers from the Aïr Mountains in the Sahara of northern Niger south to the Niger River.

Fulbe migrants began to settle in the Boboye region in the eighteenth and early nineteenth centuries. According to Zarma oral sources, many of the Fulbe lived peacefully as herders and as Muslim religious leaders until some time between 1804 and 1808. Bambakar Louddouji, a Fulbe chief and an ally of the great Fulbe empire builder Ousman Dan Fodio in Sokoto, 250 kilometers southeastward in present-day Nigeria, began to impose his will on the region at that time, a move that generated resistance among Zarma warriors. They united to drive Louddouji into exile in Sokoto. But his son, Abdoul Hassane, returned to defeat the Zarma in 1831, reestablishing control over them and also over the Tuareg in the region.

The Zarma suffered not only from Fulbe hegemony but also from drought, raids by the Tuareg, and wars between different Zarma chiefs. Issa Korombé, like so many other epic heroes from the Sahel, left home around 1840 to learn the arts of war with the hope of returning some day to help his people. He fought against the Tuareg and the Fulbe in the Songhay area on the right bank of the Niger River 200 kilometers to the west as well as in the northern Zarma region of Zarmaganda on the left bank nearer the current Niger-Mali border.

In 1854, he returned to the Boboye, settling with his brother Daudu in Karma, a village about twenty-five kilometers northwest of Dosso. He then appealed to all Zarma *wangaari* ('war chiefs') in the region to join him in a sustained effort to defeat both the Tuareg and the Fulbe. His successful campaign to free the Zarma from external hegemony lasted for ten years and ended in 1866 with the signing of a peace treaty that guaranteed the independence of Zarmatarey, the land of the Zarma.

Because of his great skill as a military strategist, Issa Korombé was accorded the title of *wangougna*, "mother of the science of war," by his people. He was typical of a class of war chiefs of his epoch who did not seek political power but lived instead for combat and the opportunity to drive traditional enemies out of their region. For the next thirty years, he offered his services as a skilled commander to a series of clients in the region and participated in wars against the western Zarma, whom he considered to be the allies of the Fulbe. In 1895, at the age of eighty-five, he decided to return to Koygolo. But Bayero, son of the Fulbe leader Abdoul Hassane, who had reestablished control over the Zarma in 1831, set out to reassert his family's influence in the region. With support from other Fulbe leaders being pushed eastward by the French from Senegal and Mali, his army defeated the Zarma force of Issa Korombé in August 1896 at Boumba, located at the confluence of the Niger and the Dallol Bosso. The attackers were armed with rifles while the Zarma were still fighting with spears, swords, and arrows. Issa Korombé died of gunshot wounds in that battle. The victory of his enemies was short lived, however, because the French soon moved into the region to establish their own colonial empire for the next six decades.

This 805-line text from which the following excerpts are taken is one of a collection of four narratives about Issa Korombé assembled for comparative study by Ousmane Mahamane Tandina. Two are in prose while two others are in linear form. One of the linear texts is 2,355 lines long and is recounted by an elder based on his memory of a written account owned by his father. The shorter version that serves as the source here came from an elder in the home town of Issa Korombé. None of the four texts was recounted by a griot because the Zarma people do not have griots who recount long epics, only genealogists and town criers. But the Golé people are known locally to share many of the traits of griots. For example, they are seen as particularly talented with words to describe their heroes. For this reason as well as because of the content and form of the text, Tandina argues that the narrative by Samba Gâfisso is indeed an epic.

	Issa in reality
	Is not a prince.
10	Nobody was a prince
	In those days when the Whites had not yet come here.
	But one used to become a chief and was succeeded in turn by others.
	Korombé[1] was a big producer of millet.
	He became a chief because of the quantity of millet he produced.
15	The mother of Issa was of blacksmith origin.
21	She ask Korombé to marry her.
	They got married and produced Issa.

---

1. The father of the hero.

141

	Daudu[2] came to ask Korombé for the boy.
	Daudu said to him:
	"Korombé, will you allow me to take your son?"
30	"What will you do with him?" he asked.
	"My child, you see, does not work with his hands.
	"He does not farm.
	"I don't want him for farming.
	"I will take him at the risk of sacrificing him
35	"Because I, I only fight wars,
	"And it is in war that I will engage him.
	"So that he can become my squire.
	"Is he capable of it?"
	"Discuss it with him," replied Korombé
40	He called him to talk about it.
	"My boy, do you like me?
	"I want to make you my follower.
	"But you must know that I have no other occupation except war
	"If you want to join me, say so."
45	"Yes," agreed the boy.
	"Do you understand all the consequences?"
	"I accept them," replied Issa.
	So then they went off on the warpath against the Tuareg, who
	were bothering them.

[Issa and Daudu go off in different directions, fighting their own separate wars against the various enemies of the Zarma. Issa returns from one war with much booty.]

	Issa alone brought back forty horses.
	"All these forty horses," he explained,
	"Come from warriors who abandoned their mounts
85	"And from warriors whom I killed."

[The chief of Kolman invited all of the warriors to march through the village to his palace to choose among the eligible young women. Suffering from an unexplained sense of unhappiness, Issa declined the offer and then left for Wanzerbé, a town in the Songhay region near the Niger-Mali-Burkina Faso border that is known as the capital of Songhay magic. He seeks help from a single-breasted woman who is widely known for her powers. She proposes to solve his problems by placing his head on her knees and having him suckle her breast.]

	He suckled, he suckled, and then fell asleep.
150	She wanted to remove his head from her knees.
	But he gripped her breast.

---

2. A warrior friend of the family.

He suckled again, suckled until he went back to sleep again.
She wanted to free his head from her knees again.
155 He again grabbed his breast.
"My child," she said, "this, my breast,"
"I have not given it a single time to someone
"Who suckled it, fell asleep,
"And I wanted to sleep,
160 "And he tried to stop me, continuing resolutely to hold on to
     it."
"My mother," replied Issa, "it is because I suffer from a great
     problem."
"If that is the way it is, continue to suckle."
After six more sessions with her, she tells him that he does not
     need to suckle anymore.

196 "If it is the world that you desire,
"Everything that you want,
"Know that you will have it.

200 "The only thing left, I think,
"Is to give you a few small things."
She made him some *gris-gris*.[3]
She made him
Some magic powders.

[She warns him that when he leaves he will encounter a woman with a
calabash containing seven measures of food. He must take the food, eat
four measures of it, give the other three to his horse, and destroy the
calabash. He then encounters some Tuareg, engages them in combat,
defeats them, and continues on his way. He arrives at a village where
the chief wants to buy his horse for the price of ten captives. Issa demands twenty. When the two fail to agree on a price, the chief then
bars the gates of the village to prevent Issa from escaping. Issa simply
jumps with his horse over the walls and goes on his way, eventually
meeting up with his old patron, Daudu. When the two decide to settle
down, no city or town will accept them. Only after they arrive at the
town of Bankassam are they finally accepted by threatening violence to
the local people. Later, after an incident in which they kill a Fulbe boy
who insulted them, the Fulbe in the region set out to attack Issa
Korombé.]

Issa posted scouts in the bush.
To warn him of the first sign of their arrival.
410 They saw the dust far away.
They came to warn Issa,

---

3. Charms.

To warn him that the Fulbe were coming.
He then ordered
That a horseman remain with him,
415   That ten others go out on the road
To wait for them,
That the ten horsemen go off a little distance,
To a point where they could see the enemy,
And that they should wait for them there.
420   The assailants arrived.
They encountered the ten horsemen.
Issa and the one horseman are hiding in ambush.
The skirmish takes place.
It goes on, it goes on.
425   When anger arose in him, Issa shouted.
He shook the magic gourd
(Provided by the woman of Wanzerbé)
And the Fulbe retreated.
They pursued them.
430   They harassed them.

[Some time after the victory, Daudu dies, Issa Korombé attends his funeral, and then assumes the leadership of the Zarma military forces.]

He looted here,
He pillaged there.
460   He destroyed such and such a city
He consumed another city
Until he gained control of the entire region.
Now the ancestor of the Fulbe,[4]
As soon as Issa heard of him,
465   He[5] was forced to retreat to the right bank of the river.
To spend three months there,
Four or five years,
Before returning.
Issa did not accept the idea of coexisting with him.

[The Fulbe plan to attack Issa Korombé. His *marabout* recommends that he retreat some distance to a tree on the horizon because the religious leader and diviner foresees danger that day.]

"May Our Lord save me from doing that," declared Issa.
"Nobody will ever say that behind my back!"
485   He stood up and made several leaps forward,
About five steps forward,
And sat down.

---

4. Bayero. 5. Bayero.

-" Me, I am your *marabout*," continued Gounou.
"I have spoken to you,
490   "Because today is not your day.
"If ever the opposing army possesses a *marabout* of my talent
"They will attack shortly,
"If they don't, you will be spared,
"But I repeat that if they have one of them,
495   "In an instant, they will find us here."
Before this meeting was over,
The people of Ziji[6] betrayed Issa
Because they declared:
"We thought that
500   "You came to fight and then run,
"When actually you came to deliver us as prey to the enemy.
"We, we will no longer follow you."
As soon as the Ziji people had turned in the opposite direction,
The Fulbe attacked.
505   The battle started,
Mayatchi Téko[7] and Marou[8]
Charged into the melée,
Made a path among the attackers,
Sent them into retreat,
510   Pushed them back.
Mayatchi Téko returned, Marou continued,
Mayatachi Téko returned, then he said,
"Father of Bibata,"[9]
"Naam!"[10]
515   "Let's withdraw, today's encounter
"Is turning out as Alfa Gounou had predicted.
"Let's retreat.
"A man, if he does not flee one day, does not return another
        day!"

520   Issa said that he would not know how to flee,
That he would never flee.

[After his son Marou dies in battle and Mayatchi Téko and other warriors counterattack, Issa Korombé single-handedly chases the enemy
down to the edge of the Niger River. The retreating Fulbe decide that
only a hunter's child who has not reached puberty will be capable of
killing Issa Korombé. He hides in a tree and succeeds in shooting Issa
Korombé with a poisoned arrow that penetrates the forearm and the
armpit. The child reports his feat but also says that the hero did not

6. Region to southeast of Boboye. 7. Chief lieutenant of Korombé. 8. Son of
Korombé. 9. Term of respect normally used by the first wife to her husband.
10. "Yes."

145

fall. The Fulbe decide to wait until the poison takes effect. When Issa Korombé weakens, he lies down on his shield and wraps himself in a white sheet. When the Fulbe approach, he transforms himself first into an elephant and then into one lion, two lions, and three lions in order to pursue them till late at night. At this point, a hunter takes the initiative to take a closer look. He discovers green flies all over the trees near Issa Korombé.]

	"Really!" he exclaimed.
	"It is a cadaver that is chasing us!"
595	He went off to tell everyone else.
	They got up.
	"We are the victims of a hallucination," they declared.
	"It is not a living person,
	"Let's reassemble and go there.
600	"If it is a lion, let him eat all of us at once.
	If it is an elephant, may we all be fodder for him."
	So, they got together and marched off
	To the cadaver.
	He transformed himself into a lion without hunting them.
605	He transformed himself into an elephant without pursuing them.
	Finally, they came closer.
	Then
	They cut off his head.

[After displaying his head, the Fulbe are shamed into burying it and they also spare the life of his *marabout*. Soon thereafter, the French arrive and demand that all wars cease.]

	"No more war.
700	"We have come to stay.
	"So that you listen to us from now on,
	"Anyone who doesn't want to listen to us,
	"Must know that he has no place here on earth.
705	"Because we, our fire,[11]
	"No fire can equal it.
	"May everyone here follow our orders,
	"For we are here."
	Since that time, they submitted to the Whites;
710	The Whites became their masters.

[The presence of a small French force does not prevent the Tuareg from harassing the Zarma after the death of Issa Korombé during a period of some instability that lasts until the First World War.]

---

11. That is, guns.

Fulbe Epics

THE FULBE ARE A CATTLE-HERDING PEOPLE who are now to be found across the Sahel, that region of Africa just south of the Sahara desert from the Atlantic coast of Senegal, Mauritania, and Guinea in the west, to Cameroon, Chad, and southern Sudan in the east. Pastoralists and nomads in origin, they have followed their herds over vast distances. They have also followed their faith. The nineteenth century saw several outbreaks of religious fervor among the Fulbe in various portions of West Africa and the establishment of Islamic states: Ousman dan Fodio in northern Nigeria (where the Fulbe established their rule over the Hausa); Cheikou Amadou in the Macina; and later and most spectacularly Al-hajj Umar Tal in Senegal. This latter's career brought him into conflict with the French, so that he was forced east and into conflict with both Cheikou Amadou (a sectarian struggle within Islam) and with the Bamana state of Segu (a holy war against unbelievers). He perished in 1864 when his conquered subjects revolted; he took refuge in a cave and someone set fire to the gunpowder.

Over this vast sweep of West Africa, there are many subgroups of Fulfulde-speakers who go by many different names. Their language remains recognizable, and so do certain of their traditions: Muslim and non-Muslim, the Pullo (singular) and cattle raising are intertwined. They have settled down and formed states, most notably in Guinea (the Futa Jallon) and in Senegal/Mauritania (the Futa Tooro), or attached themselves to other groups as herdsmen and neighbors. But cattle-herding (and cattle-raiding) are an essential element of Fulbe tradition, as one sees in their epic poetry.

The literature, oral and written, of the Fulbe is abundant and complex. Pre-Islamic initiatory traditions are represented by *Kaydara* or *Koumen*, poems collected and presented originally by Amadou Hampaté Bâ and Lilyan Kesteloot, and by an abundant tradition of songs and poems. Evidence suggests that the Fulbe of Macina took their epic-singing tradition from their neighbors, the Bamana of Segu, or possibly from the Soninké. The various linguistic traditions become intimately connected in the area north of the Niger, in the former Bamana kingdom of the Kaarta.

Among the Fulbe, as elsewhere in the Niger River valley, epic narration is the function of professionals known by a variety of names. Musicians in general are *awluube* (sing. *gawlo*); the specialized singers of epic are *mabuube* (sing. *mabo*), a term that also refers to weavers. The sedentarized Fulbe appear to observe the professional status groups common in the Mande world, including such occupations as blacksmith, leatherworkers, woodcarvers, and others. For example, one repeated poetic passage describes a hero mounting his horse by using the names of these professions as metonymies for the products of their labor: the blacksmith represents the stirrups and the bit, the leatherworker the reins and parts of the saddle, the woodcarver the saddle-frame. The musicians are generally considered to be of foreign origin.

In the process of appropriation, the epic as a borrowed form

147

loses its historical value. Where the Malinké traditions of Sunjata, who founded the Empire of Mali, or the Bamana traditions of Segu deal with purportedly historical events, the Fulbe songs deal fairly consciously with an admitted never-never land of heroic deeds and gestures, and their purpose is entertainment. There is, however, a nuance to this statement. Early in the first epic (*Hambodedio and Saïgalare*), we hear of "praise-names" (*jammoore* or *noddol* in Fulfulde), which are traditional praises associated with celebrated individuals or, through them, with their clans. These praises are a source of self-identification for the individual Pullo; to hear them is to be sent into a paroxysm of family pride, to be swept up into the glory of one's tradition (see Seydou 1977). Besides the praises, the epics serve also as the classic demonstration of *pulaaku*, the quintessential quality of the Pullo hero in his (or her?) former arrogance and prowess. These qualities are demonstrated through a variety of heroes, all significantly pre-Islamic. Hambodedio and Silâmaka, neighbors and contemporaries in Macina, are associated with the Bamana kingdom of Segu of the late eighteenth century, before the establishment of an Islamic *dina*, or rule of faith, by Cheikou Amadou; Samba Gueladio, a hero of the Futa Tooro, is dated by Senegalese scholars to the early eighteenth century.

14. The Epic of Hambodedio and Saïgalare
Narrated by Hamma Diam Bouraima

Recorded in Douentza, Mali, February 23, 1970, by Christiane Seydou.
Transcribed and translated into French by Christiane Seydou. Edited by
Christiane Seydou and published in La geste de Hambodedio ou Hama le
rouge *by Armand Colin in 1976. This excerpt edited and translated into*
English by Stephen Belcher.

HAMBODEDIO AND SAÏGALARE IS AN EPIC POEM from the region of Macina, in the modern republic of Mali, and it tells, in Fulfulde, of the legendary hero Hammadi Paté Yella, also known as Hambodedio or Hama
the Red. There are many stories about Hambodedio; this is only one of
them, and perhaps one of the least historical. It is also one of the most
delightful, and versions of this story are reported in other regional languages.

The historical Hambodedio lived at the time of Monzon and Da,
kings of Segu between 1790 and 1828. Legend and epic performances
attach him to the time of Da (c. 1808-18), and he is said to have been
the ally and son-in-law of the king of Segu. He probably lived somewhat earlier; we can date him by reference to the battle of Noukouma
in 1818, between Segu and Islamic Macina. Around that time, his son,
Gueladio, was the leader of the Fulbe of the Kunaari and eventually
came into conflict with Cheikou Amadou, founder of the Fulbe Islamic
state of Macina. Gueladio then led a migration of Fulbe to the southeast,
across the arc of the Niger bend, to what is now Niger and Burkina
Faso, around 1818. A German traveler met Gueladio (Gelaajo) there in
1853, and his descendants are still to be found there.

The story is a long and episodic one, revolving essentially
around Hambodedio's quest for reputation (through "his" tune "Saïgalare") and the consequences of that quest; he shares the stage with his
griot, who acquires the tune from the jinns, and with his wife Fadia,
who incites him to great deeds. As the story starts, we consider the
praise-names of the hero.

Now, we—Hamma Diam Bouraïma and Ousmane Amadou
    Ousso are from Time,
But I, Hamma Diam Bouraïma, I am from Koysa—
We are going to record a little.
We will record Saïgalare of Hambodedio Hammadi Paté Yella.
5   This is the tune for Nyanyi Hammadi, for Wel-Hore Hammadi,
For Fadia Hammadi, Kummbo and Umma Haani!
Hammadi rose and trampled through the dew.
At noon he had made the land a dark waste,
The stranger-guest in the morning, the master of the house at
    noon.
10   He said, "Oh, no! Don't name me by those worthless praise-
    names!

"Those are the praise-names of the low-rumped hyena!
"I, Hammadi, am no hyena."
They told him, "Well, shall we call you the Peredio
"Who gathered no monkey-bread fruit with his pole,
15   "Who gathered no wild duck eggs,
"Who drank no watered milk in Barbe,
"Who drank no water from Hoore-Gennde!
"You are the Pullo who rules Bumaani and Budaande,
"And Aada-Wadda and Nama Nawre and Kanel Jeeje and
        Wandu Jeeje and Humbaldu-Jeeje and Ngappere Wumbere
        Jeeje,
20   "Or yet that you are the Pullo of Delbi and of Bubdo Njaree.
"You are the man who, if he goes to Segu, is the son of a red
        Pullo; if you squeezed his throat, the man would spit sour
        milk.
"But back in Kunaari he is the son of a Bambara and the grand-
        son of Da Monzon."
He said, "Ha! Now you have spoken God's truth of me.
"The night when I, Hammadi, am no longer in this world,
25   "Then for sure Saïgalare will be sold across the counter,
"And Saïgalare will be played for any peanut seller."

[Hambodedio then tells of the only three times he had felt fear: once
when a snake crawled over him while he was sitting with a woman;
again when he encountered a woodcutter whom he mistook for a jinn at
night; and a third time when he forded a river filled with wild beasts to
punish a shepherd who had insulted him. The last two incidents
occurred while he was fulfilling a request by his wife Fadia that he raid
some cattle for her from Samba Bongouel Samba, her old beau, and
while he was accompanying her on a boat ride: these incidents intro-
duce characters and themes which will reappear.]

And when did Saïgalare come down here?
It was on a Wednesday night that Saïgalare came into this
        world.
At the time, there was no Saïgalare, so that one might speak of
        the Saïgalare of Hambodedio Hammadi Paté Yella.
295   From Yeli to Yelikapa,
That is where people had settled.
One Wednesday night, a male genie,
An elder, came out of Yelikapa, over there,
And was brought into the entrance hall of Hambodedio, here in
        Gundaka.
300   He sat, plucking out Saïgalare.
It was a Wednesday, in the night.
While he was playing Saïgalare, Hammadi was upstairs, lying
        down.

He woke up with a start, he heard Saïgalare being played.
Hammadi rushed down, armed with his wide spear, he tum-
    bled down the stairs and came into his entrance hall.

305   The genie stopped playing his music
And called "silence."
Hammadi returned upstairs immediately;
He lay down again.
Once again, the genie began to play Saïgalare.

310   Hammadi rose up with a double-barreled rifle of tempered steel
    and moving breech; he loaded it with powder and ball; it
    never left him by night or day.
He came down again to the entrance hall.
The genie stopped playing Saïgalare.
He went back upstairs
No sooner was he back upstairs

315   Than the sun was driven by sticks, pushed from the East,
    drawn over the lands of China.
He turned over Karsana, he spread himself over Baghdad, he
    came down over Hanjiwa
And Hadeijiya
And Doogonduci and Kaedi, the little *guiguili* trees of Tamba-
    counda.
In Dakar they say that he is slow to come but that shading your
    eyes will not hide him.

320   Hammadi rose, sounded the great drum
From Kassa
To Kuna,
From Denga
To Mondio.

325   Everyone in the country assembled in Gundaka.
He declared that he needed none but the pluckers of strings.
All he needed was a player of the lute.
So the musicians who were there that day assembled,
Numbering a thousand.

330   He said, "Musicians!" The musicians answered, "Yes."
He said, "Last night,
"I heard a tune.
"Never, since God made me,
"Never have I heard its like.

335   "I do not know if it was one of you musicians who played,
"I don't know if it was a genie playing,
"I don't know if it was the Devil playing, but in any case I
    heard it.
"And all I know is that if, when the time comes around
"For the prayer of *salifana*[1] on the next Thursday,

---

1. Noontime.

151

340 "If I have not heard it again,

   "Then that evening, there will be no live musicians in this
     world.

   "If I have not heard it,

   "Then that evening, no musicians will be left in the world."

   The musicians asked, "What is it named?"

345 He said, "Eh!

   "Exactly! I don't know what it is named.

   "All I know is that if I have not heard it again

   "By the time of the prayer of *salifana* on the next Thursday,

   "Then that evening there will be no musicians living in the
     world."

350 The musicians asked, "How is it named, Hammadi?"

   He said, "We have talked enough!

   "Let each of you decide which way he will go,

   "And leave at once to look for it.

   "I do not know how it is named."

355 The musicians dispersed.

   Each left, looking for what he did not have at his fingertips,

   Without knowing how it was called.

   They left that Thursday morning,

   None of them having found it then,

360 And by the time of the *salifana* prayer on the next Wednesday,

   Not a single one of them had yet found it.

   Each one of them came back. Then came the turn of Ko Biraïma
     Ko, alone.

   Each on his return played for Hammadi what he had found.
     Hammadi said it was not the tune he had heard.

   As for Ko Biraïma Ko,

365 That Thursday, God's sun had already risen and he still had
     not found it.

   And when the time for the *salifana* prayer came and the people
     played,

   Then that evening not one would be left alive in the world.

   And Ko Biraïma Ko himself that Thursday

   Found nothing the whole day long.

370 He said, "Well, I will go back now. This is bad luck."

   Ko left

   And prepared to return to Gundaka.

   Soon he came where the Black River and the White River join.

   There was a rise of wooded land;

375 A termite mound stood on it.

   Soon he came, and he was going past

   When the genie came out and hailed him.

   As soon as he hailed him, Ko turned his head to see.

   The genie hid.

380 Ko said, "Ho! You!

"You, who called me, whoever you are! If you would stop then
    I could see you.
"Nothing can bother a man who is doomed to die today!
"The rice will be well cooked tomorrow.
"As for me, what awaits me in Gundaka terrifies me far more
    than you, who called me and then hid."

385   He went on his way. The genie called to him again.
He turned his head and saw him.
He touched heaven with his head, with his feet still on earth.
He did not falter, did not waver,
Did not turn, did not retreat,

390   But went on until he touched him.
The genie sat up, and they were face to face.
They greeted each other.
The genie said, "Ko Biraïma Ko!" He answered, "Yes!"
He said, "I am the one who called you."

395   He added, "As for why I called you,
"It is just that I have in my hands the thing you are looking
    for."
He said, "What is it that I must look for?"
He said, "A tune that was played in the entrance hall of
    Hambodedio,
"Last Wednesday night," he said. "That is what you seek."

400   He said, "That's true, that is what I must find."
The other said, "Come, here it is in my hand."
He said, "Sit down." He sat.
The genie pressed on the termite mound, and the lute came
    out. They tuned their instruments.
They began to play Saïgalare again and again.

405   He said, "That is what you are seeking." He said, "Rise and go.
"We the genies call it Saïgalare.
"All of God's creation living here below, all the sons of Adam,
    will only hear the tune from you. Rise and go."
Ko rose.
He went off a bit further.

410   He sat and began to pluck the strings.
He realized that what he had learned by heart had slipped
    from his fingers, and even more so with Saïgalare. He
    realized that nothing was left.
Ko turned around,
He came back
Where he had left him. He came and said, "Peace upon you."
    The old man answered, "And upon you, peace." He said,
    "If you are not a joker,

415   "Then, for that gift you gave me,
"Help me to know it,

"Give me back what I had before, let me once again play my
   instrument."
The genie said, "Ko!" And he said, "Yes!"
The genie said, "Raise your lute above your head and break
   it."
420 Ko struck his lute on the ground. It split.
The genie pressed on the termite mound.
A lute came out.
He pressed upon the termite mound, and another lute came
   out.
He pressed the mound, and a spring flowed out.
425 He pressed on the mound,
A bag of magic charms came out. He pressed the mound,
A calabash came out.
He took the calabash, he drew water,
He took the charms,
430 He undid them over the calabash, he told Ko to drink. Ko
   drank.
He told Ko to wash; Ko washed.
He told Ko to take up . . .
One of the lutes. He took one of the lutes.
Together, they played the first chords of Saïgalare.
435 Then they played Saïgalare again and again.
He said, "Ko!"
Ko said, "Yes!"
He said, "Rise and go home."
He said, "Rise and go home. Now you have it!
440 "No one will ever now be able to take Saïgalare from you; even
   I could not, no other could take it from you now.
"As for any one of God's creation,
"It is from you he will hear the tune."
Ko rose.
He took the hem of his robe in his teeth,
445 He gave himself to God, hoping he would reach Gundaka as
   noon came.
From point to point, from point to point, at last he reached Gun-
   daka just at noon.
He arrived.
They received him with open arms, they greeted each other,
   they announced, "Ko Biraïma has come! Ko Biraïma has
   come!
"He was the last we were expecting."
450 He came.
You know, one Jawando in a village is a cure.[2]

---

2. Someone skilled in diplomacy and intrigue.

Two Jawandos in a village are a sickness, and if the number
    rises to three, then it's an epidemic.
Hambodedio had one Jawando.
He said, "Now, Ko has come!
455   "Bring him food,
"And dry onion,
"And those little yellow things,
"And fish oil: it slips into the hand, it slides, it's swallowed,
"It sends the food down smoothly and sweetly. Bring him
    some!"
460   He asked for curdled milk and fresh milk; they were brought.
He asked to have a white kola nut, and he was given one.
He collected his wits.
Ko picked up his lute, he went to the entrance hall of Hambo-
    dedio,
He came and he found sitting there nine hundred—I tell you
    the truth—and ninety-nine men, all musicians.
465   The musicians said, "Well, well! Ko, come! Play us whatever
    you may have found, and let us all die. Because certainly
    you, all by yourself, cannot have found whatever we all
    together could not find."
Ko sat down, tuned his *hoddu*[3]
Began to play Saïgalare,
And played Saïgalare over and over again.
Hambodedio said, "That is it! That is the tune I heard last
    Wednesday night!"
470   The musicians said that as for them, they had never heard any-
    thing like that tune.
Hammadi said to him, "Ko!" He said "Yes!"
He said, "What you have accomplished just now is magnificent.
"I will make you a gift of a ten-count of everything, even the
    base of stew."
What is the base of stew?
475   He meant even ten chickens.
And with that, Hammadi picked up the double-barreled rifle,
    which he loaded with bullets.
He said that any musician he came across just then would travel
    to the next world, except for Ko Biraïma Ko.
The musicians pushed and shoved each other, struggling to be
    the first through the door.
The powder charge coughed.
480   Four slipped into that everlasting slumber; most succeeded in
    escaping
And returned to Gouyel.
Ever since those musicians left Gundaka to get back to Gouyel,

---

3. A four-stringed lute.

Any musician you see who claims to come from Gouyel,
They really come from here, from Gundaka, even though they
    may have settled in Gouyel later.
After that, Saïgalare belonged to Hammadi and to him alone,
    and no other could listen to Saïgalare as a piece of music.
Hammadi said, "Ko!" and he answered, "Yes!"

515   He said, "Saïgalare
"Has become my very own particular Saïgalare.
"You must not play Saïgalare for any of God's creatures
"Except for me.
"If ever I learn that you have played Saïgalare for anyone but
    myself,

520   "I will make of you a cold corpse."
He said, "I have two wives:
"I have one named Fadia,
"I have another named Tenen, daughter of Da Monzon.
"I also have two sons: I have one named Gueladio Hambodedio
    Hammadi Paté Yella,

525   "And one named Ousmane Hambodedio. Even for them,
"Let me not hear that you have played the tune. If I learn
"That you have played it for them, I will make of you a cold
    corpse."
He said, "Truth!"
He said, "I have heard, I agree.

530   "For none of God's creatures, whoever it may be, will I play the
    tune."
And from that moment on, it was for Hammadi alone that it
    was to be played,
There in his entrance hall.
Fadia lived upstairs, on the second story.
Tenen Da Monzon was here, on the ground floor.

535   But there! For Hammadi, the music was played in the entrance-
    way here,
When a little old woman servant who was on the ground floor
    heard it being played.
The little old woman servant climbed upstairs, she found Fadia.
She said, "Fadia!" Fadia said, "Yes!"
She said, "They have made up a tune for Hambodedio."

540   Fadia said, "Really? They have composed a tune for Hambode-
    dio?" She said, "Yes, they have composed a tune, in truth."
Fadia said, "And yet I have not heard this tune."
The old woman said, "If you haven't heard it, that means you
    are not the preferred wife.
"Tenen Da Monzon, the concubine, is dearer than you; she
    hears it every day, while you have not yet managed to
    hear it."

Fadia answered; she said, "Old servant," and the other said "Yes!"

545 She said, "As for me, since they have composed a tune for Hambodedio, I will hear it!

"Whether because I have earned the right, or because money enables me to hear it,

"But nevertheless, I will hear it."

The servant went back down.

At length, one fine morning,

550 Ko left the ground floor

And climbed upstairs to the second story.

He greeted Fadia, and Fadia answered him.

Fadia said, "Ko Biraïma Ko!" He said "Yes!"

She said, "I hear that you have composed a tune for Hambodedio."

555 He said, "Indeed, I have composed a tune."

She said, "But won't I get to hear it?"

He said, "You will not hear it."

She said, "And why not?"

He said, "Hammadi has said that if he learns I have played the tune for any other person, whoever it may be, he will kill me and the other person."

560 Fadia told him, "Well, Ko, if you have composed a tune for Hammadi, I will hear it,

"Whether I am worthy of hearing or not,

"I will hear it.

"And meanwhile, as for you, Ko,

"Take these fifty *mithqal*[4] of gold!

565 "By God, I will hear it!"

Ko took the fifty *mithqal*;

He made a hole in his trousers, he placed them there;

Ever since that time there have been pockets in the pants.

Ko went downstairs.

570 On Saturday, Hammadi was launching a campaign.

All evening long, Ko drowned Hammadi in music.

Hammadi said, "Tomorrow, when the morning rises,

"I launch my campaign,

"I go off to get the tawny cattle of Bongouel Samba,

575 "Drank-no-dust, Never-walked-on-foot, the Little Man of Gaïssoungou.

"I wish to bring them back here to Gundaka."

The morning rose.

They were busy harnessing the horse

When Ko rose up alone in his place.

---

4. Thirty grams.

580   He put ashes into the water, and pepper, and then splashed it
        into his eyes.
    At the last moment, as the horsemen were leaving,
    They realized he had not left, that his eyes must be treated.
    And so he would have a way to play Saïgalare for Fadia,
    So that Fadia could hear the tune at that time.

585   When morning came, all the horses were harnessed.
    Ko Biraïma Ko was the only one who did not come.
    They asked, "How is Ko today?
    "He hasn't yet come, has he?"
    They said, "Someone should go look in his sleeping place."

590   They found him wide awake, but his eyes—as you
        know—were sick.
    They said that his eyes were sick.
    They said, "And now what?
    "We aren't going to put off the departure
    "Because Ko isn't feeling well."

595   Hammadi told the riders to saddle their mounts; they saddled
        them.
    They set off, they left on the raid noiselessly, before the dawn,
        and rode through Kunaari.
    As soon as she was sure they were really off and away,
    Fadia came down
    From the upper story. No one was left in Gundaka,

600   Save for Ko; he was the only man left behind.
    Fadia came down,
    She took some sour milk, she splashed his eyes and rinsed
        them out,
    And the eyes were completely healed.
    Ko took his *hoddu*,

605   Slipped up to the upper story and found Fadia there.
    He seated himself across from Fadia,
    And began to beat out Saïgalare as best he could, while Fadia
        drank in Saïgalare.
    Hammadi's horsemen had ridden out on their raid.
    Soon they came to Dena.

610   Hammadi turned about.
    He did not hear Saïgalare.
    He looked far away before him, and he heard no Saïgalare.
    Hammadi told the riders to turn around immediately;
    On that day, he knew that if he met Bongouel, Bongouel would
        defeat him; he said that he had not heard Saïgalare all
        morning.

615   He told the horsemen to go back;
    On that day, the other would defeat them.
    If ever he met Bongouel on that day, Bongouel would defeat
        him.

He told them to return.
He said the rearguard should lead the way, and this was one.
He said the vanguard should take up the rear.
620 They turned about face and lined up to ride back to Gundaka.
Soon they reached the outskirts of Gundaka.
Soon, they came and entered Gundaka,
And as they entered, the griots began to praise them. He said,
"No!"
Not one should praise him.
625 "I have not seen Ko Biraïma Ko, my own griot, the only one I
care for, for some time. He is not in good health.
"Let each of you other griots go home to his house, while I in
turn return to my own house."
Hammadi went straight to his house,
And as his steps led him there, he heard Saïgalare
Being played above on the upper story.
630 You might think that pepper juice had been dropped into his
eyes.
Here, Hammadi comes to the door of the entrance hall, dis-
mounts,
Leaves Mad Mane,
Leaps forward with his broad spear,
Takes the stairs.
635 He had almost reached the upper story:
They heard his feet pounding the stairs.
Ko Biraïma Ko leaped to his feet, dropping his *hoddu*.
Fadia said, "Sit down! Where are you going?
"No matter how high the Lord may have raised you, you are
only his dog, while I am his wife. You're playing for me
here. Sit down.
640 "You may curse me, if he kills you today."
Hammadi burst into the upper story rooms.
He said, "Ko!" Ko said, "Yes." "Didn't I tell you that you
should not play Saïgalare
"For any of God's creatures? Didn't I tell you?" He said, "Yes,
you said that."
He said, "And why then?"
645 He said, "Fadia told me to play for her.
"She gave me fifty *mithqal* so that . . .
"That is why I was playing for her."
He said, "If God wills, you will pass on right now."
He brandished his broad spear. The crested cranes screamed,
650 They spoke with Dibi.
He said, "Where will they land?
"Where should this spear fall? Will it fall on the woman, or will
it fall on Ko?"
The woman said, "Really, Hammadi!

159

"It's not proper for it to fall on Ko.
655   "Ko is your griot. He composed Saïgalare for you.
"Your spear can only fall on me."
He brandished it again.
He asked, "Where must it fall?
"Will it fall on the woman, or on the griot?"
660   The woman answered more strongly, "Heavens, really,
        Hammadi!
"It is not proper to it to fall on Ko, for he is your griot.
"It must fall on me, yes, on me. It's on me, your wife, that it
        must fall."
He brandished it again.
He told her to show him where it should fall.
665   The woman drew back her skirt.
Showed him her thigh.
He pierced it through to the straw mat, and he withdrew it.
He said, "That is not the only blow!
"Where should it strike for the second?"
670   "Will the second blow fall on the griot, or will it fall on my
        wo . . . , my woman?"
The woman said, "The second blow must fall here, on me. It
        would be wrong if you struck him on the second blow."
He said to show him where this second blow should fall. The
        woman drew back the skirt from her left thigh and showed
        it to him.
He struck and he hit the bone.
He pulled.
675   He pulled so hard that he fell over.
Fadia did not stop chatting and laughing.
Ko Biraïma Ko had not stopped playing the *hoddu*.
The blood streamed out.
The blood streamed so much that it was going to trickle down
        the stairway,
680   The sound was that of a punting pole that sobs.
He said, "Ko!" Ko said, "Yes!"
He said, "What is that I hear now? Is it rain falling?"
Ko said, "No."
Ko said, "It is your wife's blood dripping."

[Hammadi then sends for holy men and healers, and makes of them the same demand he made of the griots: cure her, or else. The most notable among them succeeds; the others are dispersed with gunfire. Once healed, Fadia twits Hambodedio. "Brrrrr!" she cries. All you can do, she says, is stab women and griots, and she challenges him to attend the market at Kuna where the heroes meet on market day to drink beer.

    Hambodedio sends Ko first, and Ko comes to Kuna and is re-fused beer by Nyamoy, the woman who brews and sells the beer drunk by the heroes. One after another, the heroes come: Djenne Wor-ma Djenne, Hama Alseini Gakoy, Silâmaka, and especially Bongouel Samba 'Drank-no-Dust,' Fadia's former suitor. Each of them intercedes on Ko's behalf, but Nyamoy remains adamant: she does not know Hambodedio, still less his griot. Ko returns and reports his mission. Hambodedio rides off to Kuna. On the way, he consults the omens; riding into town, he shoots a pair of lovers emerging at dawn. He comes to the market-place and settles down. The other heroes ride in, learn who is sitting in the market, and ride off without drinking beer, except for Bongouel. He buys some beer for Hambodedio, and then they play "tioki," a local board game. Hambodedio beats Bongouel, and he responds by cuffing Hambodedio. Finally, of course, they come to a duel. Neither can injure the other with weapons: swords, guns, spears all fail. At last, Hambodedio pulls out a hobble and begins to beat Bongouel with it, and Bongouel flees, leaving Hambodedio the field.

And so Hambodedio accomplishes the boast he had made to Fadia: he has gone to the market, he changes the market-day for Kuna, and he marries Nyamoy to Ko.]

15. The Epic of Silâmaka and Poullôri
Narrated by Maabal Samburu

Collected by Amadou Hampaté Bâ. Published by Amadou Hampaté Bâ and Lilyan Kesteloot in "Une épopée peule: 'Silâmaka,'" L'homme 8 (1969), 1-36. Reprinted in Lilyan Kesteloot, Da Monzon de Segu: L'épopée bambara (Paris: Fernand Nathan, 1972; reissued by l'Harmattan, 1993). English version by Stephen Belcher.

THE STORY OF SILÂMAKA IS A MAJOR ELEMENT OF THE TRADITIONS of Macina, where it seems to have become the common property of the Fulbe and the Bamana: the epic is sung (with differences) in both languages. Historically, the narrative places itself in the time of Da Monzon, ruler of Segu in the early nineteenth century, but this connection is hardly essential. While the story fits the pattern of revolt and conquest typical of many elements of the Bamana tradition, the most interesting dynamic is the relationship of the master, Silâmaka, with his retainer Poullôri, and the questions of social status and human worth involved.

A number of versions were collected in the colonial era by Leo Frobenius and Gilbert Vieillard. The following excerpts are taken from a version collected by Amadou Hampaté Bâ from the *mabo* Maabal Samburu, about whom we know nothing except that Hampaté Bâ (himself a figure of some importance) considered him the greatest *mabo* he knew. This version was published in French translation by Hampaté Bâ and Lilyan Kesteloot in 1969 and thus marks one of the first salvos before the explosion of collecting and publishing of African epic of the 1970s and 1980s.

[The Ardo Hammadi and his household captive Baba both marry; their wives conceive on the same day and give birth on the same day. The noble son is named Silâmaka; the captive is Poullôri.]

> Da Monzon was the lord of Ardo Hammadi.
> He sent one day for the "price of the honey-beer."[1]
> The tax gatherers were three young Bambaras.
> They went to Hammadi and told him why they had come.
> 5   The Ardo went into the chamber where he kept his cowries.
> He saw his son's mother nursing the boy.
> He called to Aissa; she put the baby on a mat
> Near the three emissaries who stood waiting.
> The baby was then exactly forty days old.
> 10   A horsefly suddenly landed on his forehead
> And began to suck his blood.
> The three messengers from Da Monzon
> Watched this infant, barely forty days old,
> Who didn't even bother to raise his eyes.

---

1. The tribute.

15   Silâmaka did not move.
He did not blink.
He did not weep,
Before the horsefly, sated with blood, fell off him.
Then blood flowed over the face of Silâmaka.
20   When the father and mother returned,
They gave the emissaries a measure of gold for the "price of
          honey-beer."
Hammadi said to his wife, "See the naughty boy!
"A horsefly drinks all his blood,
"And he doesn't even cry to warn us."
25   Silâmaka's mother crushed the insect.
The three emissaries observed this scene.
The three emissaries returned to Segu,
They told their master, "We are afraid,
"That son of Hammadi, as we saw him,
30   "Will certainly give us grief."
And they told him the story of the horsefly.

[Da Monzon summons diviners and they tell him that a terrible child
has been or will be born in that year; they tell him what magical measures to take against him, but these involve conditions almost impossible to fulfill. The *jeli* of Da Monzon comforts him.]

      So Da understood that on the horizon of Macina,
A black cloud rose to threaten
35   The throne of the Master of Waters in Segu.
Silâmaka and his captive grew up;
Soon they were old enough to spend their afternoons at *niallo*.[2]
Within the chiefdom of Ardo Hammadi was a woman,
The most beautiful of the land.
40   One hundred young Fulbe horsemen came every afternoon
To spend some time with her.
Silâmaka was among them, and the young woman
Showed him more favor than others.
Each time he appeared with Poullôri,
45   The young Pullo woman set out two mats,
Finely woven and well adorned;
She set one on the ground for herself,
The other was for Silâmaka and his captive.
The two friends sat comfortably,
50   While everyone else was crushed together like faggots of wood.
One day Silâmaka and the young woman had a lover's spat.
They reproached each other and spoke hard words.
The woman said to Silâmaka, "You make me mad.

2. In dalliance.

163

"People say you are brave, and so you claim to be,
55   "But all those who flatter you in this way
"Have no choice about it.
"Because you are a chief's son, they eat from your bowl
"They are clothed in your robes!
"If you really are brave, you should not prove it through me,
60   "But rather go and prove your valor to Da Monzon.
"It is to him your father pays a measure of soft gold,
"The price of your breathing.
"Da Monzon only uses it to buy honey-beer."
Poullôri came between them and reconciled them.
65   The next day, the horseman and his captive came back to the
       niallo,
But as soon as the woman recognized the tread of Silâmaka,
She hid a sharp thorn under his usual mat
So that the point rose just where Silâmaka would sit down.
The mat bulged from the thorn.
70   When the Fula arrived, he saw the bump,
But instead of moving aside, he sat directly on it,
There in his usual place,
Without even bothering to look and see why the mat was mis-
       shapen.
So he sat down on the thorn as though it were a tuft of wool;
75   The point entered his buttock,
But Silâmaka did not blink or flinch.
He chatted as though nothing were wrong
And never stopped chewing his kola.
Blood stained his trousers and his robe,
80   As well as the mat on which he was seated;
Poullôri saw it and cried, "Silâmaka!
"Blood is running from under you!"
Silâmaka said, "Continue pouring out your words,"
And they bantered until the usual time.
85   When Poullôri wished to leave,
His master wanted to wait until the time of *lasara*.[3]
When *lasara* came, Poullôri said, "Let's go."
Silâmaka said, "Then you go first."
The captive rose, and then Silâmaka.
90   The thorn and the mat came with him,
Stuck to his behind and clotted with blood.
With a single motion, Silâmaka tore them away.
Poullôri said, "Wait, let me treat you."
Silâmaka replied, "No need.
95   "My horse's saddle will bind my wound,

---

3. The evening prayer.

"And tomorrow I shall find the master to make me invulnerable."

[Silâmaka consults a diviner who tells him he must make a talisman from the skin of the black snake of Galamani, king of the bush spirits. Silâmaka sends warriors to kill the snake, but they fail. He goes himself.]

Soperekagne was saddled.
Soperekagne was a pure white horse.
Silâmaka trod on the blacksmith,
100   He seized the leatherworker,
He sat on the woodcarver,
He spurred his mount and made him rear,
The tail swept the sand,
The hundred horses started to move.
105   See the stallions, the strong males,
So handsome when grazing in the pasture,
But changed to murderers in the battle!
They set off, growling like the thunder.
What was high, they flattened.
110   What was low, they bestrode.
What was green, they tore up.
What was dry, they broke.
They galloped, *kerbekerbe,*[4]
The blades of grass bent over.
115   Silâmaka was on the move.
The young animals knew some great deed was to come,
And wildly ran to their mothers for shelter.
A griot sang the praise-song for Gueladio:
        Samba, should a man dare say your eye is white
120   You split his skull on the spot.
        You cannot see the cartilage
        Which separates the hippo's nostrils.
        You cannot see Gueladio
        When he charges the hippo!
125   Gueladio, he rides the horse,
        Ummu Latoma,
        The mare who crushes vermin,
        Who tramples and flattens termite hills.
When Silâmaka came to the grove,
130   He found the snake in its favorite spot,
For already it was used to killing a man each time.
Silâmaka said, "Stop the horses."
He dismounted and handed the animal to faithful Poullôri.

---

4. Onomatopoeia for speed.

The snake was facing the group.
135   Silâmaka went around the grove,
He walked with quiet little steps.
He seized the beast suddenly by the neck;
The snake wrapped itself around his arm,
And beat his ribs with its tail.
140   Then Silâmaka rejoined his horsemen.
All of them fled, except Poullôri.
The valiant Pullo mounted his horse,
Still holding the great black snake by the neck.
All Poullôri had to do was tell the others
145   That Silâmaka had captured the snake of Galamani.

[They make belts out of the snakeskin and test them at a village: the population is terrified. Then follows an extended interlude in which three griots visit the Fulbe heroes of the region, asking who is considered bravest. Djenne Vere names four: Silâmaka, Hambodedio, himself, and Hamma Alaseyni Gakoy; Silâmaka claims to be braver and says he will visit Hambodedio. When he visits Hambodedio, he is insulted, and to take revenge he and Poullôri raid Hambodedio's cattle. When Hambodedio rides after them, he also listens to the advice of an old man and approaches Silâmaka peacefully. The two heroes make up and Silâmaka returns home. Da Monzon sends for the tribute; Silâmaka takes the gold from the messengers and tells them Macina will no longer pay tribute. The messengers return and tell Da Monzon that the child they had warned him about has grown up. Da Monzon sends the three men to capture Silâmaka, but they are beaten and mutilated: one loses a tongue, the other an ear, the third an eye. They inform Da Monzon and he sends cavalry.]

The horses flew through Segu like arrows
And their hooves pierced the ground.
The news reached Silâmaka.
"How many are they?" asked the son of Hammadi.
150   "Fifty," he was told.
Silâmaka exclaimed, "Allah blast Da Monzon!
"He cannot write me off with fifty horses!"
Silâmaka could count on men of solid worth in Kekei,
They were divided in five companies, each of a hundred
        bridles,
155   All members of his age group,
All members of the Ferobe clan.
But Silâmaka told his five hundred riders,
"You may rest today,
"Poullôri and I can handle this.
160   "Do not worry, your turn shall come."
He ordered that Soperekagne be saddled;

166

It was done so well the noble horse raised its hoof in greeting.
Silâmaka trod on the blacksmith,
He seized the leatherworker,
165   He sat upon the woodcarver;
Poullôri did the same,
Together they rode down the hill from the village.
Silâmaka was wearing his talismans of war.
West of Kekei is a tamarind tree.
170   Silâmaka's magic charm is buried at the foot of the tree.
Before it grows a thorn tree, facing the plain.
It was on that plain that Silâmaka was accustomed
To draw his enemies if he wanted a sure victory.
So the Pullo waited in the shade of the tamarind tree.
175   The horses of Segu crossed the plain of Wougouba.
Silâmaka was smoking his pipe
When he saw the horses racing toward him.
He placed his pipe in his mouth and drew,
He blew out the smoke and made a cloud
180   Which divided into three other clouds.
Then he rode forward, with Poullôri close behind.
As soon as the warriors of Segu saw them,
They drew up into battle array and charged.
Their arrows pierced the air,
185   The echo came whistling in answer.
Silâmaka and Poullôri sat leaning on their mounts,
As though listening to tuneful music,
And Silâmaka continued to smoke his pipe.
Their enemies shot so many times
190   That the powder made a cloud, blocking their sight,
A fog which masked them from their opponents.
But the wind blew, dispersed the cloud,
And the fighters were face to face.
Silâmaka and Poullôri went through the horsemen
195   Like a needle through cotton.
They tore the column, as a *pirogue*[5] parts the waters.
The horses of Segu panicked and ran together.
Silâmaka and Poullôri scattered them a first time
And then returned to the plain of Wougouba.
200   The horsemen reunited but could not control their mounts;
They fled to the village of Gandekorbo
And were forced out.
The Bambara piled up like flies in Kobikoboro;
Silâmaka and Poullôri winnowed them there.
205   They pursued them and flayed them
As far as the village named "Skinning."

---

5. A dugout canoe.

The horses of Segu fled to Kondo,
But the Fula followed after to thrash them
With their fish-bodied spears and their barbed arrows.
210 The horses of Segu hid in Nene,
But found no peace there.
They entered the village and got lost.
With difficulty they found their way,
They fled to Dierma, they fled to Temougou,
215 But nothing good awaited them there.
All night through they marched,
To the village of Goumougatchamare,
The village of defeats.
That is where Silâmaka and Poullôri defeated them,
220 Silâmaka who feared shame but not spearheads.
Poullôri killed thirteen and Silâmaka twenty-seven.
Only ten returned to Segu to bear the news to Da Monzon.

[They return and give the news. A warrior of Da Monzon, trained in
Fulbe warfare, rides against Silâmaka. On the first day he puts him to
flight by brandishing a tether, i.e., by threatening to beat him like a
slave. On the second day, Silâmaka seizes him and cuts off his head,
which he brings back to his sister. Meanwhile, Poullôri has defeated the
other riders. Da Monzon sends a thousand horsemen against Kekei.]

Silâmaka asked, "How many are there?"
His griots began to sing his praises.
225 Da Monzon has sent many horses.
Silâmaka, you are *Garba mama*,[6]
Segu has crossed the river
With large and agile horses;
Their number blackens the bush.
230 We ask God to watch over Kekei in the night,
For the daytime, we shall take over, we shall guard.
Segu has crossed Senokorbo.
Segu has crossed Gande Korbo.
Segu has crossed Kondomodi.
235 Segu has crossed Siromodi.
Segu has crossed Konotamamodi.
Segu has crossed Kuma Wedu.
Oh, Kuma, pond of lily pads,
Segu has crossed you too.
240 Where we used to collect the bulbs,
We find the heads of Segu's warriors.
Where the women would do the wash,
On the banks where the white clothes were spread,

---

6. The name of a tune.

245   Today we spread the fat flesh of the men of Segu
               On the banks of the pond of Kuma.

[The first force of Segu is defeated by Silâmaka and Poullôri. Da Monzon sends another army. Silâmaka anticipates the end and consults a diviner who foresees his death. Da Monzon fetches *marabouts* (Muslim holy men) who instruct him in the occult measures to take to defeat Silâmaka. Da Monzon takes the measures, which involve sacrificing a bull in a tree and entrusting a weapon to an albino boy. He then sends another army. Silâmaka sends Poullôri away to Hambodedio to inform him of their revolt.]

          When day came, the army of Segu had just reached Kekei.
          Silâmaka ordered his horse saddled as usual,
          He went out as he was used to go,
          He placed himself in the shade of the tamarind tree.
250   He faced Segu, he puffed on his pipe,
          Then he charged the enemy cavalry,
          Which he put to flight as usual.
          Then he came to rest under the tamarind tree.
          Then the horsemen of Segu wondered
255   Why the child hidden in the tree
          Had not fired at Silâmaka.
          All began examining the tamarind tree under which he was.
          The Fula understood there was something unusual.
          The child had indeed tried three times to shoot the arrow,
260   But fear paralysed him.
          Then Silâmaka raised his eyes.
          He saw the child, the child trembled.
          The arrow fell from his hands.
          It wounded Silâmaka.
265   It struck his hip.
          It pierced through to the saddle.
          The child fell like a ripe fruit.
          Soperekagne trampled his body.
          When the arrow touched Silâmaka,
270   The poison entered his veins.
          He felt dizzy
          But his horse raced for the village,
          As though it knew its master would die,
          So his body would not fall into enemy hands.
275   It carried him to the door of his compound.
          That is where the dying Silâmaka collapsed.
          The enemy horsemen, rejoicing, returned to Da Monzon in
               Segu.
          They told him, "Silâmaka is dead.
          "Macina is ours once again."

280   When Hambodedio had read the letter,
     And Poullôri had understood its content,
     He immediately took off for Kekei.
     He cried out, "My disgrace! Silâmaka goes
     "And will spend his first night without me in the other world."
285   When he arrived, he found the irreparable.
     He said, "Today, I have lost my master.
     "The one to whom I belonged,
     "But who never made me feel that I was his captive,
     "His whole life long—save for three times.
290   "The first came when we went to greet Djenne Vere at Borigo-
         ral.
     "Djenne Vere was a renowned hero,
     "Owner of many goods.
     "Silâmaka's greeting made him exuberant.
     "He bought boots worth fifty thousand cowries.
295   "He gave them to my master, who entrusted them to me.
     "I was going to try them on, but Silâmaka said,
     "'Don't stretch my boots!'
     "That day, Silâmaka showed me
     "That mine was not the small foot of a noble.
300   "The second time, we had gone to bathe,
     "And we saw arriving men of rank,
     "Before whom we must show modesty.
     "Silâmaka told me, 'Hide your sex with your hands,
     "'And fetch my clothes.' There again,
305   "He made me feel that I was a captive:
     "I had to expose myself, while he remained in the water.
     "And the third time is today.
     "Silâmaka knew he was to die.
     "He did not want me to witness his death,
310   "And sent me to Hambodedio.
     "He showed me that I am his captive,
     "He stopped me from sharing his fate."
     Da Monzon sent a thousand horses
     And ordered them to plunder Kekei.
315   Poullôri saddled his steed;
     He went to thank his master's family
     And to take leave of his relatives.
     He wept. He said, "It is time now
     "For me to join Silâmaka."
320   He took their two sons and mounted them with him,
     Silâmaka's son before, his own son behind.
     He took Silâmaka's enchanted spear.
     He charged the thousand horsemen of Segu,
     He divided them into two groups.
325   He pursued five hundred and five hundred pursued him.

Thus he was in the midst of the thousand horses.
This was at the time the sun was setting,
And night swallowed them all. No one ever learned
Where this procession disappeared.
330   Those thousand horses, in legend,
Rose to the sky with Poullôri.
And today, as clouds march by
As thunder strikes and the rains pelt down,
When lightning flashes and the echo answers,
335   The Bambara say, "There is Poullôri,
"Still chasing the horsemen of Segu."
Ardo Hambodedio went to Segu.
He begged Da Monzon, so that Macina
Would not be enslaved; the king agreed.
340   This is how the *Masinanke*[7] escaped their captivity
Under the empire of Segu.

---

7. The people of Macina.

16. The Epic of Silâmaka and Hambodedio
Narrated by Boubacar Tinguidji

Published by Christiane Seydou in Silâmaka et Poullôri *(Paris: Armand Colin, 1972), pp. 175-213. English version by Stephen Belcher. N.B. Seydou's published text incorporates elements from a second performance by Tinguidji; these elements are indented in what follows.*

BOUBACAR TINGUIDJI, THE PERFORMER, WAS A *MABO* from the region of Niamey; for much of his life he was the retainer of Mossi Gaïdou, a local chief, and he recalls those days as the proper manner for a *mabo* to live (see Seydou 1972 for his career). He accompanies himself on the *hoddu*, the four-stringed lute.

Sometimes incorporated into the longer account of Silâmaka's revolt (see the previous text), this epic tells the lighter story of his encounter with Hambodedio. This piece is representative of a wider genre of narratives concerning cattle-raiding confrontations between two heroes of substantial reputation, and is well represented in Macina and in the Futa Tooro. The following piece was performed by Boubacar Tinguidji as a piece separate from the fuller story. It presents virtually the same emotional range as the longer narrative, beginning with the pride and valor of the two heroes and ending with Poullôri's statements of outrage about Silâmaka's deception.

> Here is another story about Silâmaka, *ardo*[1] of Macina, and
>   Poullôri, *ardo* of Macina.
> Silâmaka's father had become old; he had no strength any
>   more.
> Poullôri had become Poullôri and Silâmaka, Silâmaka.
> They learned that a great war was about to start between
>   Macina and the people of Bandiagara.
> 5   Silâmaka set off, Poullôri set off.
> They mounted their horses.
> They dressed in light-colored clothes, they headed for Gun-
>   daka.
> They said they were going to put themselves under the protec-
>   tion of Hambodedio, Lord of Gundaka.
> "I want to entrust to you my father, the Lord of Macina, who is
>   very old.
> 10   "I am just the son of a village chieftain, not the son of a king.
> "I entrust my father to you."
> A war was about to start; they did not know if they could with-
>   stand it.
> A king is more powerful than all the village chiefs in the world
>   united.
> If he lost, in that war, Amiiru Gundaka would assist him.

---

1. Ruler.

15   If he didn't lose, no harm done, it would be to Amiiru's credit.
They straddled their horses in the first rains.
They talked to a *marabout*, asked him to divine for them at
    home.
This war about to start—how should they wage it that year?
The *marabout* consulted the table, and after a long moment de-
    clared that he couldn't see anything.
20   The only thing he saw was that this year, Macina would flee.
Every last man would die.
He couldn't see a single one of them standing up!
The dead and the fleeing—that was what he saw!
Poullôri slapped the *marabout*; he fell.
25   Poullôri said, "Rise and speak!" He got up.
He continued. "Speak. If you miss again, we will kill you."
The *marabout* said, "By God, if you must kill, kill me.
"I did not see a single one alive; everyone flees.
"Some die in the bush, others are killed in the village."
30   Silâmaka slapped the *marabout*, and he fell down again.
He said, "Look! You didn't examine all the squares.
"Look again, maybe you'll see."
He said, "And now, if you make a mistake, I'll send you where
    you'll make no more mistakes. You'll see where I take
    you."
That is what Poullôri said to him,
35   So spoke the slave.
He looked for a long time at his divining table.
He said, "That day,
"Poullôri and Ardo Silâmaka, I see you in the cemetery, I see
    you dead and buried."
Then they said, "That's what we wanted you to say.
40   "But us, fleeing with the others—that, you didn't see."
They got on their horses and left for Gundaka.
The road was long enough to dry out.
They arrived and found Hambodedio's herdsmen behind the
    village, a bit further. There were seven.
They said, "Hey, you, whose are those cows?"
45   The others, all seven, answered, "The cattle
"Of Hambodedio, Lord of Gundaka."
They went on, and when they arrived at Hambodedio's gate
    they called, "Peace be with you."
Hambodedio said, "And on you, peace.
"Oh, you strangers!
50   "Is it you they call Poullôri?" He said, "That's me."
"Is it you they call Silâmaka?" He said, "That's me."
Amiiru Gundaka asked, "Do you really come in peace?"
They said, "That is our only desire."

One of Hambodedio's slaves said, "Bah! Even if you hadn't said
'Salaam,'[2] we knew you came in peace.

55 "No one among you could come here and cause trouble.
"Whoever comes here to bring trouble, for sure, trouble comes
on him.
"Here, trouble is named Gundaka."
For slaves to talk that way
And Amiiru Gundaka didn't rebuke the slaves,

60 He didn't reprimand them—
That he did not rebuke or reprimand them—
That inflamed Silâmaka and inflamed Poullôri.
If your wife insults someone,
Or your child insults someone,

65   And you sit there laughing,
Without shutting them up,
Then you have insulted the person, not your wife or your child,
What a shame!
When the slaves told them they could not cause trouble, the
heart of Silâmaka leapt, the heart of Poullôri leapt.

70 They said, "We came filled with deference, but you have made
this deference a duty.
"Well, now you will learn that we can bring trouble.
"Doing evil is not hard; doing good is."
Silâmaka signaled Poullôri, and they went back without saying
a word to Amiiru Gundaka of what brought them.
The evening was cooling, the sun was about to set but hadn't
yet.

75 They went back to the herders
Who were guarding Amiiru Gundaka's cattle.
They went to Hambodedio's cattle;
There were seven herds,
Each of a hundred head.

80 They arrived and dismounted; they told Hambodedio's
herders, "Come here to us."
Of the seven herdsmen,
They killed five.
They cut off their heads.
They left two.

85 They took a spear.
They took the eye of one
And cut off one hand.
With the other, they cut off an ear
And cut off one hand.

90 To the two mutilated survivors,
They said, "You survivors,

---

2. Peace.

"Report to Amiiru Gundaka
"I, Silâmaka Ardo Macina,
"And I, Poullôri Ardo, we are here.
95   "Tell him we will spend the night here with his cattle!
"We are the evening visitors
"Whom his slaves insulted—
"And he didn't say a word—
"They said we couldn't cause any trouble.
100 "That's who we are.
"And that is why we have taken your eye and his hand.
"Tell him we are here and we won't move, we will go no
      further. We will wait for all of Gundaka, we will wait for
      him here.
"Tell him that he will not drink his cow's milk until the day he
      dies.
"We heard his slaves insult us and he laughed."
105 One left with one eye and one hand,
The other left with one ear and one hand,
To show themselves to Hambodedio.
They spent the night there, drinking their milk till dawn.
Amiiru Gundaka left in the early morning.
110 He set off with his horsemen,
A hundred horsemen; he reached them, he found Silâmaka and
      Poullôri.
These two rose, they pounced upon them.
They killed and they killed,
Until few were left
115 To reach Gundaka.
Only a few survivors reached Gundaka.
Silâmaka told Poullôri to collect all the cattle, as many as there
      were,
The cattle of the seven herdsmen,
And to take them away,
120 To go a bit further,
And to stay there with them.
He should make a big corral.
He should wait there with them.
And then Gundaka,
125 And even beyond Gundaka—
Up to ten villages—
If they found him there,
Himself, Silâmaka Ardo Macina,
They would have to kill him to get by "and reach you, Poullôri,
130 "I myself say this,
"If you see people come to you, then you will know,
"You can swear by the Book, that I am dead."

There was a young woman whom Silâmaka had courted. To-
gether they had flirted and talked since they were teen-
agers.
Her name was Bandado Abdoulaye,
135 Bandado Suleimana.
Silâmaka courted this woman,
Hambodedio courted this woman.
Hambodedio
Drove off Silâmaka Ardo Macina.
140 He married her.
The king of the land, he drove off Silâmaka and married the
woman.
Silâmaka courted her, but didn't get her.
Amiiru Gundaka married her.
She was in his house
And he still did not know
145 That Silâmaka had courted the young girl he had married.
As for Silâmaka, he was very touchy about the whole thing.
If a woman comes between two men, they'll never ever agree
again.
All the horsemen who came, Silâmaka slaughtered them.
All the horsemen who came, Silâmaka slaughtered them.
150 And that lasted
Seven days.
In the morning at dawn,
Poullôri would set off.
He brought milk where Silâmaka was.
155 Then he went back to the cows.
He was named Poullôri Benana, the slave who died without
being anyone's thing.
A pile of blue *bougue* cloth for him alone!
Let his neck bend beneath the weight of the *bougue* cloth!
A shelter of unshattering steel!
160 Gorbal
Ali Mansore! The most cunning of the cunning!
Katiel says, "Milk."
Poullôri answers, "Mildew!"
He would tear something,
165 To have God sew it up again.
He would dry something,
To make God wet it.
Poullôri said, "Two things can't stand a third.
"Generosity and war
170 "Cannot stand deliberation.
"If you deliberate
"Then generosity and war will be hindered."
So spoke Poullôri.

Amiiru Gundaka's *mabo* said,
175 "You want your cows, don't you, Amiiru Gundaka?" He said,
"I want them."
He asked, "You want them?" He said, "I want them."
He said, "If you want them, tomorrow I'll bring them. No need
for spear or gun; they will come tomorrow."
Amiiru Gundaka said, "You lie."
He said, "By God! They will come tomorrow—my lute and my
quality of *mabo* will bring them."
180 He said, "Go."
The next morning at dawn—
Amiiru Gundaka
Had not spent the night with Bandado Abdoulaye.
Bandado Abdoulaye had belts made of what you call coins:
185 Two
Of silver.
You go to jewelers.
They melt them.
They make a sort
190 Of rosary.
The two belts
Were hung over her bed.
She said, "Silâmaka was my suitor. He courted me when I was
young.
"He and the king were rivals for my hand.
195 "That king—I didn't love him. He held power.
"That's why he carried me off and married me
"So tomorrow at dawn—since Hambodedio won't spend the
night in my room—
"Take what hangs over the bed in my room,
"My two belts.
200 "Take down my two belts from above the bed: two belts of
silver.
"Take them down.
"Take a strip of cotton—"
Her head-scarf—
"Take it down and roll it up like a turban. I give it to you.
205 "Take the belts, carry them to Silâmaka Ardo Macina—
"You will find him in the bush.
"Ask him if he knows these belts—my belts—or not.
"If you show them to him, he'll give you the cattle and you will
come back.
210 "He will understand that none other than I send him those
belts;
"He will understand from them that you do come to him from
me.

177

"At any rate, if you don't take them, the cattle won't come
back. No spear will bring them back."
The *mabo* got up early, and at dawn he came.
The *mabo* went into Amiiru Gundaka's hut.
215 He stole the two belts
He stuck them in his pocket.
He left to find Silâmaka.
He followed the road alone, with his little lute, and soon he
arrived as though begging before Silâmaka Ardo Macina.
He greeted Silâmaka and he greeted Silâmaka.
220 "Dikko, did you have a good night? Dikko, did you have a
good night? The night was propitious for you! You are like
a fine winter season without growls or claps of thunder; you
are like a harvest without chaff or nettles. You will come
down
"Where there is no softness;
"Where it is otherwise
"You are not to be found.
"You have no bad luck, no unfortunate days, no ill-omened
times.
225 "Fortunate Lord of Macina!
"I call down peace on you.
"I am only a messenger; I did not come on my own account."
Silâmaka said to him, "Heh!
"Man, did you come to lie?"
230 He said, "By God! I did not lie! If I lied, cut my throat,
"Silâmaka."
He said, "Be careful. If you lied, I will cut your throat."
"By God," he said, "If I lied, cut my throat." So spoke the *mabo*.
He said, "I hear this past month that you have only been kil-
ling *mabos*.
235 "Don't you care for killing free men?"
He answered, "What! Come on!
"Who would kill you?
"You aren't worth the effort. Would one kill a dog?"
He came up to Silâmaka, bowed to him.
240 Silâmaka bent his legs
And sat down on his cloth.
The *mabo* said, "Well, I was sent."
Silâmaka asked, "Who sent you?
"Shouldn't I rather believe that you and Hambodedio agreed
that you would come here to mock me?"
245 He said, "Bandado Abdoulaye sent me,
"Hambodedio's wife."
Silâmaka said, "What did she say to you?"
"She told me to tell you that her neck hurts,
"That she drinks no milk,

250   "That her hair is falling out,
         "That she has no butter.
         "She will not take the butter from another man's cows; she will
             not take the milk of another man's cows.
         "The cows you took
         "Do not belong to her husband, they belong to her.
255   "Her father and mother brought them behind her; she brought
             them here.
         "And so these days she is ready to die!
         "She does not want Hambodedio's butter!
         "She does not want Hambodedio's milk!
         "Those are her cows you stole.
260   "She said, 'Can't you find someone other than me to rob?'"
         Silâmaka laughed.
         For sure, then, the cows would return to their pen. Of course!
         There are things one cannot resist!
         He said, "Hey, little dog!
265   "You're still lying. You have no proof."
         And he heaped abuse on the *mabo*.
         He said, "By God's will! Praise be to God! If you don't stop
             your lies, I'll kill you on the spot."
         The *mabo* answered, "Bandado Abdoulaye told me to show you
             proof.
         "If it's a lie you may kill me."
270   He put his hand in his pocket,
         He pulled out the two belts—
         They were of silver.
         Silâmaka had known them well, once upon a time
         When the world was sweet to him.
275   He said, "Bandado said that if you didn't know them, you
             should kill me, but if you knew them you would know the
             cows are hers."
         As soon as he showed them to Silâmaka, Silâmaka smiled.
         He said, "You know that when you go back Hambodedio will
             certainly kill you.
         "Here you are, involved in trickery."
         That is what he said to the *mabo*.
280   He said, "When you go back, tell
         "Bandado Abdoulaye
         "That cattle are not my affair, I don't want any cattle.
         "My cattle
         "Are at my spear point,
285   "Any man I see is mine, him and his cattle.
         "I came to pay my respects to him,
         "But a black does not appreciate respect.
         "I stopped at the gate of his house, Poullôri and I, we wanted to
             tell him that we were entrusting my father to him.

"He is very old.
290   "Nobody knows if he will win or lose.
"And when I greeted him, the slaves said to me,
"'Is it peace,
"'Or is it not peace?'
"And since I answered, 'Peace,'
295   "And his slaves insulted me, he should at least rebuke them.
"If he had rebuked them, I would have been satisfied, I would
      have said why I had come.
"His slaves offended me, and he laughed!
"He did not abuse them!
"He did not rebuke them!
300   "That is what angered me.
"So I will show him
"That anyone can cause trouble.
"That is why I have turned back, and why I tell him
"That anybody who wants can cause trouble.
305   "Evil is hardly as difficult as good.
"Anyway, as for his cattle, tell him that tomorrow morning,
      whenever he wants, he can come get them.
"For my part, I will stop this fighting.
"If he comes,
"I will give him
310   "The means.
"The cattle—
"There are seven hundred cows—
"I gave them to Poullôri Benana.
"He took them on,
315   "To the Tree of the Captives.
"Poullôri went on with them, he went ahead.
"Poullôri is far away.
"But Poullôri is mean, you know, and he doesn't think.
"If I don't go,
320   "The cattle won't return.
"He will think that I was killed.
"So let come to me,
"Hambodedio in person.
"Tell him that his cattle are over there, further on. I will give
      him a letter and he can go get his cattle. I didn't want cattle!
325   "I just came to make arrangements with him for my father, who
      is old."
The *mabo* went back to tell this to Hambodedio.
Hambodedio didn't know that the cattle were coming back
      because his wife's belts were gone!
He told the *mabo* he was a trickster, he said to him: "You're
      lying! You want me to go out there and be killed! All you
      do is plot!

"I know your trickery very well!"
330 The next morning at dawn,
Amiiru Gundaka went riding off with a hundred horsemen,
The *mabo* was the leader.
As he was leading them, the *mabo* said, "Come on!
"We'll have no trouble with Silâmaka."
335 Soon they came to the place where Silâmaka was.
Amiiru Gundaka stopped.
He said, "Come, let's go."
He stopped and waited until the *mabo* had reached
Silâmaka Ardo Macina. Silâmaka stood up; he wore only his
     cloth
340 And his pants,
He had no spear
Or staff.
He said, "You are permitted! Approach!"
He said, "I have called you.
345 "I am not a traitor.
"I will not betray your trust."
Amiiru Gundaka came near, they vied in greetings. When the
     greetings were at last ended,
Silâmaka said, "I don't need cows, but your slaves offended me,
     and you didn't answer them—because a slave is dear to
     you!
"You should have rebuked them a bit,
350 "Even if it annoyed you.
"If you had rebuked them, I would have calmed down.
"This is why I showed my anger. But I don't need your cows
     any more, I have no claim to your cows.
"I don't even want your cows.
"But Poullôri is further on there, with the cattle.
355 "I'll send one of my boys on,
"He will go ahead and tell him that we have come to terms.
"If he is informed, he will bring back the cows.
"If you went yourself, or one of your men, things would not
     work out.
"He who knows nothing is aggressive!
360 "So let me give you a spear, let me give you a messenger;
"You will go find Poullôri—
"He is my captive—
"You will tell him that I said to give you your cattle, that I per-
     mit it, that he should let you lead them back to their pen.
     They are a woman's cattle. I do not want cattle taken from a
     woman."
Hambodedio said, "No! Since you know, by God! that we
     agree, and since you are frank with me, I am content. A
     slave is merely a rope's end.

181

365 "Show him the rope, and that's enough for him!
  "You are the one that we fear."
  He said, "What, Poullôri?"
  Silâmaka said, "Take my offer." Hambodedio said, "No!"
  He said, "Silâmaka, since you have agreed,
370 "The one over there doesn't concern us.
  "Isn't Poullôri a slave? A slave means nothing to us."
  He said, "All right. I warned you, but have it your way.
  "Since you set no store by my warnings and call him a rope's
   end,
  "Take my spear and go your way."
375 Here is the drumbeat of Silâmaka Ardo Macina and Poullôri
   Ardo Macina!
  For the day they defeated Amiiru Gundaka and his men!
  These are the vultures devouring the bodies!
  It is that morning . . . Tinguidji plays that tune today!
  Silâmaka had told Poullôri,
380 "The day you see Hambodedio's men,
  "You will know that I have died.
  "They cannot pass unless they kill me. No horseman will come
   to you.
  "The day you see them, you will know that I am dead."
  Poullôri had a spear named "Gaping Wound."
385 Silâmaka had a spear named "Evil Doer."
  One had a horse named Golden Scarab.
  The other had a horse named Lethal Hoof.
  Hambodedio continued, walked, walked, walked.
  Poullôri, standing in the middle
390 Of the enclosure,
  He looked behind him, his head turned; he was named Poul-
   lôri, he was the slave who would die being no man's thing!
  A pile of blue *bougues* for him alone!
  His head bows beneath the weight of *bougue* cloth!
  Shelter of unshattering steel!
  Gorbal!
395 Ali Mansore! Most cunning of the cunning!
  Premier piper!
  God tears
  And he sews it up behind him.
  Poullôri makes dry,
400 God makes wet!
  He said, "Generosity and fighting can do without thought and
   advice.
  "To action! To deeds!"
  When Poullôri saw Amiiru Gundaka and his men come up,
  Coming to get the cattle,
405 With that spear held high,

He said, "God is great! A slave acts as a slave!
"Whatever a slave does will have no end.
"Silâmaka must have been killed, since they brandish his
    spear.
"No doubt they come to show me they have killed Silâmaka."
410   He opened the cattle pen.
He paid no more attention to the cattle.
He charged straight at the men of Gundaka and at Hambo-
    dedio.
Hambodedio
Brandished
415   Silâmaka's spear.
He said, "Listen! We did not kill him! It is he who sends us!
    Silâmaka sends us!"
The men who were coming—
The men of Gundaka—
Called out, "We don't come to fight!
420   "We don't come to fight!
"We have reached an agreement! We have made peace!"
Poullôri wasn't listening.
He was charging.
He was coming straight at them!
425   He reached them, he attacked them furiously!
Poullôri never dismounted.
He thrusts his spear and withdraws it.
Driving them like a herd,
He runs them on.
430   When they reached Silâmaka,
Of the two hundred horsemen,
Poullôri has vanquished a hundred and fifty, he has beaten
    them down.
Silâmaka cannot see them.
The fifty others manage to reach Silâmaka,
435   They stop exhausted.
Hambodedio's horse is running away, the rein is slack,
He doesn't check it.
Each man, reaching Silâmaka, leaps from his horse, falls to the
    ground,
Lets the horse run on, for the horses are runaways!
440   They drop!
Come what may!
Poullôri comes up, he reins in his horse suddenly before Silâ-
    maka.
He says, "Silâmaka, shame on you!
"This lie is your making! You said that if I saw people coming
    to me, you would be dead!
445   "You are not dead!

183

"You are alive, but now you will live a life of shame.

"You knew that if I saw your killer, he wouldn't have—this you
    knew—the time to tell me why he came."

Silâmaka answered, "By God! I warned them!"

Hambodedio said, "By God! You did! Everything happened as
    you said!"

450   Then he sent his men to get the cattle, to return them to Gun-
    daka.

That time, they understood at last.

That is how Silâmaka and Poullôri dealt with Hambodedio.

That is what I know. This is the end of their story.

17. The Epic of Samba Gueladio Diegui
Narrated by Pahel Mamadou Baila

English translation by Amadou Ly and Stephen Belcher from unpub. work of Amadou Ly. French translation by Amadou Ly, L'épopée de Samba Gué-ladiégui (Paris: Editions Nouvelles du Sud, I.F.A.N./U.N.E.S.C.O., 1991).

THE STORY OF SAMBA GUELADIO BELONGS TO THE FUTA TOORO, the Fulfulde-speaking area on the middle reaches of the Senegal River. Various dates have been proposed for the confrontation of Samba Gueladio and the uncle who usurped his place on the throne, and the most likely historical identification appears to be with a Samba Galadiegui who appears in French commercial records of the early eighteenth century. Some time later in the 1790s, an Islamic government, the Almamate, was established in the Futa Tooro. Samba's story is considered historical by some scholars, but we should note that it contains the classic pattern of the dragon slayer which goes back to Perseus and before, and that the same story is widely told of Hambodedio, a hero of Macina in Mali. Clearly, legend has gone to work on the historical material.

Samba Gueladio may have a claim to be the earliest recorded West African epic; in 1856, Commandant Anne Raffenel provided a lengthy prose version of the story, which has had a remarkable literary life. It is only relatively recently that Senegalese scholars have begun to record their oral traditions, and the following excerpts are taken from one of several recent versions.

[Pahel Mamadou Baila begins with the early ancestry of Samba, and the origin of the Deniyanke dynasty in the Futa Tooro. A noble named Tenguella asked the Malian emperor Sunjata for gifts and was given Sunjata's pregnant wife. She became the mother of Koli, known as Koli Tenguella, who led a migration from Mali into the Futa Tooro. Then he tells how Gueladiegui, father of Samba, was without children. His slave, Doungourou, performed a divination and identified the sort of woman his master should marry. But the child would be born after Gueladiegui's death. Gueladiegui assigned to Sewi Malal, his griot, the task of finding the woman, and eventually he did: Coumba Diorngal, a hunchback. She became pregnant and Gueladiegui died. His brother, Konko Boubou Moussa, succeeded him. He ordered that any of his brother's wives who was pregnant should be put to death, to avoid giving birth to a future king. Sewi Malal, the griot, tricked him by bloodying a cloth so that he thought Coumba Diorngal was menstruating. Coumba Diorngal gave birth, and Konko Boubou Moussa's daughter Rella (aged seven) discovered this.]

The baby whined; at the cry,
Rella came and leaned over them.
She said, "What! But you,
"You said no woman in this house was pregnant.
515 "But my aunt Coumba was certainly pregnant,

185

"And now she has given birth to a boy-child!
"I shall go and tell my father."
The *gawlo*[1] said to her,
"Well, go and tell your father!
520 "I know I am only a *gawlo*—
"You see, here is my instrument.
"But if you tell your father, and he kills this child, he will have
killed your brother!
"As for me, I will go to the court of some other king and pay
suit to some other noble who will grant me gifts.
"But if this child—your brother—grows up,
525 "And if one day he becomes king, then you can profit together
from his success.
"And if he becomes rich, then you can enjoy the wealth to-
gether,
"And if he becomes famous, he will owe his fame to you."
Rella said, "Yes, but I have a small condition,
"That you should give me your word"—
530 We in the East say *laayidu*,[2]
It is something extremely important for us,
Giving your word—
"Give me your word that you promise me that if he grows up
he shall have no other first wife than me,
"And that even though I am several years older than him,
535 "It is I he will make his first wife.
"I shall be his *diewo*."[3]
"Bah!" said Coumba Diorngal, "that isn't so hard.
"God willing, we swear by God, we swear this to you—
"If he grows up he shall have no other first wife than you!"
540 Then Rella said,
"Leave it in my hands,
"I will take care of it."
She went back to her father.
She said, "Father, you know, that man Sewi really has no idea
what a pregnant woman is!
545 "As it happens, my aunt Coumba Diorngal was pregnant!
"But she had a girl!"
Konko Boubou Moussa said, "What did you just tell me?" And
she said, "She had a girl."
He said, "Well! Go tear off a piece of cloth,
"And tie it to the baby
550 "In the name of your brother Samba Konko.
"Tell him he has found his future wife,
"That they are sort of engaged."
Rella tore off a piece of cloth,

---

1. Bard. 2. To swear. 3. Senior wife.

And she tied it to the child's wrist.
555 A week went by.
Konko Boubou Moussa kills ten times ten of all sorts of animals
for Samba's naming ceremony.
But instead of Samba, he called him Fatimata Gueladiegui,
Since Rella had told him he was a girl.
That is why he named him Fatimata Gueladiegui.
560 Gueladiegui had never had a child,
And since this was the first born to him, they called the child
Fatimata.
They dressed him in *belefete*,[4]
They pierced his ears and put gold in them,
They put bracelets on his wrist.
565 After that, Rella would carry him on her back all day long.
When she had carried him all day, until the evening, she
would bring him home to sleep,
Until the time he learned to walk and could accompany Rella.
Then they dressed him in *biftoje*[5] such as Rella wore.
They used to go have their hair plaited at a woman black-
smith's house;
570 She was named Thiedel the blacksmith.
She was their hairdresser.
When they came, Rella had planned things out.
She would lie down first and have her hair plaited.
After her, Samba would lie down in his turn.
575 While he was lying there, she would arrange the folds of his
biftoje.
When the job was done, they left and went off.
But Samba had no idea
Why he was wearing bracelets, or why his ears were pierced.
He thought it was simply an old Denianke custom.
So things went until he reached his seventh year.
580 One day they went off to have their hair done at the black-
smith's.
"Well," said the attendants on Samba son of Konko, "your be-
trothed is having her hair done at the blacksmith's house;
let's go there for a chat."
And the others agreed, "Let's go!"
When they got there, they found that Rella had finished having
her hair done and that Samba, in fact, was lying there.
They said, "We've come to talk with our fiancée."
585 Our fiancée? But since Rella was a young girl,
Samba thought that perhaps they were talking of Rella.
In old times, young warriors carried bows and arrows,

---

4. A short skirt. 5. A fancier skirt.

And it happened that Samba Konko had his bow and arrows
    with him.
A cat chased a mouse.
590   He drew the bow and struck the cat with an arrow, *fatt!*
The cat fell.
Meantime, the mouse had climbed up on a beam,
And from where Samba was lying having his hair plaited, the
    mouse was just overhead.
He said, "My brother, lend me your bow and arrows."
595   When Samba Konko hit the cat,
He said, "Enemy of the heir of Konko Boubou Moussa!"
He meant, 'Enemy to me, heir of Konko Boubou Moussa.'
He had extolled himself, he had praised himself.
Samba borrowed the bow and arrows from Samba Konko.
600   The mouse was right above his belly.
He hit it with an arrow and it fell on him.
He said, "Me too, enemy of the heir of Gueladiegui!"
They said, "What? You're saying that, but you're a girl!"
"It's a girl!" "It's a girl!" The questions filled his ears.
605   He rose and stood.
He said, "Who said I was a girl?"
He took his *biftoje* and broke the belt. He took his gift from God
    and showed it to Samba Konko.
He said, "Who told you I was a girl?"
The other said, "My father told me you were a girl."
610   He said, "Your father lied!
"I am no girl!
"Ah! That is why he gave me all this[6] and named me Fatimata
    Gueladiegui!
"Well! I strip off the braids that were made,
"And I will do my own hair.
615   "Yesterday I was named Fatimata Gueladiegui,
"Today I name myself Samba Gueladiegui,
"Samba Konko Boubou Moussa,
"Samba Gueladiegui Konko Boubou Moussa
"Samba Wouri Tjilmang Gadiaga,
620   "Samba Coumba Diorngal Ali Hamadi Bedinki."
He also named himself "Samba-among-the-bandits, Samba
    Lion's-tooth."
The hero is my Samba. The toads may croak as loud as they
    wish, they will not stop the elephant going down to the
    pond.

[He goes angrily to his mother and she explains that he was disguised
as a girl to save his life. He says that henceforth there will be no doubt

---

6. His ornaments.

about his manhood. Konko Boubou Moussa learns of the revelation and
sends people to see; Samba shoots the first man to look into the compound. Sewi the *gawlo* calms him down. Konko Boubou Moussa then
plans how to kill Samba, and it is decided that there shall be an accident at the circumcision ceremony. Sewi the *gawlo* forestalls this plot by
having a smith perform the circumcision at Samba's house. Samba goes
into retreat with the other boys. At the end of the retreat, in a mock
attack, Samba kills Hamadi Konko, a son of Konko Boubou Moussa.
Despite this tendency to violence, Samba is a good boy; he brings food
to an old woman, and she warns him that Konko Boubou Moussa is
preparing a magic dish; whoever eats the marrow bone in it will succeed him as king. The next day, at the meal, Samba seizes the bone
and eats it. On the following day, Konko Boubou Moussa divides his
wealth. Rella tells Samba that her father is doing this, and he asks for
his share.]

	Konko asked him, "Where were you?"
	He said, "I was sleeping."
	Konko said, "Well then, I give you sleep."
	He came back, told his mother, and his mother began to weep.
1045	He spoke to Doungourou, and Doungourou began to weep.
	He said, "Why are you weeping? My father has granted me sleep?
	"Well, if you are given something you become its master!
	"So tonight no one will sleep.
	"Let us go into the bush."
1050	They went into the bush and cut *kelli sticks*.
	After eight-thirty, whenever he found anyone in bed,
	He stripped off the bedclothes to bare his head,
	And putting his back into it, whacked him with the sticks.
	Doungourou and he did this throughout the town,
1055	And complaints rose up all around the town.
	People got up and came outside.
	They asked, "What? What does this mean?" and he answered them, "My father gave me sleep,
	"So I am master of sleep.
	"No one will sleep unless I allow it."
1060	His father called him and asked, "Why are you doing this?"

[Konko Boubou Moussa takes back sleep and offers Samba all things of
beauty; Samba immediately takes one of his wives, and Konko takes
this gift back. He gives Samba handfuls of gunpowder and bullets,
saying that is how his father became king. Samba says that he will
regret this gift. He marries Rella, and then he leaves. He has with him
his horse, Oumou Latouma, his mother, Doungourou, and Sewi. He
asks Sewi who furnished the magical protection to his father, and Sewi
tells him it was a jinn. Samba goes to the jinn, and obtains magical

protections from him, as well as a rifle named Boussi Larway, which never misses. He then kills the jinn, to prevent him giving such protection to anyone else. They then leave town.]

1325   They traveled all day, they traveled until evening time.
        A storm threatened.
        It was a bit before dusk; they slipped under a tree of the sort
            named *tialli*.
        This is when he gets the *Lagya*, his tune.
        Some, who do not know, call it *Lagya*,
1330   But *Lagya* isn't a name.
        When they had slipped under the tree—and at that time, they
            played the *Ana* for them—
        The *gawlo* women sang the song *Ana*, which is also called the
            Alamari!
        The *Alamari* was the tune for the Denianke.
        Those are the tunes that were played or sung for them.
1335   So when they had slipped under the tree,
        A green woodpecker—it's a bird with a long beak—
        Yes, the Wolof call it *toxxo*, and we Poular call it *lori*—
        This bird was at the top of the tree calling out the *Lagya*.
        "I made my nest in the *dieri*,[7] and I was rousted out.
1340   "I made my nest in the *waalo*,[8] and I was rousted out.
        "This time when I make my nest, I shall not be displaced."
        He also sang, "*Diala Waali Ndende*,
        "*Diala Waali Ndende*,
        "Between the Poure waters and the Manimani waters!
1345   "*Diala Waali!*
        "He who dares not cause trouble will not rule."
        The bird said that and played the tune.
        Samba had his staff, he was beating out the time on the tree.
        Sewi had fallen asleep.
1350   His mother had fallen asleep,
        And Sewi's mother had fallen asleep.
        He called out, "Father Sewi! Father Sewi!" His father Sewi
            answered, "Yes?" and he said, "Quick, wake up!"
        Sewi got up.
        Samba said, "Listen carefully to this."
1355   Sewi said, "I've listened carefully."
        He said, "Have you heard what is happening?"
        Sewi said, "I have heard."
        He asked, "Can you play that on your lute?"
        "Well," said Sewi, "I shall see, my Samba."
1360   Sewi stretched his strings and tuned them to the words of the
            bird

---

7. Rarely flooded land. 8. Floodplain.

Until he was able to play the tune.
Then Samba said, "Do you know it?" "I know it," he said.
"You can play it?" "Yes, I can play it."
Samba asked, "You know it?" He said, "I know it."
1365 Samba said, "Every task must have its wage.
"I offer the bird up to you."
Sewi said, "Now? In this night, my Samba?"
He said, "I'll bring it right down."
He touched his brow and said, "Enemy of the heir of Gueladie-
gui!"
1370 He fired a shot!
And the *lori* fell to earth.
Samba said, "Collect the blood and moisten the strings with it."
Sewi collected the blood and moistened the strings.
Samba said, "Well, I have just offered a sacrifice in your honor."

[He then says that he will return and kill Konko Boubou Moussa that
night. Sewi expresses some doubts. Konko Boubou Moussa is listening
to his *gawlo* name the great heroes; the *gawlo* does not name Samba, and
so Konko Boubou Moussa sings Samba's praises. He does so just as
Samba is creeping up on him, and so Samba refrains from killing him:
one may not kill someone who sings one's praises. He returns to Sewi.
They continue on their way. Samba leaves a half-*muid* [a measure] of
gold with the ruler of Tiyabu to take care of the two mothers, his own
and Sewi's, and continues with his retainers. In a clearing, he and Sewi
exchange wishes, and Samba then engages in a horse race with a Moor,
for which the stakes are the loser's life. The Moor loses. The Moor's
father acknowledges that his son was arrogant and hotheaded, and
gives Samba his daughter as wife; Samba eventually becomes restless,
mutilates his pregnant wife, burns her father's village, and goes on his
way. He comes to the land of El Bil Djikri and he and his retainers put
up with an old woman, Mint Hobere.]

She brought them water; the water was twelve months old.
It stank.
Samba leaned over the water to drink; the stench filled his nos-
trils and he threw the gourd away.
He said, "We asked you to bring water, and you have brought
us piss!"
1705 She said, "Alas, my son.
"You are doing me wrong!
"If we weren't just about to come on the time—
"Tomorrow we must give the king's daughter to the Crocodile.
"He will eat her and give us water—
1710 "You would have done me a great wrong!"
He said, "How is that?"

She said, "A crocodile lives there in our river; unless we adorn
    a princess every twelve months, and give her to him as
    food—
"And that is how we get our water; everyone takes enough for
    twelve months—
"Otherwise, we have no water, Samba."
1715   He said, "And this river right here?"
She said, "One cannot touch it!"
He said, "Doungourou, lead Oumou Latoma.
"Father Sewi, wait for us."
They put a halter on Oumou Latoma.
1720   They walked to the river.
When they came to the river—
Oumou Latoma couldn't drink unless her hocks were entirely
    in the water, and her belly touched the water.
Only then would she drink; otherwise, she would refuse to
    drink.
Doungourou led her into the water as far as she was accustomed
    to go—
1725   For we all have our habits,
And her habits had to be satisfied before she would drink.
She began to drink, *farak!* as horses do,
And already the *Caamaaba*[9] came out of the depths of the river,
And the whole river went up in flames.
1730   The *Caamaaba* came toward them.
Samba was behind the mare, Oumou Latoma.
Doungourou held her by the bridle.
Doungourou didn't blink.
Samba didn't blink.
1735   Oumou Latoma didn't blink.
When the *Caamaaba* was some five to ten meters from him,
Samba pulled out Boussi Larway.
He touched the middle of his forehead.
He said, "Enemy of the heir of Galadiegui!"
1740   He shot at the *Caamaaba.*
The bullet found that the *Caambaaba* wasn't fully protected.
The *Caamaaba* dove, but without its soul.
Already, Doungourou had closed his fist—
We say *womre,*
1745   The Whites say "fist"—
He struck the *Caamaaba* on the head,
And his hand went through to the water and withdrew.
He said, "My Samba, if I had known that you didn't even want
    me to kill it,
"When you told me to come, I wouldn't have come,

---

9. Here, a crocodile.

1750   "For you should have left this to me.
      "I am the *Diagaraf*,
      "I am he who gets angry and reigns,
      "I am he who gets angry and establishes reigns,
      "I am he who gets angry and dethrones.
1755   "I do not butcher,
      "Or trap,
      "Or hunt lizards.
      "I am *Doumbooy Daali*, Hunts-no-lizards."
      In Macina, they are called *maram marooji*.
1760   In the East, the lizard is called *maram mara*.
      We in the Futa call it *gunndo*.
      He said, "I do not butcher, or trap, or hunt lizards.
      "I am the one who has noble parents—
      "Meaning that noble parents give birth
1765   "And noble women carry children on their back,
      "But these are gift giving nobles; these are the women who
          carry me on their back and with whom I spend my child-
          hood."
      He really praised himself fully, did Doungourou, as he struck
          the head of the *Caamaaba* with his fist.
      They drew the *Caamaaba* up on the bank,
      And Samba cut off fifty centimeters of his tail.
1770   He took off one of his shoes
      And left it near the beast.
      They went back to the house.
      Oumou Latoma had been watered and groomed.
      They filled the old woman's calabash up to the rim with fresh
          water,
1775   And they brought it back to the Moorish woman. . . .
      The next morning, at dawn,
      The daughter of El Bil Djikri,
      Named Soueina,
      Soueina was adorned
1780   And covered with gold.
      "Your sister died in such and such a year, without fear;
      "Another sister died, in such and such a year, without fear,
      "We were given our water.
      "Your other sister died here. . . . All told, seven princesses.
1785   "And you, today.
      "And if you show no fear, we shall have water.
      "But if you run away,
      "The town will die of thirst!"
      They sang her praises, and she sang her own praises as well.
1790   She said, "When I get there today,
      "I shall give myself first to him,
      "And you shall know me for a king's daughter,

"For the daughter of a hero,
"As a descendant of Someone, son of Someone, son of Someone,
      going back to the Arabs."
1795 They came and were twenty meters from the river.
They saw, floating on the surface, the Crocodile.
"Ha!" they said, "Today,
"Today, he is impatient.
"Today, if you show no fear,
1800 "The people will have water early!
"In the past people had to wade into the water to their waist,
"Only then would he appear. But today he is already out!"
The young girl Souëina was so brave
That she leaped from her horse
1805 And walked to the Crocodile.
She came to him, climbed over him, and began to trample him.
Her clothes were stained with blood.
She came back and said, "That one is dead!"
Then all sorts of people like us sat up:
1810 "It was me, Someone son of Somebody!
"I came last night with the thought that a young Moorish
      woman like you
"Should not die in this way in front of everybody.
"I am the one who fought with him in the night,
"And I inflicted insults worse than death upon him,
1815 "So that you wouldn't die."
And everyone boasted about themselves.

[They inspect the carcass and notice the missing piece of tail and the
shoe. Mint Hobere suggests the hero might be her lodger; when they
try to wake Samba in Moorish fashion, however, by pinching him, the
attendants are killed. Finally he rises and is identified as the slayer of
the Crocodile. Samba asks El Bil Djikri for an army with which to re-
gain his kingdom. El Bil Djikry imposes some other tasks first. Samba
breaks a wild horse that no one could tame and is lost for a time in the
bush. The Moors enslave Doungourou and Sewi while Samba is gone.
When Samba and the horse emerge, the Moors quickly buy the silence
of Samba's retainers. He then battles various Moorish groups and finally encounters a great hero named Baayo, who has famous herds of cattle. At first Samba only takes a fraction of the herds, but El Bil Djikry
complains, and so Samba returns and kills Baayo. El Bil Djikry fulfills
his promise and gives Samba an army: enough horsemen so that the
procession, passing over three large logs, cuts through them. On the
way back Samba and Sewi encounter their mothers, who have been
evicted by the ruler of Tiyabu and are living in poverty in the bush.]

2250 Then Sewi sang, "Has-no-herdsman,
"Sire Gansiri Sawalamou Ndioubou Diom Koli Tenguella!

"Those who saw Samba leave in the morning will see him re-
turn
"Samba did not leave in vain, Samba has not labored for
nothing, Samba!
"The hero, the son of Gueladiegui!
2255 "Samba!
"Samba was best at the court of the Wali Counda, Samba was
the best at the court of El Bil Djikry!
"Samba goes with purebloods, and so does Oumou Latoma!
"So come out in the morning, admire the departure of Samba
Galadiegui, Samba who must be greeted as an equal!"
"My God!" said Tourou Tokossel, "Is it possible?
2260 "Oh, welcome! Beloved voice!"
Sewi's mother called out, "Coumba Diorngal?"
Coumba answered, "Yes?" She asked, "Did you hear Sewi's
voice?" She said, "Which Sewi?" She said, "Sewi my son!"
Coumba said, "What are you saying?" She said, "That voice I
heard,
"That voice—I bore it.
2265 "That voice is the voice of my Sewi!"
"Bah!" said Coumba Diorngal. "Let's try to sleep, all right?
"Do you imagine the Tounka would have treated us so badly,
"If he hadn't learned of Samba's death?
"Sleep!"
2270 The next morning,
Sewi said again, "Has-no-herdsman! Come out and admire the
departure of Samba Galadiegui-Konko Boubou Moussa!
"Let all who thought that Samba was dead learn that he is
alive!"
"Ah!" said Coumba Diorngal, "You were right!
"That is the voice of Sewi,
2275 "And Sewi sings for no one but Samba Galadiegui!"
After eight days, the vanguard of the purebloods
Broke into the clearing which they had come through.
Sewi had forgotten it!
But Samba was a prince
2280 And a hero: he forgot nothing.
He said, "Father Sewi?
"Do you remember this clearing?"
"Ah," said Sewi, "I have forgotten, my Samba."
He said, "When we were coming here, me alone with you and
Doungourou and our three horses,
2285 "And today we lead five thousand purebloods—
"Not counting the goats, the sheep, and the cattle,
"When we came through here, what did you tell me about this
clearing?"

Sewi said, "I said, about this clearing, that I would be happy if
    it were full of cattle, of goats, and of sheep that someone
    was giving me."
Of each sort, Samba selected some:
2290   A flock of goats,
A flock of sheep,
A herd of cattle,
And even a herd of horses.
He said, "This, Sewi, is a gift to you.
2295   "But what I wished for,
"God has not granted me here.
"I wished for someone to try to compete with me!
"What you asked for, God has granted you. But what I wanted
    God has not granted."
The next morning they went on
2300   Until they found Tourou standing in the middle of the road.
She said, "You have no reason to sing your praises,
"You have no cause for pride!
"It is now two years, two months, and ten days
"That we have been living next to an anthill."
2305   Samba, on Oumou Latoma, faltered and fell to the earth.
Pieces and pieces of cloth—
They took a hundred to make tents.
We call them *gidwar*, some say "tent."
They were comforted warmly; Samba asked his mother's for-
    giveness,
2310   And he asked forgiveness from the mother of Sewi,
Saying, "Mother, I am the cause of this,
"Please accept my apologies and forgive me."
They stayed there for eight days.
Meat was cooked for them, and they ate it.
2315   They were washed, with good water.
They were given milk to drink.
They were rubbed and consoled for all the troubles they had
    suffered, which were completely erased.
They put soft pillows on camels for them.

[They come to Tiyabu and are told by the townspeople that their mothers have died. Samba punishes the town by demanding, as tribute, a
pile of cloth as tall as he can reach while standing on Oumou Latoma's
back. The *Tounka* of Tiyabu dies of his punishment. While his army is
crossing the river, Samba shoots a hero, Boisigui. On the other side, he
gathers allies for the battle with Konko Boubou Moussa. The night before the battle, Samba rides into the enemy camp to sleep with Rella,
his wife. His presence is discovered, but Konko Boubou forbids any
action against him. The next day comes the battle.]

In Poular, a proverb says that if your father cleared an acre, you
should clear a furlong more.
That is true.
Do you know there are three sorts of sons?
"You aren't worth your father,"
2535   "You're as good as your father,"
And "You are worth more than your father."
"You're worth more than your father,"
That's a good state to be in, but it's not nice to hear "You are
worth more than your father."
"You're as good as your father," that is a good state,
2540   And it's nice to hear it said:
"You're as good as your father."
"You aren't worth your father"—
That's not a good state, and it's not nice to hear.
So Samba had three forms of protection:
2545   The protections of his father,
The ones he had gotten himself,
And those he had snatched from the hands of the heroes killed
by him, Samba Gueladio, Samba Konko Boubou Moussa,
Samba Coumba Diorngal Ali Hamadi Bedinki,
Samba-among-the-bandits, Samba Lion's-tooth, Samba the hero,
my hero,
Grandson of Birama Ali and Dianga Ali and Bira Mbaba
Ndiouga Dianga Youman Bele. . . .

[They come to fight on the field of Bilbassi. Over several days there is a
series of single combats].

Sewi called: "Has-no-herdsman! Courage! Courage!"
2650   He said, "Cheer him! Cheer him!"
He said, "The master of the town has met his equal.
"You can tell! Samba has met Mawndo Gali Coumba Kagnina!"
Samba slew Fouybotako Ali Maham Daouda Mbarya Sokoum
Ya Allah
At Bilbassi.
2655   As he advanced on Fouybotako,
Samba said, "Ford the pond at Gawdoule!"
Fouybotako said, "I will not ford the pond at Gawdoule!
"My clothes are white,
"My rifle stock is of white *dabadji* wood,
2660   "My thoroughbred has a white coat.
"If I dipped into the pond at Gawdoule,
"You might wash them, but they would not be clean.
"You might perfume them, but they would stink.

197

      "People would ask me, 'What happened to you?' and I would
          answer, 'I was running away from Little-Samba-won't-
          rule.'"

2665   He tied his pants legs together.
       Samba fired a shot at him—*karaw*!
       And said, "I've killed a Mbegnoughanna!"
       That was Fouybotako Ali Maham Daouda Mbarya Sokoum Ya
          Allah.
       Samba killed him at Bilbassi.
2670   He gave no work to the washers,
       He did not wear out the mourners;
       The fish carried him off.
       Samba fought with Sam Maïram Molo Baroga, who might have
          trouble with the beauties but always makes a day of deeds.
       They met in a deadly duel.
2675   Samba killed him.
       He fell at Bilbassi.
       He didn't tire out the mourners or the washers; the fish carried
          him away.
       Samba did the same with Biram Gaal Segara Ali Mousse.
       He was so tough that when he went into battle he would only
          take a single bullet.
2680   He would say, "When I've killed someone, I'll take his bullets
          and powder."
       That's the sort of man Biram Gaal was.
       Samba met him in deadly duel, and fired a shot at him—*tall*!
       Biram fell, without his soul.
       Samba slew him at Bilbassi.
2685   He didn't tire out the mourners or the washers, the fish carried
          him away. . . .

[Samba continues his deeds. The battle ends on the seventh day.]

       Samba advanced on his father,
2760   Konko Boubou Moussa.
       He chased him into a pumpkin field.
       He shot at a pumpkin.
       The pumpkin flew into the air and landed on the father's head.
       Samba said, "I shall not kill you, but with that squash.
2765   "I've given you a green pumpkin hat."

[Samba becomes king and kills Konko Boubou Moussa's children—except for his own wife, Rella—and grandchildren to establish his own
position. Samba rules for ten years, plundering his neighbours; Konko
Boubou Moussa lives on by begging. Samba moves into the Fulbe
kingdom of Bondou and lives there for a time; Sewi and Rella, traveling, are captured by Moors from the northeast. Samba eventually res-

cues them. There are other minor adventures. Finally, Samba dies as
the jinn had foretold, from eating a forbidden food. And there is a story
that a man who threw a stone onto his tomb later died. Even in death,
Samba is terrible.]

Wolof Epics

THE WOLOF CONSTITUTE THE LARGEST ETHNIC GROUP IN SENEGAL, with nearly forty percent of the population. Their history is rooted in the Jolof empire, which flourished from approximately the twelfth century to the sixteenth century and covered much of what is known as modern Senegal on the western coast of West Africa. Jolof was heavily involved in trade beween the Moors of Mauritania to the north and the Mali empire to the south and east. With the arrival of the Portuguese in the mid-fifteenth century, Jolof began to decline, a process that led to the independence of successor states Baol (Bawol), Walo (Waalo), Kayor (Kajoor, Cayor), Sine (Siin), Ñaani, and Wuli (Woulli) in the sixteenth and seventeenth centuries. Kayor became the strongest of these new states, dominating a coastal strip of land from the Senegal River in the north to Rufisque in the south. These states experienced internal conflicts, wars between each other as well as against other states farther east, and resistance against the French, who conquered the region in the latter half of the nineteenth century.

The oral memory of that tumultuous past remains quite vivid today, especially the events of the nineteenth century. Jacques François Roger's *Fables sénégalaises recuéillies de l'ouolof* (Paris: 1828), Jean Baptiste Bérenger-Féraud's *Recuéil de contes populaires de la Sénégambie* (Paris: Leroux, 1885), and Victor-François Equilbecq's *Contes populaires d'Afrique occidentale* (Paris: Maisonneuve et Larose, 1913) are among the early collections by Europeans. By the twentieth century, the Senegalese were beginning to record their own oral tradition, especially the veterinarian Birago Diop (published as *Les Contes d'Amadou Koumba* [Paris: Présence Africaine, 1961], in English as *The Tales of Amadou Koumba*, trans. Dorothy Blair [London: Oxford, 1966]). But it is not until relatively recently that scholars have managed to record, transcribe, translate, and publish major examples of the Wolof epic tradition.

The two texts that follow convey interpretations of the founding of the Walo kingdom and the last days of resistance of the Kayor state at the end of the nineteenth century. The richness of these texts, and in particular the many episodes of Kayor from which *The Epic of Lat Dior* is taken, suggest that we have much more to learn about the Wolof epic from the other states that developed after the fall of Jolof.

18. The Epic of Njaajaan Njaay
Narrated by Sèq Ñan

Recorded in six sessions starting January 12, 1990, in Rosso, Senegal, by Samba Diop. Transcribed and translated into English by Samba Diop. Edited by Samba Diop and published in The Oral History and Literature of the Wolof People of Waalo, Northern Senegal: The Master of the Word (Griot) in the Wolof Tradition *by Mellen Press, Lewiston, 1995. This excerpt edited by Thomas A. Hale.*

THE HISTORY OF THE WOLOF PEOPLE of Senegal is marked by the rise and fall of several empires, kingdoms, and states. Waalo, based at the mouth of the Senegal River, developed rapidly in the seventeenth century as the result of the slave trade. Many European countries vied for control of the region, but the French and the British were the principal competitors. By the late eighteenth century, the French had outlasted the English and gained a trade monopoly in the area that served as the foundation for the nineteenth-century colonial conquest of Senegal.

This 975-line epic about the founding of the Waalo empire was recorded in Wolof by the Senegalese scholar Samba Diop from the griot or *guewel* Sèq Ñan during a series of sessions beginning on January 12, 1990. Diop also translated the epic into English. A retired veteran and truck driver of *guewel* origin, Ñan lived in Xuma, a village fifteen kilometers east of the town of Richard-Toll, 150 kilometers upriver from Saint-Louis near the mouth of the river. The recording took place in the home of Mapaté Diop, the father of Samba Diop, in Rosso, Senegal, a town on the left bank of the Senegal River just east of Richard-Toll. The audience was composed of Mr. Diop and his son Samba, two other men, and occasional visitors who dropped in from time to time. According to Samba Diop, Sèq Ñan sometimes stopped the narrative to play the *xalam*, a five-stringed lute, eat meals, drink tea, and pray during recording sessions that lasted from 5 p.m. to midnight on the first day and from 10 a.m. to 5 p.m. the next day (Diop, 33-34).

As with any epic, the genealogy of the hero is particularly important. At the outset the narrator traces Njaajan Njaay's heritage back to a past that has echoes from Islam, Judaism, and Christianity. These excerpts also emphasize the role of the hero in creating both political and family relationships with other peoples in the surrounding region, from the Serer to the Peul. Finally, the *guewel's* narrative refers often to the importance of transmission of knowledge from father to son.

Tradition says that,
75   One day,
   Noah fell asleep;
   Ham the eldest son was laughing.
   Sham asked him:
   "Why are you laughing?
80   "Are you laughing about our father?"
   Right at that moment,

Noah woke up.
Noah said:
"From today on,
85   "You,
"Ham!
"You will be the precursor of the black race.
"You,
"Sham!
90   "You will beget all white people."
Thus Sham begot two persons called Yajojo and Majojo.
Ham begot a son called Anfésédé.
Anfésédé addressed Ham his father in these terms:
"Noah is my grandfather,
95   "You are my father.
"I am asking for your grace to fall upon me."
Anfésédé himself begot a son called Misrae.
Misrae himself is the founder
Of a town called Misrae.
100   Ham also begot two black children:
One male and one female.
One day, Ham went into exile.
He arrived at the shores of the River Nile
When he went into exile,
105   Ham said to his wife:
"These two children are not mine."
The wife replied: "What? You are the father.
"Remember that it takes two people
"To make a child: me and you."
110   Ham went into exile.
That was the beginning of the black race.
Thus, Ham went into exile.

115   Ham's children grew up.
They became very strong.
They didn't know their father.
They asked their mother:
"Mother, where is our father?"
120   The mother replied:
"I don't know where your father is."
The two children left in their turn.
They journeyed for many many months
Until they arrived at the banks of the River Nile.
125   There they met Ham.
The latter asked them:
"Where are you going?"
They answered: "We are looking for our father."
Ham said: "What is your father's name?"

130   They replied: "Our father's name is Ham;
        "We were told that Noah is Ham's father;
        "Noah is then our grandfather.
        "We were also told that
        "Our father went into exile;
135   "He went to exile just after our birth.
        "Now we are fully grown up.
        "That's why we are journeying;
        "We want to find him."
        Ham replied:
140   "The man you have in front of you is your father.
        "I am Ham."
        Ham created a settlement on the banks of the Nile.
        The settlement was called Nobara.

[A descendant of Ham named Bubakar Umar, father of the hero, along
with a retainer named Mbaarik Bô, migrated first to the Ghana Empire
and then to the Waalo Kingdom in the lower Senegal River of northern
Senegal.]

        They arrived in the River Senegal area,
        More precisely, up the river.
        There, they found Abraham Sal;
        They converted Abraham to Islam.
270   Abraham thought that Bubakar was Bilal.
        Bilal himself was the companion of the prophet Muhammad;
        (Peace upon him)
        That's why Abraham didn't fight Bubakar.
        Abraham Sal is the ancestor
275   Of all the people bearing the name Sal.
        Among the Lamtoro, the Tukulor people.
        Thus, Bubakar was the one
        Who converted Abraham to Islam.
        Abraham begot Fatumata Abraham Sal.
280   Fatumata was Abraham's daughter.
        Her father gave her in marriage to Bubakar.
        She became Bubakar's wife.
        Thus, Bubakar converted the Serere people.

[But some leaders were reluctant to convert.]

        Bubakar called on Hamar-the-scolder-of-old-people.
300   He said to him: "Come here!
        "I am going to shave your head;
        "I am going to convert you to Islam."
        "Hamar-the-scolder-of-old-people replied:
        "Can you let me go to the outhouse first?"

203

305   Bubakar said:
       "Yes, you can."
       Hamar-the-scolder-of-old-people did not enter the outhouse.
       He went behind a nearby tree.
       His bow and quiver were hanging there
310   With many arrows inside.
       He took the bow;
       He adjusted an arrow;
       He then hit Bubakar on the forearm.
       The latter quivered, quivered, and quivered;
315   He was in pain.
       He went to his wife Fatumata and told her:

       I am going to die,
       As a result of the wound
330   Caused by Hamar-the-scolder-of-old-people.
       The arrow is poisoned;
       I don't want to die here.
       I want to die back East where I am from.
       I am going back East

[Bubakar then leaves his wife.]

345   At that time, Fatumata was pregnant with Njaajaan Njaay,
       His given first name was Muhamadu;
       It wasn't Njaajaan.
       A few days later Bubakar left the village.
       He headed back East to his native homeland.
350   He didn't make it back east;

355   He died halfway through his journey.

[His son, the hero, then accomplishes what his father failed to do.]

       Muhamadu, Njaajaan was born.
380   When he was eleven,
       He fought Hamar-the-scolder-of-old-people
       In a very celebrated combat;
       Njaajaan smote him with his swift hand behind the ear;
       He smashed both jaws killing him instantly.

[But the hero continues to enjoy a normal childhood, playing with other children, until his mother remarries his father's retainer, Mbaarik Bô. Njaajaan Njaay's friends make fun of him for this reason.]

450   Njaajaan Njaay was playing in the river.
       He was with his young friends.

They were splashing water on each other;
They were running after each other.
On the bank of the river.
455 The playmates started teasing him;
They said to him:
"Oh! Poor boy!
"Your mother couldn't find any man to marry;
"That's why she fell back on the man
460 "Who accompanied your father.
"What a shame!"

[Njaajaan Njaay becomes so upset by this taunting that he leaves home, goes into the river and becomes a water spirit. He reenters the human world when he finds children fighting over fish. He demonstrates his wisdom, kindness, and concern for others by helping resolve the dispute over the fish.]

580 After seven days and three days,
He came out of the river.
In those days in Waalo,
The children went fishing in the river.
When one caught a fish,
585 He would throw it several feet away from the bank.
In those days,
They had not yet learned the technique
Of taking a rope,
Of running it through the gills of each fish,
590 Of linking all the fish onto a single rope.
After they finished fishing, they would gather the fish;
They would start fighting.
For no one would recognize his fish.
One would say: "This is my fish";
595 Another would say: "No;
"It's not your fish,
"It's mine."
They would keep quarreling and fighting.
When Njaajaan saw the children quarreling,
600 He came out of the river.
He walked toward them.
When the children saw him,
They were scared.
They started running away.
605 He raised his hand;
He signaled them to stop.
He reassured them that
He wouldn't do them any harm.
When the children stopped,

610   Njaajaan came.
He took all the fish;
He divided them in equal piles.
After that, he took a rope.
He ran it through the gills of the fish of one pile;
615   He then put it down.
He did so until all the piles were done.
My father told me that
He would look straight into the eyes of one child;
He then would point to a pile;
620   The child would grasp the rope,
The rope from which the fish were dangling.
He would then walk away.
He would do so
Until all the children had their fish
625   And peacefully walked home.
For three days.
He divided the fish in this manner.
He did so after the children had finished fishing.
If you add the three days to the previous three,
630   You come to a total of six days.
The older people were amazed at the children's behavior.
They asked: "Well! Whenever you went fishing,
"You used to quarrel and fight about the catch.
"Now, you come back here in peace,
635   "Each one holding an equal amount of fish.
"What's happening?"
The children answered in unison:
"There is a man who comes out of the river.
"He equally divides the fish among us.
640   "He has been doing so for the past three days.
"He has hair all over his body,
"Except on his palms and around his eyes."
The older people held a council.
One of them said:
645   "We are going to set a trap;
"We should catch that man;
"We want to know more about him.
"Some of you are going to take reeds.
"Get them from the river bank.
650   "Then make a round fence near the fishing place.
"When he comes to divide the fish among the children,
"You should step inside the fence.
"He will certainly follow you.
"If he is a noble man,
655   "He will not jump over the fence
"Once he steps inside it."

A few strong men were chosen to do the job.
After setting up the fence,
They hid behind a nearby tree.
660   After the children caught some fish,
They went inside the round fence;
Then they started quarreling.
Njaajaan was watching them.
After a while,
665   He stepped inside the fence.
He calmed the children down.
He then proceeded to divide the fish.
He wanted to divide them equally among the children.
After he finished,
670   He was walking back to the exit door.
At that moment, a gang of men jumped on him;
They immobilized him.
After that,
The old people were called to see the prisoner.
675   My father told me that
Njaajaan had killed three men among
Those who were trying to catch him.
He was a very strong man;
He had supernatural powers.
680   After they caught him,
They tied his hands behind his back.
A man of the Council of the Elders asked him:
"What's your name?"
Njaajaan didn't answer;
685   He was silent.

Maramu Gaaya came to the council and said:
"If you give me this man,
"I'll take him to the kitchen.
"If you give me two stones,
705   "A cauldron,
"Some flour,
"Water,
"And fire,
"I'll make him talk."
710   What Maramu asked for was given to him.
Njaajaan sat on a low stool;
He was staring at Maramu.
Maramu mixed the water and the flour;
After he finished the mixing,
He took the two big stones;
He then put them half a foot apart.
720   He then lit the logs

207

In order to make a cooking fire.
He then took the cauldron;
He filled it with water;
He then put it on the two stones.
725   But as soon as he put the cauldron down,
It fell and the water spilled out.
He started again;
He filled the cauldron with water;
He then put it on the two stones;
730   But the cauldron fell on the ground;
The water splashed all around.
Njaajaan was very hungry.
He said to Maramu in Peul:
"You need three stones,
735   "Not two,
"In order to hold the cauldron straight above the fire."
Maramu replied:
"Oh, really?"

[After several other incidents in which Njaajaan Njaay offers advice to Maramu, the "cook" announces the news.]

Maramu Gaye left the kitchen.
He ran out;
775   He called the people and said:
"My dear villagers, come here;
"Come and witness the man speaking."

[The discovery that the strange mute can speak prompts the elders of Waalo to seek advice from the King of the Serere, who advises that they should make Njaajaan Njaay chief of the army and ruler. Njaajaan later rediscovers a long lost younger brother named Mbarak, whom he designates as his successor. Njaajaan Njaay establishes a democratic government and expands his influence over the region.]

When the white Europeans came here long ago
895   They found here, in Waalo,
A true model of government,
A democracy.
They also found here a well-organized
And very efficient army headed by the Mbarak.
900   Njaajaan was the first Mbarak:
He was the first chief of the army.
Njaajaan begot Gèt Njaajaan,
Saré Njaajaan,
Dombur Njaajaan,
905   Nafaye Njaajaan,

Fukili Njaajaan.
All in all,
He had five children.
Fukili went to the Saalum region.
910   Njaajaan left Gèt in Tundu Gèt
On his way to Jolof.
When he arrived in Warxox,
His horse was very tired,
That's why he named the place Xoox.
915   He named the place Xoox.
After that,
Njaajaan arrived in Yang-Yang.
He got there at sundown,
At the time darkness was covering the land.
920   There,
He was given in marriage a Peul woman called Këyfa.
They spent the night together.
At the break of dawn,
Njaajaan left the room.
925   He left Këyfa and Yang-Yang.
He really did not want to have her as a wife.
But Këyfa was pregnant.
She is the ancestor of all the Peul people
Who bear the name Njaay.

Njaajaan had been chief of the army for sixteen years in Waalo
Before he was transferred to Jolof.
945   Before he came to the Waalo region,
The Waalo Empire had been in existence
For four hundred and thirty years, before Njaajaan came into
        existence

950   There,
In Jolof,
He begot Biram Njèmé, Kumba, and Albury Njaay.
Albury was later going to be ruler of the Jolof kingdom;
But when Njaajaan got to Jolof,
955   It was unsettled.
There was no authority,
No chiefdom,
No kingdom,
960   Njaajaan installed authority in Jolof.
In the same order of things,
The region of Bawol,
Of Kayor,
Jolof and Siin were part of the Waalo Empire.

965   That empire covered a vast area going from Ganaar to Casa-
          mance.
        This is how the story of Njaajaan Njaay
        Was handed down to me
        By my father and my ancestors.
        This is also how I learned the traditions,
970   Customs,
        Events,
        And history of the Waalo Empire.
        This is exactly
        How my father narrated to me
975   The story of Njaajaan Njaay.

19. The Epic of Lat Dior
Narrated by Bassirou Mbaye

Recorded in 1985 in Sakh, Senegal, by Bassirou Dieng. Transcribed and translated into French by Bassirou Dieng. Edited by Bassirou Dieng and published in L'épopée du Kajoor by Editions Khoudia in Dakar in 1993. This excerpt edited and translated into English by Thomas A. Hale.

LAT DIOR DIOP (1842-1886), ONE OF THE MOST FAMOUS HEROES of Senegal, was the last great *damel*, or ruler, of the Wolof kingdom of Kayor in the northwest part of the country. He died in battle during the final French drive to conquer Senegal. He is viewed as the hero who incarnated both traditional values and the newer beliefs of Islam at a time of great change. The Senegalese government has designated him as a national hero for his resistance against the French conquest of Senegal. After the breakup of the Jolof empire in the sixteenth century, Kayor, Baol, Sine, and Saloum developed as smaller states in the area near the frontier between the Arab-Berber cultures north of the Senegal River and the black African cultures in Senegal. Each maintained its own identity until the French conquest.

A French commercial presence in the region dates back to the seventeenth century, although it was only in the nineteenth century that French colonial expansion began to impact more directly on these kingdoms. But the story of the conflict between Lat Dior and the French is rooted in a rather complex family history that reflects the importance of women in the Wolof political system. Birima Ngoné Latir, son of a woman of royal origin and a man named Makodou, ruled Kayor from 1855 to 1859. He and the French administration in Saint-Louis, the colony's capital located on an island at the mouth of the Senegal River, signed the first of several agreements for the construction of a railroad that would link Saint-Louis with Dakar, a growing port 300 kilometers to the south. After Birima Ngoné Latir's death, his father, Ten Makodou, was elected ruler of Kayor against the opposition of those who preferred Lat Dior, a son of Ngoné Latir and another man. Lat Dior withdrew from the political arena to build a powerful army. In the meantime, Makodu renewed the railroad construction treaty, violated it at one point, and came into conflict with the French at the battle of Mekhé. He was defeated by the invaders, who replaced him on the throne of Kayor with Madiodio and a resident French supervisor in 1861.

At this point Lat Dior reasserted his claim to the kingship by unseating Madiodio in 1862 and forcing the French to recognize him as the Damel. They responded by driving him into exile in 1864. He retreated south to the Saloum region where a Muslim leader, Maba Diakhou Ba, was fighting both the French and other non-Muslim peoples in the area. It was during his stay there that Lat Dior converted to Islam, a process that included circumcision. He and Maba then mounted a fierce campaign of resistance against the French and forced them to retreat at the battle of Pathébadiane in 1865. Maba was killed in 1867

211

and Lat Dior retreated to Kayor. With new Muslim allies he defeated the French at Mekhé in 1869 but then had to retreat after a split with his closest ally. He reached an agreement with the French in 1871 and reassumed the kingship of Kayor. In 1874, he was defeated by his former allies and then joined the French and a Jolof ally, Albury, to defeat Alhajj Umar Tal, leader of the Tukulor empire. Two years later, Lat Dior expanded his kingdom to include Baol, a neighbor to the south of Kayor. When construction began in 1883 on the long-planned Saint-Louis-Dakar railroad, a project that would cut through Kayor, Lat Dior scrapped earlier agreements, fought the French, and then retreated. He was killed in battle in 1886 by the French and their allies, including some of his former supporters, at a place called Dékhelé.

The Wolof epic that includes the story of Lat Dior differs from the earlier forms in several ways. Instead of the sweeping history of a single hero who marks a turning point in history (for example, Son-Jara), *The Wolof Epic of Kayor*, collected from two griots and edited by Bassirou Dieng, is composed of a series of episodes that cover four centuries and the major political developments of this long period. Each episode focusses on a particular ruler and his effort to solve a political, institutional, or social crisis. Power in the region was originally based on ownership of land as well as the concept of the master hunter, a source of both magic and military strength. Kayor came into being as the result of the merger of these two notions. But the growth of Islam in the region and the impact of European colonization led to the destabilization and eventual collapse of the Kayor kingdom.

This 1074-line version of *The Epic of Lat Dior* was recounted in Wolof by Bassirou Mbaye, a thirty-five-year old royal *guewel* of Kayor, in 1985 at Sakh, a small village two miles from Mboul, a town that was the capital of the kingdom. Mboul is approximately halfway beween the cities of Thiès and Louga in eastern Senegal. In the larger *Epic of Kayor* it appears as text number twelve of a series of thirteen that, collectively, tell the story of the Kayor Kingdom from the early sixteenth to the late nineteenth centuries. Given the importance of the maternal lineage in the transfer of power from one generation to the next, it is not unusual that Lat Dior is often referred to as the child of his mother, Ngoné Latir. In the text the original spellings of names and places from the French translation are maintained.

       The son of Ngoné Latir,
       We lost him in order to become solders for the Whites.
       We lost him in order to pay taxes to the Whites.
       Ngoné Latir, his mother,
5   Commanded in the battle of Ngangaram for her father, the
         Damel Maysa Tend.
       It is the mother of Birima Ngoné Latir and of Khourédia Mbodj.
       She fought for her father, the Damel Maysa Tend,

The master of cavalrymen Darnde, Goreel, and Nambaas.
After the battle of Ngangaram,
10   All of Kayor spoke only of her.
All of Baol spoke only of her.
All of Jolof spoke only of her.
Troublemakers paralyzed one of her legs;
Thus, since she could not find in Kayor a nobleman from the
    same lineage,
15   They gave her to Sakhward Faatma Mbaye, a freeman land-
    owner.
But Njibi Koura, his mother, is the sister of Tiam Mbaye.

Ngoné Latir told them:
25   "Even if you give me to the Lawbé,
"I will give them a *Maalaw*.[1]
"That is why Lat Dior will make 'Maalaw' the name of his
    horses."
Some say that a Maalaw does not have to be big, provided that
    he be instead a skillful woodcutter.
Others say: "As skilled a woodcutter as he may be, he should
    never cut the trunk of his father."
30   Ngoné Latir had affirmed that
"Even among the Lawbé,
"I will give birth to a *Maalaw*."
Maalaw will be therefore the last warhorse of Lat Dior.
When Birima Ngoné Latir died,
35   Madiodio Déguène Kodou took power.
He conquered all of Kayor brought together at Loro;
Conquered them at Diadji Daaro;
Obliged them to work in his fields in the middle of the dry
    season;
He made all of Kayor flee across the Tan stream.
40   Birima Ngoné Latir
Had made a gift of a horse to Lat Dior, then an adolescent.
He spurred it,
And the horse threw him.
Birima predicted then that "You will never become king.
45   "The day I leave this world
"The Gedj lineage will lose power forever.
"When a prince
"Is incapable of controlling a horse,
"He will not be able to govern an entire country."
50   The son of Ngoné Latir left the royal court
And went to Koki, the land of Amadou Yalla,

---

1. Chief of the woodcutters.

The fiefdom of his father, in order to learn the Koran.
Madiodio Déguène Kodou, he moved into the capital,
    Nguiguis,
Where he kept a vulture spirit named Njëbb.
55   When the vulture flew over the houses,
Madiodio interpreted the event: "He still would like some
    human flesh.
"Call the people to a meeting."
He stared for a long time at someone in the assembled crowd
Before killing him with a gunshot.
60   "Throw him out for Njëbb to feed on," he added.
The vulture opened the chest of the victim
To feed on his innards.
Kayor was deeply shocked,
Without any means to remedy the situation.
65   Demba War Dior Mbaye Ndéné said one day:
"I can no longer put up with the tyranny of Madiodio Déguène
Kodou;
"I, the eldest of the Gedj lineage,
"I can no longer endure this:
"I am therefore going to look for Lat Dior."
70   He found the son of Ngoné Latir with Serigne Koki
Who was teaching him the Koran.
Lat Dior still had his hair done in the three-tuft style of Diop
adolescents.
The tablet of wood for learning the Koran was between his
hands.
Demba War greeted Serigne Koki
75   And said to him, "Entrust Lat Dior to me.
"I will install him at Mboul.
"Thus, tomorrow he will make you the *Barget*[2] of Guet."
"I cannot do it because Lat Dior is a religious chief and you are
still non-believing warriors."
"Entrust Lat Dior to me," insisted Demba War.
80   "Take him, if that is the way it is," concluded Sérigne Koki.
With Lat Dior mounted behind him,
Demba War rode to Nguiguis
And proclaimed, "Here is the new king."
Kayor replied, "No Damel named Diop,
85   "With his three tufts of hair,
"Will spend the day here."
Madiodio Déguène Kodou said to them,
"You, Demba War with Lat Dior mounted behind you,
"Don't spend the day at Nguiguis,

---

2. Governor.

90   "Or else I will reduce you to ashes."
Demba War left with him on his horse called Kuddu, "the
      spoon,"
Repeating all the while, "One who has a spoon doesn't get
      burned while cooking."

[Next comes Lat Dior's circumcision.]

They brought Lat Dior into the "men's house"
At Khabnane.
Laba[3] sat down.
They told this to Madiodio Déguène Kodou:
125   "Some blood of a noble has been spilled on your land."
He commented, "One who dares to spill the blood of a noble on
      my land without my authorization
"Will not set up his compound for circumcised men here."
Demba War said then to the son of Ngoné Latir: "After all,
      Madiodio Déguène is your grandfather."
Madiodio sent to him a final emissary bearing this threat:
130   "I will come to burn down his compound for circumcised men."

160   Demba War sent the emissary back with this message:
"Even if he is riding a wooden mortar, he will find me here."
The first name of the horse of Lat Dior is "Dondo-Neeri."
It is not a Wolof adage, rather it is Tukulor and means:
"Let someone else take care of your bleeding wound."
165   This was the motto of his first horse.
He was still circumcised
When Demba War told him:
"They should saddle a horse for you
"So that you can train it yourself."
170   They saddled a horse for him and handed him the reins.
"Dondo-Neeri" he named it,
"Let someone else take care of your bleeding wound."
He rode it and spurred it;
His blood of a newly circumcised man wet him all the way
      down to the stirrups.
175   Demba War said to him:
"You are now capable of fighting any king."

They followed Lat Dior
And booed him all the way to Kër-Madiop,
215   The frontier between Kayor and Baol.
Lat Dior said to them:

---

3. Praise-name for Lat Dior.

"You could have installed an exit door for the future,
"Because I will come back soon."
Laba[4] continued his quest.

[Dressed in the clothing of a young man who is circumcised at the age
of seventeen, Lat Dior wins his first battle but loses the second against
Madiodio, who has the support of the French. He then goes off into
exile. His itinerary includes battles against the armies of neighboring
kingdoms. A victor over Baol, he is defeated at Sine. Finally, he arrives
at his destination, the kingdom of Maba Diakhou Ba, who gives him an
army.]

	The son of Ngoné Latir continued on his way
315	And went to Maba Diakhou in the Saloum region.
325	He sent emissaries to Maba Diakhou,
	Telling him that it was Lat Dior who greeted him.
	Maba, who was in the middle of a big meeting,
	Spoke to the assembled in these terms: "I have a great dilemma today.
	"For Lat Dior, who has just asked me for asylum here,
330	"Seeks only power on earth.
	"While I, I lead a holy war,
	"Only for the greatness of God.
	"Morever, he who fights for God
	"Must be neither an ingrate
335	"Nor someone who disappoints hopes.
	"How could I give asylum
	"To Lat Dior, who is fighting for worldly benefits?
	"I who fight for the glory of God?
	"One remembers that Makodou Yandé Mbarou asked me for asylum here, in the same circumstances.
340	"I fought with him
	"In order to advance him to the throne
	"And surprised him afterward drinking wine!
	"That is why I don't trust Kayor people."
	An elder stood up in the assembly and proposed:
345	"Ask him to convert,
	"To cut his hair
	"And to present it as a sign of humility.
	"In that way you will give him exile.
	"And when he will be strong enough,
350	"You will let him return to Kayor."
	Lat Dior remained for a long time at that place and said one day:

---

4. Praise-name for Lat Dior.

"A disciple must go look each Wednesday for the pittance he
    gives each week to his master."
The son of Ngoné Latir assembled his army.

365   And raided Sasa Ndoukoumanae,
Raided Waliyaar,
Raided Sabakh
Raided Diaba Kounda
Before going to find Sàmba Diabaye at Ndiaw Mame.

370   He refused to convert.
Lat Dior put his foot on his head and slit his throat.
In fact he asked for Demba War Dior Mbaye Ndéné, and told
    him,
"Go greet Mame Samba Diabaye."
This man, at that time, had pierced one of his nostrils, where he
    hung a golden chain.

375   And at his feet was a vessel full of wine.
When he shouted "The nobles have heard,"
They pulled on the golden chain and he took a long drink of
    wine.
When he got up, his eyes bulged from his head.
He replied to the emissary, "I thought there was no other king
    but me,

380   "And you speak to me of a certain Lat Dior, king of Kayor."
Demba War said, "I will not reply to him before consulting
    with Lat Dior."
He went to report to Lat Dior,
Who said, "Nobody ever showed his own death to the door.
"Return and present my greetings to Mame Samba Diabaye

385   "And point out to him that it is Lat Dior, king of Kayor, who
    greets him."
He returned,
And said to Mame Samba Diabaye, "Lat Dior greets you.
"The king of Kayor also demands from you hay and water for
    his horses."
He cried out, "The nobles have heard."

390.   They pulled on the chain and he took a long drink of wine;
He stood up, saying:
"I thought there was no other king but me."
Demba War returned to report to Lat Dior.
The people of Kayor said to Lat Dior:

395   "For three days, we are feeding only on *nduur*[5] plants
"While drinking water from the stream.
"We rustle some sheep from herds
"That we encounter.

---

5. A kind of bush.

"We will slaughter them, we will roast them to satisfy our
    hunger,
400   "Before meeting Mame Samba Diabaye at Ndiaw."
Then a *jeli*[6] named Samba Koumba Kalado
Played on his *xalam*[7] the tune *lagya*, while seated on the ground,
And composed that day this song: "Niani refuses to be subjec-
    ted.
"O descendant of Dior Saala Faatma Khourédia,
405   "The son of Ngoné Latir swept down on Mame Sàmba Diabaye
"And burned Ndiaw.
"He knocked down all the stockades
"And burned the entire country,
"Bringing everything there back as booty.
410   "He finally returned."

[In the service of Maba Diakhou, Lat Dior leads a series of battles
against non-Muslim peoples and French-led armies.]

Maba Diakhou, the Foutanké,[8] warned him, nevertheless:
455   "I taught you the letter 'B,'
"Which should remind you of my taboos.
"I taught you the letter 'S,'
"Which should remind you never to fight against the people of
    Sine;
"These are peaceful people,
460   "Living by the sweat of their brow,
"Who never commit aggression against anyone.
"I will give you, too, two kinds of land:
"This red earth,
"And this white earth.
465   "If the soil of the field where you must fight is red,
"You will not survive this campaign."
Maba, who had to fight a battle, looked at the white earth that
    had become red.
He decided nevertheless to follow his destiny;
But he called Lat Dior
470   And said to him, "I know you very well;
"A noble has a sense of honor;
"You will want to follow me till death.
"I am undertaking my last campaign against the ruler of Sine.
"With Sayeer Mati, my elder,
475   "To the Sayaan of Somb.
"You, Lat Dior,
"Today you are the elder of the Gedj lineage,
"And you have still not yet been installed at Mboul.

---

6. Mande griot. 7. Lute. 8. Someone from the Fouta Toro region.

"Many people have followed you into exile,
480 "Abandoning women, children, and goods;
"Thus, if you die with me in this war,
"They will not know how to return to Kayor.
"I order you to saddle a mare when we go to the Sayaan of
Somb."
That is why Lat Dior did not die during that battle.
485 Maba Diakhou was killed, with Sayeer Mati, his eldest son.
Lat Dior came back to Kayor.

The son named Lat Dior finally returned.
505 It was the beginning of the rainy season.

On the third day of the rainy season,
510 The people of Kayor were going to sow peanuts and millet.
He declared, "From Koki, fiefdom of Amadou Yalla,
"To Kër-Madiop, the frontier between Kayor and Baol,
"I plugged all of the wells,
"I burned all the villages.
515 "I burned all of the silos.
"Today the country is called 'Diop'
"Or 'Ndiour'
"Where the forest returned for seven years."
Madiodio Déguène Kodou
520 Supported, by the *Jawrin-Mboul*[9] Mador Diagne,
Also said, "The country will answer to 'Faal,'
"Or 'Ndiour,'
"Or will become forest for seven years."
That is the cause of the battle of the wells of Kalom.
525 The battle raged for a full day.
On that day, at Ndande,
The Madior lineage was decimated.
Madiodio Dior Lobé fell at Ndandé;
Ten Lat Déguène Kodou was killed with An, "The luncheon."
530 Ma Bigué Faati Lobé was killed with Boo-dëdde-nuul.[10]
All the great compounds of Ndiémbale on that day.

535 They are lineage of Madior.
The night before, Madiodio Déguène Kodou had proclaimed:
"Tomorrow, I will eat my own flesh!"
"Why?" he was asked.
"When one speaks of the Madior lineage," he explained,
540 "One refers to Dior who had come from Njiguène.
"I will kill them at the Wells of Ndande."

9. Ruler of Mboul. 10. "You-turn-black-when-you-turn-around."

219

"While tomorrow, Weyndé Nakk and Tanor Nakk,
As soon as the sun rises,
Madiodio Déguène Kodou killed Weyndé Nak and Tanor
    Nakk.
545   As for the *Jawrin-Mboul* Madior Diagne,
The heroes of the army of Madiodio Déguène Kodou,
As brave as Demba War in the army of Lat Dior,
The lineage of Demba Tioro cast a spell on him,
Magically plunging his body into the well,
550   Maintaining it between the bottom and the curb. His body had
        no more strength.
He could neither fight nor raise his gun.
He who, like Demba War at the side of Lat Dior,
Was the pillar of the army of Madiodio Déguène Kodou.
Lat Dior conquered Madiodio Déguène Kodou.
555   Who took refuge in Saint-Louis, with many relatives.
Lat Dior returned
And called again to the people of Kayor, "What is your deci-
        sion?"
"We refuse," replied the people of Kayor.
He was going to slit the throat of Sérigne Gatiratte,
560   Exterminating all those who were on the surrounding hills.

[The hero thus completes the cycle of traditional heroes of the Sudan
that is made up of a conquest or reconquest of power. Son-Jara is the
model for this type. The tragic epic of the hero's resistance against the
French and the colonial penetration into the region follows next. Lat
Dior fights unceasingly against both the French and the Muslim Tukul-
ors who want to build a federation of traditional kingdoms. He will die
alone in combat against the French and part of his own original army,
led by his general Demba War, whom the invaders have succeeded in
bringing over to their side.]

785   He returned to Kayor.
That is why, when one talks about the battles of Lat Dior
One can estimate that there were forty or thirty of them,
But to tell about each one, where it took place and what he did,
Nobody would dare recount in detail.
790   He encountered, for example, Sidiya Ndaté Yalla at Bangoye.
It was a lightning battle.
Bouba Mbaye succeeded in killing rapidly Sidiya Ndaté Yalla,
Who raised himself up on an arm and moaned,
"God All Powerful!"
795   Ngoté Niasse in his turn fired his gun at Bouba Mbaye,
Who was projected into the air,
Sticking his tongue completely out:
His heart came out of his arm;

Lat Dior turned his head and cried.
800   Nevertheless, that didn't stop the son of Ngoné Latir.
He encountered Cheikhou Amadou at Tiowane.

825   Lat Dior called for the French to help
—this is the origin of their long conflict—
And said to them:
"Help me to conquer Amadou Cheikhou.
"If he leaves my kingdom for good,
830   "What you ask from me,
"The railroad from Ndar to Dakar,
"I will grant it to you."

Kayor betrayed him, one man after another.
910   Some of his closest men
Said to him goodbye.
Others advised him to go into exile:
"Lat Dior, why don't you go into exile?
"Why not go to the Sine Kingdom?" they asked him.

930   "I can't go there!
"What should I do with you?" he asked himself;
"Anyone who does not want to die should not follow me."
One cavalryman said goodbye to him on that day.
And Lat Dior took his horse and said:
935   "There is *licin*—the Hawk—take him!"
"What does *licin* mean?" he asked him.
"One flies easily with him," he replied.
The son of Ngoné Latir got himself ready at Thilmakha.
The tamarind tree where they hang their guns
940   Is still full of nails.
He took off all of his magic charms
And buried them at the foot of the tamarind tree.
He went to greet Khadimou Rassoul,
Who said to him, "You have had all of the powers of this world.
945   "Come prepare with me your rule in the other world!"
He replied, "If people ask me for protection,
"And if I begin to look for protection myself,
"That will seem like cowardice.
"A noble must never retreat.
950   "I don't want to tarnish the honor of my lineage.
"But there is Mbakhane, my son,
"I make him your disciple."
The Marabout said, "Mbakhane, I name you Abdou Khafor,
"'The pardoned slave.'"
955   That is why Sérigne Bamba never cursed Mbakhane.

He took off his *boubou*[11] and gave it to Lat Dior
And prayed for him.
Lat Dior got ready and ordered,
"Saddle my companion."
960 Every horse that they presented to him,
He said, "That one is not my companion."
Until there were none left except Maalaw,
Who pawed the ground with his right foot.
"Have you understood this augury of Maalaw?" he asked.
965 "No," they replied.
"He pawed with his right foot; it is my tomb that he is digging.
"I will pray the *tisbaar*[12] prayer today with Maba Diakhou,
my guide, in the world beyond."
At daybreak they arrived at Dékhélé.
Khadim had recommended one thing to him:
970 "However rough the combat may be,
"Don't sing your praises.
"Always say, 'God is All Powerful!'
"As long as you praise him, you will not fall."
He left with many relatives from our village.
975 None returned.
That is why the village is so barren.
All those who left here on that morning
Fell on the field of battle.
Even we griots.
980 At daybreak,
Lat Dior went out of Dékhélé.
When the Whites arrived,
The White placed his hand on the shoulder of Demba War and
asked him:
"Who is Lat Dior?"
985 "Lat Dior? There are the tracks of his horse," he replied.
"Lat Dior has fled!" he said to him.
"Lat Dior does not flee!
"I witnessed his birth, I educated him!"
"By the way, what is your tie with Lat Dior?"
990 "We were together for a long time," he replied.
"Are you relatives?"
"To be linked for a long time suffices for a family relationship.
"I saw Lat Dior born:
"I brought him up;
995 "It was I who had him initiated into the 'house of men.'
"We participated together in twenty-nine battles.
"This is the thirtieth and we are fighting against each other.
"What is turning white down there,

---

11. Robe. 12. Early afternoon prayer.

"We Wolof call the sun.
1000 "When it reddens, I will see his blood.
"You will know then that Lat Dior does not flee."
They advanced again, arriving near the well;
They planted their flag and decided to prepare a meal.
It was at this moment that the son of Ngoné Latir swept down
       upon them
1005 And cried *"Tuuge waaye!"*13

[Lat Dior's enemies now carefully prepare to kill him.]

They had prepared the bullet magically
Before giving it to the one who was to kill Lat Dior.
A bit of gold,
A bit of silver,
1025 A bit of copper,
A bit of iron.

1030 They had prepared two bullets.
Lat Dior never looked behind him.
The first bullet hit his horse Maalaw on the white spot on his
       forehead.
The second cut down Lat Dior,
Tearing out his right eye.

1051 The son of Ngoné Latir
Is the only one for whom the people of Kayor say:
"We lost you in order to become soldiers for the whites.
"We lost you in order to pay taxes to the whites."

1070 But the great deeds of Lat Dior
No one has equaled them.
To be the last born
And to have the greatest reputation,
If it is not due to virtues, it is certainly the sign of greatness.

---

13. Exclamation when catching a criminal.

PART TWO

NORTH AFRICA

Egyptian Epics

AT LEAST A DOZEN ORAL EPICS have existed at different times in the Arab world. Some, such as *Sīrat ʿAntar ibn Shaddād* (the *sīra* of the pre-Islamic black poet-knight, ʿAntara son of Shaddād), *Sīrat Dhāt al-Himma* (the *sīra* of the heroine Dhāt al-Himma and her wars against the Byzantines), and *Sīrat al-malik Sayf ibn Dhī Yazan* (the *sīra* of the Himyarite king, Sayf ibn Dhī Yazan and his wars against the Abyssinians) have ancient, pre-Islamic roots. Others, such as *Sīrat al-amīr Ḥamza al-Bahlawān* (the *sīra* of Ḥamza, uncle of the Prophet Muḥammad), and *Sīrat al-Zīr Sālim* (the *sīra* of the Bedouin warrior, al-Zīr Sālim) are set at the beginning of the Islamic era. Still others, such as *Sīrat al-Ẓāhir Baybars* (the *sīra* of the thirteenth-century Egyptian ruler and folk hero, al-Ẓāhir Baybars) and *Sīrat Banī Hilāl* (the *sīra* of the Banī Hilāl Bedouin tribe and their eleventh-century conquest of North Africa) are tied to more recent historical events. Several of these were still performed up to the nineteenth century; today, however, only *Sīrat Banī Hilāl* exists in the oral tradition.

Arabic written literature has left us a fragmentary record of the emergence of these epics, their stories, and the poets who performed them. The epics are often cited in medieval collections of religious sermons in which the devout are warned not to waste time with such frivolous pastimes and are encouraged instead to devote themselves to prayer and the study of religious works. Occasionally, a scholar or a market-place scribe would record a fragment of one of the poems: such is the case of Ibn Khaldūn, the famous fourteenth-century Arab historiographer, who quoted pages of *Sīrat Banī Hilāl* in his treatise on the nature of history, *al-Muqaddimah* ("The Introduction"). In later centuries we even find versions of the oral epics in Classical Arabic, part of the "popular literature" of the day. These texts, however, were usually written on inexpensive materials which have not easily weathered the passing years. For this reason, it is very difficult to determine what role these "pulps" may have played in the development or preservation of the epics.

Since *Sīrat Banī Hilāl* is the last of these epics to survive, it has received more attention from modern scholars than the other epics. This epic, though well known in much of the Arab world, is now sung as a versified epic poem in only two regions, northern and southern Egypt. Elsewhere it is currently found as a cycle of folktales occasionally punctuated with lines of poetry.

Dwight Reynolds

20. The Epic of the Banī Hilāl
Narrated by Shaykh Tāhā Abū Zayd

Recorded in June 1987 in al-Bakātūsh, Egypt, by Dwight Reynolds. Transcribed and translated into English by Dwight Reynolds. This excerpt edited by Dwight Reynolds.

The Birth of the Hero Abū Zayd

THE FOLLOWING EXCERPT IS FROM THE ARABIC ORAL EPIC POEM *Sīrat Banī Hilāl*, the epic history of the Arab Bedouin tribe of the Banī Hilāl (literally "sons of the crescent moon"). This recording was made in the village of al-Bakātūsh in the Nile Delta region of northern Egypt. The poet was Shaykh Tāhā Abū Zayd, who was about seventy at that time. Since Tāhā is an epithet of the Prophet Muḥammad and Abū Zayd is the central hero of the epic as it is sung in Egypt, the poet's name itself is emblematic of the connection between the Islamic nature of the epic and the close bond which is understood to exist between epic singers and the epic heroes of whom they sing. The performance was held in the home of Aḥmad Bakhtātī and was the first of a series Shaykh Tāhā Abū Zayd sang over a period of two months in which he provided a full rendition of the epic as he knew it. The resulting version was fifty-four hours long; it numbers well over 12,000 verses of *qasīda*-style poetry, a form in which each verse is twenty-eight to thirty syllables long with a medial caesura and closes with a mono-endrhyme. In this tradition the poet can maintain the same rhyme for a hundred verses or more before moving on to a different rhyme. The poet accompanies himself musically on the *rabāb*, a two-stringed, spike-fiddle, the same instrument on which the heroes in the epic perform, providing a tangible link between epic singer and epic hero.

At the beginning of this performance the audience consisted of six men from the village and myself; several more men, however, arrived after verse 68. Had they been high-status guests the poet would have interrupted his singing to greet them in improvised poetry; this group, however, consisted of men who regularly attend all epic performances in the village, aficionados of the tradition, and as "regulars," they were greeted simply with a nod. The beginning of most performances is rather sedate, with audience members providing only desultory comments and sounds of approval. As the scene foretelling the birth of the hero, Abū Zayd, approaches, the listeners begin shouting comments at the end of every line; and from verse 95 onward many verses are even interrupted and one listener makes a display of placing a handful of cigarettes in front of the poet, which elicits the poet's thanks. The epic opens on a common theme: the most valiant warrior of the tribe does not yet have a son. He has married nine women before he encounters a Sufi dervish who predicts the birth of a son if only he marries the daughter of the ruler of Mecca.

228

[Spoken:]

After praise for the Prophet of the tribe of ʿAdnān, and we do not gather but that we wish God's blessings upon Him, for the Prophet was the most Saintly of the Saintly, the Seal of God's Messengers, and on the Day of Resurrection He shall smile on the faces of all who wish God's blessings upon Him.

The author of these words tells of Arabs known as the Arabs Banī Hilāl, and their Sultan at that time and that era was King Sarḥān, and their Warrior was Rizq the Valiant, Son of Nāyil, for every age has its nation and its men. And the guardian of the maidens was a stalwart youth, his name was Prince Zayyān, and the protector of the Zaghāba clan was the courageous Ghānim, warrior among warriors.

Rizq had married women, yes, eight maidens, but he had not yet sired a male heir. He sat in his pavilion and some lads passed by him (lads, that is, of the Arabs, the lads, that is to say, the little boys, if you'll excuse me). His soul grew greatly troubled over the lack of an heir, so Rizq sat and sang of the lack of a male heir, words which you shall hear; and he who loves the beauty of the Prophet increases his wishes for God's blessings upon Him.

All: *May God Bless and Preserve Him!*

Voice: *You mean you're not going to have supper tonight?*
Shaykh Tāhā: *Why do you say that, brother?*
Voice: *The food!* (gesturing to the food being laid out in the next room.)
Shaykh Tāhā: *Praise be to God!*[1]

[Music on the spike-fiddle.]
[Sung:]

I am the servant of all who adore the beauty of Muḥammad,
All: *May God Bless and Preserve Him!*
Tāhā, for whom every pilgrim yearns.

Listen to what said Rizq the Valiant, Son of Nāyil;
Tears poured forth from the orb of his eye, flowing.

Ah! Ah! the World and Fate and Destiny!
All I have seen with my eyes shall disappear.

5   Fate make peace with me, 'tis enough what you've done to me,
I've cast my weapons at thee, but my excuse is clear.

---

1. That is, We have already eaten.

229

I do not praise among the days one which pleases me
 But that its successor comes along, stingy and mean.

My wealth is great, O men, but I am without an
   heir;   Voice: *Allah!*
 And wealth without an heir after a lifetime disappears.

I look out and find Sarhān when he rides,
 His sons ride with him, princes and prosperous.

I look out and find Zayyān when he rides,
 His sons ride with him and fill the open spaces.

I look out, ah!, and find Ghānim when he rides,
 And his sons ride with him and are princes, prosperous.

10 And I am the last of my line, my spirit is broken,
  I have spent my life and not seen a son, prosperous.

I have taken of women, eight maidens,
 And eleven daughters followed, princesses true!

This bearing of womenfolk, ah!, has broken my spirit,
 I weep and the tears of my eyes on my cheek do flow.

So Ghānim said to him, "O Rizq I have a maiden daughter,
 "Marry her today and you shall achieve your desires."

He signed the marriage contract with the maiden Jallās,
    Shaykh Tāhā: *Wish God's blessings on the Prophet!*
      All: *May God Bless and Preserve Him!*
 They held the wedding, O Nobles, and slaughtered
  slaughtering beasts.

15 The first year Jallās bore him a daughter,
  That rounded out a dozen daughters for him, true!
               [Laughter]
 But Ghānim said, "Be patient! There is benefit in patience,
  "With patience, Royal One, you shall achieve your desires.

"One who bears a daughter may also bear a son,
         Voice: *That's right!*
 "And if my Lord God wills, from her will come children to
  people the open spaces."

The second year passed and the third she became pregnant,
At the pregnancy of the Zaghāba girl perfumes were
released.　　　　　　　　　　　　　　　Voice: *Allah!*

Her months went by, ah!, and she bore him a boy!
But his two arms were crippled and his legs were lame.

20　　It became a wonder amongst the Arabs,
And those coming and going did speak of it.

So Rizq said to the maiden Jallās: "Take your son and move off
from here, "I want no women, by God, in this camp."

She took her son on her arm and her daughter, O Nobles, with
her,
And this is the way of the husband when he is mean.

So Sarhān said, "Let us go, O Rizq, you and I, out into the desert and wilderness,
"To hunt gazelles, O Friend, in the wide, open spaces."

They set out, then, the two of them,
　　　　　　Shaykh Tāhā: *Wish God's blessings on the Prophet!*
　　　　　　　　　　All: *May God Bless and Preserve Him!*
And they found a man, a shaykh, in the wilds wandering.
　　　　　　　　　　　　　　　　　Voice: *Allah!*

25　　They found this man, a shaykh, in the desert and the wilderness,
The foam on his chest was like the billowing sea.

"O Rizq, my son, your need, ah yes, is clearly for a boy,
"Who will, after your lifetime, honor those coming and
going.

"The day the pilgrims set forth from Egypt to the Prophet,
　　　　　　　　　All: *May God Bless and Preserve Him!*
"Pack up the Hilālī Arabs and offer up slaughtering beasts.

"Go marry Khadra, daughter of Qirda the Sharīf, Son of
Hāshim,
"From her shall come a lad, O Courageous One, who shall
prosper.

"From her shall come a lad, God shall cause his memory to live
on.
"He shall be a strong boy of ominous determination."

231

30   They took in the <u>sh</u>eik<u>h</u> and invited him for three full days,
          And each night, O Nobles, the *dhikr*[2] rang out.

      The day the pilgrims set out from Egypt to the Prophet,
          Rizq said to them, "O Hilālī Arabs, I intend to Visit the
          Prophet, Possessor of shining light."
                        All: *May God Bless and Preserve Him!*

      The Hilālī nobles then packed up with the Son of Nāyil,
          O fortunate is he who yearns and then makes pilgrimage.
          <u>Sh</u>ay<u>kh</u> Tāhā: *Wish God's blessings on the Prophet!*
                  All: *May God Bless and Preserve Him!*

[Spoken:]

      Said the *Rāwī* [reciter]: After praise for the Prophet of the tribe of ʿAdnān, they reached the land and the country of Mecca. They erected their tents and their pavilions and hoisted their banners, and they occupied the country from every side and direction. Then Qirda [the <u>Sh</u>arīf of Mecca] welcomed them with the warmest of welcomes and showed them every consideration. He invited them to rest for three days. After three days he asked them about their origins. So King Sarhān said, "We are Arabs from the land of <u>Sh</u>arīfa the High-born . . . [<u>Sh</u>eik<u>h</u> Tāhā corrects himself] . . . from the land of Najd, O Warrior among warriors, and our desire is the hand of <u>Sh</u>arīfa the High-born. Our goal is a maiden of noble descent and good lineage, O Warrior among warriors." So Qirda said to them, "Welcome to you, O Arabs of Hilāl. You have honored us and graced us in our land and our country." Then he moved them to his own area of the camp and placed them in tents of honor and hospitality. Then the Hilāl *Qādī* [religious judge] came forth, Fāyid, father of Badīr, and Sarhān said to him, "Speak, Qādī, speak of the brideprice for the maiden" [aside to audience: The brideprice, that is, the dowry]. See what the Qādī will say, and he who loves the beauty of the Prophet wishes God's blessings upon Him.
                  All: *May God Bless and Preserve Him!*

[Music.]
[Sung:]

      I am the servant of all who adore the beauty of Muhammad,
          Tāhā, who asked for intercession and obtained it.

      Listen to what the Qādī Fāyid said and what he sang:
          "My *eye* aches and sleep frequents it not in this state.[3]

---

2. Sufi chanting. 3. Metaphor for the soul.

35   "It goes to sleep with good intention, but awakes filled with
        caution,
      "As if all the hooks of life lay in sleep's domain.

    "If my burdens lean, with my own hand I set them straight,
      "But if the world leans, only God can set it straight.

    "Happy is the eye which sleeps the whole night through,
                          Shay<u>kh</u> Tāhā: *Ah yes, by God!*
      "It passes the night in comfort, no blame is upon it.

    "But my eye is pained and keeps vigil the whole night
        through,
      "It passes the night troubling me with all that has befallen
        it.

    "Listen to my words, O Qirda, and understand,
      "These are the words of princes, not mere children.

40   "We wish from you a maiden, high-born,
      "Of noble ancestry from both grandfathers, paternal and
        maternal uncles, too.

    "We shall give her a dowry, a dowry of nobles, O Hero,
      "We shall dress her in the finest and purest of silks.

    "Perhaps she'll bear a son, a prince awe inspiring,
      "He shall emerge from the vessel whose waters are pure.

    "If he comes and speaks in the mosque a word, they will say,
      "'That is the son of Rizq who came to us and said it.'

    "We'll take not the fair maid for the fairness of her cheek,
      "If the fair one goes astray, her menfolk are blamed.
                                   Voice: *True!*

45   "We'll take not the dark maid for the greatness of her wealth,
      "If her wealth decreases she'll blame you for her loss.
                                   [Laughter]

    "We'll take not the foolish maid or the daughter of a miser,
      "Flustered on the day of the feast, we won't even approach
        her.

    "We'll take not one who scrapes the pot with her hand,
                                     [Laughter]

"If a few days of want come,
    "She'll vie with her own children [for the food]!   [Laughter]

"We shall only take the high-born princess,   Voice: *Allah!*
    "Who honors the guest of God, yes, when he comes to her.

50   "She who receives the guest of God with welcome and greet-
            ings,
    "So that her man may sit honored among men.

"We shall give you, O Qirda, a hundred horses, and a hundred
        sheep,
    "And a hundred slave girls, and one hundred camels.

"And a hundred slaves, O Kindest-of-the-Arabs,
    "And one hundred fair slave girls to serve their men.

"And on top of all of this, one thousand pieces of gold,
    "Wealth is useful and the years are long.

"This is our dowry, O paternal uncle, in our country,
    "And we are Arabs, the poorest of its men.   [Laughter]

55   "Have pity on us, ah!, O Son of Hashing,   Voice: *Allah!*
    "Nobles are not thanked except for their actions."

Then Qirda said, "Write this down, too, O Qādī of the Arabs,
    "From me, I give its equal for the Lady Khadra.

"Perhaps Fate will change toward her;
    "And if she sets aside her wealth,   Voice: *Allah!*

"Even if Fate and Destiny and Time change toward her,
    "She need not rely on the least of her menfolk." [Laughter]

The Courageous One signed the wedding contract,
            Shaykh Tāhā: *Wish God's blessings on the Prophet!*
                    All: *May God Bless and Preserve Him!*
    They slaughtered young camels and they invited all her
        men.

60   The Arabs packed up that very day and travelled,
    They placed the heavy loads on their camels.

They went home, ah, ah, to their land and their territory,
    Their land was that of Taifa, may its men always thrive!

They brought the burdens, all the men, every single one of
them,
They brought the burdens to Rizq in their entirety.

But then there was <u>Gh</u>ānim, who felt wronged,
O Hero, that Rizq had left Jallās and left her children with
her.

The first year went by the Lady <u>Kh</u>adra,
And the second passed, and the third just the same.

65   And the fourth passed by the Lady <u>Kh</u>adra,
And the fifth passed without the fulfillment of her desires.

And the sixth passed and was finished,
The elders spoke of it, as did even their children.

Seven years were completed with the Son of Nāyil,
She neither gave birth nor grew pregnant, nor fulfilled her
desires.

<u>Gh</u>ānim heard the talk and he grew light hearted.
He was the bringer of evil, <u>Gh</u>ānim, among the men of the
tribe.

He came to Rizq in order to tell him,
"Listen to my words," so hear now what he said to him:

70   "You married *al-<u>Sh</u>arīfa*,[4]
"O Rizq, to increase your honor. It turns out she's barren,
cannot fulfill her desires."

[Music while additional guests enter and are seated.]

"You married al-<u>Sh</u>arīfa, O Rizq, to increase your honor,
"It turns out she's barren, cannot fulfill her desires.

"You've taken a line of barren women, O Rizq, what a pity,
<u>Sh</u>ay<u>kh</u> Tāhā: *Your line of barren wives is a pity, O Rizq!*
"Rizq, divorce this one and take yourself another."

Rizq heard these words and his mind grew greatly troubled,
"O fire of my heart whose flames are not slackened!"

---

4. Literally "the honorable."

He went to K̲h̲adra as she sat in her pavilion,
  O how beautiful were her features.

75   As soon as she saw Rizq,
          S̲h̲ayk̲h̲ Tāhā: *Wish God's blessings on the Prophet!*
                  All: *May God Bless and Preserve Him!*
      Tāhā, the pilgrims pelerinated and came [to Him].

She stood up on her feet, her hand lovely,
  Her face fair and oh so comely.

So he said to her, "K̲h̲adra, you're a whore,
  "By God I married you but there are no sons in you.

"I married you an honorable woman[5] to increase my honor,
  "It turns out you are barren, in you there are no offspring.

"Seven years, O K̲h̲adra, you have been in my dwellings,
  "And I have not seen from you any sons."

80   "She heard this fury from him, she gestured to speak to him,
      "Stop there, man, and put your faith in God!   All: *Ah!*

"By God, the bearing of children is not in my hands,
  "Everything, O Rizq, comes about by the will of God."

He heard from her these words and gestured and said to her,
  "My mind from me, O S̲h̲arīfa, has strayed.

"I am like a crazy man in the desert and the wastelands,
  "Woe to him whose strength Fate has destroyed!"

He struck her with his palm upon her comely cheek,
  Her fair cheek, its sweetness fled.

85   So K̲h̲adra began to complain to those in the encampment,
      "By God I am a stranger, I have no dignity of rank."

She passed by S̲h̲amma, wife of King Sarhān,
  She was also a stranger with little dignity of rank.

And S̲h̲amma was the daughter of King Zayd the Virtuous
  From the land of Tubbaʿ, from righteous men.

---

5. S̲h̲arīfa.

She said to her, "O Khadra, who has caused you to weep?
  "Who is capable of this to a stranger, to cause you such suf-
    fering?"

She said to her, "Rizq reproaches me about offspring,
  "About the lack of a son and heir."   All: *Ah!*

90   She said to her, "You are barren, and I am just like you,
        "My sustenance [*rizq*] and your sustenance are both up to
          God.

    "Come, come, you and I, let us go out into the wilderness,
      "Let us go out and wander beneath the face of God."
                                                        Voice: *Ah!*

They passed a short night, the two of them,
  While Sarhān kept Rizq company.

And it was Friday morning,
              Shaykh Tāhā: *Wish God's blessings on the Prophet!*
                    All: *May God Bless and Preserve Him!*
  As for the oppressed, God hears their prayers.

She said to her: "Let us go, you and I, to the sea in the wilder-
    ness,
  "Let us go calm our blood in its emptiness.

95   "When you look at the salten sea you shall encounter wonders,
        "You shall encounter wonders, by the will of God."

They set out, the two of them along with their slave,
  Saʿīda, wife of Najjāh, oh so beautiful.

Suddenly a white bird . . .   Voice *Yes!*
                        . . . from the distance came to them,
      A white bird, beautiful to behold.

He landed and did not take flight again, the bird in the waste-
    land,
  All the other birds flocked round him.

Said Shamma, "O Lord, the One the Everlasting,   Voice: *Allah!*
  "Glory to God, there is no god but He.

100   "Grant unto me a son, like unto this bird,
        "And may he be handsome and the Arabs obey his [every
          word]."

237

Her request was completed, O Nobles, and the bird rose up,
    The bird took flight, it climbed up toward the heights.

Then suddenly a dark bird from the distance came to them,
                      Laughter—Voice: *This is Abū Zayd!*
    A dark bird . . .   Voice: *Yes!*
        . . . frightful to behold.   Voice: *Heavens!*

He beat his wings at the other birds,
    And each one he struck did not [live to] smell his supper.

Said Khadra, . . .   Voice: *Yes!*
    . . . "O how beautiful you are, O bird, and
    how beautiful your darkness.
                          Voice: *Allah!*
    "Like the palm date when it ripens at its leisure on the tree.

105   "O Lord, O All Merciful, O One, O Everlasting,
                Voice: *May God be generous to you!*
                Shaykh Tāhā: *May God reward you!*
    "Glory to God, veiled in His Heaven!"

[Audience member lays cigarettes in front of poet.]

              Shaykh Tāhā: *Wish: May you always have plenty!*
                May you always have plenty, we wish you!

"Grant unto me a son, like unto this bird,
    "And may each one he strikes with his sword not [live to]
    smell his supper."   Voice: *My heavens!*
                Voice shouting: *That's Abū Zayd!*

The two of them requested. Then Saʿīda said, "O Lord, grant
    unto me a son like my mistresses,
    "He whose satisfaction is with the Most Generous fears
    nought."

They went home, O Nobles,
              Shaykh Tāhā: *Wish God's blessings on the Prophet!*
              All: *May God Bless and Preserve Him!*
    O how fortunate is he who requests, and the Most Generous
    [grants] its fulfillment.

Said King Sarhān to Rizq the Hero,
    "O Cousin, listen to my words and to their meaning,

110   "Make peace with Sharīfa, Rizq, O Kindest-of-the-Arabs,
       "Honor her for she is of the line of God's Messenger.

      "Honor her, O Rizq, or escort her back to her people
        "For honor is like tilled land, honor is dear, honor is dear,
          and the Arabs know this."   Voices: *Allah! Allah!*

      He made peace with her and escorted her to her pavilion,
        And the Most Generous willed that he be rightly guided, O
          how beautiful!

      And on this night the three became pregnant,   Voice: *Allah!*
        O how fortunate is he who requests, and the Most Generous
          grants its fulfillment.

      Her months passed, Shamma of noble ancestry,
        she gave birth to a son, O Nobles,
        Of rare features, a boy handsome of face, O how beautiful!

               Shaykh Tāhā: *Wish God's blessings on the Prophet!*
                    All: *May God Bless and Preserve Him!*
                    Voice: *May God provide for you!*
               Shaykh Tāhā: *May God reward you!*
                      Voice: *Listen . . . .*
               Shaykh Tāhā: *May God bless you!*

      [Tea break]

21. The Epic of the Banī Hilāl
Narrated by ʿAwadallah ʿAbd al-Jalāl ʿAli

Recorded in 1983 in Gūrna (Qēna Governorate), Egypt, by Susan Slyomovics. Transcribed and translated into English by Susan Slyomovics. This excerpt edited by Susan Slyomovics.

Milād Abū Zēd: The Birth of Abū Zayd

ʿAWAḌALLAH ʿABD AL-JALĪL ʿALI IS AN ILLITERATE EPIC POET and singer who recites in Saiʿidi Arabic, the dialect of his native Upper Egypt. He was born in the village of Najʿ al-Hajis, Aswan Governorate, in southern Egypt, and at the time of this recorded performance on January 23, 1983 (ll. 1-414) and March 5, 1983 (ll. 415 to the end), he gave his age as sixty-three or seventy-three years old. He is the son and grandson of epic singers and he accompanies himself on the large Nubian frame drum (*ṭār*), following the musical tradition of his family. He sings during weddings, circumcisions, Ramadan fast-breaking ceremonies, in local cafes for public audiences, and in private homes for evening command performances. For additional material on the poet, see Susan Slyomovics, *The Merchant of Art: An Egyptian Hilali Oral Epic Poet in Performance* (Berkeley: University of California Press, 1988), and her article "Arabic Folk Literature and Political Expression," *Arab Studies Quarterly* 8:2 (1986), 178-85.

An epic poet characteristically recites isolated tales and episodes either according to audience request or by prior economic arrangement with a patron. ʿAwaḍallah claims he has never performed the birth sequence, because listeners prefer the love stories or the battle sequences. However, even when reciting to a Western ethnographer, he follows performance protocol in opening with a praise-poem (*madīḥ*) and closing by invoking the Prophet Muḥammad. Opening praise-poems occur at ll. 1-14, 81-84, 179-84, and 310-31.

This section is from "The Birth of Abū Zayd," the first part of the traditional tripartite division of the epic. Part one begins the Banī Hilāl cycle with an account of the marriage of Rizq, the Hilāli Bedouin, to Khaḍra Sharīfa, daughter of the Sharīf of Mecca, and the miraculous circumstances surrounding the birth of their baby, the hero Abū Zayd. When the Hilāli Bedouin Arabs discover his black skin color, mother and infant are banished to the desert. There they meet al-Khiḍr (literally, "the Green Man"), called the "Pillar of the Turbaned Ones" (l. 249). In Egyptian and much other Islamic folklore, he is a man who achieved immortality in this life. He is thought to be without a bone in his right thumb, and if this is discovered as one shakes hands with him, one may demand that he grant a wish. Al-Khiḍr protects Abū Zayd from early exile in the wilderness until his first youthful battle against the Koranic schoolteacher (*faqi*). This first part of the cycle ends with Abū Zayd battling his father until the hero is accepted back into the Banī Hilāl tribe. Note how the poet uses the term "tribe" (*qabila*) to evoke the particular ethos and glory of the Bedouin desert peoples.

240

How happy are you who praise the Prophet
Ahmad Muhammad, Who dwells in the city of Yathrib.
I took as my heavenly merit a poem of praise to the
    One with kohl-darkened eyes.
I adore the beauty of the Prophet while praising Him.

5   I adore His beauty, I adore the beauty of the Prophet to
    whom we utter "peace."
O Protector of the oppressed against those who oppress,
I praise a Prophet Ṭāhā;[1] His light is consummate,
Muhammad of the ʿAdnān, clouds came sheltering
    Him.
My next words, my words, about the Prophet of good
    lineage,

10   Ahmad was led by Gabriel on the night of Rajab.
I create and make art about the Arab horsemen,
With my art esteemed only by clever minds,
With my art esteemed only by perfect minds:
The community of our Prophet, the Hashemite, peace
    be upon Him.

15   Said the horseman, Rizq son of Nayil, emir of valiant men:
"I want to wed, O bold ones of Hilāl,
"I want to wed because I am perfect.
"I wish to have a girl or a boy."
Said the horsemen who are the brave Hilāl:

20   "The daughter of Sharīf Gurḍa, king in his house,
"The daughter of Sharīf Gurḍa, from perfect people,
"A descendant of our Prophet, the Chosen One, peace be upon
    Him."
The brave horsemen of Hilāl saddled up.
Rizq headed to Sharīf, to Mecca, made straight for Sharīf Gurḍa,

25   "I am Sharīf," and Rizq journeyed to his place.
They were prosperous nobles, fortunate people of times past.
When Sharīf saw the horsemen descending upon the *diwan*,[2]
He slaughtered for them a plump she-camel for their supper,
He slaughtered for them a she-camel, even honored them more:

30   At Sharīf's, they attained happiness and their desire.
Sharīf Gurḍa said: "Welcome, O Arabs,
"What you request, God will provide,
"What you request, we will bring you in excess,
"It will be brought to you, whether near or far."

35   Said Rizq the Hilāli: "I come to you desiring
"Kinship with you, O you the spring pasture for passers-by,
"Kinship with you, O you who give spring pasture to guests,
"And your lineage will increase my honor above the rest."

---

1. Another name for the Prophet Muhammad. 2. Special meeting room where men
share coffee, talk, and listen to oral performances.

So said the Hilāli, Rizq son of Nayil.

40 Sharīf Gurḍa said: "I want four thousand in money,
"Five hundred strong camels and two hundred young she-
camels,
"Five hundred choice horses
"And four hundred to carry the loads.
"All these, O clever-minded ones,
45 "All are gifts for the servants and envoys,
"All are gifts for the servants and slaves.
"This as a dowry for Khaḍra Sharīfa—to meet her is a joy:
"A hundred Abyssinian women from the land of Upper Egypt,
"A hundred Mamlukes must come to us here,
50 "These hundred Mamlukes to meet the need
"To serve the emirs who have high rank.
"If, O Hilāli, these lineages are linked,
"Khaḍra's dowry in wealth is a full coffer,
"Khaḍra's dowry in wealth is a coffer of gold
55 "Like the dowry of her mother. Ask the Arab elders.
"If, O Hilāli, your intention is kinship
"On the wedding night, the meal is my duty,
"On the wedding night, by God, dinner is my duty—
"The dowry of Khaḍra, who came from my loins.
60 "If she gives birth to an infant and he grows and matures,
"He will grow to be a brave youth, lionlike, he will vex the
enemy,
"He will grow to be a brave youth, of good descent, he will vex
valiant men,
"A descendant of our Prophet, peace be upon Him."
Said Rizq the Hilāli, emir of valiant men:
65 "Were you to say something more, God would requite;
"Were you to say something more, I must say to you, it would
be my duty."
They brought him the *maˀzūn*[3] and they counted the gold.
She became his wife, from among the women,
The daughter of Sharīf Gurḍa became his wife,
70 Khaḍra Sharīfa, her honor was pure.
They set up for her an elegant royal litter.
From atop a high palace whose heights are decorated,
From atop a high palace spaciously built,
She passed the night telling him: "Your company is a delight,
O love."
75 The white chemise was stained with blood,
O night,
The white chemise was drenched with blood.
A descendant of the Prophet, praise be upon Him.

---

3. Official authorized to perform marriages.

Khadra Sharīfa lived there an entire year. She bore and gave
    birth to Shīha, with God's leave.
80   Muhammad let us pray for Him.

[Pause.]

    Praise for Tāhā, a poem of praise for the Messenger
    To whom his Lord gave happiness and acceptance of
        prayers.
    One who praises Ahmad, my Beloved, the Prophet, I
        start to tell,
    My art esteemed by clever minds.
85   Khadra gave birth, she gave birth to Shīha,
    May happiness increase!
    She remained with Rizq the Hilāli in harmony,
    But she spent eleven years
    Barren. This is the destiny intended by God.
90   Barren—this is the destiny intended by my generous Lord—
    Imposing His judgment, light or heavy.
    They requested horses for Rizq and Hilāli, the prince
    To meet with the princes, horsemen and warriors
    To meet with the horsemen of the Banī Hilāl.
95   Their children came out
        [The Arabs were seated in the *diwan*.]
    Happy and prosperous. Their sons delighted him,
    Their sons upon the cushions playing
    Like leopards in the vast desert,
    Like lions in the vast plains.
100   Their fathers' happiness and delight grew greater.
    Rizq and Hilāli eyed them and his wound increased.
    Inside his tent tears poured again.
    Inside the tent tears poured again.
    He cried, wet his cheeks and his handkerchief.
105   Khadra Sharīfa left, her tears a canal.
    Beautiful as she was, she loved him to the point of death,
    Beautiful as she was, by God, unique,
    She cried and felt hardship each night he was absent:
    "Tell me, what is the reason for laments, O love,
110   "O Rizq, you cry, why, why?
    "What good has weeping done you?
    "O Rizq, O you so dignified, why do you cry?
    "The tears upon your cheek are flowing swiftly."
    He said to her, "O Khadra I beheld during the day
115   "There is no warrior, knight, nor courageous horseman who has
        not his son to play with him—
    "No knight, nor horseman who has not his son beside him on
        the cushions.

"I looked, I found myself among them, worthless."
"Khadra Sharīfa's tears fell like hissing droplets.
"Rizq son of Nayil's turmoil was so great, this answer softened her,
120   "Rizq, son of Nayil's turmoil was so great, he gave this answer.
"Khadra had had reason in her head, but reason departed.
"Then came Shamma, a maiden of noble descent and lofty lineage.
"She gathered her robes, with cheeks resembling roses touched by dew,
"With cheeks resembling roses but touched by dew,
125   "She entered and found Khadra weeping, tormented.
"She said, O Sharīfa why are you like this?
"You have lost nothing, my cousin, and none has gone astray.
"You lost nothing from the exalted homeland.
"O Khadra, why do you weep, why do you have tears flowing?"
130   Khadra said to her, "O Shamma, I have a problem,
"It rends the core of my heart and my womb aches,
"It rends the core of my heart and the tears are flowing—
"I, if I complain, I, if I complain, O the nights!
"If I complain to the mountain so that it bends,
135   "If I complain to the river so that its waters stop,
"Saddened for my sake, and my tears a riverbed,
"My tears pour down upon the bed, O Shamma, they wet my cheeks."
"O my cousin, O Khadra, your Lord feels compassion and He will bestow.
"Whoever abandons something lives without it,
140   "Whoever seeks something of God, he will obtain.
"My Lord is to be trusted to grant bountifully."

> *He is to be trusted with what? With the granting of supplication. When one says, "O lord" he is entrusting Him with ample supplication, that is the one who invokes Him, may He be praised and exalted.*

She said to her: "O Khadra, arise and cast aside burdens!
"Tomorrow we go to this river, we will see its clarity,
"Tomorrow we go to the crossing, O coquettish woman,
145   "We will show you waters that are limpid."
She gathered ninety maidens from the daughters of Hilāl
They walked alongside Khadra like sentinels,
They walked alongside Khadra until they reached the rivers;
They found translucent water surrounded by birds.
150   But among them was a bird, black and disturbing.
He scattered all the kinds of birds, and cleared them away,
He scattered all the birds and kept them dispersed,

He was black, and in his coloring were all the qualities.
Shamma says:

155   "Supplicate, O maidens, the Lord provides for His worshippers
    though they have no eyes to see.
"He provides for his worshippers though they have no eyes to
    see Him,
"The Lord provides for His worshippers from the beginning of
    the world.
"He knows the drops of dew and the walk of ants."
Khadra says: "Give me a lad like this bird,

160   "Black like this bird!
"I swear to make him possess Tunis and Wadi Hama,
"I swear to make him possess Tunis by the blade of the sword."
From this they say she bore a lad
To Rizq and Hilāli fulfilling God's favor.

165   O You who cured Job,
       O You who cured Job, he recovered from his affliction,
       O You who cured Job, he recovered from affliction,
       O You who opened Jacob's eyes from blindness,
       O You who raised Enoch to the highest heaven,

170   O You who called to our Lord Moses, O my God,
       When Pharaoh came and his army was with him,
       When Pharaoh came and his army was cut down.
       Moses lay his staff upon the ocean and it parted.
       My generous Lord, You have neither associate nor son,
         there is only You, O Knower of the waters' course,

175   There is only You, O my Lord, who knows what is in
         the wilderness.
       You subdue the wind, the clouds, and the rain.
       I beseech Thee, O light, O radiantly beautiful.
       I adore the beauty of the Prophet, let us Praise Him.

[Pause.]

How happy are you who praise the Messenger,
180   Whose God gave Him joy and granted supplications,
A praise-poem for Husayn's beauty, I begin to say.
I praise the Hashemite,
I adore His beauty to whom we utter "peace,"
O Protector of the oppressed against those who oppress.

185   Supplicate, O daughters and servants of the Hilāli Arabs!
Khadra Sharīfa—her reason failed, lost—
Khadra Sharīfa stopped bearing, but weak with desire
She came to the royal bed yearning.
Rizq son of Nayil came to her after the evening prayer.

190   Khadra wore silk brocade, she sat with him.
She wore brocade of silk, her best clothing.

Rizq asked for union with her.
She was happy! And the Lord of the Throne sent her
An infant who vexes the enemy!
195 She bore an infant who vexes valiant men!
Khadra passed the full nine months.
They approached the Emir Abū Zayd, emir of valiant men,
They found the Emir Abū Zayd was blue-black, not resembling
    his father,
They found the hero, Abū Zayd the Hilāli, the color of a black
    slave.
200 They found the boy coal black, a strange color,
Black, as if from distant Upper Egypt.
Prince Sirhān said: "God's decrees are obdurate,
"With God's mercy who shields sinners,
"With God's mercy who shields the guilty,
205 "His mother and father are both fair, whom does he take after?"
It was an insult, so the Arabs convened.
"O, the wrong of Khadra, she loves a cloak-bearing slave,
"O, the wrong of Khadra, she seduced a purchased slave."
They said "Sharīfa is from the best lineage."
210 When he heard these words, Rizq was overcome.
Azgal said to his people: "Listen, O tolerant ones,"
Azgal said to his people: "Listen, O valiant men,
"The killing and death of a son of adultery is lawful,
"No good is expected from an infant who does not take after his
    father,
215 "No good is expected from an infant born in adultery!
"Divorce Khadra, O Rizq, so that you can obtain your desire.
"Divorce Khadra, O Hilāli, during this year.
"I will give you a Zughba woman—much is said about her.
"I will give you a Zughba woman, a pleasing one,
220 "She has necklaces of silver and bracelets of gold."
When Rizq the Hilāli heard these words he was overcome.
He swore an oath and a vow. In anguish he said:
"I will not receive Khadra again nor do I want the child."
The Hilāli Arabs pleaded with Rizq,
225 They pleaded with Rizq but he did not consent.
They pleaded with Rizq but he refused to consent.
Their bold men cursed him but they returned in vain.
Then came Shīha moving slowly.
To her father, Rizq, she said these words:
230 "My mother Sharīfa is from the Prophet's lineage.
"O Rizq, you mistreat Khadra, whose sin is unseen.
"O Rizq, O father, you mistreat Khadra, who has not sinned.
"My mother Sharīfa does not know the paths to tread.
"Graciously grant Khadra a single companion,
235 "Graciously grant Khadra, by God's truth,

"Graciously grant Khaḍra, by His truth, the One, the Unique—
"He who is my Lord knows the true state of the boy."
When he heard these words, patience came to Rizq;
When he heard these words, he called out: "O Najāḥ,

240 "Listen to my words, for my thoughts are sound:
"Take the lance and the sword and depart for the vast plain,
"Cast the lance across my wealth, and your eyes will see,
"Cast it across my wealth, may your will be strong.
"Rely upon God, generous and adept,

245 "Wherever the lance falls from afar
"Give to Khaḍra, O slave, as charity—
"Lest my son among Arabs be shamed."
Najāḥ took the lance. While he rode
The pillar of turbaned ones[4] hovered and came to him.

250 The pillar of turbaned ones said to him, "Where do you go?
"I will plead for your sake, O slave."
Khidr took the lance from Najāḥ as he cast—
Half the wealth of Sirḥān, his wealth divided equally—
He took half of Sirhan's wealth, O listeners.

255 Praise Ṭāhā we have a guarantor!
He said to him: "O prince of the Arabs, in the name of the
    Prophet, the Guarantor,
"He took your wealth and half of Sirhan's to be divided
    equally,
"Half of Sirhan's wealth though not demanded."
Then came the Arabs:

260 "Find us a guardian engaged for hire
"Find us a guardian from the land of Hejaz
"He will take Khaḍra's clothes and even her trousseau
"From here to accompany her to the land of Hejaz
"For the sake of her father whose domain we have entered,

265 "For the sake of her father whose generosity is vast."
They summoned the judge, his name is Manī.
When he heard these words, he came to them obediently.
They said, "Here are the ones behind whom people pray,
"Here are the ones wanting an *imām*."[5]

270 They said, "We are with him, we will not oppose his words."
They awoke in the morning, they spread out the wide tent.
Khaḍra approached the judge and kissed his hands,
She approached the judge and said, "I am Sharīfa.
"I cannot descend to my father for this whole year,

275 "If I told him Rizq the Hilāli has abused us.
"I cannot say these words while I am in Rizq's custody,
"I cannot say these words nor speak of it,

---

4. Khidr, a man who achieved immortality in this life and grants wishes to those who discover his identity. 5. Religious leader and judge.

"Were Rizq to concede generously that I am still his wife."
"Then find me a guardian, I will go to his side.
280   "Let me raise the prince Abū Zayd in his custody.
"Find us a good man, I will raise the prince Abū Zayd with
    him.
"Let me raise Abū Zayd while he is young.
"O how fate rules over many people!
"He who has ordered our separation from each other, O prince,
285   "May he be destitute among the Arabs and his women led
    astray,
"May he be dropped from the bold ones and may he have
    children
"Who are assaulted by the vanguard Hilāl."
The judge struck his palms and said,
He said, "The land is Zahlān and I am their great enemy."
290   He said, "The land is Zahlān, I cannot pass through.
"Even if a thousand were with me they must die."
The judge accompanied them, they returned silently.
Then the Atwān Arabs came upon Khadra brandishing spears.
He said: "Attack the tent and bring it down."
295   Khadra Sharīfa emerged veiled:
"Shame on the horsemen who dishonor women,
"Shame on the horsemen who dishonor ladies.
"This deed is evil, only the wicked do it.
"Whoever is pure and his body sound,
300   "He never does hateful things,
"He never does hateful things throughout eternity.
"Whoever traverses the region travels in safety.
"I considered you a tribe with leaders of good lineage.
"You turned out to be Atwān Arabs, vile and worthless,
305   "You turned out to be Atwān Arabs, vile and greedy,
"The most cowardly of the region, you do not honor a guest!
"I beseech Thee, O Knower of languages and wild beasts,
"O Provider of the birds in the vast desert."
    Muḥammad let us praise Him.

[Pause.]

310   God is noble, His coffers full. After my words about His Beauty
I begin and make art about the Hilāli Arabs,
I turn my words to the hero Abū Zayd,
His turban tilted, his side fringe aslant,
Defender of the Zughba and the Dirayd
315   And of the horsemen of Najd Hilāl.
From his birth, a child of strength,
Abū Zayd, Abū Zayd, a courageous man,
Lacking brothers and siblings,

With his sword he vexes enemies.
320 From his birth the prince is blessed,
In the fray he thrashes his rivals,
And he enters his wars eagerly,
The battlefield, his feastday.
From his birth he descends to the fray
325 In the vanguard with a mighty armspan,
When horses clash together
He opens the gates to misfortune.
O the nights, O the night!

[The poet repeats ll. 297 to 308.]

Abū Zayd grew up a horseman riding steeds,
He seizes fools with iron hands,
He reaches his goal against his greatest enemies,
345 He reaches his goal with noble people,
I swear by the life of our beloved Prophet, the Imam of the
Sacred Precincts.
When he heard about Abū Zayd, Daghīr became angry.
He said to his tribe: "Hear me, O listeners,"
He said to the Atwān Arabs, "Hear me, O valiant men,
350 "Let us plunder her horses and even the camels.
"Do not leave with the woman or child.
"I will abandon her alone in the wild,
"I will abandon her alone in the vast desert,
"O how she will suffer humiliation and disgrace!"
355 Then there came a lion, invisible, peace be upon Him,
Khidr, Khidr, may God be pleased with Him.
Then came a lion, invisible, from the open country,
Walking, quickening his steps,
Walking, quickening, he went to her.
360 He found Sharīfa weeping; beside her, her son.
The bold Khidr dispersed and beat the Atwān Arabs with
swords.
He knew their schemes with the aid of God the One,
He knew their schemes with the aid of God the One, the
Unique,
He turned to Khadra and said, "Bring me the boy."
365 She gave him the hero, Abū Zayd,
She gave him the Hilāli, Abū Zayd,
But the strength to endure did not come to her.
"Name him *Barakat*,[6] my secrets will be his;
"Though I become annoyed with him, I will be of use to him."

---

6. "Blessed."

370   The Pillar of Turbaned Ones, peace be upon Him, from that
          time armed him.
       Khaḍra Sharīfa peered about, she beheld Khiḍr not.
       Khaḍra Sharīfa peered about, she did not see him—
       She stared with her eyes, but she could not see him.
       Then came Prince Zahlān. He saw an army;

375   He identified a green pavilion and around it banners,
       He identified a green pavilion and around it tents.
       They were not Arabs of his tribe and not northerners.
       "I will send four horsemen to her, to the mother of the lad."
       She said, "I am a guest of the king, under his protection."

380   She said, "A guest, O slaves, go bring him the news.
       "Tell him guests have arrived, O generous countenance."
       The slaves went to him right away. They told him the news.
       He came to her and said, "Arise." She entered his tent.
       He came to her and said, "Arise, you enter safety,

385   "Raise Abū Zayd in happiness and perfection."
       They remained among the Zahlān a long time.
       The hero Abū Zayd grew and God made him robust.
       The hero Abū Zayd grew up and was brought to a *faqi*.[7]
       He was clever in writing and in prayers devout.

390   He was advanced in writing before he could read.
       He was advanced in writing, he had the best answer,
       People of the Koran, because he was upright.
       There were other young lads among the Zahlān.
       From the day they went to Koran school they were together.

395   From the day they went to Koran school together, they were
          with each other.
       Then came the Emir Abū Zayd. The teacher intended to harm
          him.
       The teacher began and said to the lads:
       "Hold him down, I will give him thirty blows,
       "Hold him down, I will give it to this naughty Abū Zayd."

400   They all encircled him, even the teacher.
       Abū Zayd fled from them, no one beheld him.
       Abū Zayd fled from them, O listeners,
       He ransacked the corners of the house, left and right,
       When suddenly he found a spear many years old.

405   It weighed eighty pounds. Abū Zayd held it level in his hand.
       It weighed eighty pounds, including its spear-point.
       The Emir Abū Zayd carried it in the palm of his hand.
       Then came Khaḍra and kissed him:
       "You distract me, my son, from private sorrows."

410   She said, "You distract me from lasting passions."
       He said to her: "I will not retreat until I kill the teacher."

---

7. Koranic school teacher.

She said: "That would be villainous."
While they were talking, the teacher arrived.
Muḥammad let us praise Him.

[Pause.]

415   While they were talking, the teacher came intending to betray
him.
Abū Zayd brought him a meal that they gave him to eat.
The teacher behaved shamefully, his sin his punishment,
The teacher behaved shamefully, and his sin overcame him.
Abū Zayd went to him, to the Koranic school, as earlier
ordained.
420   The teacher said to Abū Zayd, "O ill-mannered slave."
The teacher tried to seize Abū Zayd. Abū Zayd hit him with a
spear, he threw him down.
The teacher tried to seize Abū Zayd. Abū Zayd hit him with
the spear, he was thrown,
His breath left him, and blood flowed.
Then came the teacher's brother Ruyan and wrapped him in
cloth.
425   He went to Zahlān, he requested rescue.
He went to Zahlān, he said: "O emir,
"Abū Zayd killed the teacher, the Shaykh."
The emir said: "But he is a small child!
"Go now, attend to the school, for your memory is great."
430   Abū Zayd's knowledge was perfected by God, his Lord,
And his knowledge was perfected out of piety.
Abū Zayd became the schoolteacher, and the brother, a
monitor.
If a child entered school late, he called to God,
Fearing the hero Abū Zayd would cut short his life.
435   Muḥammad let us praise Him.

[Abū Zayd kills Daghīr, leader of the Atwān Arabs who tried to humil-
iate Khadra Sharīfa when she was banished to the desert. The defeated
Atwān Arabs join forces with an Arab prince, Emir Jayel, and his tribe
to attack the Zahlān, the protectors of Abū Zayd and his mother. Emir
Jayel is invincible, because he possesses a magic necklace capable of
summoning a fighting genie. Abū Zayd flees, but when assured of divine protection by Khidr, who captures the genie, he returns and defeats his enemies. Abū Zayd and the Zahlān tribe depart for the Hilāli
Arabs. There Abū Zayd provokes a fight with the Hilāli leaders who
call upon their strongest warrior, Rizq, who battles Abū Zayd while his
mother, Khadra Sharīfa, rejoices. It is only at the intervention of Shīha
(Rizq and Khadra Sharīfa's daughter, Abū Zayd's sister) that Abū
Zayd's identity is revealed. The family and tribe are reunited.]

PART THREE

CENTRAL AFRICA

Central African Epics

QUESTIONS OF PERFORMANCE STYLE AND HISTORICAL REFERENCE may serve to distinguish Central African epic traditions from those of West Africa. History is essentially absent from the stories of Jéki, Mwindo, Kahindo, and the Mvet tradition of the Cameroon-Gabon region, except insofar as the epics reflect and preserve images of the past embedded in their social descriptions and narrative construction. Instead, we find cycles of stories centered on a given figure such as Jéki, or others not represented in this anthology, such as Lianja and Ozidi; in the case of the *mvet* tradition, an entire fictive world lies at the performer's disposal.

Performances are more visibly associated with ritual than in the Sahelian traditions, although the occasions remain overwhelmingly secular. Performers are often initiates in spirit cults, and their art is the product of apprenticeship rather than genealogy and birth to a status group as with the *jeli* of the Mande (although some Sahelian performers do claim a relation with the spirit world and one should not belittle the importance of training in the Sahel). A performance is in some sense the occasion of spirit possession, and certainly a focus of occult energy; descriptions of apprenticeship and training always include mention of the magical preparation of the performer. Women may also perform, although there is little documentation available of their performances and training, if different from that of the men.

More significant, however, are the performative differences between the two areas. In this region, epic performance becomes in a sense a group effort: the lead performer is accompanied by a team of musicians and singers (the backup chorus). Performances take place not in the private space of a courtyard but in open and public spaces; the performer him- or herself is not stationary and impassive but is passionately and dramatically involved in the reenactment of the story. The audience will participate in the songs and dances which punctuate the narrative. All these features combine to provide grounds for a general regional distinction in performance traditions between the Sahel and central Africa, although one must note that the distinction is not rigid; one may find counter examples in each region. The division reflects a sense of the prevailing performance mode for the region.

The various groups represented in the following selections may be classified as belonging to the Bantu language family, that broad label which covers the southern third of the continent; they are concentrated in the upper tier of that region (Cameroon, Gabon, northeastern Zaire), in the dense equatorial forests. The economic activities described center on hunting and fishing, although there is some mention of agriculture. The political traditions of the groups do not include states and great kingdoms, although on the local level there is a clear hierarchy of authority derived most probably from patterns of migration in which the first settlers in a region subsequently become the chiefs.

Exposure to the outside world varies considerably among the groups. The Douala of Cameroon (*Jéki la Njambè*) have been trading

255

middlemen for centuries. The baNyanga of Zaire have been relatively isolated, having migrated southwest from the region of Uganda into their present territory.

22. The Epic of Mvet Moneblum, or The Blue Man
Narrated by Daniel Osomo

*Recorded in 1967 in Yaoundé, Cameroon, on the occasion of the inaugura-
tion of the Faculté de lettres of the University of Yaoundé. Transcribed by
Arthur Sibita. French translation by Samuel Martin Eno-Belinga. First
published as S. M. Eno-Belinga, Mvet Moneblum (n.p.), Yaoundé, 1978.
This excerpt translated and edited by Stephen Belcher.*

Mvet is the term used in Central Africa, among the Fang and Bulu populations of Cameroon and Gabon, for a narrative performance style and
for the instrument which accompanies it. Performances by the *Mbom-
mvet* are public and highly animated, incorporating songs and dances
in which the audience may participate. The subject matter of the *mvet* is
not historical but imaginary or mythical: the world evoked is one of the
distant past in which the mortal men of the clan of Oku struggle with
the immortals of Engong who are ruled by the great man of power,
Akoma Mba. Stories typically develop a conflict, a complex intrigue of
mobile and airborne characters, and finally a resolution through the
decisive intervention of Akoma Mba. The knowledge required of the
performer is one of geography and genealogy, necessary for a proper
description of clan relations, but there is little evidence for standard
story lines. The performer is free to shape his or her story in this mythical landscape as he or she wills, and the results are highly creative.

The modern nation of Cameroon is a highly diverse one, prid-
ing itself on representing Africa in microcosm. Before World War I, it
became a German colony; after the war, it was divided between the
French and the British. The forced labor on the road, to which the hero
is subjected, echoes the colonial experience. The expressions of magic
and power the various warriors exhibit may also recall external mecha-
nisms. The family conflict between a son and a father over the question
of a wife is an ordinary sort of domestic tension. Fathers are expected to
provide the bride-price for a son, but they need not be eager to incur
the sometimes heavy expense.

Canto 1

     This is what happened.
     The man, Ondo Mba, had a son.
     He named him Mekui-Mengômo-Ondo.
     As soon as Mekui-Mengômo-Ondo was old enough to marry,
5   He asked his father, "When shall I marry?"
     His father answered him, "A son of Ekañ never asks his father
         when he will marry."
     His father swore an oath. "May I disappear and meet the dead
         while I mourn Ngema!
     "If you dare to ask me such a question again,
     "I will cut off your head,
10   "Or I will banish you."

Canto 2

That is why his son stayed sitting for two days,
Until again he came to ask his father, "When will you get me
    married?"
To! His father growled,
And a violent storm shook the sky nine times.
15   The courtyard was plunged into thick darkness.
And there, Ondo himself took his horn and blew it, *ko-o-o!*
The sky once again became as clear as a new dawn.
       Now we sing and dance!
       Let us sing of the deeds and exploits of the Ekañ. Hey!
20   I have come to hear you. The ears are listening.
       In truth, they are listening!

Canto 3

Then his father dressed his lower half.
He dressed his upper half.
He put on his iron armor.
25   He put on the shoes which speak of war.
He took his iron helmet, and *to!* placed it on his head.
Then he seized the great sword named *Abe-Nleme-Otyeñ.*[1]
He fixed in the earth his finger which speaks of war.
30   He rose into the clouds, and the sound of his passage was
    duk-duk-duk!
He came to the home of Akoma Mba.
To! He lay face down before Akoma Mba.
He told him, "By the tomb and all the dead, while we mourn
    Ngema-Ekañ!
"I beg you to take captive the child named Mekui-Mengômo-
    Ondo.
35   "Cut off his head, or send him into exile."

[Akoma Mba sends Abe-Mam-Ondo to fetch Mekui-Mengômo-Ondo. At
first Mekui-Mengômo-Ondo resists; there is fighting until his mother
intervenes and tells him to find out what Akoma Mba wants of him.
After Mekui-Mengômo-Ondo arrives, his father Ondo Mba asks Akoma
Mba to exile the son, and Akoma Mba summons the great men of the
clan for a council.]

Canto 7

In the morning,
Everyone came together: young and old, women and children.
They gathered before Akoma Mba at Fen.
Akoma said to Ondo Mba, "Now all the people of Ekañ are
    gathered here.

---

1. "Sword-of-the-cruel-heart."

258

40   "You have asked me to exile Mekui-Mengômo-Ondo.
       "Tell the people of Ekañ on what grounds you have asked for
           his exile."
       Ondo answered, "Since the time when our ancestors of the Ekañ
           left, one after the other, the following lands,
       "The ancient lands of Anyu-Ngom, of Biba, of Mfulu-Amvam,
           of Bivele-Vele,
       "Of Ewa-Mekon, of Ebap-Yop, of Ekutu Mintum, of Aya-
           Minken . . . .
45   "Have we ever heard of a son asking his father when he would
           marry?
       "That is why I say you are no man," he said to his son.
       "A man would never ask his father, 'When shall I marry?'
       "That is why I am banishing Mekui-Mengômo-Ondo,
       "So that no longer will he resemble a woman here among us in
           Engoñ-Zok."
50   A heavy silence sat over the assembled Ekañ-Mebe'e.

Canto 8
       Kpwo! Medañ lay face down before Akoma
       And told him, "I have something to say.
       "I address this request to Akoma.
       "Let Ondo entrust Mekui-Mengômô to me, and I shall get him
           married,
55   "For Ondo seems to me a poor man."
       Ondo answered, "That is out of the question!
       "No other man shall arrange the marriage of my son."
       Kpwo! Meye-Mengini in turn lay face down.
       He said, "It shall not be Medañ.
60   "I shall be the one to marry him off, oh Akoma!"
       Ondo answered, "I am not of that opinion."
       Kpwo! Ebi-Zok, the son of Mba-Ndeme-Eyen, lay face down.
       Otuna Mba!
       He said, "Neither the one nor the other.
65   "I shall be the one to marry him off."
       Ondo answered, "No one in Engoñ-Zok has the right to marry
           off my son."
       Then all the Great Men of Engoñ-Zok became angry.
       They told Akoma, "Exile Mekui-Mengômo-Ondo."
                 Here we sing and dance!
70   Let us sing of the deeds and exploits of the Ekañ, ehee!
                 He took pity on me! Ehee!
                 And we hear on the other side of the mountain,
                     My ears carry far, ooo!
                 O, Mba! What a marvelous story!
                     My ears carry far, ooo!

> A matter without equal, a matter of great interest,
>> My ears carry far, ooo!
> Do you hear me, people of Abaña? Ehee!
>> Ehee! Ehee!
> Ehee! Aya! The fine man!
>> Ah, the white lover has crossed Ayina!
> The lover has crossed Nkomo!
> Ahaye! It is true that Akoma will win again!
> Silence!

[Akoma Mba wonders to which land he will exile Mekui-Mengômo-Ondo, and he sends for Nnômô-Ngañ the diviner to seek out the answer.]

Canto 9

85   Nnômô-Ngañ placed his healer's bag on the ground.
     He plunged his hand into the bag,
     He withdrew a mirror and placed it on the ground.
     He withdrew a horn and a leather cushion.
     He took his magic eyeglasses and put them to his eyes.
90   He seized the horn and blew it, *ko-o-o!*
     He spoke, he said, "I ask the spirits of the people of Ekañ,
     "Of Ngema-Ekañ, of Oyono-Ekan, of Mintya-Ekan,
     "I ask you,
     "Are you willing to send Mekui Mengômo into exile over a
          question of marriage?
95   "Let your desires and your consent be known!"
     His divining tools flamed up.
     The oracle had said yes.

Canto 10

     Nnômô-Ngañ said, "How shall I know into which land to exile
          him?"
     He looked in his mirror,
100   He saw a road leading out of Engoñ-Zok.
     The road ended at a great river.
     The river split into three other rivers . . .
     His gaze crossed the forest . . . and another forest. . . .
     He saw a road which led to the land of Yeminsiñ.
105   The queen of that land is named Ntye-Ngon-Oye-Ndon.
     She has a mysterious power
     Which she uses to gain wives for her brother.
     This is how her magic works:
     She owns many, many pigs.
110   The pigs are neutered.
     Any time she desires to get wives for her brother,
     She first sends the pigs to the village she will visit

So they will eat all the foods of the village.
When they have finished eating the village's crops, they invade the village.
115 They go into the houses.
They eat the food in the kitchens,
They take the pots from the fire.
That is when all the villagers throw themselves on the pigs to kill them,
All the men and women.
120 When Ntye-Ngono knows that they are all gathered, then she sounds her horn.
Immediately, everyone is caught within an iron fence.
Ntye-Ngono appears in the middle of them.
She has a magic jewel on her breast,
And as though by magic, any man who moments before might have boasted he could marry five women, grows breasts on his chest, and on his head he has women's hair.
125 She tells her brother, "You may marry them all. There are no longer any men among them; the men have all become like women."
That is when Nnômô-Ngañ asked, "Could Ntye-Ngono keep Mekui-Mengômo in exile?"
He blew his horn, *ko-o-o!*
The shades remained silent, the oracle did not approve.

Canto 11
He stopped looking in that direction.
130 He saw a trail.
The trail led to Mvele-Mekomo, son of Mekomo-Obama, himself a descendant of the Yemiñyon.
He had announced that no longer would he tolerate meeting a smoker of tobacco, on the road or around himself,
Because tobacco disturbs the order of the world.
Any smoker he met immediately lost his head.
135 He hated tobacco for this reason.
In old times,
Only adults over thirty had the right to smoke.
But now, today,
Children of ten can smoke.
140 Women smoke.
They smoke tobacco wrapped in a leaf.
They smoke it in short-stemmed pipes.
They smoke it in ceremonial long-stemmed pipes.
People treasure tobacco.
145 Even toothless gums will chew tobacco.
Tobacco is always the medicine used for a purge.

That is why he had said to himself, "If that's the way it is,
    tobacco must disappear."
He came to limit the way in which the Ekañ consumed their
    tobacco, for there had been shocking excesses.
His encounter with the Ekañ is worth a mvet to itself alone.
150   Nnômô-Ngañ asked, "Could Mevele-Mekomo keep Mekui-
    Mengômo in prison?"
He blew his horn, *ko-o-o!*
The shades remained mute.

Canto 12

His gaze followed another path
Which led to Angono-Zok-Obama-Ndon, son of the Yemeñyiñ.
155   This was a man who had said that so long as he was alive,
He could not accept that anyone else bear the same name as he.
But he learned that another man answered to that name, a son
    of the Ekañ-Mebe'e.
He called him to a meeting at a place known as Mefan-Mevin:
"We will learn," he said, "which of us deserves to bear the
    name of Angono,
160   "And let no one else interfere in this business.
"When you come to meet me, bring also your wife Nda-
    Mengono.
"Then we shall learn which of us two deserves to be the hus-
    band of Nda-Mengono."
Only the mvet is worthy to tell what happened between the
    two men in the forest.
Then Nnômô-Ngañ asked, "Could Angono-Zok-Obama-Ndon
    hold
165   "Mekui-Mengômo-Ondo in exile?"
He blew his horn, *ko-o-o!* The shades remained silent.

[He continues to look down paths and through forests. The spirits continue to refuse the places.]

Canto 23

He looked to another side
And followed the third path
Which leads into the forest of the Yemenjañ.
170   If you go through that forest,
You come to Enye'e-Minsili, home of Ekañ-Dume-Mve, son of
    the Blue Men.
Looking to the other side of the mountain,
You see a village high up named Bengobo,
Home of Efeñ-Ndoñ, the Blue Man.
175   Then Nnômô-Ngañ asked, "Might I send Mekui-Mengômo-
    Ondo in exile to the land of the Blue Men?"

He questioned the spirits: *so-o-o!* The oracle approved.
Then Nnômô-Ngañ told Akoma,
"Send Mekui-Mengômo in exile to the land of the Blue Men, to
the house of Efeñ-Ndôñ."

[Mekui-Mengômo-Ondo and his escort travel to the land of the Blue
Men. They stop in several villages along the way, where the escort displays a ravenous appetite and wakes everyone up in the middle of the
night.]

Canto 30
180 Our young men were sleeping soundly when, in the middle of
   the night,
  Kpwañ-Ondo took his horn and blew, *ko-o-o!*
  Immediately, the animals that announce the morning greeted
   the new dawn.
  From the other side of the mountain, the master heard the first
   morning activities.
  First came the long call of the *daman*,[2] who said,
185   I went up, o!
    I came down, o!
    I went up, o!
    I came down, o!
  That was the *daman's* greeting the first glimmers of the dawn.
190 There was another call:
    I come, I move with little steps, here I am!
  That was the owl greeting the first glimmers of the dawn.
  There was another call:
    Tyorooot! bañ! bañ! bañ!
195 That was the bat greeting the first glimmers of the dawn.
  And there was another call: *Aïe! aïe! aïe!*
  Where did this call come from?
  It was the toucan, suffering from a violent toothache because he
   had eaten some *engo*.[3] He flew off to the mountaintop to be
   treated by the healer.
  His brother followed him, holding a bag of coins which he
   wasted in gambling.
200 As he pulled out the coins, one could hear him:
    Nep! Nep! Nep!
  That was the toucan greeting the first glimmers of the dawn in
   his way.
  One could hear another call:
    Vovolivo mewo! Was!
205 Those were the parrots, passing through the clouds, greeting
   the light of day.

---

2. A bird. 3. A tree.

One could hear another call:
> O, death! O, death!
> I am good hearted.
> Is that why I must eat raw mice?

210 The elegant white cat was greeting the dawn in her way.
One could hear another call:
> *Kpwraa! Ma'a!*
> Move on!

The ram was bleating while joined with the ewe in the early
morning.

215 One could hear another call:
> *Ko! Ko! Ko!*
> See how he goes!
> O-o-o!

The rooster was greeting the dawn.

220 And one could hear also:
> *We, we, we,*
> We are together!

While the mother called:
> Hurry up, hurry up, hurry up!

225 The hen was calling her chicks while greeting the start of the
day.

[The men continue on their way through other villages.]

Canto 32

There is a meeting place of three roads.
The first road leads to Akok, home of Tolo-Obama-Ngema,
The man with a single eye set into his armpit;
His face is blind and you see in it only the ears, the mouth, and
the nose.

230 The second road leads to the land of the man named Nkum-
Etye-Ndon, of the tribe of the Yemenjañ.
The third road leads to the land of the Blue Men, to the land of
the man named Ekañ-Dumu-Mve, of the people of the Blue
Men and of Efeñ-Ndôñ.
That was the land to which they were leading Mekui-
Mengômo-Ondo for his exile.
In those days, the masters would spend the night in Ngon-
Esele-Mendim.

235 When morning came,
They left Ngon-Esele-Mendim,
And headed for the forest of the Yemenjañ.
They stopped in the land called Nne-Zam, home of Ondo-Nkoo-
Ela.
Before them, they saw a country splendidly shining! The earth
was blue, blue.

264

240   The dwellings were blue.
          To! They stopped at the threshold of the men's hut.
          They took out the writing they had brought from Engoñ-Zok,
             from Akoma Mba.
          They presented it to the man named Ekan-Dumu-Mve.
          When Ekan-Dumu-Mve saw what was in the message,
245   He returned the writing to Kpwañ-Ondo and said that he was
             not Efeñ-Ndôñ.
          "Go to that wide land you see over there, up on that mountain.
          "When you reach it, go to the foot of the iron tower,
          "So that the man named Efeñ-Ndôñ can see you through the
             clouds, from the sky lands where he lives.
          "And then he will send a vehicle to fetch you," he said.
250   The young men replaced the writing in the bag.
          Kpwo! They rose above the ground.
          Up there in the clouds, they made a noise like thunder.
          Inside his house, Efeñ-Ndôñ turned his ear.
          He asked, "What is making the air mass move that way?"
255   Efeñ-Ndôñ was on the threshold of his lofty home.
          He saw the young men spinning in the clouds.
          Suddenly, they stopped at the foot of the iron tower.
          "This is the place we were told of," they said.
          As soon as Efeñ-Ndôñ looked through his glasses,
260   He saw our three young men there at the bottom of the iron
             tower.
          The master took the cushion which sows the storm, and a great
             wind shook the sky.
          The wind came from the top of the sky.
          The great wind blew to the place where our young men were
             standing.
          All at once, *mek!* the wind carried them into the air.
265   And *To!* They found themselves at the threshold of the heaven-
             ly home of Efeñ-Ndôñ.
          Kpwo! Kpwo! Our young men lay face down before Efeñ-Ndôñ.
          Kpwan-Ondo took out the writing and handed it to the man
             they call Efeñ-Ndôñ.
          Efeñ-Ndôñ took the big paper and he read.
          Efeñ-Ndôñ then asked, "Which among you is named Mekui-
             Mengômo-Ondo?"
270   *Kpwo!* Mekui-Mengômo-Ondo himself lay face down and he
             said, "I am the one named Mekui-Mengômo-Ondo."
          He added, "And these two men are Kpwan-Ondo, son of the
             daughter of the Yemingel, and Njik-Zok-Ekum-Nge."

[Mekui-Mengômo-Ondo is sent to prison. The next day, Efeñ-Ndôñ summons him to impose tasks upon him.]

Canto 33
... Efeñ-Ndôñ told him, "I am not the one who put you in
  prison.
"Akoma is the one who exiles you.
"And so now I will show you the jobs you must do.
275 "I will make you build roads,
"And all the prisoners you find in the prison will work with
  you.
"The first road you built will go from here to the land of the
  man named Nna-Beyeme.
"When that road is built, you shall start building a second road
  leading to the man named Evo-Menumu.
"When those roads are built, I will give you other jobs."
280 Mekui-Mengômo asked, "How many prisoners are there in the
  prison?"
Efeñ-Ndôñ answered, "I have three hundred prisoners."
He said, "Listen. I will work with the prisoners,
"But I don't want to see a single soldier watching over them. I
  will be with them myself.
"Also, I ask you to make sure that I am properly fed.
285 "Each day, I must have two sheep and three chickens.
"And for the prisoners, you must provide a hundred chickens
  and fifty sheep.
"And my stomach can certainly hold two bunches of pounded
  plantain.
"So much for the meals.
"Now, let me take possession of my tools, for tomorrow we start
  work."

[Mekui-Mengômo-Ondo lines up the prisoners and gives them their instructions. He collects tools. Efeñ-Ndôñ sends food to the prisoners, but
Mekui-Mengômo-Ondo instructs the women that boiled vegetables are
not acceptable.]

Canto 35
290 When day came, Mekui-Mengômo rose.
He dressed himself.
He took his war belt and bound it around his waist.
He took in his hand the flaming sword,
Assembled all the prisoners.
295 The master opened the storehouse.
He told the prisoners: "Take these tools and let's get to work."
The prisoners asked themselves, in low voices, "Who is this
  man who leads us to work? Will we come out of this
  venture with our lives? Are we rushing to our doom?
  Where does this man come from?"
Mekui-Mengômo told the prisoners, "Let us go."

And they went.

300 When he and the prisoners had come before Efeñ-Ndôñ, he
prostrated himself and said, "Today we start a great job."

Efeñ-Ndôñ told him, "First, you shall build the road leading to
the land of the man named Nna-Beyeme."

He asked, "What distance separates us from that land?"

"That land is two months' march away."

He said, "I think it will take me two days to finish the road
which leads there."

305 When he and the prisoners came to the work site, he told them,
"Place yourselves here. This is where we shall work."

Mekui-Mengômo then asked the prisoners, "Do you know my
land?"

The prisoners answered, "We do not know where you come
from, or from what land."

Mekui-Mengômo told them, "I am a man of Mbayan Bikop,
where the dwellers of Ekan-Mebe'e are accustomed to dry
human skins in the sun, like pumpkin seeds and peanuts.

"That is why I tell you, truly, that until I blow my whistle to
stop the work, you will work without a moment's pause."

310 Mekui-Mengômo said this to the men: "Take your places on
either side of the road."

The prisoners took their places.

Mekui-Mengômo drew his flaming sword.

He swung the flaming sword to one side, and *fuuum*, all the
trees were cut down.

He swung the flaming sword to the other side, and all the trees
fell.

315 He struck his breast, and vomited a golden egg.

He dropped the golden egg and sword, "Oh, my fathers
Mebe'e-Me-Ekan, Ngema-Ekan, Oyono-Ekan-Nna, give me
the strength to build this road."

He hurled the golden egg into the air,

To! It fell to the ground, and *fuuum!* the road was built in an
instant.

That day, you could see the road stretch from the threshold of
Efeñ-Ndôñ's home out of sight.

320 Then he told the prisoners, "The only work you have to do is to
sweep any litter on the road. Let no one touch the other
tools. Put all this stuff on the ground, we have worked
enough for today."

He looked at a sundial and saw they were at midday.

He told the prisoners, "We must go home."

When they got back, he told the prisoners. "Go, wash yourselves. I can't stand to have dirty prisoners near me."

He took a large block of soap and gave it to the prisoners.

325 When the prisoners had come back from their bath,

Mekui-Mengômo dipped his hand into his bag and drew out
    the little cushion that sows the wind.
He threw the cushion in the air, and *tin!* a large trunk appeared
With a ring of keys as large as a hand.
The man took the keys and opened the trunk, and *kpwin!*

330   He lined up the prisoners.
To each he gave clothing to cover the top of the body, and cloth-
    ing to cover the lower part of the body.
To each prisoner he gave a pair of sandals
As well as a headdress to cover their head.
He said, "This is the right costume for prisoners.

335   "I don't like to see badly dressed prisoners."
He left the prisoners gathered in the courtyard.
He pressed into the ground the finger which announces war,
    and in the wave of a hand he was in front of Efeñ-Ndôñ.
He said, "Come see the prisoners dressed in their finest."
Efeñ-Ndôñ said, "I will come see the prisoners today, early in
    the afternoon."

340   Early in the afternoon, Efeñ-Ndôñ joined Mekui-Mengômo at
    the prison.
Mekui-Mengômo lined up all the prisoners.
Efeñ-Ndôñ saw that the prisoners were clean and well dressed.
Then Efeñ-Ndôñ congratulated Mekui-Mengômo-Ondo thus:
    "You are a good man to take such good care of my prison-
    ers."
"When shall we have food?" asked Mekui-Mengômo.

345   Efeñ-Ndôñ answered, "When I get back to my house, I shall
    send you food."
When Efeñ-Ndôñ got back, he told the bodyguard to collect
    food throughout the village and bring it to the prison.
An instant later, you could see a crowd coming from the
    village, taking food to Mekui-Mengômo-Ondo.
After the master had distributed the food to the prisoners, he
    chose two prisoners and told them,

350   "You shall stay with me and prepare all my meals."
He also said, "I say to all the prisoners that we shall only work
    once in a day.
"Prepare all this food that people have brought you, and eat it
    without leaving the prison."
The prisoners took the food.
Then four men prepared a meal for Mekui-Mengômo-Ondo.

355   When the meal was ready, they went to tell Mekui-Mengômo-
    Ondo.
The master arose to eat.
He took two sheeps' heads and offered them to the prisoners.
Then he ate everything prepared for him, leaving no scraps.

The prisoners exclaimed, "Is it true he ate all the food and left
no scraps?"
360 Night came and the master lay down and slept.

[The next day they finished the work with the same division of labor as
before. Mekui-Mengômo goes to tell Efeñ-Ndôñ that the job has been
finished.]

Canto 36
Efeñ-Ndôñ clapped his hands, *tyoe!* and caught the fold of his
mouth between his two hands.
Efeñ-Ndôñ rang a bell, *kangan!*
A young woman answered from inside the palace.
Kpwo! The young woman lay face down before her husband.
365 He said, "See, here I present you a strange man.
"I asked him to build me roads; he is in prison here.
"He has gone twice, and now he tells me the road is finished."
The young woman asked, "What country is this man from?"
He said, "Let him tell you his tribe himself."
370 "I am a man of the Ekan-Mebe'e. My father's name is Ondo-
Mba.
"The king of the Ekan-Mebe'e is named Akoma Mba."
"And why are you in prison?"
"My father reproaches me with a lack of respect toward him,
because I answered back to him while he spoke.
"So he brought me before the court and asked for my banish-
ment,
375 "Without any further sort of process,
"And here I am in exile."
At that point, Efeñ-Ndôñ said, "Let's stop talking about that.
"Go back to your prison; I will go to the site to see your new
road.
"You say the first road is built; you must begin work on the
second."
380 Mekui-Mengômo admired the enchanting Nlem-Okele-Abum,
wife of Efeñ-Ndôñ.
Mekui-Mengômo admired her beautiful hair, glittering with
jewels bright as coins.
Mekui-Mengômo said farewell to Efeñ-Ndôñ and said, "I must
go back to my prison."
Efeñ-Ndôñ and his wife said goodbye.
Mekui-Mengômo admired the young woman a last time, staring at her. He admired her face, shining like the full moon
rising over the horizon.
385 Mekui-Mengômo said to himself, "When I have accomplished
the tasks which Efeñ-Ndôñ has set me,

> I will get this young woman as my reward, or let me die and
> see the dead whom we mourn, by Ngema!"
> And then Mekui-Mengômo went back to the place where he
> spent his nights.

[Mekui-Mengômo builds the second road as quickly as he built the first.
Efeñ-Ndôñ leaves to summon his Great Men to see the work that has
been done; he leaves his wife in charge and tells her that Mekui-
Mengômo and his prisoners should sweep up the town while he is
gone. Mekui-Mengômo dresses up and goes to talk to the woman about
his work.]

> He spoke to her with these words. "I have come to ask you
> what jobs I must do to serve Efeñ-Ndôñ and be useful?"
> She answered, "He wants you to keep order in the city, and to
> keep it clean."
> He said, "That was the first point!
390   "Also, I must admit that I am madly in love with you.
> "How do you feel about it?"
> The young woman had trouble hiding her feelings, and she
> answered,
> "What! If I tell you I love you, what should you do?
> "I am no longer a maiden; I am the wife of another man."
395   He answered, "What do you mean, the wife of another man?
> "Aren't I another man myself?"
> The young woman said, "If that is so,
> "Then I tell you I love you as much as you love me."
> He said, "I must go now, but I will come back later tonight."
400   The master went back to his prison.

[Mekui-Mengômo and the wife of Efeñ-Ndôñ carry on an affair while
Efeñ-Ndôñ is absent. Efeñ-Ndôñ returns with all the important men,
and they hold an assembly to discuss Mekui-Mengômo. They offer him
the kingship, but he refuses. He wants to be paid. Efeñ-Ndôñ says he
will not be paid.]

> Without any further ado, Mekui-Mengômo-Ondo went back to
> his chosen home and took his war belt, which he fastened
> about his waist.
> He also took a great haversack, tying the straps about his waist.

Canto 42

> Mekui-Mengômo fixed in the earth the finger that speaks of
> war, while anger rose to his head.
> He raced off toward the palace of Efeñ-Ndôñ.
405   He was heard to say to Efeñ-Ndôñ, "Pay me my wages, for I
> must leave."

Efeñ-Ndôñ told him, "I don't owe you anything."

When Mekui-Mengômo heard Efeñ-Ndôñ say he didn't owe anything, he growled, *to!* and became angry with Efeñ-Ndôñ.

After he growled, he reached out his right hand and seized Nlem-Okele-Abum, the wife of Efeñ-Ndôñ, and carried her off in his haversack, *to!*

And he said, "This woman is the price of my wages, for the work I did for you.

410   "Because of that, she is mine, and I will take her to Engoñ-Zok."

He swore by Mebe'e-Me-Ekan and Ngema-Ekan and raced off toward the courtyard, carrying the young woman in the sack;

He had tied the straps around his waist, he held the flaming sword in his hand.

He meant to go back to Engoñ-Zok.

That is when Efeñ-Ndôñ growled.

415   As he growled, thick shadows invaded the courtyard.

At that moment, Mekui-Mengômo-Ondo in turn blew his horn, *ko-o-o!*

The sun backed up on its steps and reappeared at the east, as though at dawn.

One could see Mekui-Mengômo fixing in the earth the finger that speaks of war

As anger rose to his head.

420   Immediately the young man carried the woman off above the clouds.

Then Efeñ-Ndôñ struck his breast to vomit a charm; he struck the earth with the charm, *to!* and a stone wall rose from the earth to the sky to block any ways to Engoñ-Zok.

Then Mekui-Mengômo growled like thunder, *to!* and the iron [sic] wall parted in its middle, *mek!*

The young man went through to the other side, he had the young woman with him.

As soon as Efeñ-Ndôñ realized the young man had burst the stone wall,

425   The master reached out his right hand, and with his hand as a trap cut off the path of Mekui-Mengômo and his wife. *To!* they were at the palace.

Wos! Efeñ-Ndôñ took back his wife.

Kpwo! Mekui-Mengômo again seized the young woman and put her in his haversack.

You saw him place in the earth the finger that speaks of war, and soon the master rose through the clouds.

You heard Efeñ-Ndôñ blow his horn, *ko-o-o!*

430   He took out a great iron net, he hurled it into the sky.

Mekui-Mengômo meant to head for the other side, and *vias!* the
   iron net picked·him up as well as the young woman.
And *to!* both of them were again before the palace of
   Efeñ-Ndôñ.
Then Mekui-Mengômo spoke a prayer, "Oh, Fathers of the
   Mebe'e-Me-Ekan, Ngema-Ekan, Oyono-Ekan, tell
   Nnomo-Ngan that misfortune is striking me in the land of
   the Blue Men, the land of Efeñ-Ndôñ."

[The spirits pass the word on to Nnomo-Ngan, who tells Akoma Mba.
Akoma Mba sends Mbot-Ekam to help Mekui-Mengômo; along the
way, Mbot-Ekam sells tobacco. When he arrives and tries to help
Mekui-Mengômo, he is propelled back to Engoñ-Zok. Akoma Mba
summons an assembly with a special drum, and a rescue party is
formed. Nlem-Okele is seized and brought to Engoñ-Zok. Medan Bot
wages war for two months, but eventually asks Akoma Mba for help.]

Canto 55
435   As soon as he received the message, Akoma sounded the gold-
          en bell, *kangan!*
       And then appeared Menye-Me-Akoma and Medja-Me-Akoma,
          both sons of Akoma Mba and twin brothers.
       To! They lay face down before their father.
       Their body was covered with scales from head to foot.
       They did not look like human beings.

[Akoma Mba sends them to help Mekui-Mengômo. On the way, they
ask the spirits where to find Efeñ-Ndôñ. Mebe'e-Me-Ekan comes with
them.]

440   They went to the man named Etam-Mot-Nkomo-Boto-Ovo-Boto-
          Akuk-Boto.
       There, they were working the bellows which gave Efeñ-Ndôñ
          the strength to fight.
       Then Mebe'e-Me-Ekan gave the young man the magical charm,
          holding his hand.
       He said, "Strike the earth with this object."
       As soon as the young man struck the earth with that object, all
          the bellows burst.
445   All the spirits which were working the bellows lost the light of
          their eyes.
       He said, "Strike the earth again with your charm."
       As soon as the young man struck the earth, a great trunk came
          out of the entrails of the earth.
       He said, "Strike the trunk with your charm."
       The trunk opened like a mouth.
450   Out came the statue of a man.

He said, "Here is Efeñ-Ndôñ."

He said again, "Strike him on the breast with your charm."

Then, all the magics which were in the belly of Efeñ-Ndôñ
came out.

He said, "You can go and capture him now."

455 At that moment, Mebe'e-Me-Ekan struck the young man on the
head with a cushion of bat skin, and immediately the
young man was back with Medan and the others.

He said, "I am back. Now we must capture Efeñ-Ndôñ."

Medan called Otuna-Mba and told him, "Go block off the way
in the home of the spirits.

"Meye-Mengini will go to the moon and keep watch.

"Angono-Zok will go to the sun. Let us close off every way
out."

460 They called Okpwat, and said, "Now you may go and challenge him."

No sooner had the words been spoken than Efeñ-Ndôñ
appeared at the head of his army.

As soon as he charged down where the sons of Ekan-Mebe'e
were assembled,

Medan made straight for him.

Then Medan vomited a golden egg.

465 With a sharp blow, he struck Efeñ-Ndôñ in the back, and *to!* his
backbone broke.

And *lotototo!* They captured Efeñ-Ndôñ.

They captured Efeñ-Ndôñ and took him before Akoma.

Then Akoma Mba said to them,

"My son was exiled to your land,

470 "And you made him your slave and bound him to road building.

"So I tell you that his reward shall be this woman he has
seized."

He struck him with the magic cushion,

He took away all the charms which made him so formidable.

Then they put out one eye.

475 They cut off one ear.

They cut him on the back and gave him four scar marks.

They said, "By these signs, people will know that you have met
the Ekan along your way."

At that time, they gave him a writing which raised him to the
rank of Great Man.

Now he obeys the orders of Akoma.

480 They took the young woman and gave her to Mekui-Mengômo-
Ondo.

He has already married her.

I have said all I know about this story of the mvet.

23. The Epic of Jéki la Njambè Inono
Narrated by Pierre Célestin Tiki a Koulle a Penda

Recorded in Dibombari, Cameroon, in 1972 by Lucien Endene Mbedy and Eric de Rosny. Transcribed and translated into French by Joseph-Marie Epée. Edited by Joseph-Marie Epée and François de Gastines and published as Les merveilleux exploits de Djéki la Njambè *by Pierre Célestin Tiki a Koulle a Penda in two volumes by Éditions Collège Libermann in Douala, Cameroon, 1987. This excerpt edited and translated into English by Ralph Austen.*

THE HEROIC NARRATIVE OF JÉKI LA NJAMBÈ IS PERFORMED among the Sawa-Bantu-speaking peoples of the Cameroon coast, including the community which has given its name to the port city of Douala. The epic appears to be very old, probably preceding the establishment of the long-distance trading networks which made the Douala people prominent in precolonial Cameroon history. In fact the epic contains no direct references to any historical developments and when first recorded in extensive form around 1910, its performers claimed, "Our fathers and forefathers often recited this epic but they could not discover its meaning or what it is supposed to teach us" (Ebding, 1938, 36-102).

There appears to be no immediate connection between *Jéki* and the occasions upon which it is most frequently performed, such as funeral wakes. Skilled performers are well known but they have no formal social or ritual status and the epic is also recited by various men and women in quite casual circumstances at family gatherings or fishing encampments. Recent published and televised performances (including the one from which the present excerpts are taken) have been accompanied by extensive efforts at interpretation by local intellectuals, but these seem to belong more to a contemporary discourse of ethnic, national and Pan-African identity than to any meaning the narrative may have had in earlier times. The name "Njambè Inono" can be translated in some Sawa-Bantu languages as the "Creator God, son of the Eternal," but there is little agreement as to whether such a sense is valid, still less what it might signify.

Jéki exists in many variant forms but the basic plot seems to be fairly standard: Njambè is a village chief whose first wife (here called Ngrijo) initially bears him a daughter who is soon kidnapped by the spirits of the dead. Ngrijo then becomes pregnant with Jéki but remains in this state for many years without giving birth. Njambè banishes Ngrijo to a peripheral dwelling and takes several new wives who all bear him children, male and female. Following Jéki's delayed and remarkable birth, described in the first section, he undertakes a number of dangerous quests on Njambè's behalf (see second excerpt), stakes his life on various athletic contests with his brothers or other local champions, and also in many versions, rescues his sister from the underworld. The story is consistently said to "have no end," but in some versions there is a resolution where Jéki either dies, kills his father, or takes over from him peacefully.

The source of the present version of *Jéki*, Tiki a Koulle (b. 1918), is, like most of the few coastal bards who have been recorded, a man well educated in French who earned his living as a teacher and administrator in the local Catholic school system. He learned the epic from earlier well-established bards, although he admits some episodes (not included here) are his own. Tiki is presently the only public performer of *Jéki* and has developed, especially for the project of publication, a more structured version than is common but otherwise seems to be a valid representative of the regional tradition. The songs included in the excerpts here are all performed in variants of the Douala *ngoso* ("parrot") style closely associated with the rhythms of canoe paddling. Italicized exclamations in the right margin are audience or performer interjections.

Jéki's Birth

One day Dibengelé[1] came to Ngrijo and said to her: "Ngrijo, it has been a long time since I last saw you, many years since I came here. There is such a famine at the house! It is time for us to go fishing in the river; there are great quantities of shrimp in our stream just now. We must go fishing!" "I agree! I too am beset by famine."

On her way home Dibengelé met their husband. "Dibengelé, where have you been?" "I was telling my co-wife that we ought to go fishing tomorrow morning." "Hum! That co-wife of yours, it is sterility that she will die of, that worthless thing! Can she give birth? Each of you has eleven children by now; how many does she have? Can she bear a child and see it? That worthless thing, can she bear a child and see it?"

While he spoke in this manner, Ngrijo Epée Tungum approached and heard him. She spoke to Njambè, saying: "Yes, husband!"

"If you continue to call me your husband I will kill you on the spot! Am I your husband? Are you stupid? Who told you to call me your husband?"

"Yes, husband, I too want so much to give birth. I too, it would please me to hold a child in my arms! I too want the happiness of having a child! Do you think that it is I who holds back my womb so that I do not deliver? Why then do you mock me?"

[Song:]

> I, too, let me bear a child!
> Oh husband, let me bear one and let me see it!
> Oh husband, let me also bear a child!
> Let me bear one, I too!
> Let me bear one, oh husband!
> I too, let me bear one!

---

1. The senior of eight wives.

"I too, I want so much to give birth. I want to give birth! It would please me so much to hold a child in my arms! But I cannot get there!"

[Song:]

> The heart of a sterile woman
> Cannot really be happy!
> At least have pity on me!
> Let me also bear a child
> And let me see it!
> Let me give birth to one!
> And let him also make me happy!
> Let me give birth to one!
> And allow me also to walk with him in the village!
> Let me bear one, let me bear him!
> I also, let me bear him and let me see him!
> Let me bear one, let me bear him!
> I also, let me bear him and let me see him!
>   *Eh! Eh! Engingila ye! . . . Eyese e!*

At the break of day, the women thus went fishing. Once at the river, they were as far from Ngrijo as from here to Yaoundé,[2] because her stomach pushed them away. They began to fish at the river. They fished and the shrimp were so plentiful! As they continued to fish they finally moved out onto the water. Each of them had already filled a basket of shrimp.

The tide had gone out, completely gone out. Then the wind began to blow. As soon as the wind began to blow, the water rose. And as the water rose, the wind became terrible; the waves began to break. "Let's go back" said Dibengelé to the others. "If the tide cuts off our way out of the river we will be trapped!"

So they began to go back with the waves. It was then that a voice spoke from Ngrijo Epée Tungum's womb: "Ina! Sit down in the water and give birth to me!"

"Oh, what am I to do? Shall I give birth to you on the water with these waves which are breaking so powerfully?" "Hurry up, give birth to me!"

Njambè's wives were overcome with fear. The voice sounded to them like thunder. And it said: "Hurry up, give birth to me!"

> *Inambolo e!*

"Here on the water with these waves which are breaking so violently? Gently, gently, I am going to give birth!" The voice repeated: "Have mercy, hurry up, give birth to me!"

---

2. Capital of Cameroon, 300 kilometers away.

[Song:]

> Wave, go gently, gently!
> I am going to give birth on the water!
> Wave, go gently, gently!
> I am going to give birth on the water!
> The other day
> I was going to look for firewood
> And I gave birth in the forest!
> Today I will see it in all its colors!
> I have to give birth on the water, my brothers!
> Gently, gently!
> Me, I am going to give birth on the water!
> The waves are breaking
> And covering everything, covering everything!

Ngrijo Epée Tungum was pushed against the water and she gave birth on the water, *"Poo!"* But when she wanted to touch the child it objected. "Do not touch me!"

The child began growing right away, all of a sudden. How large it became! Njambè's wives fled, they threw all their shrimp on the ground! Dibengelé ran without stopping and went to tell her husband: "Something frightening just happened! Ngrijo Epée Tungum gave birth on the water!" "Ngrijo Epée Tungum just gave birth on the water?" "Yes!"

Then Njambè went out and sat down in his courtyard. He sat down to see the child who was born on the water. His wives came running and encountered the child where he was standing on the beach. He said to them: "Where are you going? Go back to where you came from, quickly!" Njambè's wives then turned back. "Dip your baskets into the water," he said to them. As soon as they dipped their baskets into the water they filled up with shrimp. Njambè's wives completely filled their baskets.

Inambolo e!

The women who had dipped their baskets into the water filled each one of them with shrimp. Then the child said to his mother: "Ina, sit down on the water, I am going to enter your womb!" His mother sat down on the water and he returned to the womb. Njambè sat at home, in his courtyard, to see how the child was who was born on the water. Njambè's wives came, each with a basket full of shrimp. The first ones were in front, others followed, and others continued to pass by. . . .

Njambè, seated, saw the stomach arrive, passing, passing, passing. "That womb, hasn't a child come out of it at last?" The stomach passed, passed, passed. All at once he saw Ngrijo Epée and, clicking his tongue against his teeth, said to her: "What filth there is beneath the heavens! I said that this rotten woman has a sterile womb, she cannot give birth!"

277

"Dibengelé, didn't you tell me that Ngrijo Epée had a child on the water? Where is that child? This worthless thing, can she bear a child? That nasty piece of goods! That one, the witchcraft of her father, Epée Tungum Bokambo, has filled her entire womb! Can she give birth? How can she not give birth at all?!"

"Yes husband, should you kill me? Even if you go to the Whites you will find sterility; among the Grassfields[3] , likewise; among the Ewondo, likewise! Am I the most sterile of all? Must I kill myself? Tell me!"

[Song:]

> I, must I kill myself?
> Oh husband, must I kill myself?
> She said to him : "Must I kill myself?
> "Tell me now!
> "Must I kill myself?
> "Sterile women even among the Whites.
> "Must I kill myself violently?
> "O husband! Must I kill myself?
> "Should you go among the Whites
> "You would find sterile women!
> "Should you go among the Mulattos
> "You would find sterile women!
> "Should you go among the Ewondo
> "You would find sterile women!
> "O husband! Must I kill myself?
> "Tell me!
> "O husband! Must I kill myself?"

And she went on her way. Upon arriving at her house, she unloaded the shrimp and cleaned, cleaned, cleaned.

Inambolo e!

The next day, as Ngrijo Epée Tungum was seated, a voice spoke from her womb: "Ina! Ina!" She said: "Yes! Here we go again!" "Ina!" She answered: "Yes, my child, I hear you!"

He said to her: "Tomorrow morning, as soon as you awake, sit down somewhere; don't do anything. When noon comes, set out for that silk cotton tree down there; it is there you will give birth to me. Tomorrow, precisely at noon!" To make a long story short, here we are at noon; it is impossible to distinguish the sky from the land. At high noon a darkness falls, a darkness which you can feel with your hands. Thus Ina sets off to place herself under the silk cotton tree. Hardly has she come under the tree when she begins to give birth. Let everyone lend their ears and listen!

---

3. Region in western Cameroon.

At the moment of delivery—

She gave birth to fly whisks, fly whisks, and fly whisks, up to nine.[4]

She gave birth to white cloths, white cloths, and white cloths, up to eighteen.

She gave birth to velour cloths, velour cloths and velvet cloths, up to eighteen.

She gave birth to miseseko rattles, to miseseko rattles to accompany singing up to two times nine.

She gave birth to leg rattles, leg rattles, and leg rattles for singers, up to two times nine.

She gave birth to harps and harps and harps, up to two times nine.

She gave birth to ancestral cutlasses and ancestral cutlasses, up to two times nine.

She gave birth to ancestral axes, ancestral axes, axes to cut tree trunks, up to two times nine.

She gave birth again to the ancestral whetstone, for sharpening cutlasses and all sorts of tools.

Then she gave birth to the ancestral spears, the ancestral spears, up to two times nine.

She gave birth to the ancestral rifles and she also gave birth to the ancestral cannon.

Then she gave birth to the *ngalo*,[5] the *ngalo*, and the *ngalo*, up to ninety-nine.

Then she gave birth to Ebènguè Njonga,[6]

Then she gave birth to the elastic vine which freezes,
> Then she gave birth to the elastic vine which burns,
> Then she gave birth to *Tombise Dikonbinjok*,[7]
> Then she gave birth to Esidijiji,
> Then she gave birth to Esidingengesingesin,
> Then she gave birth to Esidingongong.

Then she gave birth to the canoe with the palm-leaf sail and the nine-pointed paddle.

Then a voice spoke from her womb: "Ina! Now arise from here, go and give birth to me on the broken bottle glass down there and the fragments of demi-johns;[8] it is there that you must give birth to me. Do not place dead leaves or cloth or anything on the ground or on the broken bottle glass!"

And Ngrijo went off; her womb was very much lightened. Then she gave birth to the son of Njambè Inono on the broken bottle glass and fragments of demi-johns. She said to the child, "Should I pick

---

4. Fly whisks are symbols of authority. Nine is considered the perfect number.
5. Amulets. 6. What follows is the list of Jéki's magical weapons. 7. "That-which-can-run-over-the-elephant." 8. Large glass containers.

you up?" The child replied: "Pick me up, cut the umbilical cord, pick me up! Today is the day of my birth!"

[Song:]

> I, the son of Njambè,
> I was born on the bottles!
> I come out of the bottles,
> And I will return to the bottles.
> I, the son of Njambè,
> I was born on the bottles!

Inambolo e!

[Jéki's birth does not reconcile his father and mother. On the contrary, Njambè develops a violent hatred for his son and orders him to undertake a series of dangerous quests which he hopes will cause Jéki's death.]

Ngando ["Crocodile"]

[Early on the following morning, just as dawn was breaking and light appeared on the horizon, Budubudu and Eboy[9] appeared at the house of Jéki and his mother.]

"Toc, toc, toc! Father wants you to come!" Jéki went out, started on his way a few steps, then stopped and sent this message to his mother: "Ina! Father wants me to come this very day. I am going!"

When he arrived at Njambè's house, his father said to him: "Now listen to me, my son! In two days I will have visitors here, but there is nothing in the house for them to eat. There are plenty of crocodiles in the river. If you kill one of them for me, even a small one, I will have what I need for my guests!" "Very well!" said Jéki.

When he returned home, Jéki said to his mother: "Ina! Father wants me to go down the river and kill a crocodile for him!" Jéki's mother rose up off her feet and then landed hard on the ground. "Haven't I told you that your father does not like you. He has placed an enormous crocodile in the river and he hopes that when you go down there, the crocodile will kill you. Haven't I told you that your father does not like you?"

Jéki replied: "Not me! The panther did not kill me[10] and the crocodile cannot kill me either. Don't worry about me!"

At the crack of dawn "our man" took his canoe, his palm-leaf sail and his nine-pointed paddle. As the canoe got under way he tried to move slowly, slowly, slowly out of the river mouth. He guided the canoe, gradually, gradually, gradually moving in a curved path. He came out into the open sea, set up his palm-leaf mast, looked up at the

---

9. Jéki's half brothers. 10. In a previous episode.

sky, took hold of the rudder, and watched where he was going. Then he called out, asking for the great sea wind, asking it to come and carry him along.

[Song:]

> Take me, me, I am on my way! Take me . . .
> Great wind, take me! Take me . . .
> Yes, I am on my way! I am dying [of joy]! Take me . . .
> Even if it is to the west of the ocean! I am dying! Take me . . .
> Yes, I am always on my way! Take me . . .
> Great wind, take me along! I am dying! Take me . . .
> Even if it is to the west of the ocean! I am dying! Take me . . .
> So take me! Take me. . . .

And the wind came in floods, in gusts, blowing hard, filling the leaves of the mast very full and moving Jéki along at a very rapid pace.

The canoe now cut hard through the water: "*Wai, wai, wai, wai, wai, wai, wai!*" And the waves broke and spread out: "*Wea, wea, wea, wea, wea!*" And the canoe moved along at a dizzying speed!

Jéki then stopped the great wind short and took hold of his nine-pointed paddle. Then he called to the *ngalo*[11] "Now bring me my paddle!"

[Song:]

> My paddle! Oh my paddle!
> Bring me my paddle! Oh my paddle!
> My paddle! Oh my paddle!
> Bring me my paddle! Oh my paddle!

He barely thrust it into the water and "*Vongom, vongom, vom, vom,*" the canoe flew off like from here to Yaoundé.

He paddled: "*Vongom, Vongom, vom, vom!*" and the canoe took off at full speed and the water split: "*Wai, wai, wai, wai, wai!*" and the waves rose: "*Wea, wea, wea, wea, wea!*"

Eh! Eh! Eh! Inambolo e!

Then he saw something standing up in the sea like a wall, a wall which thrust straight up into the sky. He could no longer see before him, the wall having cast the whole place into darkness; so he stopped paddling. He gave his *ngalo* a brisk shake to consult them, saying, "Tell me what kind of wall this is!"

The *ngalo* replied, "You really do ask questions! The crocodile you have come to find, the enormous crocodile, isn't that him? Dear boy, it is surely your father's crocodile."

"So then! Is that crocodile really so big?"

"And how! A crocodile who swallows entire boats! Do you

---

11. Amulets.

know what your father is like? Njambè is such a one that, when you go into the waters, you find him there; when you go into the forest, you find him there; when you go into the clouds, you find him there again. Do you know what your father is like?"

Jéki said to himself: "Let's see, how will I get done with the crocodile now? Can I approach this beast?"

He shook his amulets and they said to him: "Listen, lay your paddle down in the canoe and let yourself be drawn nice and gently by the current. The crocodile, on his own, will thunder very loudly at you. Do you understand?" "Yes," he answered.

As he was told, he laid his paddle down in the canoe, which began to sail along. Then the crocodile clacked his teeth: "*Kwako-kop-kop-kop-kop!*" A blinding lightning bolt appeared in the east and flashed. The crocodile thundered, "What is going on here?!"

Jéki said to him, "Cousin, I have come to look for you because there is to be a meeting at our uncles' place which requires your presence!" The crocodile laughed and said, "There you are! Didn't I say so? If I do not come to my uncles, what kind of meeting could they possibly hold there?" He asked further, "To the east, to the west, to the north, or to the south, where are we going now?" "To the east," answered Jéki.

And the crocodile began to turn. He turned very, very clumsily toward the east and said to Jéki: "Now take your canoe, you will lead me with slow strokes of your paddle, slow paddle strokes to pass the cape, slow paddle strokes to pass the cape. Do not make any rapid little strokes at all. Lead me with slow paddle strokes, calmly, gently; that is how I will travel through the water with you, do you understand?" "I understand," answered Jéki.

So Jéki thrust his paddle into the water: "*Vongom, Vongom, vom, vom!*" And the canoe set forth slowly with the crocodile.

[Song:]

> Slow paddle strokes to pass the cape!
> > Motor-power paddle!
> > Oh, motor-power paddle!
> > Motor-power paddle!
> Slow paddle strokes to pass the cape!
> > Motor-power paddle!
> > Oh, motor-power paddle!
> > Motor-power paddle!

The canoe moved forward lightly with the crocodile. You should have seen them coming from the west out of the great ocean!

[Song:]

> Oh, motor-power paddle!
> Motor-power paddle!

Slow paddle strokes to pass the cape!
Oh, motor-power paddle!

He traveled a long time with the crocodile, lightly, lightly, lightly; straight, straight, straight, and finally grounded on the sand!

Inambolo e!

When they were grounded on the sand, Jéki shook his *ngalo* to consult it. The *ngalo* told him: "Listen, this crocodile should not stop on the beach; send water right up to the village!"

Jéki called the water; the water came in great quantities; it began to enter the village in waves, great waves. The water came like a hurricane. When Njambè himself noticed this water, he fled and entered his house. He said to his children: "Everyone get into the house! Something terrible is on the way!" How the water did come into the village! It even flooded the houses.

The crocodile came in, very, very clumsily. He came in with the water. Then Jéki stopped the water and told it to return to its bed . It returned completely and the crocodile was grounded on the sand. The crocodile was grounded among these houses, preventing the people to his right from seeing those who were to his left, because his back stood right up to the sky. He was so furious that when he saw a duck, he ate it; if he saw a dog, he ate it; a goat, he ate it; even a child of Njambè or whatever else came beside him, he wanted to eat it.

Njambè said, "No, Budubudu and Eboy go through the forest,[12] only through the forest and go to tell him to take back the crocodile!"

Budubudu and Eboy now departed, walking only through the forest. When they saw him [Jéki] they said, "Brother this is going very badly; the crocodile wants to exterminate us. Take him back quickly!"

Jéki and his mother exploded with laughter and said, "Didn't we tell you so? You cannot do anything more with the crocodile?" He went then and called the water, asking it to come. The water came in great, great quantities and the crocodile began to float again. Then Jéki said to him, "Go back now!"

[Song:]

Crocodile, go forever.
Crocodile, go forever.
Crocodile, go into the river.
Crocodile, go forever·

The crocodile reentered the river easily, easily, and went off.

Crocodile, go into the river!
Crocodile, go forever!

---

12. To Jéki at his mother's house.

The crocodile went away and descended deep into the water down, down, down, until it disappeared.

Eh! eh! eh! Inambolo e!

Njambè's hatred for Jéki and his mother became greater and greater. In effect, Jéki had annihilated the crocodile, he had so stultified it that it would not do anything, that it had become like a corpse.

baNyanga Epics of Zaïre

THE BANYANGA ARE A BANTU-LANGUAGE PEOPLE of northeastern Zaïre, dwellers in the equatorial forests; their lifestyle remains based on a mix of hunting, fishing, foraging, and limited forms of agriculture. They did not develop states or kingdoms; local communities are governed by hereditary chiefs. They coexist with the Pygmies of the region, from whom they have acquired many of their forest-dwelling skills, and who appear in the epics as servants of the chiefs.

The performance tradition from which Mwindo and Kahindo spring is rooted in the hunting camps which lie outside the settled communities. In that venue, the occasion for performance is simply the need to pass the time away from one's home and family, although Biebuyck and Mateene do note that a performance may be commissioned for the town as well, as a conspicuous and lavish entertainment put on by a person of means and prestige. Performers are initiates in the *Karisi* spirit cult, but in other regards performances are entirely secular affairs. The epics published by Biebuyck and Mateene were collected in the 1950s, at which time the baNyanga numbered some 27,000; we have little information on modern conditions and performances.

In the 1950s, there were few expert epic performers left among the baNyanga; nevertheless, in contrast to the neighboring Mongo and Nkundo traditions of Lianja, the Mwindo epic tradition seems vital and fertile. Biebuyck has published four different versions, each quite distinct in its presentation of the story. We find few signs of the contraction of material, the standardization of episodes, and the repetitiveness which mark Lianja and the modern Jéki tradition of Douala. Mwindo is a far more polymorphous vehicle for a variety of artistic and social concerns, while still sharing certain identifiable regional traits of which the principal one may be his reliance upon an older female relative for assistance and support in his adventures.

Biebuyck and Mateene have published the texts as prose, rather than with line divisions as is the case for most of the other texts presented in this volume. The performance does, however, involve a rhythmic or musical accompaniment like the others presented in this book, and the texts themselves have been termed "epics" since their first publication. We present the texts in prose, then, with the reminder that these are textualized translations. We have also omitted Biebuyck's extensive annotation.

24. The Mwindo Epic
Narrated by Mr. Shekwabo

Recorded in Mera, Zaïre, in 1954 by Daniel Biebuyck. Transcribed and translated into English by Daniel Biebuyck. Edited by Daniel Biebuyck and published in Hero and Chief: Epic Literature from the Banyanga (Zaire Republic) *by the University of California Press in 1978. This excerpt edited by Stephen Belcher.*

THE HERO MWINDO, "LITTLE-ONE-JUST-BORN-HE-WALKS," is in some regards a culture hero for the baNyanga; his exploits define the limits of their world and the modes of their life style. He is an utterly exceptional being, from his mode of birth to his departure from the world. In many regards his story conforms to "universal" hero-models: after his exceptional birth, such a hero often encounters considerable hostility from his father; his exploits lead him to the underworld, following either his father or a lost sister; he also travels to the sky. Throughout, he is often assisted by his paternal aunt.

The following excerpt is taken from the second of the four texts published by Biebuyck and presents a recurrent episode in Mwindo's career: his encounter with the supernatural being Nyamurairi and his daughter Kahindo. In this case the encounter is complicated by the presence of Mwindo's father Sheburungu in the underworld.

[The story starts with the miraculous birth of Mwindo and his sister. His sister is then married to Lightning, who lives in the sky; she brings down the knowledge of cultivation. She and Mwindo then find an egg, which hatches into a huge and ravenous bird that devours the village. The sister destroys it from within. Mwindo then draws the enmity of other chiefs.]

After Mwindo had distributed buffalo tails[1] to his peers, the chiefs, these peers harbored hatred against him because he ruled in fame surpassing them. Where Itewa dwelled, he pondered in his heart, saying that because Mwindo surpassed them, because his fame surpassed theirs, he wanted to go and fight a war of spears with him. Having spoken to himself in this manner, Itewa said to his people: "You all, each man a spear! Let him take it up to fight war with Mwindo, for tomorrow we shall set out to fight with Mwindo!" When his (Itewa's) people heard this, they prepared themselves with the spears. Where Mwindo remained, when he heard this news of warfare with Itewa, he was deeply grieved, saying: "Truly this is rough! The bad thing is that Itewa summons war to fight with me, and I am the one who gave him the chieftainship that he now holds. Indeed, on earth there is no good. So, he shall come to know me; tomorrow he shall know how strong I am." He said to his people: "Tomorrow we shall be

---

1. Symbols of authority.

attacked by Itewa. So, then, prepare yourselves!" After he had spoken to his people in this manner, they remembered it; they prepared themselves with the spears, saying: "Indeed tomorrow we shall set out to fight." When sky had changed to dawn, Little-call-of-Itewa left his village with his people; as he went to fight with Mwindo Mboru, he was singing:

> Little-call-of-Itewa, Little-call-of-Itewa
> Is being trapped, Little-call-of-Itewa.
> His antelope,
> Little-call-of-Itewa.
> His warthog,
> Little-call-of-Itewa.
> His waterbuck,
> Little-call-of-Itewa.

Where Mwindo dwelled, when he saw Itewa marching against him with the war of spears, he said to his people: "Leave your spears; just go like that. I shall take my scepter; it will fight with Itewa." They went like that. They went to the place where Itewa made his appearance. As they confronted each other, the people of Itewa hurled their spears against the people of Mwindo. The people of Mwindo were annihilated; they died. After they had died, Itewa took all the things of Mwindo and climbed with them and his people to his village. He was calling loudly for Munkonde, the one who had forged the spears for him, saying that where he had gone to war he had won. And he was singing:

> E! Munkonde, forger of large spears,
> Forger of spears.
> Munkonde, forger of large spears,
> Forger of spears.
> Munkonde, forger of things that are feared,
> Forger of large spears.
> Forger of things that are feared.
> E! Munkonde, we are going to Roba-Land,
> But not we.

After Itewa returned home, he took one goat; he gave it to the blacksmiths of Munkonde, saying that they had forged for him the spears with which he had fought. After he had finished giving this goat to Munkonde, the people entertained him; they played the drums and the horns for him. Four days passed and they still kept on dancing without going to sleep, because of the joy of winning the war.

In the place where Mwindo had remained, after he had been overcome in the war, he returned to his village, he himself and his dogs, Ndorobiro and Ngonde, and his scepter; that is all. His people are

decimated. And his father Shemwindo still dwells in his village of Tu-
bondo. Mwindo meditated by himself, saying that the one who overcomes a strong one, let him not say that he overcomes (someone else),
(rather) that he is overcoming himself. Having had this kind of medi-
tation, he said: "What now, a true man does not die on the ground. Act
first! I, Mwindo, I am not rubbed twice with the sign of war!" He stood
up in order to fight with Itewa. He went with his two dogs and his scepter; he went singing:

> I shall overcome the Snails.
> I shall fight over there, in the place of
>   Chunks-of-meat.
> I shall overcome the Snails.
> I shall fight over there in the place of
>   Chunks-of-meat.

Where Mwindo Mboru went, as he arrived at the entrance to the village
of Itewa, he threw his scepter on the ground. As he arrived in the middle of the village place, he looked around here and there: all the people, together with their chief, Itewa, were dead; and all the chickens,
the goats, and the flies—all these things had perished! Mwindo Mboru
praised himself in the middle of the village, saying: "Itewa, wake up
now. He who went to sleep wakes up again. You usurped power and
force for yourself, thinking that you would be capable against me.
Today, you here are the one whose fang is stuck in the ground. I had
told you that a young man cannot be saved by playing with his elder
brother. Lo! He is miserable, the one who tries to measure up to me; he
climbs on a difficult tree." After he had thus praised himself in the middle of the corpses of the people of Itewa, he took all his goods; he cut off
two of Itewa's fingers, and his tongue, and his penis. He returned home
with all these goods, singing:

> Mburu passes through the hunting grounds with good things.
> Nyamasangwasangwa is not dead.
> *Muntindi* bird passes through the hunting grounds with good
>   things.
> Nyamasangwasangwa is not dead.
> Mburu passes through the hunting grounds with goodness.
> Nyamasangwasangwa is not dead.

After he had returned home, Mwindo said: "My dogs are dying
of hunger; what shall I do now?" He spoke to his scepter, saying: "You,
scepter, because I was born already possessing you, up to now you
have overburdened me like a *murimba* stone and a *mutero* stone." He
said: "Produce food for me now so that these dogs of mine may eat it."
After he had spoken in this manner, he looked beside him: cooked

foods were already there! While giving this food he made a proclamation, saying: "You, Masters-of-the-subterranean-world, you who are on earth, and you who are in the sky, and you who are in the air, come to appear here to meet with me here where I am; give me heroism and much force and honor to surpass the other so-and-so chiefs who are next to me." Having finished speaking like that, he gave the food to his dogs. Having finished feeding the food to his dogs, he coughed, saying: "What now (about) my people? How now, you, my scepter?" He took his scepter; he threw it on the ground: all his people woke up; they were completely saved! When they had finished recovering, they went to bathe, and they were singing:

> We are like the ones throwing one another in the pools.
> We will throw Karunga in the pools.
> We are like the ones throwing one another in the pools.
> We will throw Karunga in the pools.

On leaving the river where they had bathed, they went, singing:

> E! Batondo,
> My kinsman, yoyo.
> My senior father,
> My kinsman, yoyo,
> Said that I shall not eat banana paste,
> Unless I eat the banana paste with meat.
> My kinsman, yoyo.

When they were now back in their village, all the houses were standing up again; they had finished building themselves! Mwindo Mboru was the one who had said to his scepter to erect the houses again. When Mwindo went to sleep he placed his scepter underneath his armpit.

When Mwindo's village was filled again like that—his children had been born, chickens were scurrying around like locusts—he said to himself that he, Mwindo, had not yet arrived at the place of God, being fully alive; that he was not himself, that it was befitting for him first to go and see God, so that he might meet with him. He said to his people: "Remain here, you all, together with those my dogs. When you will be met by difficult things arriving at the end of the village, those my dogs will fight against them; they will bring me the news in the place where I am. I am with you, however; I do not go far."

Having spoken like that, he grasped his scepter and a long bill-hook knife; he went with them. He arrived at a *kikoka* fern; he pulled it out; he entered at the place where he had pulled it out. Where he went, he appeared at a wading place. There he met with the daughter of Nyamurairi, called Kahindo. Mwindo was singing, saying:

E! Hawk, the termites destroy the trees.
Hawk, the termites destroy the trees.
E! Hawk, the termites destroy the trees.

After Mwindo Mboru had finished meeting at the river with Kahindo, daughter of Nyamurairi, (he noticed that) scabies covered her entire body: it begins at the big toe of the foot and arrives at the tussock of the hair. This Kahindo, daughter of Nyamurairi, when she saw Mwindo Mboru arriving for her, the heart burned her while she was scrutinizing him. She said: "Truly! A splendid young man, how beautiful he is, this one. Truly!" Having spoken like that, this Kahindo said to Mwindo: "You, young man, clean for me this scabies." Mwindo began cleaning her entire body, removing the scales very well. When Mwindo had finished cleaning her, Kahindo said to him: "May you be healed, you, Mwindo." She asked him inquisitively: "You, where are you going?" Mwindo answered her that he was going to Nyamurairi. Having finished bathing Kahindo, Mwindo fainted. (Mwindo) having fainted, Kahindo shook him, saying: "E! Mwindo, wake up! A hero does not die from one spear throw." Mwindo returned to life; he sneezed. While Mwindo was going to Nyamurairi, Kahindo shouted on the road, saying: "Go over there and when you arrive at Nyamurairi's, go close to the men's house where he is (seated). My father Nyamurairi will show you water that is in a jar, asking that you wash with it. You say to him: My father, the beer from which you drink, is that for me to wash with? You refuse firmly, even though he goes on pressing you, saying that you should wash with it. You go on refusing until he stops pressing you with it." Kahindo also said to him: "When you arrive at my father's place, then you sing for him this song:

"I am not with those who have killed Ringe,
"Ringe of the chief, Ringe."

After Mwindo had been briefed in this manner by Kahindo, he went and sang while climbing the mountain (road) to Nyamurairi:

Kabira, beat the drum for me.   Kabira, beat the drum for me.
This one here is Waterbuck.   This one here is Waterbuck.
Kabira, beat the drum for me.   Kabira, beat the drum for me.
This one here is Warthog.   This one here is Waterbuck.

After Mwindo had climbed up to Nyamurairi's village, he mounted the steps near the house of Nyamurairi. He arrived at the men's house. When Nyamurairi saw him, he said to Mwindo to bathe in the water that was in the jar. Mwindo replied to him, saying: "E! My father. I cannot wash myself in the beer that you drink." Having spoken to him in this fashion, he sang for him the song:

I am not with those who have killed Ringe,
Ringe of the chief, Ringe.

When he (Mwindo) had finished singing this song for him, Nyamurairi was full of joy, saying: "I rejoice, my father, because you have arrived here, but tomorrow morning I want you to go harvesting honey for me which is over there at the entrance to the village." After he had finished speaking to Mwindo like this, they cooked banana paste for him. When the banana paste was ready, it was brought to the men's house where Mwindo was. This banana paste was of the *kitehe* variety; it contained frogs that were cooked; they were the garnish of it. It arrived there; Nyamurairi told Mwindo to sample the paste. Mwindo refused it, saying: "You, my father, your followers say about you that you do not eat them (the frogs) with banana paste. This now is difficult!" After Mwindo had spoken to him like this, the frogs stood up; they clapped their hands (in astonishment), saying: "Yes, our Mwindo. We are saved. Lo! You also know things after they had spoken in this way." Nyamurairi said to Mwindo: "So now go into the house of Kahindo, my daughter, to sleep therein." Mwindo went into it (the house). When he arrived there, Kahindo stirred banana paste for him. This banana paste, Mwindo ate it. Having finished eating the banana paste, the sky turned dark; he slept with Kahindo in her house. When the sky had changed to dawn, in the early morning, Nyamurairi said to Mwindo: "You, my son, go to harvest the honey for me which is there on the tree." Mwindo went there. When he arrived at the foot of the tree, Bat gave him nails to stick fast to the *mpaki* tree; and Spider gave him cobwebs (to serve) as ropes to climb the *mpaki* tree. They gave him these things because Mwindo had made a blood pact with Spider and Bat. As he was going to climb the tree, Nyamurairi gave Mwindo his belt (stitched with cowries), saying that he should climb with it. And Mwindo left with Nyamurairi his billhook knife, saying that he should remain with it on the ground. On the belt of Nyamurairi there were cowries. Mwindo climbed up. When he had arrived near the honey, Nyamurairi sent a call to where he was, saying: "You, my belt, bend him." The belt smashed Mwindo; his mouth was smashed against the tree; Mwindo's breathing found no way to come out. The strands on which he had climbed were completely still.

As Mwindo was troubled to death there in the sky, he implored Lightning, saying: "E! My friend Lightning, bring me help and counsel." The scepter that was on his back turned itself toward the face of Mwindo; it removed his mouth from the trunk of the tree. While Mwindo was now dropping excrement because of the fear of being bent against the tree, where Mwindo had sent his call for help, he had called for Lightning. Lightning came down; he cleaved the *mpaki* tree twice; the honey fell to the ground. Mwindo made a call, saying: "You, my billhook knife, may you also smash Nyamurairi." Where Nyamurairi dwelt in his village, the billhook knife of Mwindo smashed him and

291

planted him with his mouth on the ground: excrement and urine, coming from where Nyamurairi was, dispersed everywhere. After Mwindo had climbed down, he reached the ground; he collected the honey; he arrived with it in the village. As he saw Nyamurairi (with) the mouth planted on the ground, Mwindo snatched his scepter from the back; he beat Nyamurairi with it on top of the head, saying: "E! Nyamurairi, everyone who went to sleep wakes up again. Why have you imperiled Mwindo? Why?" When he had finished beating Nyamurairi on the head with his scepter, Nyamurairi came to life again; he recovered; he stood up; he said: "Long life! Long life (to you), Mwindo!" All the honey that Mwindo had brought went into the house of Nyamurairi; and Mwindo on his side went into the house of Kahindo, daughter of Nyamurairi, to sleep in it. When he arrived in the house of Kahindo, Kahindo stirred banana paste for her lover. Mwindo ate it; he went to sleep having placed it on his chest.

[This pattern of task and trap continues with two other attempts by Nyamurairi on Mwindo's life. Mwindo is sent to clear a banana grove and again the belt crushes him against a tree; he is sent to a pond. In both cases, he calls on Lightning and is released and then punishes Nyamurairi.]

Nyamurairi said to Mwindo: "You here who have recovered from this danger, tomorrow in the early morning you shall go to play the dice with Sheburungu. When you have beaten Sheburungu in the game of dice, then you may carry off your father." At night Kahindo cooked five dishes of banana paste for Mwindo; she placed meat on them; she said to Mwindo: "Go tomorrow with these banana pastes; traveling on the road you will meet with newborn babies who are collecting the eleusine of Nyamurairi. You will give them these banana pastes, together with the meat, and they will show you the way to go to Sheburungu."

When the sky had changed to dawn, Mwindo began the journey; he took the five banana pastes together with the meat. He first left to Nyamurairi his billhook knife, and Nyamurairi gave Mwindo his belt, saying to go with it. Where Mwindo went, as he arrived at the entrance to Sheburungu's village, he met two thousand children collecting the eleusine of Nyamurairi. Nyamurairi had poured out that eleusine there so that he (Mwindo) would not recognize the road leading to Sheburungu. When Mwindo met those children, he removed the banana pastes from his shoulder bag; he distributed them together with the meat to all the children. After the children had finished eating the banana pastes, they clapped their hands, saying: "May you be healed! May you be healed, Mwindo!" Mwindo told the children to show him the road to Sheburungu. They showed him the road, saying: "In that cave dwells Sheburungu, but the men's house is located inside the cave; that is the place where you will play dice." Mwindo Mboru went;

he arrived at the men's house of Sheburungu where his father Shemwindo was hidden. When Sheburungu saw Mwindo, he took a hide; he spread it on the ground; he poured the dice on it. When the dice were on top of the hide, Sheburungu said to Mwindo: "Take up the dice now." Mwindo took up the dice. In the place where Nymurairi remained in his village, he said: "You, my belt, see to it; bend him." Where Mwindo had gone, the belt of Nyamurairi bent Mwindo; all the dice threw themselves into his mouth; they made his cheeks swell. It (the belt) planted him with the mouth on the ground on the hide; excrement and urine could not find the one who could clean them; the breath failed to find a way to come out. As the belt was bending Mwindo in this way, his scepter turned around; it came before his eyes; it removed Mwindo's mouth from the ground: the breath was released. Mwindo shouted loudly to Lightning: "My friend, I am dying." Mwindo stood up; he removed the dice and the hide; he went to place them into the mouth of Sheburungu: excrement dropped down. His people said that Sheburungu was dead. Mwindo stood up; seeing Sheburungu, he said: "Now why does Sheburungu imperil Mwindo?" He (Mwindo) said to his (Sheburungu's) people: "Give Sheburungu water to drink." They answered him: "How shall it pass through? Look how the dice are stuck in his mouth; he does not know what to do, and excrement are stuck to his buttocks; they fail to find the one that can remove them!" Sky became dark without Sheburungu having sneezed. His people said: "Bring Shemwindo out from the place where you have hidden him in the cave, because this Sheburungu has no life left; he is close to expiring." Where Shemwindo remained they went to take him out; they arrived with him. They gave him to Mwindo, saying: "Your father here." Mwindo got hold of his father; he took his scepter; he beat it on top of the head of Sheburungu, saying: "Now, Sheburungu, everyone who went to sleep wakes up again. Wake up now. Now you have stuck Mwindo onto you; you have carried him on the back." As Sheburungu was being beaten by Mwindo with his scepter, Mwindo said: "Sparrow is Shebireo, and Katee is crackling of dried leaves."

After he had been beaten by Mwindo's scepter, Sheburungu recovered completely; he stood up. When Sheburungu had recovered, Mwindo returned with his father; he returned with the wives of Sheburungu and the goats of Sheburungu because he had beaten Sheburungu and taken all his goods from him. Returning with his father, he went to arrive at Nyamurairi's. Nyamurairi gave Mwindo his billhook knife, and Mwindo gave Nyamurairi his belt. Mwindo slept in the house of Kahindo. Among the spoils that had come from Sheburungu were two maidens. Mwindo took one maiden; he gave her to Kahindo, his lover, because she performed very many nice things for him.

[The story continues with a number of seemingly disconnected incidents involving a dragon-ogre and hunting adventures in the forest, and at the end Mwindo is made a chief.]

25. The Epic of Kahindo
Narrated by Muteresi Shempunge

Recorded in January 1952 in Mutakato, Zaïre, by Daniel Biebuyck. Transcribed and translated into French by Daniel Biebuyck and Kahombo C. Mateene. Edited by Daniel Biebuyck and Kahombo Mateene and published as "Anthologie de la littérature orale Nyanga," in Mémoires de l'Academie Royale des Sciences d'Outre-Mer (1970). This excerpt edited and translated into English by Stephen Belcher.

THIS TEXT WAS THE SHORTEST OF THE EPICS BIEBUYCK RECORDED among the baNyanga; it is also unusual in that the protagonist is female. Women are a constant presence in the epic traditions of central Africa but rarely move into center stage; more often they are content to guide, to motivate, and to assist the hero. Here, Kahindo and her supernatural namesake play a role in a mythical drama which reflects some notion of how the universe became organized and the human world defined. The name Kahindo occurs in the Mwindo texts; she is there the daughter of a supernatural being whom Mwindo must manage to defeat. (See the *Mwindo Epic* for an example.) It seems likely that despite the tale-like quality of the plot, we are here faced with deep cultural roots.

Because of its brevity, the text is presented in its entirety.

There was a chief named Muhuya. He lived well and quietly with his people in his village, and his subjects made him ecstatic, for his rulings improved their own lives. As he and his people did so well, he married many wives. One of the wives was the mother of a young girl. The girl's name was Kahindo, one who spreads joy, an only child. The other wives had no children; they were barren. The father made bells for his child, and a *sanza*;[1] he gathered bunches of hairs and tied them into an *ndorera* bracelet which he put on her. And that day, she was shut within a fence and she did not leave it.

When she grew up, her father named her Ngarya, and her mother called herself Nyangarya. Some days later, her father decreed that no one should ever take his daughter to the fields. Any one who did so would have to deal with him! And he told his daughter that she should never try to go into the fields; her only job was to stay within the fence.

When some seasons had passed, one day when her father and mother had gone off to the fields, some girls from her age group came by. They suggested she could come with them to bathe in the river. She agreed. They went off to bathe. When they came to the river, they all undressed. Ngarya piled up all her precious things apart from the others. They plunged into the river. When they finished bathing, they dressed again. Ngarya forgot her calabash and the *ndorera* bracelet. They went off; Ngarya had only her water jug and the *sanza*. And her age mates didn't remind her about the other things; they were running

---

1. A thumb piano.

to the village, afraid of being scolded for having taken someone else's child without permission.

Near the path to the river lived a little old woman, a *Mpaca* spirit who had killed off the men and who had a girl-child who was also named Ngarya. She wore large clothing, which dragged on the ground. As this little old woman of the forest was coming down the river looking, she came to the place where the girls had bathed and she saw the things that had been forgotten. She picked them up and wrapped them in her clothes that dragged on the ground, since she had just heard the noise of the young girls. So the little old woman waited for the owner of the objects.

On the way back, the girls had come half way. They had gone over two plateaus when the owner of the objects remembered them; she said to herself that she had left the things where they had bathed in the river. She asked her companions to go back with her to pick up the things; they refused to go with her and went back to the village. After they said no, Ngarya went back alone to pick up the things she had forgotten by the river.

When she reached the place where she had left the things, she found the little old woman sitting there. The old woman said to her, "What are you doing coming around here at this time? Always, when night falls, this place belongs to the others who live in the forest." The girl said to her, "It's you, old woman, who have taken my things." The little old woman said, "The things I have belong to my daughter." The girl came crying up to the old woman, and the old woman moved aside. She said, "Gently, gently! Is it my fault that at this time night is falling on you in the forest?" The little old woman slipped off, she ran away, and the girl followed her. They chased each other. The girl put sound in her voice and sang,

> The little old woman went off with Ngarya.
> I am pursuing them, ooo!

When they came to the halfway point (where are you coming from? where are you going?), still pursuing each other, they rested. They abused each other; the one said the other had stolen her things, the other answered that the things belonged to her daughter. After they had rested, the old woman took flight again, putting her legs 'around her shoulders,' and the girl raced after her, following. They chased each other. Chasing each other, they came to the village of the little old woman, where her daughter was.

They saw each other: one was named Ngarya, the other was named Ngarya. When the old woman's daughter saw that her counterpart's body was suffering, covered with scratches, and that her clothes had become rags because of the thorns, she made a gift of what she was wearing. She warned her friend, saying, "My friend, the mistress of this place is hard; she wants to eat you. Each time she calls us, we shall have to answer together, and if she sends us on a task, we shall have to go together. Neither of us can be alone, or we will be eaten." This was their trick to escape death.

When the old woman saw her two children, she said to herself there must be a way to eat the girl who had just come. One day she sent the two to pick bananas. When together they came to the place, they cut down the bunch of bananas together, and together they peeled them, and they brought the bananas back to the village together. When they came to the village, together they cut the bananas lengthwise. So that was a trial they passed.

When the old woman saw them get through that trial, she made another trap with some roast boar; they got through that test also. She tested them with another trap: grilling the bananas. Again they escaped. When she saw that they had passed these tests, she asked them to sing for her. Just as they were about to sing, the daughter of the ogre told her companion, "While we are singing, if you complain that the old woman ran away with you, Ngarya, you will give yourself away." So that evening, the old woman danced while they sang for her. They sang:

> Something escapes me, eh, ree-ree.
> I don't recognize my Ngarya,
> I don't recognize the child, eh, ree-ree,
> I don't recognize my Ngarya.
> You have made me happy, oh, my mothers,
> I don't recognize my Ngarya.
> My mothers, think of me with nostalgia, eh, ree-ree,
> I don't recognize my Ngarya.
> Little old woman, close to God, eh, ree-ree,
> It's tight among children.
> Someone who has gone to God will never return, eh, ree-
>   ree,
> It's tight among children.
> Oh, my mothers, what shall I do? eh, ree-ree.
> It's tight among children.
> So there you are, small bladder,
> It's tight among children.
> Saliva falls out of the mouth, eh, ree-ree,
> I don't recognize the child.
> Nostalgia says, "I am surpassed," eh, ree-ree,
> I don't recognize the child.

Hearing how the voices sounded, the voices of the children singing, the old woman hopped here and there, saying, "My mothers, sing on, I am pleased with you." When she was tired of dancing, she sent them to the river to catch her a crab. They went together. When they went there, together they turned over the stone, together they put their hands underneath; they drew out a *mungai* crab; they brought it to her. She was pleased when she saw them and said, "Thank you, mothers who feed me, thank you. Thanks to you I shall bite on crabs' legs." So once again the children had succeeded in passing the trial.

During the night, she got her knife and sharpened it, saying, "The day that dawns shall not be one of defeat. And so today my little pot will shine." Her knife was as sharp as a razor. When they went to bed, the ogre's daughter said to her friend, "If you mention the sparks, you shall die."

They got their things and put them together; they exchanged things as they dressed. Each wore the clothes of her friend. Once again, the daughter said, "When we go to sleep, you sleep on the far side and I'll sleep near the hearth; also we'll have to twine our legs together. Even if she turns us over and over during the night, if we don't let go oɪ each other so there is a space between us, she won't be able to kill either of us. And so you mustn't let yourself be startled during the night, or she will cut your throat."

In the middle of the night, when they were asleep, the little old woman lit the resin torch at the hearth; sparks and more sparks leaped out. The one warned the other in the night and said, "She is coming."

Then the little old woman burst into the house where they were; their spirits fled! They were really going to die! She turned them over and over. She wore herself out working like a chicken, turning them and turning them, thinking that one would let go of the other so that she could kill one of them.

When she was worn out, she left them there. They went back to sleep, their hearts calmed. They said, "Once again, we're safe for the moment."

When day came, she left them the task of pounding and grinding the bananas and went into the forest. When she was in the forest and they were in the village, the children said to each other, "When the wind rises it will be her about to come, and if we are talking we shall have to be quiet." All at once, there she came with lots and lots of meat. When she came, she asked the children who had stayed in the village for her pipe and some tobacco, 'to hold her breath.' They gave it to her. She told them to go butcher the animals. They went there. When they came to the butchering place, they cut up some and they left others as they were—those were the ones where she had put traps. When they finished the butchery, they went back to the village; they smoked the meat and cured it.

When night came and they were asleep again, she came once more. She touched them and touched them and said, "I am surprised! This is very hard! Which one is mine? Which one shall I slaughter?" The little old woman didn't know what to try, she didn't know which of the two she should slaughter.

The next morning, they beat the drum and sang for her while she danced up a storm. The night after that, she told the girls to put the drum in her courtyard so she might bid them goodbye; she was off to find riches for them. When they heard that, the girls went all out on the drums and beat them hard. They sang,

> Oh, you children!
> Greetings, greetings,
> I'm going off today.
> Greetings, greetings.
> You stay here,
> Greetings, greetings.
> Keep this place,
> Greetings, greetings.
> Keep your hearts low,
> Greetings, greetings.
> Preserve this place,
> Greetings, greetings.
> Joyful one (whose joy) makes you grow,
> Greetings, greetings.
> Joyful one (whose joy) makes you grow,
> Greetings, greetings.

When she finished dancing, she headed out of the village after she had said goodbye to her children. Two days after her departure, as the daughters had heard nothing from the direction in which she went, the girls thought up a trick of their own. They brought red powder and an *nkuki* brush and they spread the powder all over the way she had gone, so that when she came back she wouldn't know which way they had gone. The third day they went to the whetting block and slipped in under it—those two girls! They came out at the place where Kahindo had left her clothes.

They went off and climbed up to the village, they reached it. The chief, at first, did not recognize his daughter. No one in the village went to work in the fields, and the whole village had become very quiet, thinking the chief's daughter was really dead. The father and mother had let their hair grow out unkempt, 'like this!' and they didn't eat anything anymore—they had become like the *kangerangera* bird because of their anguish. When the children came, the chief and everyone in the village were very happy. They put the two girls in a guest house.

Once she had rested, Kahindo told her daughter how she and her friends had gone to bathe and how she got lost and how she was saved by the young girl, Ngarya. When her father heard the story, tears ran down his face. He said his child had really been lost! He summoned the young girl who had saved his daughter and assigned her a number of servants and a strip of land. He told her, "We shall name you Nyamumbo, and you shall give birth to a chief who shall inherit my power."

After that, they told him the news, saying, "Chief, you must listen. When the little old woman comes back from wherever she went to find riches, if she comes to this village and you tell her we are here, we shall be slaughtered along with everything else." When the chief heard this he sent three young men off to spread the red powder with the *nkuki* brush in the direction the old woman had taken, so she wouldn't find out which way the children had gone. After they had done that, the young men went home.

A few days later, on her part, the old woman began to feel a longing and concern for her children, because they had stayed all alone in the village without anyone to watch them. She went home. When she came to the village where she had left the children and put down her loads (what a joke!), the bags of salt went one way and she another. Looking at the ground—what sadness, what pain in her eyes! The tears she shed right then gave birth to a small stream. She said, "The ones who gave me warmth have left, but whether they were taken by some eater- of-food or some other member of the clan of God, whoever it may be, I will make myself known to them." She threw herself on the ground, seven times and seven times more. Sky and earth met; rain and lightning and the hurricane came forth; trees fell; rivers everywhere filled up; in the forest the animals did not know where to go, they were caught by the night. Having accomplished this deed, she boasted and said, "The one who will knock me to the ground is not known."

In this state of worry, she feverishly sought her children here and there, at the river and among her traps, in her banana plantation— everywhere she had used to send them. She found not a trace of their passage. She said, "Did they go through heaven or by the earth?" While looking, she came to the whetting block, and she smelled something where they had gone. She threw herself on their trail.

And in the village where the girls were, they worried. They told the chief and his people, "She is coming! She has returned from her expedition. If she comes here, you will have to strengthen your hearts; tell her what we have told you. Even if she brings amazing things, refuse them. Eventually she will pass us by."

Following the track of the children, she appeared in the chief's village; she threw herself to the ground in the middle of the village so that houses almost fell over. She said,

> I return from my trip.
> I go in pursuit
> Of Sereka and Ngarya,
> I go in pursuit.

She came to the chief of the place, and she asked him to give her news about the passage of her children. The chief told her, "One day, when the sun was at its brightest, after all the men had gone into the forest, I saw your children. They passed us by; one of them was carrying a *sanza* and the other had a strap over her shoulder with a calabash holding little bells and woven bracelets."

When she heard that, she did not delay; she headed out of the village and continued her hunt. She went to Lightning. When she tried to ask Lightning where her children had gone, Lightning, as though he had not heard, fell on her seven times. She fell on the ground, belly up. She got up. When she tried to sniff Lightning with her muzzle, once again, Lightning fell upon her once more. He raised her and threw her here and there. She said, "This time it's not him. He leaves nothing on me! Are we equals? Could we be servants of the same court? He has strength and he is tough."

She went back to Lightning, she boasted. "Here I am, and by your mother, Lightning, I shall not die on earth." She seized all Lightning's servants and killed them. They stopped marching by; they died. When Lightning looked backwards, there was no buzzing behind him. At the second blink of his eyes, his partner appeared in front of him and said, "Let's throw dice."

They threw them in the air. The dice of Lightning were of copper; the old woman's dice were shaped like knives. The *kangancu* bird caught Lightning's dice in the air; the old woman's dice fell loudly on Lightning's head. So Lightning became her servant. His partner picked him up and put him into her large game bag. She picked up her dice and went on.

Continuing her chase, she came to Murimba the Roc. When she and Murimba met, each threatened the other. Murimba got angry and dropped two huge white stones on her; the old woman stepped aside and they missed. Escaping this first danger, she collected herself and then she appeared in the middle of Murimba's village.

When they met, they threw their dice. Both sets, hers and Murimba's, stayed aloft for seven suns, twined together, and neither set could make the other come down. On the seventh day, the old woman's dice fell, while those of Murimba were held above and could not descend. Coming down, the old woman's dice fell on Murimba's head; Murimba's brain ran out and spread in all directions. She boasted, "Today, their challenges are turned back upon them, they are climbing a hard mountain." She grabbed and took away as booty all the possessions of Murimba. She went off with all his men.

Continuing her pursuit, she appeared at the home of Rundurundu (Fog). As she went up, the cloud ceiling was above and below. When they met, they challenged each other, and they threw their dice. Rundurundu's dice were held in the air, they disappeared; the old woman's dice fell back down and killed Rundurundu. She took Rundurundu's skull and set it 'just so.' She went off.

Continuing her pursuit, she came to Mutero (Hail). When they met, they insulted each other, and they threw up their dice. Mutero's dice were held above, the old woman's dice came back. And so he also became her servant. As she was leaving Mutero's home, resuming her path, she heard the music of *sanzas* and the sound of singing voices. She was pleased, saying this must be her children. But when she came and saw, it was the clan of toads singing and the clan of bats beating the drums and the clan of the stars (fireflies) lighting the fire. When she came to the stars, she perished.

After the old woman died, back where the two girls had stayed, the chief sent out Pygmies as scouts. They came and found that the old woman was really dead. They came back. That is when men's hearts came down. And so the men and the chief and the two girls lived in prosperity.

> That is why:
> Spoiling a child is idiotic; you should not prevent a child
>   from playing, because this is how the child gains
>   knowledge;
> The world requires helping others; the person who helps
>   another will be helped in turn one day;
> The rashness of a single man will not fail to leave a mark; it
>   brings disaster.
> A brave being surpasses us: the all powerful.
> You have good fortune only if it is your fate.

Bibliography

I. General Works

Belcher, Stephen. *An Introduction to West African Epic*. Forthcoming, Indiana University Press.

Biebuyck, Daniel. "The African Heroic Epic." In Felix Oinas, ed., *Heroic Epic and Saga*, pp. 336-67. Bloomington: Indiana University Press, 1978.

Finnegan, Ruth. *Oral Literature in Africa*. London: Oxford at the Clarendon Press, 1970.

———. *Oral Poetry*. Cambridge: Cambridge University Press, 1977; 2nd ed. Bloomington: Indiana University Press, 1992.

Hale, Thomas A. "Griottes: Female Voices from West Africa." *Research in African Literatures* 25:3 (1994): 72-91.

———. *Griots and Griottes of West Africa*. Bloomington: Indiana University Press. [forthcoming].

Johnson, John Wm. "Historicity and the Oral Epic: The Case of Sun-Jata Keita." In Robert E. Walls and George H. Schoemaker, eds., *The Old Traditional Way of Life: Essays in Honor of Warren E. Roberts*, pp. 351-61. Bloomington: Trickster Press, Indiana University Folklore Institute, 1989.

———. "On the Heroic Age and Other Primitive Theses." In E. V. Zygas and Peter Voorheis, eds., *Folklorica: Festschrit for Felix J. Oinas*, pp. 121-38. Bloomington: Research Institute for Inner Asian Studies, 1982.

———. "Yes, Virginia, There Is an Epic in Africa." *Research in African Literatures* 11:3 (1980): 308-26.

Kesteloot, Lilyan. *L'épopée traditionelle*. Paris: Fernand Nathan, 1971.

———. "Myth, Epic, and African History." In V. Mudimbe, ed., *The Surreptitious Speech*, pp. 136-43. Chicago: University of Chicago Press, 1992.

———. "La problematique des épopées africaines." Université de Dakar: *Annales de la faculté des lettres et sciences humaines* 17 (1987): 43-53. [Reprinted in *Neohelikon* 16:2 (1989): 247-64; English translation in *African Languages and Cultures* 22 (1989): 203-14.]

Kesteloot, Lilyan and Bassirou Dieng, eds. *Épopées d'Afrique Noire*. Paris: Karthala [forthcoming].

Okpewho, Isidore. *African Oral Literature: Background, Character, and Continuity*. Bloomington: Indiana University Press, 1992.

Okpewho, Isidore. *The Epic in Africa: Toward a Poetics of the Oral Performance*. New York: Columbia University Press, 1979.

————, ed. *The Oral Performance in Africa*. Ibadan, Nigeria: Spectrum Books, 1990.

Panzacchi, Cornelia. "The Livelihood of Traditional Griots in Modern Senegal." *Africa* 64:2 (1994): 190-209.

Seydou, Christiane. "Comment définir le genre épique? Un exemple: L'épopée africaine." *Journal of the Anthropological Society of Oxford* 13:1 (1982): 84-98. [Reprinted as Veronika Görög-Karady, ed., *Genres, Forms, Meanings: Essays in African Oral Literature/Genres, formes, significations: essais sur la littérature orale africaine*. JASO Occasional Paper, 1982.]

Westley, David. "A Bibliography of African Epic." *Research in African Literatures* 22:4 (1991): 99-115.

II. Specific Traditions

A. Soninké

Bathily, Abdoulaye. "A Discussion of the Traditions of Wagadu with Some Reference to Ancient Ghana." *Bulletin de l'Institut Fondamental d'Afrique Noire* 37:1 ser. B (1975): 1-94.

Dantioko, Oudiary Makan. *Soninkara Taarixinu: Récits historiques du pays Soninké*. Niamey: Centre d'Études Linguistiques et Historiques par Tradition Orale, 1985.

Delafosse, Maurice. *Traditions historiques et légendaires du Soudan Occidental. Publication du Comité de l'Afrique Française*. Paris, Comité de l'Afrique Française, 1913.

Diawara, Mamadou. *La graine de la parole*. Stuttgart: Franz Steiner Verlag, 1990.

Dieterlen, Germaine. *L'empire de Ghana*. Paris: Karthala, 1992.

Jablow, Alta. "Gassire's Lute: A Reconstruction of Soninké Bardic Art." *Research in African Literatures* 15 (1984): 519-29.

————. *Gassire's Lute*. New York: E. P. Dutton, 1971. [Republished in 1991 in Prospect Heights, Ill. by Waveland Press.]

Meillassoux, Claude, Lassana Doucouré, and Diaowa Simagha. *Légende de la dispersion des Kusa*. Dakar: Institut Fondamental d'Afrique Noire, 1967.

Monteil, Charles. "La légende de Ouagadou et l'origine des Soninké." *Mémoires de l'Institut Français d'Afrique Noire* 23 (1953): 358-409.

B. MANDE

i. The Sunjata Tradition

Cisse, Youssouf Tata, and Wa Kamissoko. *La grande geste du Mali: Des origines à la fondation de l'empire.* Paris: Karthala/Association pour la Recherche Scientifique d'Afrique Noire, 1988.

———. *Soundjata, la gloire du Mali: La grande geste du Mali, Tome 2.* Paris: Karthala/Association pour la Recherche Scientifique d'Afrique Noire, 1991.

Diabaté, Massa Makan. *L'aigle et l'épervier ou La geste de Sunjata.* Paris: Pierre Jean Oswald, 1975.

———. *Kala Jata.* Bamako: Éditions populaires, 1970.

———. *Le lion à l'arc.* Paris: Hatier, 1986.

Innes, Gordon, ed. and trans. *Sunjata: Three Mandinka Versions.* London: School of Oriental and African Studies, University of London, 1974.

Jabaté, Kanku Madi. [Collected, translated, and annotated by Madina Ly-Tall, Seydou Camara, and Bouna Diouara.] *L'histoire du Mandé.* Paris: Association Société Commerciale de l'Ouest Africaine, 1987.

Jansen, Jan, Esger Duintjer, and Boubacar Tamboura. *Het Sunjata-epos verteld door Lansine Diabate uit Kela.* Utrecht: Published by the authors; distributed by Drukkerij Organisatie Oude Muziek in Leiden, 1994. [Translated by the authors as *L'épopée de Sunjata, d'après Lansine Diabate de Kela.* Leiden: Center of Non-Western Studies, 1995.]

Johnson, John William, and Fa-Digi Sisòkò. *The Epic of Son-Jara: A West African Tradition.* Bloomington: Indiana University Press, 1986 [2nd ed. (text only), 1992].

Johnson, John William, and Magan Sisòkò. *The Epic of Sun-Jata According to Magan Sisòkò* (FPG Monograph Series, no. 5). Bloomington: Folklore Publications Group, 1979.

Koné, Tiémoko. [Ed. Lassana Doucouré and Mme. Martal.] *Soundiata.* Bamako: Institut des Sciences Humaines du Mali; Niamey: Centre Régional de Documentation pour la Tradition Orale, 1970.

Laye, Camara. *Le maître de la parole: kouma lafôlô kouma.* Paris: Plon, 1978. [Trans. by James Kirkup as *The Guardian of the Word.* London: William Collins Sons, 1980; New York: Fontana Books, 1980.]

Niane, Djbril Tamsir. *Soundiata, ou L'épopée mandingue.* Paris: Présence Africaine, 1960. [Translated by G. D. Pickett as *Sunjata: An Epic of Old Mali.* London: Longman, 1965.]

ii. Other Mande Traditions

Bird, Charles S. "Heroic Songs of the Mande Hunters." In *African Folklore,* ed. Richard Dorson, pp. 275-93. New York: Anchor Books, 1972. [Reprinted by Indiana University Press in 1979.]

———, ed. and trans. "Bambara Oral Prose and Verse Narratives." In *African Folklore,* op. cit., pp. 441-77.

Camara, Seydou. [Ed. and trans. Charles Bird with Mamadou Koita and Bourama Soumaoro.] *The Songs of Seydou Camara: Vol. I: Kambili.* Bloomington: Indiana University African Studies Program, 1974. [Original text published as *Seyidu Kamara ka Donkiliw: Kambili.* Ed. Bourama Soumaoro, Charles S. Bird, Gerald Cashion, and Mamadou Kanté. Bloomington: Indiana University African Studies Program, 1976.]

Conrad, David. *A State of Intrigue: The Epic of Bamana Segu According to Tayiru Banbera.* Oxford: Oxford University Press for the British Academy, 1990. [Union Académique Internationale: Fontes Historiae Africanae, Series Varia 6.]

Coulibaly, Dosseh Joseph, ed. and trans. *Récits des chasseurs du Mali: Dingo Kanbili de Bala Jinba Jakité.* Paris: Conseil International de la Langue Française/Edicef, n.d.

Dumestre, Gerard, ed. and trans. *La geste de Ségou.* Paris: Armand Colin, 1979. [Classiques Africains.] [Previously published at the University of Abidjan, Institut de Linguistique Appliquée, no. 48, 1974.]

Dumestre, Gerard, and Lilyan Kesteloot, eds. and trans. *La prise de Dionkoloni.* Paris: Armand Colin, 1975. [Classiques Africains.]

Frobenius, Leo. *Dichten und Denken im Sudan. Atlantis V.* Jena: Eugen Diederichs, 1925.

———. *Spielmannsgeschichten der Sahel. Atlantis VI.* Jena: Eugen Diederichs, 1921.

Geysbeek, Timothy, and Jobba Kamara. "'Two Hippos Cannot Live in One River.' Zo Musa, Foningama, and the Founding of Musadu." *Liberian Studies Journal* 16 (1991): 27-78.

Hayidara, Shekh Tijaan, ed. and trans. *La geste de Fanta Maa*. Niamey: Centre d'Études Linguistiques et Historiques par Tradition Orale, 1987.

Innes, Gordon. *Kaabu and Fuladu: Historical Narratives of the Gambian Mandinka*. London: School of Oriental and African Studies, University of London, 1976

———. *Kelefa Saane: His Career Recounted by Two Mandinka Bards*. London: School of Oriental and African Studies, University of London, 1978.

Innes, Gordon, and Bakari Sidibe. *Hunters and Crocodiles*. Sandgate: Paul Norbury/ U.N.E.S.C.O., 1990.

Kamissoko, Wâ. [Ed. Youssouf Tata Cissé (?).] *Les Peuls du Manding*. Niamey: Centre d'Études Linguistiques et Historiques par Tradition Orale, [1974].

Kesteloot, Lilyan. "Le mythe et l'histoire dans la formation de l'empire de Ségou." *Bulletin de l'Institut Fondamental d'Afrique Noire*, ser. B 40:3 (1978): 578-681.

Kesteloot, Lilyan, ed. and trans, with Amadou Traoré, Jean-Baptiste Traoré and Amadou Hampaté Bâ. *Da Monzon de Ségou: Épopée bambara*. 2 vols. Paris: L'Harmattan, 1993. [First published in 1974 in Paris by Fernand Nathan, 4 vols.]

Thoyer, Annik, ed. and trans. *Nyakhalen la forgeronne, par Seyidou Kamara*. N.p., 1986.

Thoyer-Rozat, Annik, ed. and trans. *Chants de chasseurs du Mali*. 3 vols. Vols. 1 and 2 by Mamadu Jara; vol. 3 by Ndugace Samake. Paris: n.p., 1978. [Reprinted in Paris by L'Harmattan, 1995.]

Wright, Donald. *Oral Traditions from The Gambia: Volume 1. Mandinka Griots*. Athens: Ohio University Center for International Studies, 1979.

———. *Oral Traditions from The Gambia: Volume 2. Family Elders*. Athens: Ohio University Center for International Studies, 1980.

iii. Background Materials

Ba, Adam Konaré. *L'épopée de Segu*. Paris: Pierre-Marcel Favre/Agence de Coopération Culturelle et Technique, 1987.

———. *Sunjata: le fondateur de l'empire du Mali*. Libreville: Lion, 1983.

Bird, Charles, and Martha B. Kendall. "The Mande Hero: Text and Context." In Ivan Karp and Charles S. Bird, eds., *Explorations in African Systems of Thought*, pp. 13-26. Bloomington: Indiana University Press, 1980.

Brett-Smith, Sarah. *The Making of Bamana Sculpture*. Cambridge: Cambridge University Press, 1994.

Camara, Sory. *Gens de la parole: Essai sur la condition et le rôle des griots dans la société Malinké*. Paris: Karthala, 1992. [First published in Paris by Mouton in 1976.]

Conrad, David, and Barbara Frank, eds. *Status and Identity in West Africa: Nyamakalaw of Mande*. Bloomington: Indiana University Press, 1995.

Cissé, Youssouf. "Notes sur les sociétés de chasseurs Malinké." *Journal de la Société des Africanistes* 34:1 (1964): 175-226.

Diabaté, Massa Makan. *Janjon et autres chants populaires du Mali*. Paris: Présence Africaine, 1970.

Durán, Lucy. "Jelimusow: The Superwomen of Malian Music." In Graham Furniss and Elizabeth Gunner, eds., *Power, Marginality, and African Oral Tradition*, pp. 197-207. Cambridge: Cambridge University Press, 1995.

Hodges, Carlton, ed. *Papers on the Manding*. Bloomington: Indiana University for the Research Center for the Language Sciences, 1971. [African Series 3.]

Levtzion, Nehemia. *Ancient Ghana and Mali*. London: Methuen, 1973. [Studies in African History, vol. 7.]

McNaughton, Patrick. *The Mande Blacksmiths: Knowledge, Power, and Art in West Africa*. Bloomington: Indiana University Press, 1988.

Monteil, Charles. [Notes by Jean Bazin.] *Les Bambara du Ségou et du Kaarta*. Paris: Maisonneuve et Larose, 1977. [First printed 1924.]

―――. *Les empires du Mali: Étude d'histoire et de sociologie Soudanaises*. Paris: G.-P. Maisonneuve et Larose, 1968. [First published in *Bulletin du Comité d'Études historiques et scientifiques de l'Afrique Occidentale Française* 12:3/4 (1929).]

Niane, Djibril Tamsir. *Histoire des mandingues de l'ouest*. Paris: Karthala, n.d.

―――. *Le Soudan occidental au temps des grands empires xie-xvie siècle*. Paris: Présence Africaine, 1975.

Person, Yves. *Samori, une révolution dyula*. 3 vols. Dakar: Institut Fondamental d'Afrique Noire, 1968.

Wright, Donald. "The Epic of Kelefa Sane as a Guide to the Nature of Precolonial Senegambian Society—and Vice Versa." *History in Africa* 14 (1987): 287-309.

C. SONGHAY

i. Primary Sources

Dupuis-Yakouba, A. *Les Gow, ou chasseurs du Niger*. Paris: Ernest Leroux, 1911. [Reprinted in 1974 by Kraus.]

Hale, Thomas A. *Scribe, Griot, and Novelist: Narrative Interpreters of the Songhay Empire*. Gainesville: University of Florida Press, 1990. [2nd ed. (text only) reprinted as *The Epic of Askia Mohammed*. Bloomington: Indiana University Press, 1996.]

Laya, Diouldé. *Texts Songhay-Zarma*. Niamey: Centre d'Études Linguistiques et Historiques par Tradition Orale, 1978.

Mounkaila, Fatimata. *Le mythe et l'histoire dans la Geste de Zabarkane*. Niamey: Centre d'Études Linguistiques et Historiques par Tradition Orale, 1989.

Tandina, Ousmane Maliamane. "Une épopée Zarma: Wangougna Issa Korombeïzé Modi ou Issa Koygolo, mère de la science de la guerre." Ph.D. diss., University of Dakar, 1984.

Watta, Oumarou. "The Human Thesis: A Quest for Meaning in African Epic." Ph.D. diss., State University of New York, Buffalo, 1985. [Ann Arbor, UMI 8528296.]

———. *Rosary, Mat and Molo: A Study in the Spiritual Epic of Omar Seku Tal*. New York: Peter Lang, 1993. [American University Studies in Theology and Religion 135.]

Zouber, Mahmoud Abdou, ed. and trans. *Traditions historiques Songhoy*. Niamey: Centre d'Études Linguistiques et Historiques par Tradition Orale, 1983.

ii. Secondary Materials

Hama, Boubou. *Histoire traditionelle d'un peuple: Les Zarma-Songhay*. Paris: Présence Africaine, 1967.

Olivier de Sardan, Jean-Pierre. *Les sociétés Songhay-Zarma*. Paris: Karthala, 1984.

Rouch, Jean. "Contribution à l'histoire des Songhay." *Mémoires de L'Institut Français d'Afrique Noire* 29 (1953): 137-269.

———. *La religion et magie Songhay*. Paris: Presses Universitaires de France, 1950. [2nd ed., Éditions de l'Université de Bruxelles.]

Stoller, Paul. *Fusion of the Worlds: An Ethnography of Possession among the Songhay of Niger*. Chicago: University of Chicago Press, 1989.

Stoller, Paul, and Cheryl Olkes. *In Sorcery's Shadow*. Chicago: University of Chicago Press, 1987.

D. FULBE

i. Primary Materials

Allaye, Beidari. [Ed. and trans. by Bocar Cisse and Almamy Maliki Yattara.] *Poullo Djom Ere et le Touareg*. Niamey: Centre d'Études Linguistiques et Historiques par Tradition Orale, 1984.

Bâ, Amadou Hampaté , and Lilyan Kesteloot. "Une épopée peule—Silamaka." *L'Homme* 8 (1969): 1-36. [Reprinted in Lilyan Kesteloot. *L'épopée bambara de Ségou*. 2 vols. Paris: L'Harmattan, 1993. First published as *Da Monzon de Ségou: Épopée bambara*. Paris: Fernand Nathan, 1972.]

Equilbecq, François-Victor. *Essai sur la littérature merveilleuse des noirs, suivi de contes indigènes de l'ouest africain*. 3 vols. Paris: Maisonneuve et Larose, 1913-16.

———. *La légende de Samba Guéladio Diégui, Prince Fouta*. Dakar: Nouvelles Éditions Africaines, 1974.

Corera, Issagha. [Ed. Samba Guladio.] *L'épopée peule du Fuuta Tooro*. Dakar, Institut Fondamental d'Afrique Noire, 1992. [Initiations et Études Africaines 36.]

Ly, Amadou, trans. *L'épopée de Samba Gueladiegui*. Dakar: Institut Fondamental d'Afrique Noire/U.N.E.S.C.O., 1991. [Éditions Nouvelles du Sud.]

Meyer, Gerard, ed. and trans. *Récits épiques toucouleurs: la vache, le livre, la lance*. Paris: Karthala/Agence de Coopération Culturelle et Technique, 1991.

Ndongo, Sir Mamadou. *Le Fantang: Poèmes mythiques des bergers peuls*. Paris: Karthala; Dakar: Institut Fondamental d'Afrique Noire, 1986.

Ngaïde, Mamadou Lamine. *Le vent de la razzia*. Dakar: Institut Fondamental d'Afrique Noire, 1981.

Sare, Ougoumala. *La guerre entre Ndje Fara Ndje et Hambodedjo Hammadi.* Niamey: Centre d'Études Linguistiques et Historiques par Tradition Orale/Organisation de l'Unité Africaine, n.d. [1974?].

Seydou, Christiane, ed. and trans. *La geste de Hambodedio ou Hama le rouge.* Paris: Armand Colin, 1976. [Classiques Africains.]

————. *Silâmaka et Poullôri.* Paris: Armand Colin, 1972. [Classiques Africains.]

Sow, Alfa Ibrahim. *Chroniques et récits du Fouta Djallon.* Paris: Librairie Klincksieck, 1968.

Sy, Amadou Abel. *Seul contre tous.* Dakar: Nouvelles Éditions Africaines, 1978.

Vieillard, Gilbert. "Récits peuls du Macina et du Kounari." *Bulletin du Comité d'études historiques et scientifiques de l'Afrique occidentale française* 14:1 (1931): 137-56.

————. [Ed. Eldridge Mohammedou.] *Récits peuls du Macina, du Kounari, du Djilgodji.* Niamey: n.p., n.d.

ii. Secondary Materials

Robinson, David. *The Holy War of Umar Tal.* London: Oxford at the Clarendon Press, 1985.

Seydou, Christiane. *Bibliographie générale du monde peul.* Université de Niamey, Institut de Recherches en Sciences Humaines, 1977. Études Nigériennes No. 43.

————. *Contes et fables des veillées.* Paris: Nubia, 1976.

————. "La devise dans la culture peule: vocation et invocation de la personne." In Geneviève Calame-Griaule, ed., *Langage et cultures africaines,* pp. 187-264. Paris: Maspero, 1977.

————. "Panorama de la littérature peule." *Bulletin de l'Institut Fondamental d'Afrique Noire,* ser. B, 35:1 (1973): 176-218.

Sow, Abdoul Aziz. "Fulani Poetic Genres." *Research in African Literatures* 24:2 (1993): 61-77.

E. WOLOF

i. Primary Materials

Dieng, Bassirou. *L'épopée du Kajoor.* Dakar and Paris: Centre Africain d'Animation et d'Échanges Culturels/Khoudia, 1993.

Diop, Samba. "The Oral History and Literature of the Wolof People of Waalo." Ph.D. diss., University of California, Berkeley, 1993. [Ann Arbor, UMI 9407934.] [Republished under same title, Lewiston: Mellen Press, 1995.]

ii. Secondary Materials

Barry, Boubacar. *Le royaume du Waalo*. Paris: Karthala, 1985. [First printed in Paris by Maspero, 1972.]

———. *La Sénégambie du XVe au XIXe siècle*. Paris: L'Harmattan, 1988.

Boulègue, Jean. *Le grand Jolof*. Paris: Façades/Karthala, 1987.

Diop, Adboulaye-Bara. *La société Wolof*. Paris: Karthala, 1981.

Diouf, Mamadou. *Le Kajoor au XIXe siècle*. Paris: Karthala, 1990.

Kesteloot, Lilyan, and Bassirou Dieng. *Du tieddo au talibé: contes et mythes Wolof II*. Paris: Présence Africaine, 1989.

Makward, Edris. "Two Griots of Contemporary Senegambia." In Isidore Okpewho, ed. *The Oral Performance in Africa*, pp. 23-41. Ibadan: Spectrum Books, 1990.

F. ARABIC

Connelly, Bridget. *Arabic Folk Epic and Identity*. Berkeley: University of California Press, 1986.

Galley, Micheline, and Abderrahman Ayoub. *Histoire des Beni Hilal et de ce qui leur advint dans leur marche vers l'ouest*. Paris: Armand Colin, 1983. [Classiques Africains.]

Guignard, Michel. *Musique, honneur et plaisir au Sahara*. Paris: Geuthner, 1975.

Lyons, M. C. *The Arabian Epic*. 3 vols. Cambridge: Cambridge University Press, 1995. [University of Cambridge Oriental Publications no. 49.]

Norris, H. T. *Shinqiti Folk Literature and Song*. London: Oxford at the Clarendon Press, 1968.

Reynolds, Dwight Fletcher. *Heroic Poets, Poetic Heroes: The Ethnography of Performance in an Arabic Oral Epic Tradition*. Ithaca: Cornell University Press, 1995.

Slyomovics, Susan. "Arabic Folk Literature and Political Expression." *Arab Studies Quarterly* 8:2 (1986): 178-85.

Slyomovics, Susan. *The Merchant of Art: An Egyptian Hilali Oral Epic Poet in Performance.* Berkeley: University of California Press, 1988.

G. CENTRAL AFRICAN EPICS

Austen, Ralph. *The Elusive Epic: Performance, Text, and History in the Oral Narrative of Jeki la Njambè (Cameroon Coast).* African Studies Association Press, 1995.

Awona, Stanislas. "La guerre de Akoma Mba contre Abo Mama (épopée du mvet)." *Abbia* 9/10 (1965): 180-213; 12/13 (1966): 109-209.

Biebuyck, Daniel. *Hero and Chief: Epic Literature from the Banyanga (Zaire Republic).* Berkeley: University of California Press, 1978.

Biebuyck, Daniel, and Kahombo C. Mateene. "Anthologie de la littérature orale Nyanga." *Mémoires de l'Academie Royale des Sciences d'Outre-Mer* 36:1 (1970): 29-39.

Biebuyck, Daniel, and Kahombo C. Mateene, eds. and trans. *The Mwindo Epic from the baNyanga (Congo Republic).* Berkeley: University of California Press, 1969.

Boelaert, E. *Nsong'a Lianja: L'épopée nationale des Nkundo.* De Sikkel: Anvers, 1949. [Reprinted by Kraus in Nendeln, Liechtenstein, in 1973.]

Boyer, Pascal. *Barricades mystérieuses et pièges à pensée.* Paris, Sociétés d'Ethnologie, 1988.

Clark , J. P. *The Ozidi Saga, Collected and Translated from the Ijo of Okabou Ojobolo.* Ibadan: Ibadan University Press and Oxford University Press Nigeria, 1977. [Republished by J. P. Clark-Bekederemo, with a critical introduction by Isidore Okpewho, in 1991 by Howard University Press, Washington D.C.]

De Rop, A. "Lianja: L'épopée des Móngo." *Mémoires, Académie Royale des Sciences d'Outre-Mer. Classe des Sciences morales et politiques,* n.s. 30:1 (1964).

Eno-Belinga, Samuel Martin. *L'épopée camerounaise, mvet.* Yaoundé: n.p., 1978.

Pepper, Herbert. [Ed. P. and P. de Wolf.] *Un Mvet de Zwé Nguéma: Chant épique fang.* Paris: Armand Colin, 1972.

Priso, Manga Bekombo. *Défis et prodiges: la fantastique histoire de Djéki-la-Njambe.* Paris: Armand Colin for Classiques Africains, 1993.

Tiki a Koulle a Penda, Pierre Celestin. *Les merveilleux exploits de Djéki La Njambè*. 2 vols. Douala: Éditions Collège Libermann, 1987.

Towo-Atangana, Gaspard. "Le Mvet: Genre majeur de la littérature des populations Pahouines." *Abbia* 9/10 (1965): 163-79.

Index

Oral epics are catalogs of cultures because they contain such a variety of names, places, objects, plants, animals, customs, and references to events. Names are especially important because they reveal both the human panorama conveyed by the epic and the multiplicity of attributes for a particular hero. In the index below, the names of all the characters referred to in the epics are listed under the heading 'characters.' In some cases, different names for the same hero are grouped under a single heading, for example Askia Mohammed, Askia Mohammed Touré, and Mamar. But in other cases, the many different names for the same character have been listed separately. We have distinguished between names of characters, who are listed as they appear in the text, and names of narrators, accompanists, translators, researchers, and others, which, in most cases, appear last name first.

John William Johnson is Associate Professor of Folklore and African Studies at Indiana University. His numerous publications include an edited translation of *The Epic of Son-Jara*.

Thomas A. Hale is Professor of African, French, and Comparative Literature at The Pennsylvania State University. His publications include a translation of *The Epic of Askia Mohammed*.

Stephen Belcher is Assistant Professor of Comparative Literature at The Pennsylvania State University.

LaVergne, TN USA
23 August 2010
194281LV00001B/3/P